Noyes F. Palmer

Volume No. 1 of Palmer Records

Proceedings, or memorial volume of the first Palmer family re-union held at

Stonington, Conn., August 10 & 11, 1881, the ancestral home of Walter Palmer, the

pilgrim of 1629

Noyes F. Palmer

Volume No. 1 of Palmer Records
*Proceedings, or memorial volume of the first Palmer family re-union held at Stonington,
Conn., August 10 & 11, 1881, the ancestral home of Walter Palmer, the pilgrim of 1629*

ISBN/EAN: 9783337291242

Printed in Europe, USA, Canada, Australia, Japan

Cover: Foto ©Andreas Hilbeck / pixelio.de

More available books at **www.hansebooks.com**

VOLUME NO. 1

OF

PALMER REC

PROCEEDINGS, OR MEMORIAL

OF THE

FIRST PALMER FAMILY

HELD AT

STONINGTON, CONN., AUGUST 10

THE ANCESTRAL HOME OF WALTE

THE PILGRIM OF 1629.

Being also a part of the Genealogical, Biographical, and Histori
Family, as contained in the several Addresses, etc., de
on the occasion of the Re-Union.

IARTOTYPE ILLUSTRATIO

EDITED BY

NOYES F. PALMER,

JAMAICA, L. I., N. Y., BOX 188.

Published by BROOKLYN UNION-ARGUS, 1881. Copyrighted by NOYES F. PALMER.

DEDICATION.

It is customary to dedicate a book to some person or principle. If this work deserves a like mention among the customs of book making, it should be dedicated,

As regards its personality,

TO

LORIN PALMER, Esq.,

OF BROOKLYN, N. Y.,

the Editor and Manager of one of Brooklyn's best evening daily newspapers.

For had it not been for his co-operation, this volume would have been an imaginary one to the Author.

As regards its principle,

TO

THE PALMER FAMILY,

in hopes of eliciting interest in a subject very much neglected in America—*the preservation* of genealogical and historical family records.

THE ILLUSTRATIONS.

The illustrations in this volume are by Edward Bierstadt, Esq., Nos. 58 and 60 Reade Street, New York City, and under a new process called *artotype*, being a reproduction of a photograph in printer's ink.

The method of grouping pictures on a page enables the comparatively cheap reproduction of many illustrations in works of this class.

Where only one likeness appears on a page is noticed the most faithful use of this method, if from a large negative.

In the illustration of this volume it has not been possible to insert but a few of the many pictures kindly sent to us. As a matter of justice, the officers of the Re-Union and those who were engaged in the entertainment have been "displayed" to the best advantage, and at the same time not absorb the printer's or binder's share of the expenses. Those illustrations that are larger than the groups were specially contributed for the purpose.

PREFACE.

The first Re-Union of the Palmer family was held Aug. 10, 11, 1881, at Stonington, Conn., the ancestral home of Walter Palmer, the pilgrim from England to America in 1629.

The gathering was a spontaneous success, and beyond the most sanguine hopes of its management. At least three thousand descendants participated. But the larger proportion of the family were not present on the occasion, for want of address and proper notification. This volume is prepared to bring the Re-Union to them so far as the printer can do it, and, at the same time, furnish a memorial of the Re-Union to those who enjoyed its gathering.

Had more time been permitted, this offering to the family would have been more worthy of the event, and more *perfect* in its arrangement.

Fraternally yours,

NOYES F. PALMER.

Jamaica, L. I., N. Y., Box 188.

The Germ of the Re-Union.

On May 20th, 1879, Elisha H. Palmer, of Montville, Ct.,
addressed a letter to the writer, in regard to Palmer Genealogy.
A correspondence was kept up, until a complete record was developed of the branch of Walter Palmer's family, to which he
belonged. On October 6th, 1880, Elisha H. attended a Re-
Union of the Turners and Comstocks at Niantic, and became
impressed with the idea that a Re-Union of the Palmers would
be an interesting event. He called to see the writer, February,
1881, and, upon learning that we could send invitations from
" Palmer Genealogical Record " to over four thousand, concluded
to organize a Re-Union. On Feb. 2d, 1881, he addressed us a
letter wherein he says: " I expected to have written you before
this, " when I left your place. I have been waiting to see the
" Stonington folks, to see what encouragement I would get from
" them with regard to the family Re-Union. * * * I went
" to see some cf the Palmers you gave me the names of in New
" York. * * * As soon as I can get to Stonington and ar-
" range about the Re-Union, I shall want to get up a circular to
" send to all the Palmer descendants. We will furnish you with
" the circulars and stamps, and get you to send to all you have
" a record of." On the 25th of Feb., Elisha H. again wrote.
" If it would not be too much trouble, would like to have you
" write some of the prominent men of the Palmers, and see what
" they thought of having a family gathering in Stonington.
" We would have to hold it two days, in order to get much good
" out of it."

Correspondence was kept up, and from responses to letters to
prominent Palmers, it soon became evident that the Re-Union
would be largely attended. It was, therefore, decided to organize, which was done the following April.

MINUTES.

1653.   PALMER RE-UNION.   1881.

At a preliminary meeting of the Re-Union of the Palmer Family, held pursuant to notice in the Baptist Vestry on Wednesday, April 6th, 1881,

REV. A. G. PALMER was chosen Moderator,
and Hon. ELISHA H. PALMER, Clerk.

Upon motion of Ira H. Palmer, it was

Voted, That the matter of permanent organization and appointment of committees be deferred till the next meeting.

Voted, That while this effort is primarily for the descendants of Walter Palmer, who settled in Stonington, Ct., in 1653, the invitation is extended to all branches of the Palmer Family to participate in the proposed Re-Union.

Meeting adjourned to same place Wednesday, April 20th.

E. H. PALMER, Clerk.

Present at above meeting : Hon. E. H. Palmer, Montville, Ct.; Rev. A. G. Palmer, Stonington, Ct.; Amos N. Palmer, Norwich, Ct. (deaf man) ; Ira H. Palmer, Stonington, Ct.; H. Clay Palmer, Stonington, Ct.

At an adjourned meeting of the PALMER FAMILY RE-UNION held in the Baptist Vestry, April 20, 1881,

REV. A. G. PALMER, Moderator,
and H. CLAY PALMER, Clerk.

The matter of permanent organization was discussed, resulting in the choice of officers, as follows :

President—Hon. ELISHA H. PALMER, of Montville, Ct.

Vice-Presidents—Rev. A. G. Palmer, of Stonington. Ct.; Alexander S. Palmer, of Stonington, Ct.; Alexander Palmer, of Stonington, Ct.; William L. Palmer, of Stonington, Ct.; Noyes S. Palmer of Stonington, Ct.; Thomas W. Palmer, of Stonington, Ct.; Amos Allen Palmer, of Stonington, Ct.; Rev. Roswell C. Palmer, of Stonington, Ct.; Dr. L. N. Palmer, of Brooklyn,

N. Y.; Albert M. Palmer, of New York City; William Pitt
Palmer, of New York City; R. P. Palmer of North Stonington,
Ct.; Robert Palmer, of Noank, Ct.; B. P. Palmer, of Boston,
Mass.; Noyes F. Palmer, of Jamaica, L. I.; Ex-Gov. John C.
Palmer, of Illinois; Charles Palmer, of Albany, N. Y.; C. T.
H. Palmer, of Oakland, Cal.; Jerome Palmer, of Preston, Ct.;
Amos N. Palmer, of Norwich, Ct.; Hon. R. A. Wheeler, of Ston-
ington, Ct; C. P. Dixon, of New York City; Dr. J. H. Trum-
bull, of Hartford, Ct.; Rev. H. Clay Trumbull, of Philadel-
phia, Pa.; Rev. William Clift, of Mystic Bridge; Henry B.
Noyes, of Mystic Bridge; Rev. J. Randall Hoes, of New
Rochelle, N. Y.; Porter C. Bliss, of New York City.

Treasurer—H. Clay Palmer, of Stonington, Conn.

Secretary of Record—Alex. S. Palmer, Jr., of Stonington, Ct.

Corresponding Secretary—Ira H. Palmer, of Stonington, Ct.

Executive Committee—Henry M. Palmer, of Stonington, Ct.;
James E. Palmer, of Stonington, Ct.; Edwin T. Palmer, of
Stonington, Ct.; Theodore D. Palmer, of Stonington, Ct.; Eugene
Palmer, of Stonington, Ct.; Miss Emma W. Palmer, of Ston-
ington, Ct.; Miss Sara A. Palmer, of Stonington, Ct.; John D.
Palmer, of Greenville, N. J.; William R. Palmer, of New York
City; Courtland Palmer, of New York City; Lambert L. Palm-
er, of Chicago, Ill.; Nathan F. Dixon, of Westerly, R. I.;
Jesse L. Moss, Jr., of Westerly, R. I.; Mrs. Elizabeth P. Soper,
of Stonington, Ct.; Miss Emily A. Wheeler, of Stonington,
Ct.; Mrs. Dr. Stanton, of Stonington, Ct.; Miss Hannah Stan-
ton, of Stonington, Ct.; Miss Grace Stanton, of Stonington,
Ct.; Mrs. Maria S. Chesebro, of Stonington, Ct.; J. Warren
Stanton, of Stonington, Ct.; Nathaniel P. Stanton, of Stoning-
ton, Ct.; William Bradford, of New York City; Charles Haw-
kins, of New York City; Mrs. M. J. Pitkin, of New York City;
Miss Elizabeth Van Tine, of New York City; Miss Eliza
Palmer, of Stonington, Ct.

Voted, That Auxillary Committees be appointed at the next
meeting.

Voted, That the PALMER RE-UNION be held at Stonington,
Ct., on the 10th day of August next.

Voted, That the Hon. Richard A. Wheeler be invited to deliver the Genealogical Address of the descendants of Walter
Palmer.

Voted, That William Pitt Palmer, Esq., of New York City,
be invited to deliver a poem on the occasion. That Noyes F.
Palmer, of Jamaica, be invited to deliver an address on
" Palmer Families."

Voted, That the officers elected at this meeting be officially notified by the Corresponding Secretary.

Adjourned until April 27, 1881.

Attest : H. CLAY PALMER, Clerk.

Form of letters of Notification sent by the Corresponding Secretary to the various officials and committees elected at the meeting of April 20th :

ELISHA H. PALMER,   1653—1881.   A. S. PALMER, JR.,
Yᵉ President.   Yᵉ Sec. of Record.

H. CLAY PALMER,   PALMER RE-UNION,   I. H. PALMER,
Yᵉ Treasurer.   AT   Yᵉ Cor. Secretary.

STONINGTON, CT., Yᵉ 10TH OF AUGUST.

STONINGTON, CT., April 23d, 1881.

DEAR SIR:—At a meeting of the resident descendants of Walter Palmer, held at Stonington, April 20th, you was unanimously elected as one of the...........of the PALMER RE-UNION to be held August 10th.

It will be gratifying to us all to have your co-operation with the Re-Union, which bids fair to be large and pleasant.

The resident .... will doubtless relieve those more remote of the details of preparation.

Very truly, yours,

I. H. PALMER, Cor. Secretary.

STONINGTON, CT., April 27, 1881.

Pursuant to adjournment April 20th, a meeting was held this day in the Baptist Vestry.

Hon. E. H. PALMER, as Moderator,
and I. H. PALMER, Clerk.

Minutes of the last meeting read and approved.

Voted, That a committee of three be appointed to consider the subject of a suitable memorial to be erected to the memory of Walter Palmer by his descendants, and to report upon the matter at some future meeting.

Voted, That Wm. L. Palmer, James E. Palmer and H. Clay Palmer be that committee.

Voted, That Henry W. Palmer and Noyes F. Palmer be a committee on Invitation for New York City ; Arthur T. Palmer, for Boston, Mass.; Edwin A. Palmer and John S. Palmer, for Cleveland, Ohio; Lambert L. Palmer for Chicago, Ill., and that they be authorized to add to their members.

Voted, That a committee of Noyes F. Palmer, with the Corresponding Secretary, to get up a suitable invitation card for notification of the Re-Union.

Adjourned three weeks from date.

Attest: I. H. PALMER, Clerk.

STONINGTON, CT., May 11, 1881.

An adjourned meeting of the PALMER RE-UNION was held this date at the Baptist Vestry.

Hon. E. H. PALMER, as Moderator,
and H. CLAY PALMER, Clerk.

Minutes of the last meeting were read and approved.

Committee on "Memorial to Walter Palmer" not ready to report.

Sundry letters received by the Corresponding Secretary from non-resident descendants of Walter Palmer were read to the meeting, the tenor of them showing an interest in the Re-Union.

Voted, That Mrs. Palmer Knapp, of Brooklyn, and Miss Sara A. Palmer, of Stonington, be the Musical Committee.

Voted, That invitation to the Re-Union be sent out prior to the 10th June.

Meeting adjourned to June 1st.

Attest: H. CLAY PALMER, Clerk.

STONINGTON, CT., June 1, 1881.

Pursuant to adjournment a meeting of the PALMER RE-UNION was held in the vestry of the Baptist Church.

ELISHA H. PALMER, as Moderator,
and H. CLAY PALMER as Clerk.

The minutes of the last meeting were read and approved.

The Memorial Committee not ready with a report.

Voted, That the President, E. H. Palmer, with Edwin T. Palmer, be a Finance Committee.

Voted, That the form of invitation shown the meeting by I. H. Palmer be procured and issued soon as practicable.

Remarks were made by persons present upon the general subject of the Re-Union.

Voted, That the Re-Union be held two days—August 10th at Stonington Borough, and August 11th at Wequetequock.

Voted, That after the next meeting that the meetings be held weekly until the Re-Union.

Adjourned to June 22d.

Attest : Clerk.

STONINGTON, CT., June 29, 1881.

An adjourned meeting of the PALMER RE-UNION was held at the Baptist Vestry this date.

E. H. PALMER, Moderator.

Ira H. Palmer was chosen Clerk.

The minutes of the last meeting read and approved.

The Memorial Committee represented by H. C. Palmer were not ready to report any definite action.

I. H. Palmer, of Committee on Invitation, reported that the invitations were being sent out as rapidly as possible.

Col. Edwin Palmer, of Norwich, Conn., being present, gave the meeting his connection with Thomas Palmer of 1633.

Voted, That Col. Edwin Palmer be a committee to invite members of the Thomas Palmer family to join the Re-Union.

Various letters received by the Corresponding Secretary were read to the meeting.

The following letter to Gen. U. S. Grant, a descendant of Walter Palmer, written by the Corresponding Secretary, was read by him and approved by the meeting.

STONINGTON CT., June —, 1881.

Ex-President Grant :

DEAR SIR :—Allow me to state most briefly for your convenience the gist of what you received herewith in a few distinct heads, as follows :

First—Walter Palmer, a puritan of Nottinghamshire, England, came to Stonington, Conn., in 1653 and was one of the first settlers of the town.

Second—His descendants number many thousands and are scattered from Maine to California, over six thousand " Palmers" being recorded by a Genealogian.

Third—It is an honor and a pleasure, sir, for us to be able to state the facts that you are a descendant of the said Walter Palmer in the eighth generation.

Fourth—His descendants are to have a Palmer Re-Union at Stonington, Conn., on August 10th and 11th of this year.

Fifth—The date of the Re-Union is the anniversary commemoration of the " Battle of Stonington " in the War of 1812, our victory over the same nation that bore our worthy ancestor.

Sixth—You are specially invited to honor the occasion with your presence, and grant a thousand or more " Palmers " whom we trust will there and here assemble an opportunity to pay their respects to you, a kinsman.

Seventh—Your acceptance will allow us the pleasure of arranging to place at your disposal at that time in the Grand Central Depot, N. Y., the palace car " Palmer " to bring you hither.

Eighth—A solicitous and appreciative array of Walter Palmer's descendants await the early intimation that you will endeavor to join us on that day in the social and paternal festivities of a real Anglo-American re-union.

(Signed) IRA H. PALMER, Corresponding Secretary.

Meeting adjourned to July 13.

I. H. PALMER, Clerk.

STONINGTON, CT., July 13, 1881.

An adjourned meeting of the PALMER RE-UNION held in the Baptist vestry this date.

E. H. PALMER, Moderator,
and I. H. PALMER, Clerk.

Voted, That the President, with John C. Palmer, of Norwich, Ct., and Edwin T. Palmer, be a committee on Transportation.

Voted, That John C. Palmer, of Norwich, Ct., and B. P. Palmer, of Boston, be added to the Invitation Committee.

Voted, That the two following committees be blended as one committee. Programme—Mrs. A. G. Palmer, Miss Grace Stanton, Miss Emily Wheeler, A. A. Palmer with the Corresponding Secretary be the Programme Committee ; also Mrs. R. T. Loper, Jr., with authority to enlarge. Committee on Arrangemants—Thomas W. Palmer, Edwin T. Palmer, Dr. C. E. Brayton, I. A. Palmer and James E. Palmer, with authority to enlarge.

Voted, That Col. Edwin Palmer, of Norwich, and —— Newcomb, of New London, be added to the Finance Committee.

Dr. C. E. Brayton having tendered to the Re-Union the use of his new hall till after August 11th, it was

Voted, That the thanks of the Palmer Re-Union be tendered to Dr. C. E. Brayton for so acceptable an expression of his kindness and good-will.

Voted, That Rev. A. G. Palmer deliver the Address of Welcome on August 10th.

Voted, That the following-named gentlemen be invited to respond to name as follows:

" Cheseborough "............ Rev. Amor Cheseborough.
" Stanton "................. Dr. Geo. D. Stanton.
" Miner ".................. Ex-Gov. Miner.
" Noyes "................... Rev. Gurdon Noyes.
" Denison "................ Rev. F. Denison.

Voted, That Miss Grace Stanton, Mrs. John Chesebro, Miss Emily Wheeler, Miss Sara Palmer, Mrs. R. T. Loper, Jr., and Miss Emma W. Palmer be the Floral Committee.

The Corresponding Secretary stated to the meeting that he had used the column of the *Mirror* for the good of the Re-Union and for the purpose of creating a favorable sentiment in the community toward the Re-Union, and had made an arrangement with Editor Anderson to have the use of one column of Re-Union matter per week, with the agreement to take 100 copies of the *Mirror* at 5 cents each—$5.00 per week. Upon motion of Judge Wheeler, it was

Voted, That the Corresponding Secretary be and hereby is authorized to make arrangements as stated, or what shall be for the best interests of the Re-Union.

Voted, That the President be authorized to appoint and add to existing committees proper persons he may select from New London, Montville and Norwich.

The President stated to the meeting that since we last met, one of our number who had met with us—a Vice-President, the Rev. Roswell C. Palmer—had passed away. Whereupon it was

Voted, That the Corresponding Secretary draw up suitable resolution to the memory of our departed friend and co-worker of the Palmer Re-Union, and the same placed upon our records.

Voted, That when we again meet it shall be at Brayton Hall.

Meeting adjourned to July 20, 1881.

Attest: I. H. PALMER, Clerk.

STONINGTON, CT., July 20, 1881.

Meeting called to order.

Hon. E. H. PALMER, Moderator,
and H. C. PALMER, Clerk, *pro tem.*

Minutes of last meeting read and approved.

Resolution upon the death of Roswell C. Palmer read by the Corresponding Secretary, and ordered upon our records ; also to be inserted in the "*Mirror.*"

Upon motion of Mrs. A. G. Palmer, the programme as reported on was laid upon the table to be taken up as the first business of the next meeting.

Voted, That Mrs. F. Chesebro, Miss Brayton, I. H. Palmer, and H. C. Palmer be added to the Floral and Decorating Committee.

Voted, That H. C. Palmer, Noyes F. Palmer and Mrs. I. H. Palmer be added to the Musical Committee.

Ex-Alderman Josiah Palmer, of Brooklyn, N. Y., was present and made a very encouraging report of the interest in the Reunion among the non-resident descendants.

Meeting adjourned to July 27, 1881.

Attest :   H. CLAY PALMER, Clerk *pro tem.*

STONINGTON, CT., July 27, 1881.

Pursuant to adjournment meeting was called to order.

Hon. E. H. PALMER, Moderator
and H. C. PALMER, Clerk.

Minutes last meeting read and approved.

Programme as read from the committee was approved, subject to necessary additions and arrangement.

After some discussion upon the subject, it was

Voted, That the balance of the programme be left to the discretion of the committee.

Voted, That the caterer, Mr. L. A. Tillinghast, be arranged with according to his letter or proposition.

Voted, That the Committee of Arrangements appoint a subcommittee.

Adjourned to August 3.

Attest :   H. CLAY PALMER, Clerk.

STONINGTON, CT., August 3, 1881.

An adjourned meeting of the PALMER RE-UNION was held this date.

ELISHA H. PALMER, Moderator,
and H. CLAY PALMER, Clerk.

Minutes of last meeting read and approved.

Report of Committee on Arrangements, made by I. H. Palmer, he having been to Boston to arrange for the tents, and to Providence to see the caterer, about fire-works and electric lights. After a verbal report on each, the following was:

Voted, That Prof. Blank's proposition to furnish fire-works for the evening of the 10th for $50 and the expense of transportation be accepted.

Voted, That the Corresponding Secretary offer the Fulton Electric Light Company of New York the sum of $50 for the use of three electric lights on the evening of the 10th, we to furnish engine power and transportation of the machine from Providence.

Voted, That Miss Sara A. Palmer be a special committee to see Mr. Robert Palmer and secure the Noank Brass Band for two days and one evening—10th and 11th of August.

Voted, That Frank A. Palmer, of Westerly, be added to the Musical Committee.

Voted, That Mr. Tissington, of the Union Square Theatre, be appointed a Musical Director of the Re-Union.

Voted, Thanks to Mr. F. A. Palmer for the hymn "Battle Hymn of the Republic" composed by him; it to be left in hands of Musical Committee.

Voted, Thanks to Rev. A. G. Palmer and Miss Sara A. Palmer for hymns composed by them.

Voted, That H. F. Palmer, of Norwich, be added to the Decoration Committee.

The Corresponding Secretary read the following correspondence with the Borough authorities:

STONINGTON, CT., July 30, 1881.

To the Hon. Warden and Burgesses of Stonington :

GENTLEMEN :—I deem it proper to state to your Honorable Body that a Re-Union of the Palmer Family is to be held within the limits of the borough on August 10th and 11th, and that we have good reason to suppose there will be a large gathering of persons attending—very many from other States. Will also

mention that Gen. Grant has promised us one day of his presence, probably the 10th.

The assemblage of so large a number of persons on that occasion, and nearly all of them strangers, it may not be out of
place to thus inform you.   The invited guests will, of course,
appreciate good order and kindness on the part of the borough.

Very truly yours,

I. H. PALMER, Cor. Secretary.

STONINGTON, CT., July 30, 1881.

To the Cor. Secretary of Palmer Re-Union, Stonington :

We, the Warden and Burgesses of the Borough of Stonington, in meeting assembled this date, are in receipt of your favor
of same date, informing us of the proposed " Palmer Re-Union "
to be held August 10, 1881, within the borough limits.   After
consideration of the matter, the following was passed by this
body as its expression of good-will and feeling toward your Re-
Union :

Voted, That the courtesies of the Borough of Stonington be
and are hereby extended to the members of the " Palmer Re-
Union " and to their illustrious guest, Ex-President Grant, and
others on the days of August 10th and 11th.

Attest :   J. S. ANDERSON, Clerk.

Whereupon it was

Voted, That the expression of good feeling on the part of
the Borough authorities, as evidenced by their vote of July 30,
calls from us reciprocal thanks, which we express, by a special
invitation, to that Honorable Body to occupy seats on the Re-
Union platform.

Meeting adjourned to Monday August 8, at 10 A. M.

Attest :   H. CLAY PALMER, Clerk.

LITERATURE OF THE PRESS

BEFORE THE RE-UNION.

[EXTRACTS.]

[FROM THE NEW YORK TRIBUNE.]

A grand Re-Union of the Palmer family is to be held in Stonington, Conn., on the 10th and 11th of August, the anniversary of the battle of Stonington in the War of 1812. The Palmer family in this country is said to number now between 6,000 and 7,000, the various members of it being scattered over the East and West, but the majority residing in New-England and this State. The Re-Union is intended to bring as many of them as possible together and to make them acquainted. Walter Palmer, the original ancestor of the greater portion of the present generation, came to this country in 1629 with John Endicott, having charge of six ships filled with Puritans. After making his home in several of the New England settlements, he finally, in 1653, settled in Stonington, at the old homestead on Wequetequock Cove, where the Re-Union is to be held. His blood has flowed in the veins of one of our Presidents, and of the Governors of four different States of the Union. Among the clergymen and the doctors of the country are also several descendants of Walter Palmer. Probably no other family in the United States can count so many descendants from one ancestor as that of the Palmers. Noyes F. Palmer, of Jamaica, Long Island, has been engaged for some time in collecting the genealogical record of the family. In this record, it appears that the name of Palmer was derived from an episode which occurred during the crusades. Those who returned from the holy wars brought back, as a token and remembrance of their pilgrimage, palm leaves. In the minds of the early Christians they soon became known as palm-bearers, and this designation became perverted into the word "palmers," a name which the family subsequently assumed. In 1621 William Palmer, the first of the family, came to this country. This was a year after the *Mayflower* brought her first cargo of pilgrims to America. William Palmer settled in Salem, Mass., and from him a great many of the Palmers of New England descended in a direct line. Walter Palmer followed in 1629, and, after his final settlement at the spot where the city of Stonington now stands, died in 1661, leaving twelve children, from whom have sprung descendants numbering at the present time over 6,000 persons.　Nearly all the records of these have been preserved by Noyes F. Palmer, and such of them as are not known to him will receive invitations to the family jubilee upon sending their addresses to him at Post Office box No. 188, Jamaica, Long Island.　Gen. Grant has accepted an invitation to be present on one of the days of the Re-Union.　E. H. Palmer and Noyes F. Palmer have taken the initiative in arranging for the festival, but E. H. Palmer will have charge of the arrangements.　The first day's exercises will consist of historical addresses, poems, music, and a general acquiring of acquaintance. Judge R. A. Wheeler, of Stonington, will deliver the address; Mr. William Pitt Palmer will recite the principal poem, and the Rev. A. G. Palmer, D. D., the father of A. M. Palmer, manager of the Union Square Theatre, is also expected to contribute a poem.　On the second day a grand "tent meeting" is to be held at the homestead.

[FROM THE BROOKLYN UNION-ARGUS.]

A few days ago the *Union-Argus* published a short notice of a proposed reunion of the " Palmer Family " at Stonington, Conn., in August next.　A glance at the Brooklyn City Directory reveals hundreds of families bearing that name, and for these people, to whom the matter must be of warm interest, and to those outside likely to be reached by these columns, the following facts have been supplied by Noyes F. Palmer, of Jamaica, L. I., who has been for several years at work upon the Palmer genealogy.　The reunion is to be held at Stonington on the 10th and 11th of August, the date of the battle of Stonington in the war of 1812.　In " Palmer's Genealogical Record " are recorded over six thousand descendants of Walter Palmer, who settled in Stonington in 1653, and as he is the original ancestor of the larger portion of the present generation, it is fitting and appropriate that the family gathering should be held at the place designated. The blood of Walter, the Puritan of 1629, has flowed in the veins of one of our chief magistrates and General of the army. The same blood has warmed the hearts of Governors in four different States, also the Speaker of the House of Representatives, and in Assemblies of at least five States are among its honors.　In the professions of Divinity and Medicine, and among inventors and patentees, are also numbered many descendants of Walter Palmer.

The descendants have migrated chiefly to the East and West. Connecticut, Massachusetts and New York seem to hold the greater part, while a few are seen to be settled as far west as Nebraska, Michigan and Arkansas.　Among the direct descendants locally are found Dr. Lucius N. Palmer, Lorin Palmer, and William Pitt Palmer, the poet. In the record referred to by Noyes F. Palmer, from 1629 to 1881, are gleaned a few notes of interest as follows : "Traditionary evidences state that the name Palmer was derived during the epoch of the Crusades ; that those who returned from the Holy Land brought back, as a token of their pilgrimage, palm leaves. The perversion became palm bearers, and finally palmers. The first Palmer pilgrim to this country came in the vessel *Fortune* in 1621, the following year after the *Mayflower*, and was named William Palmer, and settled at Salem, Mass. From him many New Englanders are descended. In 1629, then followed Walter Palmer, who came with John Endicott, he having charge of six ships filled with freemen from England, bound to the Western Continent. Thus any Palmer who can trace their lineage to Connecticut or Massachusetts are in all probability descendants of those two early settlers.

After various removals from place to place, Walter Palmer settled on the site of Pawcatuck, now Stonington, and was appointed "constable" in 1658. He was almost a giant in physique, weighing over 300 pounds, and standing six feet high. He died at Stonington in 1661, leaving twelve children, Grace, John, Hannah, Elihu, Nehemiah, Moses, Benjamin, Gershom, Jonas, Elizabeth, Rebecca and William. From these children have sprung over 6,000 Palmers, whose records are preserved except in a few instances. The family "jubilee" is to be held on the "Old Homestead" in Stonington, and the following is the outline of the proposed proceedings : The first day's exercises will consist of historical addresses, poems, music and general acquiring of acquaintance. The second day a large "tent" meeting will be held at the Homestead, where stands the ruins perhaps of one of the oldest dwelling-houses of stone on the continent, with its old "Balm of Gilead" trees still growing, under whose branches have passed ten generations.

The Re-Union is in charge of E. H. Palmer, President ; H. Clay Palmer, Treasurer ; I. H. Palmer, Corresponding Secretary ; A. S. Palmer, Secretary of Record, and Noyes F. Palmer, Committee on Invitations. The latter gentleman invites all of the family name to send him their addresses to box 188, Jamaica, L. I., in order to secure a card of invitation and further particulars in regard to transportation, etc. Messrs. E. H. and Noyes F. Palmer are the primal movers in this affair, and from present indications it promises to be an unqualified success. It is expected that Judge R. A. Wheeler, of Stonington, will deliver the first address, and Mr. William Pitt Palmer the principal poem, while Rev. A. G. Palmer, father of A. M. Palmer, the well-known theatrical manager, of New York, is expected to write a poem for the occasion. Any genealogy of the family will be thankfully received by Mr. Noyes F. Palmer, at Jamaica.

[FROM THE BROOKLYN DAILY TIMES.]

I am a palmer, as you see,
Which of my life much part have spent,
In many a far and fayre countrie,
As pilgrims do, of good intent.   —*Sir Walter Scott.*

A family re-union which is expected to arouse much interest the coming month is that of the Palmers. The representatives of the family are widely scattered in many States of this country, and there has never been a gathering of them together. Very many of the families can trace their descent to Walter Palmer, the Puritan, who settled in Pawcatuck, now Stonington, Connecticut, in 1653. Largely through the efforts of Elisha H. Palmer, a wealthy manufacturer of Montville, Ct., the Re-Union to take place at Stonington, Ct., August 10th and 11th, has been arranged. This date is chosen from the fact that it is the anniversary of the battle of Stonington in the War of 1812, the chief event in the history of this quiet New England town.

The Palmers were among the earliest settlers of this country. While none of the name came over in the *Mayflower* in 1620, William Palmer came in the *Fortune*, in the following year, from Nottinghamshire, England, and landed in Salem, Mass. His descendants are chiefly in Rhode Island. Most of the present representatives of the name are descendants of three of the early immigrants. The most numerous branch is that descended from Walter Palmer. He came to this country in 1629, landing at Salem. After living at Charleston and Rehoboth, Mass., he went to Stonington in 1653. He was made constable of the town in 1658, being physically a large man, his weight being 300 pounds. He left twelve children at the time of his death in 1661. Most of his descendants are found in Connecticut and New York. A branch of the family in Norwich, Ct., is descended from Thomas Palmer, who came from Ipswich, England, in 1635, and the descendants of William Palmer, who settled in Hampton, N. H., in 1638, are numerous in that State, Vermont, and northern New York.

Among the descendants of Walter Palmer, in the eighth generation is General Grant. The well-known representatives of the Palmer name at present are General John M. Palmer, ex-Governor of Illinois; Dr. John W. Palmer, of Baltimore, the poet and magazine writer, author of several books; the Rev. Dr. Ray Palmer, Secretary of the Congregational Union, who is best known as a poet and hymn writer, author of " My Faith Looks up to Thee ;" Erastus D. Palmer, the well-known sculptor, whose " White Captive" is perhaps the best work of a native American sculptor; George W. Palmer, member of Congress from 1859 to 1863 ; Frank W. Palmer, founder of the *Inter-Ocean*, of Chicago; General Joseph Palmer, of Massachusetts; William Pitt Palmer, the venerable poet of this city; and A. M. Palmer, of Union Square Theatre. Most of these trace their lineage back to Walter Palmer.

Among his descendants in the female lines are ex-Governor Miner, of Connecticut; Dr. J. Hammond Trumbull, of Hartford; and the Rev. Frederick Denison.

Among the best-known bearers of the name in England are Sir Roundell Palmer, Baron Shelbourne, the distinguished states-man, and Dr. Edward H. Palmer, Professor of Arabic at Cambridge University, one of the most learned Oriental scholars in the world, and whose books are undisputed authority.

The origin of the family name is not lost in the mists of antiquity. The Crusaders in their marches to Jerusalem in the Middle Ages, from the time of Peter the Hermit to the close of the Fourteenth Century, had many followers who sought to see the tomb of Christ from sacred motives. Many of these pilgrims on their return wore palm leaves in their hats or carried staves made from palm branches. They thus came to be called Palmers, or bearers of the palm. Some were also distinguished by the scallop shell, worn twisted in their hat band. The name soon passed into literature. Shakespeare frequently uses the word, as these quotations show : " My sceptre for a palmer's walking staff." " Where do the palmers lodge, I beseech you ?" In Spencer's " Farie Queene " we find the following description of an aged pilgrim :

> " Him als accompanyd upon the way,
> A comely palmer, clad in black attire ;
> Of ripest years and hieres all hoarie gray,
> That with a staffe his feeble limbs did stire
> Lest his long way his aged limbs should tire."

The distinction between a palmer and a pilgrim gradually grew up, and Sir Walter Scott, in his antiquarian researches, states that the pilgrim was one who visited a shrine and then returned home, while the palmer visited shrine after shrine, going from place to place and living on alms. As these palmers settled down, their surname was assumed from what they had been, as in the case of most common surnames. The family motto relates to the palm as the reward of noble service. It is *Palmam qui meruit ferat*—" Let him who has won it bear the palm."

A tastefully gotten up invitation to the coming Re-Union has been sent to each representatives of the family whose address could be learned by Mr. Noyes F. Palmer, of Jamaica, L. I. Mr. Noyes F. Palmer has been the leading spirit in arousing the family interest which has led to this Re-Union. He has been engaged for twenty years in collecting and collating material relating to the genealogical history of the Palmers, and has already secured more or less information relating to upwards of 7,000 of the name, and has traced many branches of the family successfully. The result of his researches will be published shortly.

The plan of the Re-Union was devised by him and E. H. Palmer, of Montville, Ct., who is President of the Re-Union. The other officers in charge of the matter are A. S. Palmer, Jr., Secretary of Record; H. Clay Palmer, Treasurer, Ira H. Palmer, Corresponding Secretary, and Noyes F. Palmer, Committee on Invitations. The back of the invitations bears the name " Walter Palmer," ancestor of the majority of those who represent the names, and the dates 1653 and 1881. Palm leaves and the family motto, together with the date of the Re-Union, are also delineated. The invitation proper begins with a quotation from Shakespeare. It is ornamented with an engraving of the old homestead of Walter Palmer, at Stonington, a solid-looking house with eaves near the ground, and an old-fashioned well sweep and Balm of Gilead trees in front. It stands on Wequetequock Cove. The vessel in which the Puritan ancestors crossed the ocean is also depicted, and the dates at which Walter Palmer established himself at different places—Charlestown, 1629; Seekonk, 1643, and Pawcatuck (now Stonington), 1653.

It is expected that the exercises will be largely social, but arrangements have been made for speaking, reading of poems, and music. The first meeting will be held in the Congregational Church, if its capacity is not exceeded. Otherwise the meeting will be on the green adjoining. Judge R. A. Wheeler, of Stonington, will make the leading historical address: Different branches of the family will be spoken for by various clergymen, doctors and lawyers. William Pitt Palmer, who is seventy-six years of age, has promised to write a poem for the occasion, which will be read. The Rev. A. G. Palmer, father of Messrs. A. M. and W. R. Palmer, of the Union Square Theatre, will read a poem which he has written for the day. Mrs. Joseph F. Knapp, of this city, whose maiden name was Palmer, and whose musical abilities are well known, is expected to sing several solos.

A homestead meeting under a tent provided for the purpose at the old Palmer house on Wequetequock Cove, one of the oldest houses in the country, will be the feature of the second day, August 11. A delightful family Re-Union is expected.

The arrangements for transportation have been well made. All of the railroads in the State will furnish tickets at half fare to all who have the invitations to the Re-Union. The same arrangement has been made with the Stonington line of steamers from New York. It is also hoped to arrange for a special excursion steamer from New York, in which those who secure their passage can hold their state-rooms and secure their meals while at Stonington. If a sufficient number of persons will arrange to go by this from New York, Brooklyn and vicinity, the boat will be provided.

General Grant has been especially invited to attend the Re-Union, and it is hoped he will accept. The number of representatives of the name Palmer in Brooklyn, as shown by the Directory, is 123; in New York the number is more than twice as great. It is expected that these will be well represented in Stonington, August 10 and 11. Invitations can be secured by addressing Noyes F. Palmer, Jamaica, L. I.

[FROM THE STONINGTON MIRROR.]

NEW YORK CITY, July 27, 1881.

Ira H. Palmer, Esq.:

DEAR SIR—In answer to yours of July 21st, in regard to the Palmer Re-Union, I will say that I shall be very glad to attend at Stonington for one of the days mentioned, if it is possible for me to do so at that time.

Yours, truly,   U. S. GRANT.

There was a good deal of disappointment at the absence of Gen. Grant, who is a direct descendant of Walter Palmer's oldest daughter, and who had promised to be present a part of one day at least. Arrangements had been made for a special train to bring him from New York to Stonington. He was compelled to be absent, however, on account of the death of his brother. On Monday Mr. Ira H. Palmer received the following dispatch in response to one which he sent to the ex-President on Saturday:

NEW YORK, August 8, 1881.

To Ira H. Palmer:

Domestic reasons will prevent my attending the Palmer Re-Union.   U. S. GRANT.

This dispatch was read by Ira H. Palmer just before the close of the morning exercises.

If possible, the Re-Union grounds will be lighted with three electric lights; arrangements to that effect are being made. To do so will require much special effort, but it is hoped the obstacles can be overcome.

The caterer tables will be 200 feet long, and covered by canvas. On Monday morning work will commence on the Re-Union lot, and everything to be in order on Tuesday.

All Palmers, or descendants of Walter Palmer, without regard to family name, that have been omitted in the issuance of invitations to the Re-Union, will please consider themselves hereby invited, and, upon application to the committee at Brayton Hall, can receive one. It should be distinctly understood that the management does not intentionally omit the inviting of any descendant of the patriarchal Walter Palmer.

To the descendants of co-progenitors of ancestral families of this town, we say :

The subject of family re-unions is becoming popular in this country, and being laudable, and of a beneficial nature, is really entitled to consideration by those persons having an interest in them respectively. The Palmer Re-Union has from its inception and recent growth been the subject of study upon the part of the management, to introduce moral and interesting features, and as far as possible remaining blind to the experiences or plan of any former re-union. Any future family re-union will therefore have' the benefit of our experience as regards defect and lost opportunities, and we trust a criticising public will treat us charitably.

[FROM THE PROVIDENCE JOURNAL.]

Stonington is to have a good time, in a good way, and for a good purpose. The knightly Palmers, by the thousand, under the banner of "*Palman qui meruit ferat,*" with detachments of the Stantons, Chesebroughs, Minars, Noyeses, Denisons, and the like, are to assemble on the 10th and 11th of August, to recall the deeds of the fathers and the history of the town. Walter Palmer, a prince in physique as in sterling character, measuring six feet and some inches, came from England and settled first in Charlestown, Mass., in 1629, afterwards in Seekonk in 1643, and finally at Stonington in 1653. Having lived on both sides of Rhode Island, and being well acquainted with Roger Williams and John Clarke, he became almost a Rhode Islander. Rhode Island, therefore, will gladly claim stock in the grand Re-Union and festive celebration, taking along a few clams to be spiced with nutmegs.

The 10th of August also signalizes the spunky battle of Stonington, which occurred in 1814. when Commodore Hardy's bomb-brig, *Despatch*, got her despatch in having her hull handsomely perforated and severely splintered by cannon played by Stonington volunteers. Doubtless some of the Palmer braves will " shoulder crutch, and show how fields are won." The celebrations are to be in tents, halls, and open fields, and all the doors of Stonington will be ajar. The order embraces processions, orations, poems, annals, incidents, songs, toasts and feasts, to all of which efforts the descendants of Walter Palmer are fully equal, and so Stonington, for once, will get socially and intellectually stirred to her heart.

General Grant, who is a palm from the stalwart palm-root, Walter Palmer, will be present one of the gala days, probably the 10th, coming from New York and returning in the splendid palace car " Palmer," and he will unquestionably find a more encouraging reception at Stonington than he found in the Wilderness of Virginia. And multitudes of people will say, " When he doth ride abroad, may we be there to see."

Such re-unions and patriotic celebrations have in them a large residuum of positive good : they increase our sacred love of home ; they hallow the memories of our deserving ancestors ; they purify and quicken our bond of brotherhood, and deepen and strengthen our love of country, and our devotion to all our republican institutions. The Palmers are to be congratulated on the spirit, enterprise and order manifest in the arrangement made for this great gathering. F. D.

[FROM THE CORTLAND (N. Y.) DEMOCRAT.]

The Palmer family of this county, of which Irving H. Palmer, Esq., is a worthy member, is descended from the old stock, and have been invited to attend the Re-Union.

[FROM THE HOPE VALLEY ADVERTISER.]

We glean from the press, the great interest awakened all over the country in the coming Re-Union of the Palmer family, at Stonington, Ct., on the 10th and 11th of August next. It promises to be the greatest event in this section for many years, and will only be eclipsed by the Groton Centennial that follows in September. About three thousand invitations have been sent out, and the responses being daily received are numerous and full of appreciative expressions.

[FROM COOLEY'S WEEKLY.]

The Palmer Re-Union, which is to take place at Stonington, August 10th and 11th, 1881, is assuming quite large proportions.

Permit me to say a few words concerning it in your paper, which circulates so extensively. I will only venture (as Hon. Richard A. Wheeler is to give a genealogical record of the Walter Palmer families) that Walter Palmer came to this country from England in 1629 and was sworn a freeman in the Massachusetts colony, May, 1631. He removed in the year 1642 to Rehobeth, Plymouth colony. Here he purchased large tracts of land and filled various town offices. The next we hear of him he is in Connecticut purchasing land of Gov. Haynes. The possession was given July, 1653. In 1655 he had one thousand one hundred and ninty-one acres. His lands were situated on the shore of Wequetequock cove in Stonington, where we propose to have appropriate services on the 11th of August, near the house he built, a part of which is now standing, and also near where his remains were laid. His descendants are very numerous and reside mostly in Connecticut, Massachusetts, Rhode Island and New York States, and a few in almost every State in the Union. Noyes F. Palmer, of Jamaica, Long Island, N. Y., has gathered the lineage of nearly six thousand Palmers. There will be over five thousand invitations sent out. There are other Palmers that came over soon after Walter, and to whose descendants we extend a cordial invitation to participate in our Re-Union. Walter Palmer brought with him his daughter Grace (his wife having died in England). She married Thomas Miner in 1634, by whom she had twelve children. From one of these Hon. Richard A. Wheeler has accurately traced the lineage of General Grant. He will be invited to attend. There have been several meetings, at which officers and committees have been chosen to to carry out a programme for the occasion. At the next, to be held in Stonington, in the vestry of Doctor Palmer's church, at 2 P. M., the 29th inst. (Wednesday), it is desirable to finish as far as practicable the arrangements that will make the Re-Union a complete success. To this end all Palmers in New London County and vicinity that feel a special interest in the matter are requested to attend. Any further information can be obtained by addressing Ira H. Palmer, of Stonington, the corresponding secretary, or the subscriber, E. H. PALMER, President.

MONTVILLE, Conn., June 24, 1881.

[FROM THE MYSTIC PRESS.]

Interest is growing in the Palmer Re-Union, which will take place in this village, August 10th and 11th. Correspondence is almost daily received from members of the family, who are deeply interested in the affair. The treasurer visited Mr. Noyes F. Palmer (one of the vice-presidents) at his residence at Jamaica, L. I., last week. Mr. P. is very pleasantly situated only eight miles from Long Island City, at Maple Grove Cemetery, a large tract of ground containing nearly one hundred acres. Mr. P. acts in the capacity of superintendent and civil engineer of the same. The corporation was opened about five years ago, and has at the present time some four hundred lot owners from Brooklyn, New York, and the surrounding villages. Among some of the most remarkable features of the cemetery are the chapel and superintendent's lodge, built of stone, with steep French roofs. In the chapel building there is a chapel hall for the accommodation of funerals; also waiting rooms, and office of the superintendent. The lodge is situated at the main entrance, and is as convenient as pretty in design. Mr. P. has been for the past twenty years writing up the genealogy of the descendants of Walter Palmer, and has to-day some six thousand names of the family.

[FROM THE NEW YORK EVENING POST.]

The position occupied by the family in the modern world presents many points of interest to science; and anthropologists will therefore not need to have their attention called to the approaching " Re-Union of the Palmer Family," which is to take place at Stonington, next month, and to which General Grant has received an invitation. The letter sent to him calls his attention to the fact that he is one of the descendants of Walter Palmer, who was one of the " first settlers " at Stonington; that his co-descendants number "many thousands," scattered "from Maine to California;" that they propose to have a " Palmer-Re-Union," on the 10th and 11th of August, at Stonington; that the ex-President is therefore specially invited to allow a thousand or more " Palmers " on those days to pay their respects to him as a kinsman; that the palace car " Palmer " will be placed at his disposal for the occasion; and that "a solicitous and appreciative array" of his co-descendants are longing to have him join them on that day in " the social and fraternal festivities of a real Anglo-American Re-Union." The invitation bears the well-known motto: *Palmam qui meruit ferat.* Communal reunions of this kind are peculiar, we believe, to the United States, and have become of late years a noticeable feature of social life here. In older countries, where the family exists as a sort of private corporation, such meetings of the entire body of the descendant of a common ancestor are unknown, and would probably be considered undesirable, as calculated to bring together in an enforced and unpleasant intercourse people widely separated by birth, wealth, social position and breeding. It would, perhaps, also be urged that these re-unions would be chiefly useful and profitable to such members of the family as had been unsuccessful in their struggle with the world, and needed external support and recognition, and would therefore be likely to " run " the re-union in their own interest. None of these objections—to judge by the growing popularity of the custom—seem to be applicable to the circumstances of this country, and such re-unions afford interesting proof of the survival of a primitive sentiment which carries us back to the times when the Aryan or Pelasgian ancestors of " the Palmers " and other families gathered together not once in two hundred years, but three times a day, for purposes of commensal enjoyment. Thus far on all like occasions perfect harmony has prevailed, and the rigid exclusion of " politics " has greatly tended to promote this end. General Grant will, we presume, recollect that he is invited simply as a co-descendant " Palmer," and refrain from saying anything of a political nature calculated to eclipse the gayety of the Re-Union or to stir up passions, which, even in the most closely united families, often produce such unhappy consequences.

Wequetequock Cove.

Walters Homestead

"Where do the Palmers

Stonington, (

A Re-Union o:
is to take place at Stoningt
and 11th days of Auguft,
of the battle of Stonington
You are moft cordiall;
in the re-union and feftiviti(
with, which it is hoped will
attend.

WALTER PALMER came
and was one of the firft fett
defcendants number thoufa
of them together on the 10t
focial acquaintance and enj(
May we have the pleaf(
Truly you)
E.)

A. S. PALMER, JR., *Secretary of*
H. (
IRA H. PALMER, *Corresponding*
NOYES F. PALMER,

1653

PALMER

At Stonington

PALMER

"Palmam qui meruit ferat."

Conn.

H. CLAY PALMER, DEL.

INVITATIONS.

Invitations to the number of six thousand, were executed by the New York *Graphic* from a design by H. CLAY PALMER, of Stonington, Ct. There was a first edition of three thousand printed on light paper, with typographical errors, and it was not intended to use many of them, but it became necessary to send out the whole six thousand. Of this number, about one thousand envelopes were directed at Stonington, Ct., by Corresponding Secretary IRA H. PALMER, from lists prepared there. The other five thousand envelopes were directed at Jamaica, L. I., N. Y., from "*Palmer Genealogical Directory*," by Noyes F. Palmer : some eleven hundred of the latter envelopes were mailed from Stonington.

The limited time to mail these invitations, did not permit of all being sent to names coming only a few days before the date of the Re-Union. No one was intentionally slighted.

RESPONSES TO INVITATIONS,

BEFORE THE RE-UNION, FROM PALMER DESCENDANTS THROUGHOUT THE LAND.

[BRIEF EXTRACTS FROM LETTERS.]

NOTE.—Hundreds of other letters besides those following were received, equally interesting, but space will not allow of their insertion in this volume. In many cases but brief extracts have been made even of those selected to appear.

Captain A. S. Palmer, writes from Illinois: "I went into the navy in 1839, resigned after the Mexican war. I want a memorial invitation, on account of the name Palmer."

Dr. George C. Palmer, of Kalamazoo, Mich., writes: "It will give me great pleasure to be in Stonington."

Attorney Jewett Palmer, of Marietta, O., writes: "I do not see how I can stay away."

C. P. Palmer, of Winsted, Ct., says: "Will endeavor to be present."

John Palmer, of Warwick, N. Y., says: "I intend to meet with you." Note.—He will bring and show deeds, relics, etc., of interest belonging to Palmers.

Mrs. E. A. Abbe, of Mass., says: "Hope to be in Stonington at Re-Union."

Lawyer Palmer, of Cortland, N. Y., writes: "I intend to be present at the Re-Union. * * * ."

Mrs. Lucy Palmer Marshall, of Mass., writes: "Please accept thanks for your beautifully gotten up invitation card for the Palmer Re-Union. Shall attend. * * * ."

E. A. Palmer, of Indiana, writes: "Wish the participators a hearty good time, and many returns of the day."

T. W. Russell, of Hartford, writes: "Having had most pleasant relations with members of the family for twenty-five years, as a son by adoption, I very naturally feel an interest in the proposed gathering, and shall be pleased to be one with you at said meeting."

S. L. Palmer, of C. & N. W. Railway, writes: "Am in possession of a genealogy that dates back several hundred years of the Palmer family."

An aged Palmer from Jewett City says: "Am an old, feeble man. * * * My daughter may attend and represent the family. Wish you all a pleasant and enjoyable time."

A descendant in the Green Mountain State writes: "To those inland as far as Vermont, a vision of the open sea would be more wonderful than a vision of the mountains. * * * I predict a joyful occasion."

Prof. Daniel C. Eaton, of Yale College, writes: "Anything I can do to help the Re-Union, will be a pleasure to me."

A descendant writing from Fayetteville, N. Y., says: "I hope and expect to meet you in person next week, as will several from this place, and aid as far as possible to make this occasion a great success."

A re-unionist writes before coming: "Hope the gathering of the many descendants of one of the most noted families in this glorious old commonwealth, may be every way satisfactory to all concerned." He further writes: "I married one of the very best Palmer girls ever raised in Eastern Connecticut."

Colonel Wessel, of Litchfield County, writes: I came down from Walter straight as a string, and the Palmers are a stock one need not be ashamed of, either."

L. A. Palmer, of Honeoye Falls, N. Y., sends the following:

"A kindly greeting to you all
Gathered in this memorial hall;
A kinship to you I would claim,
By virtues of your honored name.—
A name that's known through all the land
From Western plain to Eastern strand.
"Survival of the fittest," then,
Gives us the chance to live 'mong men;
To live for God, for truth, for right,
And keep our ancient name still bright;
For I could never strike the lyre
To degenerate son of honored sire.
My best respects to all I give,
And may we each so faithful live,
That when on earth our time shall cease,
And we from labor have release,
Be this the meed that we have won—
A consciousness of duty done."

J. L. Moss, Jr., of Westerly, writes: "It will give great pleasure to some of our family to attend the Palmer Re-Union. With best wishes, etc."

Mr. A. M. Palmer cables from London, England, to his father, Rev. Dr. Palmer of Stonington, expressing his regret at not being able to return from Europe in time to be present at the Palmer Re-Union, and sends his greetings to the members of the Palmer family, who may be present on the tenth.

L. H. Palmer, agent Fall River line steamers, says: "Although I can claim no relationship to the descendants of your patriarchal "Walter," yet the fact, that my father was a genuine importation from England during this century, is sufficient for me to join in a Palmer family Re-Union."

Ex-Governor Minor states: "I shall be with you, etc." His maternal ancestor was Grace Palmer, eldest daughter of Walter.

Stockbridge (Mass.) descendants write: "Many thanks for the very enticing invitations to the Palmer Re-Union, which we accept with unfeigned pleasure. * * * Chaucer has told us the Palmers lodge "all over creation," and that means Stonington to every home-bound Palmer."

Rev. A. S. Chesebro' writes: "I shall be happy to be present and to represent William Chesebro', who with Walter Palmer and their fellow planters laid the foundation of society in our beloved native town, long ago."

Rev. Gurdon W. Noyes writes:

"The Re-Union you propose is well suited to keep alive the laudable family pride, to cement old friendships, and form new ones, and in every way to profit the mind and heart. Meeting as you do, near my birthplace, and where my youth was passed, recalling attention to my worthy and much revered ancestor, Rev. James Noyes, it would give me special satisfaction to be there, and share with you in the reminisences, jubilations, and outlooks, of that occasion, etc."

Amos Palmer Barber, of Rahway, N. J., writes: "Shall be happy to be present. Am a direct descendant from Walter."

B. G. Palmer, of Middleton, N. Y., writes: "Shall be one of the happy family."

R. H. Palmer writes: "Am very much interested in the Re-Union, as are all of our family."

Rev. Frederick Denison writes: "My response to the call of

" Denison " will be short, since brevity will be the soul of wit,
in your great gathering. * * ."

As to a poem:

> " Responsive to your favors shown,
> If I may haply touch the string,
> In filial strains I fain would sing,
> The merits of our Mother Town."

[932—From ALVAH PALMER.]

HOME, SOUTH BYRON, FON DU LAC CO., WIS.

Stonington was my birthplace, June 7th, 1801, the place
where my eyes first caught the light on this mundane sphere.
Oh! friend, don't doubt the great happiness it would afford my
declining years to visit the place made sacred to me, and mingle with those of kindred blood. No doubt it will be a " feast
of fat things " to those in attendance. May the God of our
fathers and of all good be present, and direct the assemblage
to His honor and the happiness of all present. My best
regards for all who are congregated on that festal day.

And now to yourself receive my hearty good wishes, and also
to all associated with you.

[1335—From ANDREW PALMER.]

JANESVILLE, WIS.

Nothing could be more agreeable to my wishes than to be
present and join with you in the Re-Union and festivities about
to take place at the old Walter Palmer homestead.

While as descendants of a race largely composed of men
noted for their brave and devout pilgrimages to the sacred
shrine of the Redeemer, it would ill comport with a due regard
for our own self-respect to base, upon that ground alone, a
claim to the respectful consideration of others. History still
verifies the fact that, among the six thousand or more names
already upon the record as descendants of the earlier Palmer
emigrants to this country, is a worthy array of able and distinguished divines, and members of the different secular professions, including many names that have elevated the callings
they have severally chosen, and from among whom have been
taken some of the wisest and most equitable of our law-makers
and chief magistrates. And while it is also a noteworthy fact,
and one of no ordinary significance, that the name by which
we are known is barely second in numerical force to any by
which the English-speaking race is designated, and embraces
among those who have borne it some of the ablest jurists and
state counsellors of the old world, rare indeed are the cases in
which it is to be found upon the records of our criminal courts,

or among the hungry herd of office seekers and official spoils-
men, so degrading to the moral condition of this people, and so
imminent in its bodings of an early and ignominious termina-
tion of our national greatness and glory.

Assuring you, that while I deeply regret my inability to join
with you in the festivities of the occasion, it is only in person
that I shall be absent, as my heart and every good wish will be
with you throughout the entire period of the gathering.

[From MRS. FRANCES PALMER BROWN.]

ELMIRA, N. Y.

My father, Nathaniel Palmer, received an invitation to the
Re-Union of the "Palmer Family" at Stonington, Ct.   It
being quite a task, at his time of life, to write letters, he sent me
the invitation and wished me to write for him thanking you for
the invitation.

About twelve years ago, a daughter of John Palmer came to
Brockport from Madison County, bringing with her a gold-
headed cane which had been her father's, and was to be handed down to each John Palmer in his line.   She said it was given
to a John Palmer away back by one of the "Georges of England," for meritorious conduct.   I saw the cane, and I believe
she said it had been in the family two hundred and fifty years.

[From B. FRANK PALMER.]

PHILADELPHIA, PA.

Your esteemed invitation to the Palmer Family Re-Union is
at hand ; and in accepting it I must beg you to allow me to add
to my acceptance the last line found in that of General Grant
—" I will be with you in thought, if not in person."

It is not probable that our English cousins—Sir Roundell
Palmer, Baron Selbourne, Prof. Edward H. Palmer of Cambridge,
or others of the line—can well come so far, across the ocean, to
be present on the occasion ; and yet you expect the ablest one
of all the Palmer crusaders, not excepting Peter the Hermit, in
the person of Ulysses S. Grant, whose " line," whether dating
from the root of the genealogical tree or from the trunk of some
sturdy old sheltering oak in the " wilderness " of Virginia, we
are more than honored in honoring, and more than justly proud
in boasting of, genealogically.

I will, if required by the record, ignore all others of the line
(ten thousand strong), for three hundred years ; and then (placing General Grant in his *true* position as the *Patriot-warrior*),
still claim for the family in which he is descended a name equal
to the best on two continents.   England would not ask of her
most illustrious family, in three hundred years, more than one

Wellington. America will not ask of any one family a more distinguishing honor than the Palmer line presents in Ulysses S. Grant. There are others in the line, who even in the presence of the great captain (whose deeds must, for a time, obscure all lesser names in *patriotic warfare*), stand forth ready to honorably contend for the palm, with our transatlantic cousin, in all the avenues of art, invention, science and literature ; and covet a warfare in the science of *peace*, in which it is hoped both will excel. The names of many honored descendants of Walter Palmer will appear, and in honoring them, I claim, for one, the Spartan epitaph (little changed)—" Walter had many a worthier son than he."

[1212—From A. S. CHESEBROUGH.]

DURHAM, CT.

There are some of the descendants of the first settler, as you know, who have changed the spelling of their name to *Chesebro*. The original William always wrote his name in full, and so do a large portion of his descendants, most of whom are not now residing in Stonington. May I ask you to see that in your programme for the Re-Union, and in any history of it you may publish, you will be particular and spell the name in full. We do not fancy this *bob-tailed* spelling.

[900—From FANNY CHESEBORO.]

STONINGTON, CT.

Dr. Nathan Palmer owned the farm and house now occupied by Joseph Chesebro, Sr., in the immediate neighborhood of the place where Walter Palmer built his home.

The land was never sold until my father bought it, after the death of his uncle, Denison Palmer.

The house, now owned by my uncle, Denison Palmer Chesebro, in Stonington Boro., also belonged to Dr. Nathan Palmer, originally. A part of my father's house, which has always been a Palmer homestead, is more than a hundred and fifty years old.

[676—From COURTLAND PALMER.]

NO. 151 EAST 18TH STREET, NEW YORK.

As I belong to the Stonington branch, I presume you need no statistics.

I shall attend the meeting on 10th August, unless absolutely prevented.

[1201—From REV. FREDERIC DENISON.]

NO. 28 SOUTH COURT ST., PROVIDENCE, R. I.

Please accept, in behalf of the palm-bearing family, my special thanks for the kind invitation sent me, to attend your grand family Re-Union, of August 10th and 11th, of the current year.

As my great-grandmother, Bridget (Palmer) Gallup, wife of Deacon Benadam Gallup, of Groton, Ct., was a lineal descendant of Walter Palmer, I naturally feel the pulse and pride of the palm-wearers; and since "blood will tell," even to the "third and fourth generation," I shall count it a pleasure and an honor to "put in an appearance," if possible, on the occasion of the great family festival.

[617—From Gen. George W. Palmer.]

137 East 124th St., New York.

I gladly accept the kind invitation to be present at the Re-Union of the Palmer Family on the 10th and 11th prox., at Stonington, and desire to convey my thanks for your courtesy.

I shall endeavor to be present with my wife, and join in the festivities of the occasion.

[1050—From Madame de Giverville.]

St. Louis.

I have gathered some items respecting the Palmers from American and English sources : " There have been about sixty families at a time in England of this very surname, differing in their armes, and no wise related but by marriage. The paternal coate is 2 bans gules, each charged with 3 trefoils of the field. Most one in chief, a greyhound—convent table. The crest is a demi-panther or demi-leopard; argent-spotted azure, fire issuing from his ears and mouth and holding in his paws a holly-bough with leaves and berries proper." " The family, whose patriarch, William le Palmer, was a crusader under Richard Cœur de Leon, was from a remote period established in the county of Sussex, but a branch of it settled in Marston as early as 1559." A descendant of the crusader, Thomas Palmer, came to Boston, married Abigail Hutchinson, and had two sons, Thomas and Eliakim, and a daughter Sarah, who married Mr. Lewis. My grandfather, who was six feet two inches, was said to have derived his stature from the Palmers.

You will notice the name was originally *le* Palmer, as in France; the family bearing the name *le* Pelerin (the pilgrim) have in their armes three scallop shells, and tradition tells their pilgrimage to the Holy Land. The palm is also an emblem of the followers of Christ, and is attributed to the Christian martyrs.

[204—From Edwin Palmer.]

Norwich, Ct.

I am not a descendant of Walter, but of Thomas of Rowley; and yet, as your committee are kindly inviting all Palmers to the Re-Union, I feel at liberty to accept, and shall probably be present. "Palmers all our fathers were," even if there were some thirty different original ancestors for those who bear the name in New England alone, making it thus an impossibility for Walter to be appropriated, much as we may desire to do so, by more than half of us, at the most. But from whomsoever sprung, we are all coming, for you design, of course, the Re-Union, although given under the auspices of Walter's descendants, to be a PALMER Re-Union, do you not? And therefore, you ask to join you in this "gathering of the clan," those who look back to William, passenger in the *Fortune*, 1621, the oldest of us all; and to the other Williams; to John of Charlestown, 1634, and to the eight other Johns; to Henry, to Edward, to George, to Barnabas; to Nicholas of Windsor; to Thomas of Rowley; and the rest.

[717—From ELIHU J. PALMER.]

CARBONDALE, ILL.

The tradition talked into me by my grandmother and grandfather, and confirmed by the "big ha' Bible" which they read, and orally by my father, was that three brothers left old England about the same time, previous to 1688, and I think before the restoration of the Stuarts. That one of them settled in New England, one in the Middle States, perhaps Pennsylvania, and one in what was once called the northern neck of Virginia. I am a descendant of the last, and am able to trace my lineage directly to him with but little trouble. The traits of the family are well interpreted as far we are concerned by the motto—"*Palmam qui meruit*," etc., for my grandfather followed Washington for seven years in the Revolution. My father followed Harrison, 1812.

And may the "returned Crusader descendants" give a good account of themselves on the 10th and 11th prox., is the wish and hope of one of them.

[1029—From HENRY PALMER ENSIGN.]

MOBILE, ALA.

To one who entertains such high veneration for the historic annals of a family whose lineage dates so far back as that to which we belong, the occasion suggested would be fruitful of pleasure and gratification. The reminiscences, which such a re-Union will necessarily call up, put into imperishable record and transmitted to futurity, revivified and modernized, will be treasured by all the participants with an intensity of affection grandly commensurate with the object in view.

The place of rendezvous, too, made by the hand-marks in

peace, and the blood in war, of those whose scions we are proud
to be to-day, will add the glamour of their legendary testimony
to the happiness that awaits those whose good fortune it may
be to give the inspiration of their presence.

[1014—From REV. EDWARD PALMER.]

BARNWELL, S. C.

I cannot refrain from saying that I am proud of the name of
Palmer, and happy in belonging to a lineage of such importance, as to justify the remarkable "Union" proposed. If it is
not too late, I will write to express my regret at not being able
to make one of your favored number. One-third of the way
among the "nineties," and feeble in strength, and at a distance
so remote, I do not feel that it would be practicable or prudent
to mingle in such a vast concourse as will swell your numbers.

But I send my hearty congratulations to you all, and wish the
richest pleasures and the happiest results from the grand
"Union." Still more, I heartily echo the *Palmer Family Motto*:
"Let him, who has won it, bear the palm." May the emblem
"Never get less."

[From FRANCIS A. PALMER.]

NEW YORK CITY, N. Y.

DEAR SIR—It will afford me much pleasure to accept your
kind invitation to meet the Palmer family at Stonington.

[970—From BENJAMIN FISH.]

NEW YORK.

I regret very much that I can only be with you in spirit on
the occasion, for it is a matter of pride with me that some of
my ancestry sprung from the good old tree. And even if there
ran in my veins no drop of Palmer blood, I should still com-
template with the rarest interest a gathering which cannot fail
to awaken anew the most honored memories belonging to my
birthplace and early home, since no history of old Stonington
can begin or end without the name of Palmer.

[897—From GEORGE H. PALMER.]

My father (the late Edmund Palmer) was born in East Haddam, Ct., in the year 1809. Often have I heard him in most
affectionate terms tell of the old homestead. The pleasure of
visiting his birthplace has so far been denied me.

[876—From PROF. ASAPH HALL.]

WASHINGTON, D. C.

My great-grandfather, on my mother's side, was Andrew
Palmer of Stonington, Ct. I knew but little of him, but had

been told that he had a brother Robert, who was a privateer during the Revolutionary War. My grandfather, Robert Palmer, was born in Stonington, and when about 21 years old he moved to Goshen, Ct., where he married and had nine children, my mother, Hannah C., being the oldest. She was born August, 1804, and died in Goshen, March, 1880. My uncle, Andrew Palmer, now about seventy-three years old, is living in Goshen. The next brother, Robert, is in California; and the other, Lemuel, is in Michigan. A younger brother, James, was killed in the Civil War; and all the rest of the generation are dead.

I should be very glad to attend the Re-Union of the Palmer family, but probably it will not be possible for me to do so.

[880—From JOHN B. PALMER.]

CONCORD, N. H.

As I cannot be present on the occasion, I desire to say that in heart I shall be with you all, in all your works and undertakings, and that, as long as life lasts, my doors will be opened wide (as they always have been) to all who bear the name of Palmer.

[686—From JAS. D. PALMER.]

HAVANA, N. Y.

With regret I inform you that I cannot meet at Stonington, August 10th and 11th, and participate in the Re-Union. I don't know as I am a descendant of Walter Palmer. My grandfather, Dan'l Palmer, once lived in Massachusetts; had sixty acres of land near the place Gen. Putnam rode down the stone steps.

[564—From J. C. PALMER.]

QUINCY, ILL.

The occasion will doubtless be one of great interest to all participants, and, circumstances favoring, I should be delighted to be present.

[993—From JOHN H. PALMER.]

SALEM, ROANOKE CO., VA.

It would afford me very great pleasure to visit the home of our ancestors, and mingle with the happy company upon this pleasing occasion; to take by the hand the many we have never seen, but who are of the same blood and of the same honored name.

Please accept, on your own behalf, and of all who may be present, my regrets in not being permitted to be with you (circumstances will not admit of my absence from home at this time), and my earnest desire that this may be an occasion of great rejoicing, the promotion of happy and enduring acquaintances, long to be remembered.

[971—From L. W. Kenyon.]

GOSHEN, CT.

Accept my sincere thanks for your kind invitation for August 10th and 11th. It is with much regret that I find myself unable to attend, although to participate in the exercises on such an occasion would give me very great pleasure.

[1234—From Isabel Grant Meredith.]

My grandfather, the late Billings Grant, was the second son of Dr. Minor Grant, who was a native of Stonington, a surgeon in Washington's army, and a sister of whom married a Palmer, and, I think, settled in Stonington. The families of Hewett and Wheeler, of Stonington, were also related by marriage to my grandfather. My mother, Mrs. Julia Grant Dowe, now living with me, is the eldest daughter of Billings Grant. His only other surviving child is Mrs. Lyman W. Crane, of Stafford Springs, Ct.

[933—From Roswell Randall.]

CLINTON, MICH.

I regret very much that circumstances forbid my attendance at the Walter Palmer Re Union. What a numerous progeny that Walter has at this time! The living members at this time number many thousands, after 228 years. Jacob went down into Egypt with seventy souls, and the Israelites that came up out of Pharaoh's realm have been estimated at six millions. Perhaps after the same length of time, the descendants of Walter may number up in the millions. The Palmers are a law-abiding people. It is presumed that a search of the records of all the jails, penitentiaries and prisons of the country would find very few Palmers among them. Fifty or sixty years ago the Palmers had not become famous, but they are coming to the front : they can now rank among their number, governors, generals, statesmen, college professors, eminent divines, etc., etc. In Stonington and Voluntown, Ct., the Palmers and Randalls intermarried, living in the same locality. Subsequently a portion of them emigrated to Lenox, Madison Co., and to Bridgewater, Oneida Co., N. Y.

In these localities they intermarried still more, but the spirit of emigration has scattered them over all the Western and Northwestern States.

They may be found in all professions, in all pursuits, in all enterprises.

Through my paternal grandmother I am grafted into the family tree.

Let the old tree continue to flourish and extend ; planted on the shore of the Atlantic, its branches have spread over the Rocky Mountains, and taken root on the Pacific coast.

Long may the name in honor shine,
From Eastern to the Western brine ;
And Walter's fame strike deep and high,
While circling ages onward fly.

[855—From MARY DANA SHINDLER.]

NO. 5 WAVERLY PLACE, NEW YORK.

My great-grandfather was pastor of a church in Falmouth, I think, and my grandfather, Job Palmer, went to South Carolina in early life and settled there. He lived to be 97 years of age, and died from influenza—not from old age. He had two sons who were clergymen, my father, Rev. Benj. M. Palmer, D. D., for more than twenty-five years pastor of the largest Congregational church in Charleston, and indeed, in the whole South ; and Rev. Edward Palmer, now 95 years of age and still preaching. My uncle Edward has two sons in the ministry, the well-known and celebrated Dr. B. M. Palmer of New Orleans, and Edward, settled in Alabama. My aunt Sarah (Mrs. Axson), has also a son in the ministry, and one a physician in New-Orleans. I suppose I belong to you, and mean to be present at the Re-Union.

[195—From GEO. D. STANTON.]

It may be safely asserted that none of the offspring of the Pilgrim Fathers can lay claim to more merited eminence in the varied fields of theory, law, physic, the art and science of war, and statesmanship, than the descendants of that sturdy old pioneer settler of my boyhood home, Walter Palmer.

[From LUCRETIA P. SPENCER.]

DOVER, DEL.

As the traveler halting for his noonday meal looks back upon what he has accomplished, and marks well his successes and their causes, also his failures and their causes—the one to copy in the future and the other to avoid—he also looks ahead, searching eagerly for the most direct path for the goal of his ambition. In like manner would it not be well at our family gathering to note well the successes and failures, and their causes, for our future benefit ; and earnestly encourage among our members to religiously labor for the high ambition of attaining perfect physical, mental and moral growth.

[685—From MRS. GEORGE SHERMAN.]

NORWICHTOWN.

My father and two brothers and two sisters are buried at Wequetequock, in the old burying ground. I suppose my grandfather lived there, and perhaps in the old Walter Palmer house. I have in my possession his old Bible which he bought the same day he was drowned.

[931—From HULDAH P. SAFFORD.]

SYRACUSE.

I deeply regret that I am not young enough to accept your kind invitation to the Palmer Re-Union, at Stonington, the place of my birth, and where my forefathers have been educated and spent the best of their days, and where our ancestors have fought for their freedom and obtained liberty, and left for us a free and glorious country. It makes me feel young again when I think of my birthplace and home, and were I fifteen years younger I would be with you at your gathering. I am the youngest and last one left of twelve of my father's family and am in my ninety-sixth year, and do not feel quite as nimble as once : but if I live to see the 10th and 11th of this month, my heart and mind will be with you, and that it will be a glorious meeting of the Palmers is the wish of your aged friend.

[646—From THOMAS R. PALMER.]

OTISVILLE, N. Y.

My grandfather's family consisted of five sons—Samuel, Aaron, Stephen, John and Daniel—all of which are dead. I could enumerate their descendants, but they are legion. I am a son of Stephen, and am in my seventy-second year ; have not been able to get my coat on unassisted for a year and a half, but I shall try and attend the Re-Union of the Palmer family, August 10th and 11th.

[103—From H. CLAY TRUMBULL.]

NO. 725 CHESTNUT ST., PHILADELPHIA.

Returning from a journey which has included Europe, Asia, Africa and America, I find here your invitation to attend the Palmer Re-Union in Stonington next month, and I take pleasure in accepting it.

All the world over, there is no place to a man like his childhood's home for its permanently impressive associations, and I shall be glad to revive my many memories of my native place by a return to it on this noteworthy occasion.

[697—From THEODORE J. PALMER.]

NEW YORK.

I shall take great pleasure in being present at the " Palmer Re-Union " on the 10th of August, and hope the affair will be a great success.

[1275—From William Pitt Palmer.]

FREYEBURG, ME.

Your favor of 13th ult. was forwarded me here by my son, two days since. He found it at my old place of business, from which ill health banished me some three years ago. My physician willed that I should try the air of the mountains for one Summer at least, and I am here accordingly. And just to think that I cannot join you and my other kindred, nine days hence, to honor the memory of our common ancestor at the house by Wequetequock, where his long pilgrimage found a peaceful and honored repose! I regret exceedingly that I cannot be with yon on an occasion so interesting. I should feel myself overpaid, if permitted to occupy the humblest seat among all my kindred. The poem which the papers accord to me, I should be delighted to prepare with all my might, if only the fates had left me some little tuneful ability. To prove my filial interest in the Re-Union, I have sent to the care of Doctor H. G. Palmer, as my representative, a small volume of verses, which perhaps may fill a little chink in the memorials of the celebration. It is but a trifle at best.

[1232—From Mrs. Alice S. Wheeler and Mrs. Elizabeth Easton.]

BOSTON.

The undersigned, great-granddaughters of General Joseph Palmer, of Revolutionary memory, and granddaughters of Joseph Pearce Palmer, his son, would be pleased to meet the various branches who will be present at your gathering, should you think proper to send an invitation.

[919—From J. B. Wood.]

WARWICK, N. Y.

I have a sort of historical record from which I briefly copy. The Palmers of Rockland County are but one branch of the family from New England, and is of English origin. (Gives reference to New York genealogical record and biographical, under the name of Palmer.) John Palmer, as early as 1750, lived near New City, Rockland County; had three sons John, Joseph and Jonathan.

John Palmer, Jr., continued near New City; his children's names are John, Sarah, Joseph, Barbara, Jonathan, Elizabeth, Mary, Catrina and Rebecca.

John Palmer, third, removed to Warwick; his children are David, Uriel, Annie, Sarah, Maria, Hannah, Rebecca and Elizabeth. Maria and Elizabeth are the only ones living. This family came from City Island, as is known by old deeds in their possession.

[1086—From GRACE B. WILGUS.]

BUFFALO, N. Y.

Have received an invitation to the Palmer Re-Union. Am a descendant of Walter Palmer in the straight line. Was born at Stonington, on a farm deeded to my grandfather, Nathaniel Palmer, by Joseph Noyes, February 10th, 1772, and for forty years lived on the farm, and in the borough of Stonington. My brother, Luke Palmer, of Burlington, Iowa, and all of our nephews and neices, I hope, have not been overlooked. Am proud of my ancestry and the old family name of Palmer. Regret that I cannot be with you at this gathering, but believe me heartily in spirit with the occasion.

[1653.] *"PILMAM QUI MERUIT FERAT."* [1881.

WALTER PALMER RE-UNION,

AT

STONINGTON, CT., AUGUST 10 AND 11, 1881.

ORDER OF EXERCISES.

AUGUST 10th.

10:30 A. M.

MUSIC,   -   -   -   -   -   BAND.

PRAYER.

MUSIC.

ADDRESS OF WELCOME,   -   -   REV. A. G. PALMER, D. D.

MUSIC.

INTRODUCTION OF PRESIDENT ELISHA H. PALMER, ESQ.

MUSIC.

INTERMISSION TILL TWO O'CLOCK.

AFTERNOON.

MUSIC—"HOME, SWEET HOME."

HISTORICAL ADDRESS,   -   -   -   JUDGE R. A. WHEELER.

MUSIC.

POEM,   -   -   -   -   REV. A. G. PALMER, D. D.

MUSIC.

"PALMER FAMILIES,"   -   -   NOYES F. PALMER, OF JAMAICA, L. I.

MUSIC.

TENTH OF AUGUST — ANNIVERSARY BATTLE OF STONINGTON; SHORT
ADDRESS BY EX-WARDEN WILLIAMS.

MUSIC—"OLD HUNDRED,"   -   -   -   BAND AND AUDIENCE.

EVENING.

7:30 O'CLOCK.

MUSIC—"AMERICA,"   -   -   -   BAND AND AUDIENCE.

POEM,   -   -   -   REV. FREDERICK DENISON.

MUSIC.

IMPROMPTU SPEECHES OF FIVE MINUTES BY NON-RESIDENT DESCENDANTS OF
WALTER PALMER.

MUSIC—"AULD LANG SYNE,"   -   -   -   BAND AND AUDIENCE.

FIREWORKS BY PROF. BLANK, OF PROVIDENCE.

AUGUST 11th.

PALMER EXCURSION TRAIN TO WEQUETEQUOCK DRY BRIDGE, LEAVING THE
RE-UNION GROUNDS AT 11:30 A. M. PROMPT.

MARCHING, MUSIC "BATTLE HYMN OF THE REPUBLIC," TO WALTER PALMER'S
HOMESTEAD SITE, THENCE TO THE ANCIENT WEQUETEQUOCK BURYING
GROUND, WHERE APPROPRIATE SERVICES WILL BE HELD.

MUSIC—"SWEET BYE AND BYE."

RETURN TO STONINGTON AT 3:30 P. M.

RESPONSES BY DESCENDANTS OF ANCESTRAL FAMILIES OF STONINGTON, CT.

CLAM-BAKE ON THE RE-UNION GROUNDS.

Evening and Closing Exercises to be Announced from the Platform.

PROCEEDINGS.

FIRST DAY—AUGUST 10th.

When morning came upon Stonington the town was full of Palmers. By four o'clock the previous day no hotel accommodations could be obtained, and Palmers lodged upon the hospitality of the residents of the borough. At a preliminary meeting on the 9th, resolutions were adopted by the Re-Union Palmers from various sections of the country, to pay a regular fee to all who furnished accommodations, and the enthusiasm soon became contagious and all seemed to join in endeavoring to lodge the Palmers. The crowds that wended their way on the morning following to the grounds, were evidence that a host of people had been furnished a temporary abiding place. The saying among all was, " *Where did the Palmers lodge ?*"

A large tent with open sides had been erected in the western part of the town near the railway station, and only a few blocks from the Hotel Wadawanuck, and here the public exercises were held. Seats were provided for over a thousand persons, and all were occupied before the exercises began. The tent was furnished by R. M. Yale, of Boston, on the lot between the Hotel Wadawanuck and the upper depot. We may say here that many thanks are due Mrs. Charles P. Williams of this place for her kindness in giving the use of the grounds to the Re-Union Committee. The exercises opened at 10:30 A. M., the tent being crowded. Not only Palmers, but a large number of borough-ites joined in the festivities with a right good will. Music by the Noank Brass Band, A. L. Spicer, leader, was followed by prayer by the Rev. E. B. Palmer, D. D.; the band played again, and Rev. A. G. Palmer, D. D., delivered the Address of Welcome, and after more music came the introduction of Hon. Elisha H. Palmer, of Montville, Ct., the president of the Re-Union.

The afternoon session opened with the singing of " Home, Sweet Home," by the audience, with band accompaniment.

Judge R. A. Wheeler was then presented to his assembled kinsmen and read an extended sketch of Walter Palmer and his
family, which was full of interest and well received. After
more music by the band, the Rev. A. G. Palmer, D. D., of
the borough, delivered a poem prepared for the occasion in his
usual able manner, its delivery occupying a half hour. The
band again assisted, and an interesting paper on the Battle
of Stonington was read by Ex-Warden Ephraim Williams, of
Stonington, the anniversary of which was celebrated by the
Palmer Re-Union. He closed by repeating the following verse:

Soon you will cross the unknown sea,
And reach the heavenly haven if pure you be.
Palmer and friends who have gone before,
Bid kindly welcome to that peaceful shore.
So should we who here remain,
Toil on, in faith " that to die is gain."

The afternoon exercises closed with the singing of " Old Hundred " by the audience.

The evening meeting opened with prayer by Rev. E. Barnebas Palmer, of Boston, with singing " The Palmers' Hymn,"
composed by Miss Sara A. Palmer, of Stonington, to the tune
of "America." Rev. Frederick Denison, of Providence, R. I.,
then recited an original poem. This was followed by an
address on Palmer Families, by Noyes F. Palmer, of Jamaica,
N. Y. After this were short, stirring impromptu speeches by
Ex-Gov. Wm. T. Minor, Francis A. Palmer, Esq., of New
York, Gen. Geo. W. Palmer, who presided temporarily, and
others.

In regard to the exercises on the first day, the Rev. Fred.
Denison wrote to the Providence Press:

" The Palmer Re-Union is a big thing. The Palmers are here
by the thousand, from Penobscot Bay, Puget Sound, the Gulf
of California, and the palmy shores of the Gulf of Mexico. One
might as well think of numbering the children of Israel. They
press upon the borough of Stonington like the ground-swell of
the Atlantic. They are here in houses, halls, tents, cars, carriages and steamboats. The grand pavilion and caterers' tents

make a beautiful cantoinment in full view from the railroad
station on the north margin of the borough.   The town never
before looked so beautiful and lively.   The celebration is a
double one ; it recalls the marvelous evolution of the ancient
Palmer stock, and repeats the memory of the gallant defense
of Stonington in 1814.

"The arrangements, not few or unlaborious, for this monster
Re-Union were made by some of the spirited tribe, particularly
the Hon. E. H. Palmer, of Montville, Ct., president of the occasion ; Ira H. Palmer, corresponding secretary; H. Clay Palmer, treasurer, both of Stonington ; Noyes F. Palmer, family
genealogist, of Jamaica, L. I., N. Y.; and the Rev. A. G. Palmer,
D. D., poet, preacher and orator, of Stonington.   Of course
these leaders had their lieutenants, and their correspondence
reached over all the country.   In short, it is the biggest family
gathering probably that has taken place in Connecticut, if not
in New England.   Of course the newspapers of the country
have duly noticed the plan and purpose of this pilgrimage of
the Palmers to their ancestral shrine, and the columns of the
Stonington Mirror have overflowed with the fullness of even
the preliminary proceedings."

The opening prayer and various addresses of the first day
follow.

PRAYER,

BY REV. E. B. PALMER, D. D., OF BRIDGETON, N. J.

Great and holy God, we thank Thee for Thy mercies unto
our fathers, and for Thy blessings to us, their children.   We render thanksgiving to Thee, that Thy bountiful providence has
attended us through the generations of the past, and brought
so many of us here to greet each other in this fraternal hour.
We acknowledge Thy goodness in the cheer of this bright and
sunny day, and for the transparent air that refreshes us with its
breeze.   We pray for Thy blessing upon us in this great family
gathering.   Direct us in all the services and festivities of this
joyful occasion.   Forgive us our many transgressions in Thy
holy sight.   We acknowledge our sins before Thee, and we

would not forget, at this time, that the hand of chastisement is upon us, as a nation. We humbly beseech Thee, that Thou wouldst look upon our Chief Magistrate, the President of these United States, and restore him again to perfect soundness of body. Grant to bless the means used for his recovery. May Divine wisdom guide those who attend him, that no mistakes may occur, and may it please Thee to raise him up to be a blessing to this nation and to the world. Command Thy blessing upon us for the years to come. May we and our children give heed to Thy word, so that, living in Thy fear, we may continue to share Thy mercies. So guide and direct us, all through the vicissitudes of this life, that at last we may form a part of the great family on high, redeemed through the everlasting covenant by Jesus Christ, our Lord. And to Thee, the Father, the Son and the Holy Spirit, shall be praise forever. Amen.

ADDRESS OF WELCOME,

BY REV. A. G. PALMER, D. D., OF STONINGTON, CT.

Ladies and gentlemen, descendants of Walter Palmer, all who bear the Palmer name, and in whose veins flows the Palmer blood. The pleasant duty has been assigned me of welcoming you to this town, the last home of Walter Palmer, to which he removed in 1653, and where he died in 1661. While not insensible to the honor of this trust, and by no means disinclined to the service, still I could have wished that it might have been committed to lips better able to embody in befitting words, the worthy aims and generous impulses of those with whom this enterprise orignated, and in answer to whose call you are here in such imposing and gratifying numbers to-day.

It had long been felt by many of the Palmer name, and especially by the descendants of Walter Palmer in this town and in towns adjoining, that a family gathering of this kind was very much to be desired, to be held either in this village, or in some place more central and convenient to the largest number of those supposed to be interested in such a movement. And so the matter had been discussed again and again, in all the phases of its desirableness and possibility, but always without any decisive conclusion, or any definite conception of what was wanted, certainly with but very imperfect ideas of how it was to be accomplished, and what the proprieties of the case demanded ; but just at this point of chaotic indecision and inaction, where so many splendid schemes collapse and fail, and so many beautiful day dreams vanish into nothingness, the Hon. E. H. Palmer, of Montville, Ct., came to the front, and by his splendid physique, build, height, manner and spirit, and, above all, by his intense self-reliance and personality, was at once recognized as a Palmer of the Palmers, every way worthy of this service and as one who could be safely trusted and followed therein—indeed as the long-looked-for man for the occasion.

Some three months since he said to two or three persons whom he chanced to meet on our streets that he wished to bring about, this Summer, a Re-Union of the descendants of Walter Palmer. He said that he held last year at Niantic a re-union of the two branches of his own family, the Palmers and Turners, with so much pleasure and interest, that his appetite was sharpened for a more sumptuous and numerously attended feast. He wanted to know who the Palmers were, who he was himself, and where the Palmers lived, and he knew of no better way to settle these questions than to have a re-union of the household in a general Palmer council, for shaking hands and mutual recognition and acquaintance. All this was said with that simple straightforward positiveness peculiar to men of strong purpose and self-reliance—men who, in the successful handling of secular interests, have come to believe in themselves, and to assume that what needs to be done, ought to be done, and what ought to be done *can* be done.

Well, we listened, if not with suppressed incredulity, yet with silent admiration for the sanguine faith of our new leader, and we at once yielded ourselves to his guidance, became his disciples, and awaited orders. We said, " If you will take us, we will take you ; if you will lead, we will follow, and we will see what will come of it." I doubt if the soldiers of Bonaparte, or

Washington, or Grant, or Sherman, had a more enthusiastic confidence in the ability of their leaders than we had in ours; but when I tell you that the significant "we" was limited to two or three very unpretentious and uninfluential persons, you will see how exceedingly unpromising was the outlook for the success of the enterprise. We comforted ourselves, however, with the thought that if we had but a small assembly, we might at least have a pleasant one, and it might be the beginning and nucleus of something better for the future, perhaps for another year. So the first meeting was appointed, and duly advertised to be held in the lecture-room of the First Baptist Church for taking the preliminary steps toward inaugurating a re-union of the descendants of Walter Palmer, to be held at such time and place as, after consultation, might seem befitting. When the day came, five persons attended. At the adjourned meeting, a week after, for a permanent organization, only the same persons were present; we, however, organized and modestly voted ourselves into office, no one dissenting. But we proceeded orderly, and gravely too, for we were not insensible to the importance of the work we were handling. Of course, this beginning was so small as to seem to ourselves almost like presumption, and I do not wonder that those who looked on, thought the affair was "all talk," and must fail from sheer feebleness. But they did not know our leader, and did not take into the account that he was a Palmer of the old, unadulterated stock and that if we were weak in faith and purpose and resources, he was not; so he said to us, "This small beginning does not discourage me in the least. A few will have to handle this matter and put it in motion, anyhow. In fact, a few are better than many; they will all have to work, and can work to better advantage because there will be less waste of time and strength from conflicting interests and counsels." He said everything had to grow, and growth took time. The momentum would be slow at first. A train did not start off at full speed of sixty miles an hour. We should, by and by, get this Re-Union under such headway that we should have to "put on the brakes, or be carried past the station from the pressure of the heavily loaded cars in the rear. The Palmers were a heavy train, and besides we must remember they were on an ascending grade." We knew this was sound logic and good preaching ; and I am glad to see that his strong Palmer good sense and grit and courage have been so abundantly confirmed and rewarded, as the surroundings of this morning, and this great gathering indicate.

It is but just to say that he has been vigorously sustained by his lieutenants, and if his disciples have been few, they have been the more abundantly earnest. Ira H. Palmer, corresponding secretary, and H. C. Palmer, treasurer, with a select number of women, if few, yet very honorable, have rendered timely and efficient aid. The amount of correspondence which Mr. Ira H. Palmer has so successfully handled is simply wonderful, and indicates an ability of dispatch in work of this kind of great practical value. Mr. Noyes F. Palmer, of Jamaica, L. I., has also brought to the work his long experience in the field of genealogical research and his rich treasure of the Walter Palmer literature, which he has been for years accumulating, and the whole movement has been cheered and quickened by his unflagging energy and never-wavering enthusiasm. If any man living can tell " where the Palmers lodge " that man is Noyes F. Palmer. He knows where they lodge by hundreds and thousands. If in his physique somewhat below the old Palmer type, for there were giants among the Palmers in olden times, yet he has somewhere stored away resources of vital force and endurance well nigh exhaustless, making him superior to weariness, and almost incapable of fatigue.

It seems needful to refer to these details of our preliminary work that you may the more readily sympathize with the difficulties with which we had to contend, and so be prepared to make due allowance for any want of completeness or fullness of preparation for the demands of this occasion, and especially that you may know under whose leadership the campaign has been so courageously conducted. And now, having according to our best wisdom brought it thus far, we take great pleasure in laying our assumed responsibilities at your feet and in committing the future of this Re-Union to the wisdom of your counsels and decisions. Our own proud desire has been and is that it may become a permanent organization and go down through the generations to come, binding the Palmers together as one great family; one in culture and literature and not less one in social, moral and religious progress. And now it only re-mains that I should say with the blunt honesty and warm-hearted-ness of the olden times: Friends, we are glad to see you, and are proud to recognize all who bear the Palmer name, and in whose veins flows the Palmer blood, as our own kith and kin, and as belonging to the great Palmer family so widely scattered over this continent, that constitutes so positive a factor in our national life and that from the War of the Revolution through each succeeding conflict has contributed so heroically to the national defense, integrity and perpetuity. We welcome you to the old town, as rugged in its history as in its rocks and hills, and in its more marked epochs, as sublime and grand as the storm-driven waves that dash and break upon its rocky shore. It is the soil that Walter Palmer and his compeers, the Chese-broughs, the Minors, the Stantons, the Noyeses, and others broke up from a wilderness state and made into homes for them-selves and their children. You are here from every part of the land, especially from the West, to which many of the Palmers from this town early removed, and laid there the foundation for that golden prosperity in wealth and liberal culture and also in social and religious relations for which the family is now as distinguished as any other family in the land, and which we are proud to see so fully represented here to-day."

And now, if any still ask, in the quotation from Shakespeare, " Where do the Palmers lodge, I pray you," the answer from the four thousand invitations sent out by the Secretary of the Pal-mer Re-Union is, " They lodge everywhere on this broad conti-nent, from Maine and the Canadas on the north, to Oregon and California on the west, sweeping the Southwestern States and Territories, back by the Carolinas and Virginia to the old camp-ground in Stonington where we are met in council to-day."

And so we welcome you to the very soil which " the old giant," as Walter has been not unfitly called, broke and worked with his own hands for the support of himself and his numerous old-time family. You will find not a few objects of interest, chief among which will be the site of the Walter Palmer home-stead at Wequetequock, and the old burying-ground where his huge grave will be shown you, and where most, if not all, his children were buried.

It is a rough looking, neglected old place, but it is where the " rude forefathers" sleep, and I am sure its hallowed associations will commend it in all its barreness to your profoundest regards, and will justify your pilgrimage to this shrine of our earliest family, life and death.

And now with another hearty welcome to all that may be enjoyable on this memorable occasion, and especially to our ocean views, cool sea breezes and the fruitfulness of the sea if not of the land, I close with the earnest prayer for the prosperity and unity of the great Palmer Household in this world and for a final re-union in the world to come.

ADDRESS

BY HON. ELISHA H. PALMER, OF MONTVILLE, CT., PRESIDENT OF THE RE-UNION.

Great-grandfathers, grandfathers, uncles, aunts and cousins, I bid you a good morning. If ever I was thankful for any one thing it is that at this time I see the beginning of the end of this Re-Union. I have seen it in the papers that I was to take charge of the Re-Union, so I have felt that I was, to some extent, responsible for it. Thank God, the obstacles that arose in our path have all been overcome, and now I am only troubled to know where the Palmers will lodge to-night. Daniel Webster once said, in one of his great speeches, or rather in a speech which he expected to deliver, that some previous speaker had stolen his thunder. I expected to give an account of the Re-Union from its inception down to the present time. But the Doctor has done that and left me nothing to say. It is a wise thing that Providence never lets us see into the future. If I had foreseen the trouble and anxiety that was to attend the preparation of this gathering, perhaps I should never have gone into it. It is the same in moral movements. If Jefferson Davis could have looked ahead, he never would have attempted to

establish a republican form of government on a platform of
slavery. What man ever stood in the position I do to-day—president of this family? Never was there such a gathering on the
globe—perhaps that is saying too much, but it is safe to say
that never was there such a gathering in the United States.
How do you suppose I was chosen? If they had chosen a president as they do delegates to political conventions, do you suppose I ever would have been the man? [Cries of yes! yes!] A
man from a little country town in the backwoods? I told you
I couldn't make a speech. Some men are born great, some
achieve greatness, and some have greatness thrust upon them.
I have had greatness thrust upon me. I consider it a greater
honor to be president of this Re-Union than to be president of
the United States. I should have told General Grant the same
thing if he had been here. I want to encourage the young
Palmers—I want them to multiply and replenish the earth.
What makes great men? I say there are better men in this
Re-Union for senators and representatives than some who are
there now. If these men were in Congress it would give them
the chance to develop their ability. I should have been in
Congress long ago if I had only received votes enough. [Mr.
Palmer has for years been the Prohibition candidate for Congress in his district.] It is the circumstances that surround a
man that makes him great. Because Grant has been President,
and general of the army, it does not prove that there are not
other Palmers who would have been just as great under favoring circumstances. What would he have amounted to if he had
never left his tannery? If there had never been a rebellion,
Grant would never have been heard of. The speaker then referred to the sculptor Palmer as having achieved success by
circumstances. His talent was first discovered by his taking
to a jeweler, to have reproduced in gold, a likeness of his wife
which he had cut out of a cameo with a jack knife. He was
simply a rude farmer when this circumstance opened to him a
new career in which he had become famous. Take the great
men of the country in the past—Washington, Jefferson, Madison,
Webster, and others—and they to-day have scarcely a descendant
who is known to the country. I have heard it said that Web-

ster had not a single living descendant. But the great family
of Walter Palmer never was more flourishing or bore more fruit
than to-day. One Palmer descendant was President for two
terms, and we could have stood him for a third term. When
I first came to Stonington and published a notice in the *Mirror*
that we would have a family Re-Union, I supposed that others
felt as I did. This is the nest of the Palmers, and I supposed
that by advertising we could get up a good re-union. At our
first meeting there were four men present and one of those was
deaf, and I had to tell him going over on the cars what we did
at the meeting. At the next meeting I supposed there would
be more, but I believe there were less. Then somebody said, if
you can enlist the ladies of Stonington, the Re-Union will be a
success. We did enlist them, and they are entitled to a large
share of the credit of this successful demonstration. After all
I have passed through, I don't regret that I have got you here.
If I had been called upon at a political convention—Republican,
Democratic, Prohibition or Greenback—with any platform under me but one of boards only, I could have made a speech.

ELISHA H. PALMER,

OF MONTVILLE, CT., PRESIDENT OF THE RE-UNION.

(BRIEF BIOGRAPHY.)

The subject of this brief sketch is a grandson of Rev. Reuben
Palmer, and a son of Gideon Palmer, the oldest of a family of
eleven, and was born the 23d day of June, 1814, in the town of
Montville, New London County, State of Connecticut. He received a common school education, and attended Bacon Academy, in Colchester, two years. It was intended by his father to
give him a college education, but sickness prevented. His father
being a manufacturer of different commodities, his son became
such, and carried on the same business, which was mostly the
manufacturing of linseed oil and paints. The first of his going
away from home was to oversee the building and starting machinery for the purpose of manufacturing cotton-seed oil in the
city of Richmond, Virginia, which was done to the satisfaction of
his employer. He was eighteen years old at this time. He was

E H Palmer

the manufacturer of the first cotton-seed oil that was made in this country, which is now one of the great industries of the South. About this time there was more important business to attend to, and he was united in marriage to Miss Ellis Loomis, Thanksgiving day, Nov. 30, 1837. The following Spring he went to Rockwell, Illinois, with his father, to erect a steam saw-mill, and sawed the first plank to construct the canal locks at the terminus of the canal near Losee. Was taken sick with fever and ague in the Fall, and had to return home. In 1840, went to Norwich, and carried on the wholesale business in oils, paints, etc., for three years. In the year 1845, got up machinery for the manufacturing of cotton rope, and went to Houston, Texas, and started it for other parties. On his return from Texas the oil business was given up, and it was changed into cotton manufacturing of different kinds of goods, and improved by him until 1876, when three of his sons bought the property and commenced the manufacturing of bedding comforters, and are doing a large business. It is on the same place where his grandfather built the dam about one hundred years ago.

In politics he was identified with the anti-slavery movement at first, and voted that ticket. In 1854, was elected represent-ative of his town; voted for the Maine Liquor Law, which was the most important question before the Legislature that session. At the formation of the Republican party he joined that—it be-ing more in accordance with his views—and was elected again by that party to represent them in the Legislature of 1864. His experience in the first Legislature enabled him to be in-strumental in getting a flowage law passed, which has been a great benefit to manufacturers of the State. He was elected to represent his district in the State Senate in 1876.

He has been a total abstainer from all that intoxicates, also from all forms that tobacco is made use of, from his youth up. He is and has been an earnest and persistent advocate of temp-erance and moral reform, both in private and public, and is known throughout the State among the temperance people as such. For the last six years has been the Prohibition candidate for Congress in his district. Feeling the need of a higher edu-cation himself, he has taken an active part in trying to elevate

its standard in his own town, for the benefit of his neighbors'
children as well as his own.   Being of the Baptist denomination, he has always done his part in sustaining the church in his
society.   Never refusing a favor to any one that was practicable
to grant ; never refused to give to the poor or to alleviate the
the sufferings of the afflicted.   He was with and of the people
—not bigoted or lifted up above them—but genial, easy to approach, social, and an enjoyable companion.   In short, Mr.
Palmer has been an active representative man in all the departments of life that go to make up good society.   His generation
will owe him a debt of gratitude for the effort and sacrifice he
he has made to elevate them to a higher plane of usefulness.

It is but appropriate to add he was the active organizer and
promoter of the first Palmer Re-Union held in America.

HYMN

SUNG AT THE PALMER RE-UNION.

We meet an old-time family
  From places far and wide ;
To answer to our pedigree
  With loyalty and pride.

Chorus·

Our fathers shall not be forgot,
  Their memory we'll enshrine,
And cherish in our latest thought
  The days of " Auld Lang Syne."
The days of Auld Lang Syne so dear
  With gladness we review ;
And pledge our children year by year
  This service to renew.

We come from North, and South, and East,
  And from the distant West,
To mingle in this household feast
  With eagerness and zest.

Chorus.

We're pilgrims all both great and small.
In faith and purpose true :
Obedient to the heavenly call
To see the conflict through.

Chorus.

With Palms in hand we'll firmly stand,
As in the days of old,
When Palmers swept the Holy Land
With conquering legions bold.

Chorus.

And when our pilgrimage is o'er,
And fought the last campaign,
In triumph on the golden shore
We'll wave our Palms again.

Chorus.

A. G. PALMER, D. D.

HISTORICAL ADDRESS

BY JUDGE RICHARD A. WHEELER, OF STONINGTON, CT.

Walter Palmer, whose descendants have met here to-day for
a family Re-Union, was of English origin, and came to this
country and joined the early settlers of Charlestown, Mass.
How and when he came is not certainly known. It had been
supposed by some that he was one of the Dorchester company,
which, forming a connection with the grantees of the Edmond,
Lord Sheffield Patent, came over in 1624, and settled at Cape
Ann, Mass., and remained there about two years. But their business operations proving unprofitable, they abandoned the place
and moved to Naumkeag, now Salem, Mass., where the most
of them remained until they were joined by other English
emigrants that soon followed them. Others have thought that
he might have been connected with a still earlier patent, issued
by the great Council of Plymouth to Robert Georges, who was
subsequently appointed by them Lieutenant-General of New

England. In 1623, he crossed the ocean to establish a colony, and thereby secure the benefits of his patent. After vainly endeavoring for a year or more to promote the success of his colony, and no supplies reaching him, he returned home, leaving his interests to the care and management of his agents. Robert Georges died soon after his return, and his interests in the patent descended to his eldest brother, John Georges who, in 1628, leased the territory embraced in it to John Oldham and John Dorrill. But they encountered so much opposition in this country and in England that they abandoned the lease, but not without a serious and protracted controversy. Most of the grantees under Georges' patent united with the planters at Salem, but some of them sought a home within the limits of the patent, where they remained until their lands and dwelling were claimed by the next comers. It is not probable that Walter Palmer was associated with any of the grantees under these patents. The Plymouth Council, which was incorporated by King James I., November 3d, 1620, had no other source of revenue than the sale of patents; so in order to increase their profits they sold on the 19th day of March, 1628, the territory embraced in all these patents over again to the Massachusetts company. In September following, John Endicott reached New England in the good ship *Abigail*, commanded by Captain Henry Gauden, bringing with him the other five associate grantees under the last patent from the Plymouth Council. Pending these proceedings, and while the grantees were greatly embarassed by the conflict of titles under so many patents— King Charles the First on the 4th day of March, 1629, granted to the "associates" and others as a body corporate and politic a royal charter, which was regarded by some as in confirmation of the patents of the old Plymouth Council. Abraham Palmer, an older brother of our Walter, was a merchant in London at the time, and one of the associates, and gave fifty pounds in aid of the object of the charter. In the early Spring of 1629, there arrived in Salam, Mass., Ralph Sprague and his brothers, Richard and William Sprague, who soon after, with three or four others, by the consent and approbation of Governor Endicott, journeyed through the woods some twelve miles, and came to a place on the north side of the Charles river, called by the Indians Mishawum, where they found an Englishman of the Georges patent living in a thatched house. He was a smith, by the name of Thomas Walford, who was the pioneer settler and inhabitant of Charlestown, Mass. Two of the four men who accompanied the Spragues through the wilderness to Mishawum, were Abraham and Walter Palmer. The following is a record of their first proceeding : " The inhabitants that first settled in this place and brought it into the denomination of an English town, were anno 1629, as follows, viz : Ralph Sprague, Richard Sprague, William Sprague, William Springer, John Meech, Simon Hoyt, Abraham Palmer, Walter Palmer, Nicholas Stowses, John Stickline, Thomas Walford, smith, that lived here alone. Walter Palmer built the first dwelling house in Charlestown. He was assigned two acres for a home lot and subsequently had more liberal grants. Walter Palmer, whose inclination tended to farming and stock raising, soon found his possessions inadequate to his business. Notwithstanding which, he continued to live in Charlestown until 1643, when he removed his habitation to the Plymouth colony. During his residence in Charlestown, Walter Palmer formed the acquaintance of William Chesebrough, who then resided in Boston and Braintree. The friendship of these men was of no ordinary character. It continued through life. They resided near each other in Rehoboth, and their houses in Stonington were within hailing distance of each other, on the east and west banks of Wequetequock Cove. Walter Palmer was a man of note in the Massachusetts colony. He was admitted a freeman there May 18th, 1631, and held various local offices. In 1643, Walter Palmer and his friend, William Chesebrough, concluded to remove to the Plymouth colony, and with others, joined in the organization of the town of Rehoboth as an independent township, which was to continue as such until they should subject themselves to some other government. Such an organization, largely composed of strangers, and situated in a remote part of the colony, was not very well calculated to secure their approval. It does not appear that they intended to run this new township wholly as an independent organization, for as soon as the preliminary steps necessary for its formation were taken, they elected and sent representatives or deputies to the general court of Plymouth ; and such was the confidence placed in Walter Palmer by his fellow-townsmen, that they honored him with the first election as deputy, and subsequently re-elected him to that office ; and also conferred upon him repeatedly the office of selectman and other local offices.

The younger Governor Winthrop, of Boston, acting under a commission of the general court of Massachusetts, commenced the settlement of New London, Connecticut, in 1645, and urged William Chesebrough to join him in organizing the new town. Mr. Chesebrough visited the place during the year, but finding the place unsuitable to his expectations, did not conclude to settle there. On his way home he re-examined our town, and selected a place for his future residence ; and on which he erected a dwelling house, and removed his family there during the year 1649, supposing that his new home was within the jurisdiction of Massachusetts. Connecticut assumed jurisdiction over this town, as well as New London, which superseded Mr. Winthrop's commission, though Massachusetts afterwards asserted her claims, and maintained them so far as this town was concerned. Mr. Chesebrough was almost immediately summoned by the general court of Connecticut to repair to Captain Mason, of Saybrook, or some other magistrates upon the Connecticut river, to give an account to him, or them, of what he was doing alone in the wilderness. Mr. Chesebrough at first disregarded this order, claiming that his new home was within the jurisdiction of Massachusetts, but subsequently acting under the advice and assurance of Mr. Winthrop, and other friends, at New London, he so far yielded to the colony of Connecticut, as to appear at the general court at Hartford, in March, 1651, and in answer to their summons, said that he was not engaged in any unlawful trade with the Indians, and also assured them that his religious sentiments were in accordance with those of the general court. That it was not his intention to remain alone, and lead a solitary life in the wilderness, but that he should endeavor to induce a suitable number of his friends to join him and establish a new township. On hearing his statement the court relented so far as to reluctantly permit him to remain, on condition that he would give bonds not to engage in any unlawful trade with the Indians, and furnish to the court before the next Winter the names of such persons as he might induce to settle with and around him at Wequetequock. The planters at New London were friendly with Chesebrough, and did not want him to remove, unless he came there to live, for they did not like the idea of a new township in this region. After repeated conferences with him, they engaged that if he would put himself on the footing of an inhabitant of that place they would confirm his title to his lands on which he then lived at Wequetequock. To this proposition he acceded, but the townsmen of New London soon discovered that they were making pledges that they could not fulfil, for the then boundaries of that town did not extend but three miles on each side of the river Thames. However, on request, the general court extended the eastern boundary of New London to Pawcatuck river, and then New London gave to Mr. Chesebrough a home lot over there which he never occupied. In January, 1652, the town of New London redeemed its promise to him, and gave a grant of confirmation to Mr. Chesebrough and his sons of all the land they claimed in Stonington. Previous to the agreement of the general court with Mr. Chesebrough, and the confirmation of his land to him and his sons, Thomas Stanton, in 1650, procured of the general court a license to erect a trading house at Pawcatuck, with the exclusive right of trade in that region for three years. He immediately built and occupied the trading house, but did not bring his family to Stonington until 1658. Thomas Miner, a former resident of Charlestown, Mass., and then of Hingham, came to New London in 1645, received a home lot there, and built a house on it the same year. He continued to reside there until 1652, when he came to this place and took up a tract of land east of and adjoining Wequetequock Cove, and during that year and the next erected a house thereon. On the 30th day of June, 1652, the town of New London granted a tract of three hundred acres of land to Governor Haynes for a farm lying together on the east side of the Wequetequock Cove. When Walter Palmer (yielding to the re-

quest of his old friend, Chesebrough, to join him in settling the
new township) came here and purchased this tract of land of
Governor Haynes, but before he took his deed he found it covered and embraced the house and lands of Thomas Miner.   So
he and the governor entered into a written agreement that
Palmer should give £100 for the place in such cattle as Mr.
Haynes should select out of Palmer's stock.   If any disagree-
ment should arise as to the price of the stock, it should be decided by indiff-rent persons.   This contract recognized the title
to the house and lands occupied by Mr. Miner, and was dated
July 15, 1653.   Mr. Miner was selected to put Mr. Palmer in
possession of the land purchased of Governor Haynes, and did so
by a written instrument, embodying therein a conveyance of his
own land and dwelling house (included in the boundaries of the
Haynes land) to Mr. Palmer, reserving the right, however, to
occupy his said house until he could build another at Mistuxet,
now Quiambaug.   The western boundary of Gov. Haynes'
land sold to Walter Palmer, including the house and lot of
Thomas Miner, rested on the cove and the rivulet that enters the
cove.   The other grants and purchases of land to, and by Walter Palmer, lay south of this purchase, and on the eastern slope
of Togwcnk, crossing Auguilla brook, and embracing the large
farms of the late Colonel William and Dudley Randalls, in all,
some 1200 acres.   Mr. Thomas Miner built his new house at
Mistuxet, in 1652-3 and 4.   Captain George Denison and family joined the new settlement in 1654, erecting his house near
Pequotsepos brook, Captain John Gallup and Robert Park, with
their families, came the same year and settled near Mystic river.
The new settlement being composed of men of note, progressed
as rapidly as could be expected under the circumstances.   Mr.
Chesebrough was now surrounded by a sufficient number of
inhabitants to claim corporate power from the general court.
The first local name that the settlement received was Mystic
and Pawcatuck.   Mystic embracing the territory between Mystic river on the west and Stony brook on the east.   Pawcatuck
embracing the territory between the Pawcatuck river on the
east and Stony brook on the west.   It being understood by the
planters here, as a condition precedent to the new settlement,

that as soon as a suitable number had joined them they should be incorporated as a new town. So in 1654, they applied to the general court for corporate powers. But no sooner made than it was opposed by New London, embracing Groton, and defeated. The planters did not rest satisfied with their defeat, and resolved to agitate the matter until they succeeded sooner or later. They were of the independent Puritan stamp, and ready to make any sacrifice in defence of the right to worship God according to the dictates of their own conscience. But to be taxed for a minister at New London, some twelve miles away, with two rivers to cross to get there, and no ferry boats, was a little too much for their Puritanism. So they were determined to have a town and a church of their own; and they continued to ask for them of the general court, but were denied as often as they applied. In the early part of 1657, the Rev. William Thompson came here to reside, and preached to planters a part of the time, and the rest of the time to the Pequot Indians. He was employed by the commissioners of the United Colonies, who were acting as the agents of the New London Missionary Society. The first religious services were held at the dwelling house of Walter Palmer, March 22, 1657. Services were subsequently held at the dwelling houses of the planters, whose efforts were continued with unremitting determination to break loose from New London, and organize for themselves a new town and church. They remembered that Massachusetts had previously claimed a part or all of the Pequot territory, embracing Groton, Stonington and a part of Westerly; so they sought the friendship of Massachusetts in their contest, and in October, the planters joined by the Rev. Mr. Thompson, prepared a memorial to the Massachusetts general court, complaining of the course pursued against them by the general court of Connecticut. Massachusetts notified Connecticut, who appointed a committee to confer with the planters here, and bring the contest to an issue, if possible. What was done in the premises cannot now be ascertained, for no records of their proceedings have been preserved. In May, 1658, Walter Palmer, William Chesebrough, and Thomas Stanton, in behalf of the planters, petitioned the Massachusetts general court again, stating that some of them were settled here by Governor Winthrop in 1649, by virtue of a commission from that court, notwithstanding which, they had been called to account for their doings under their authority, and asking for relief from such interferences from the Connecticut authorities, and also for confirmation of their lands. But this was denied them, accompanied, however, by a suggestion that the whole matter in dispute be referred to the commissioners of the United Colonies, and meantime to order their own affairs by common agreement, until provision be made in their behalf. Following out these suggestions, Walter Palmer and his associate planters assembled on the 30th day of June, 1658, and formed a compact called by them " The Association of Pawcatuck People," which was organized for municipal purposes only, and was established by them not in defiance of the laws of either colony, but with a firm purpose to maintain it until some provision inadequate to their wants should be made for them. The question in dispute between the Massachusetts and Connecticut colonies as to jurisdiction was referred to the commissioners of the United Colonies, who, in 1658, rendered a decision that all of the Pequot territory west of Mystic river belonged to Connecticut, and all the territory east of it, including Stonington and North Stonington and a part of the town of Westerly, belonged to Massachusetts. At the next session of the Massachusetts general court, after this decision was rendered, they passed an act that the English plantation between Mystic and Pawtucket rivers should be named Southerntown, and belong to the county of Suffolk, Mass., and appointed Walter Palmer and others to manage the prudential affairs thereof, until the court take further order. Walter Palmer was appointed constable, and the bounds of the plantation were extended into the country northward eight miles. Thus, after a severe and protracted struggle, they succeeded in obtaining a local government. It should be borne in mind that the Massachusetts general court did not create or even organize a new township, but simply declared that the English plantation between Mystic and Pawcatuck rivers should be called Southerntown. They recognized in part the local association of the people, and extended and confirmed their bounds. Dur-

ing the years 1659, 1660 and 1661, several town meetings were
held for the purpose of building and locating a meeting house,
which was raised May 13th, 1661, and was so far completed as
to be ready for use in September of that year, when the commissioners of the United Colonies being in town attended worship there, and were addressed by that stern old warrior statesman, Captain John Mason. Walter Palmer, whose history we
have been tracing since he arrived in New England, in 1629, was
born in England as early as 1585, and was, at the time of which
we write, an old man ripening for the grave. The rough exposure
of pioneer life had at last begun to tell upon his health and
strength, which was so much impaired that as " the November
days had come, the saddest of the year," he was gathered not
to his fathers, but laid to rest in what is now known as the old
Wequetequock burial place, dying November 10th, 1661.

Of his family it may be said that he was married in England
long before he came to this country. His oldest daughter,
Grace, of whom it is said that she was of the same age of her
husband, Thomas Miner, was born in 1608. She came to this
country with her father and family, went with him to Charlestown, and joined the church there June 1st, 1632, and was married to Thomas Miner, April 23d, 1634. They resided in
Charlestown, Mass., until 1636, where their son John was born
and baptized. Soon after which they removed their habitation
to Hingham, Mass., where four of their children were born and
baptized as follows : Clement Miner, baptized March 4th, 1638 ;
Thomas Miner, baptized May 10th, 1640 ; Ephraim Miner, baptized May 1st, 1642 ; Joseph Miner, baptized August 25th, 1644.
In 1645, they left Hingham and joined the first planters of
New London, and received a grant of a home lot, built a house
thereon, and continued to live there until 1652, when he came
to Stonington and took up a tract of land on the east side of
Wequetequock Cove, and erected a dwelling house thereon the
same year. April 5th, 1652, the town of Pequot, now New
London, granted to Governor John Haynes, of Hartford, three
hundred acres of land, which was located by the grant, east of
Chesebrough's land, and laid out by Governor Haynes on the
east side of, and adjoining Wequetequock Cove, overlapping

Thomas Miner's land.   Walter Palmer was then living at Rehoboth, and being anxious to locate himself near his old friend Chesebrough, entered into negotiations with Governor Haynes for the purchase of this land.   The bargain was made sometime before the deed was executed.   In fact, Governor Haynes gave Thomas Miner a written authority to put Walter Palmer in possession of this land, February 15th, 1653, which he did May 30th, 1653.   But the conveyance of Haynes to Palmer was not executed until July 15th, 1653.   When Thomas Miner put Walter Palmer into possession he conveyed to him in the same instrument his said land and new dwelling house, which Palmer occupied that year, though Miner continued to live there until he built his new house at Quiambaug.

William Palmer was born on the other side of the ocean, and came with his father's family to this country ; lived with them in Charlestown, Mass., but did not go down to the Plymouth colony with him.   He was admitted freeman in Massachusetts colony in 1639, and was admitted to the church there March 28th, 1641.   He remained with his brother John in Charlestown after his father removed to Plymouth, and continued to reside there until after his father's death, when soon after he sold the land that his father gave him in Rehoboth, and came to Stonington and stayed with his brother-in-law, Thomas Miner, from June 18th, 1664, to April 29, 1665, when he left him and went over to Killingworth, Ct., and received an allotment of land in the settlement of that town.   He continued to reside there during the rest of his days.   But the time of his death is not known ; nor is it certain that he ever married.   His brother, Gershom Palmer, under date of March 27th, 1697, executed the following instrument : " Know all men by these presents, that while as my brother, William Palmer, deceased, did give and bequeath unto me his house and all his lands in Killingworth, forever, I settling one of my sons thereon, and in compliance to my deceased brother's will, I do order my eldest son, Gershom Palmer, to settle in said house upon said land.   I, the said Gershom Palmer, Senior, do give and bequeath the aforesaid house and land, with all the privileges and appurtenances thereto belonging to my eldest son, Gershom Palmer, to him forever, according to the tenor of the will of my brother, William Palmer, deceased." This renders it certain that he left no wife or children. Whether he was ever married is not so clear. If he married it must have been late in life, or, what is more probable he, like his brother John, lived and died a bachelor.

3. John Palmer, born 1615, came with his father and family to this country in 1629. He was admitted a freeman of the Massachusetts colony in 1639, admitted to the church October 23d, 1640, died August 24th, 1677, aged 62 years. He left a will giving the bulk of his property to his brother Jonas, and sister Elizabeth. He was never married.

4. Jonas Palmer, was a son of the first wife, came with his father and family to this country in 1629, lived in Charlestown until 1657, when he married Elizabeth Grissill, and moved to Rehoboth, where he remained the rest of his days. They had six children. He married a second wife, Abigail Titus.

5. Elizabeth Palmer, one of the first wife's children, came to this country with her father and family in 1629, married first Thomas Sloan, and second a Mr. Chapman, but no children by either husband have been traced.

In the old church record of Roxbury, Mass., the following appears: Rebecca Short came in the year 1632, and married Walter Palmer, a godly man of Charlestown church, which they joined June 1st, 1633. The children of this union were:

6. Hannah Palmer, baptized in Charlestown, June 15th, 1634, came with her father to Stonington via Rehoboth, and married first Thomas Hewitt, April 26th, 1659, by whom she had two children, Thomas and Benjamin Hewitt. For her second husband she married Roger Sterry, December 27th, 1671, by whom she had two children. For her third husband she married John Fish. An interesting jointure between them is still preserved on our old town records.

7. Elihu Palmer, baptized in Charlestown church, January 25th. 1636, came with his father to Stonington and died September 5th, 1665. It is not probable that he left any children, for the reason that he left a will in which he gave his property to his nephews. His will was lost in the burning of New London, September 6th, 1781, and the only knowledge we have of it is

from a deed on the Stonington record, where lands were set to
his executors and vested in his nephews. If he had children
surviving him, or living at the date of his will, they would have
been the subjects of his bounty, but dying at the age of 29 and
leaving such a will, is proof well nigh positive that no children
survived him.

8. Nehemiah Palmer, born November 23d, 1637, came to Stonington with his father from Charlestown via Rehoboth, and
married Hannah, daughter of Thomas and Dorothy Lord Stanton, November 20th, 1662, and had seven children. He was a
prominent man in church and state.

9. Moses Palmer, born April 6th, 1640, also came to Stonington
with his father's family, and married Dorothy ——, and had five
children. He was deacon of the first church, and a prominent
man in town affairs.

10. Benjamin Palmer, born in Charlestown, Mass., May 30th,
1642, came to Stonington via Rehoboth with his father's family,
joined the church and became a large land holder. He married
and brought his wife home August 10th, 1681, just 200 years
ago to-day. The fact of this marriage appears in Thomas Miner's diary. But who she was and where she came from, does
not appear. He died April 10th, 1716, aged 74 years. In February, before he died, he gave a deed of his lands to two of his
nephews, on condition that they should take care of him through
life, and at his death give him a Christian burial. I regard this
fact beyond doubt that he left no offspring.

11. Gershom Palmer was born at Rehoboth, and came with his
father to Stonington ; married first Ann Denison, daughter of
Captain George and Ann Borodel Denison, November 28th,
1667. They had ten children. For his second wife he married
Elizabeth, the widow of Major Samuel Mason. They made
and recorded a jointure, which appears at large on the Stonington land records. He was a deacon of the Stonington first
church and held various positions of trust in civil affairs.

12. Rebecca Palmer, born in Rehoboth, came with her father's
family to Stonington, and married Elisha Chesebrough, son of
William and Ann Stevenson Chesebrough, April 20th, 1665, and
had one child, Elihu, born December 3d, 1668. Elisha Chese-

brough died April 1st, 1670, and his widow, Rebecca, married for her second husband, John Baldwin, of New London, July 24th, 1672. They had five children.

Walter Palmer was a Puritan of the Puritans. In England he had been denied the right to worship God according to the dictates of his conscience, and in order to escape the persecutions that were sure to follow his refusal to adopt all of Queen Elizabeth's forms of worship, " He sought a faith's pure shrine." The Puritans, while in the old country, did not design to establish a separate church. They only sought to reform and purify the church of England, and hence they were derisively called Puritans. But, seeing the utter impossibility of accomplishing their object, they left their native land to seek a home beyond " the dark, cold, heaving sea," preferring a log cabin in the primeval forests of New England, where they might live, and move, and have their being unchained by ecclesiastical machinery, to a home in affluent old England, where every religious utterance must conform to the legal standard. They had even antagonized the pilgrims, mainly because they had favored a separate church, wholly independent of the church of England. But when the Puritans had reached New England, they united with the pilgrims " in establishing independent churches." First at Salem, then at Charlestown, Boston, Roxbury, Dorchester and elsewhere, as the new settlements progressed. It was with the Charlestown church that Walter Palmer united, in 1633, and with which he sustained such relations until he removed to Plymouth colony, where he attended and united with Mr. Samuel Newman's church. There was no church here regularly organized until nearly thirteen years after his death. But it is evident, from what we can learn of him for the eight years that he resided here, that he was eminently a religious man, and so were his sons, three of whom became deacons of the first church. The first religious services in Stonington were held at his dwelling house, March 22d, 1657. During the two years services of the Rev. Zachariah Bridgden in this town, he lived with the the family of Mr. Palmer, and died while residing there, April 24th, 1662. The valley of Wequetequock was peculiarly adapted to the wants and necessities of the first comers. The marsh lands bordering on the cove furnished hay for their cattle until upland could be broken up and reduced to cultivation. The waters of the cove produced an abundance of shell and floating fish. The grand primeval forests were alive with game, from a rabbit to a bear, and from a robin to an eagle. So that a home here in those "way back" times was not entirly destitute of luxuries, much less of the necessities of life. Suppose we summon up our hero, Walter Palmer, our grand old ancestor, from the vasty deep, and let us have a talk with him about the times in which he lived, and what has happened since his departure almost 220 years ago. Well, grandfather, what think you of all these children's children's great-grandchildren, or whatever else is great and grand about them? Mark, please, the difference between our cultivated fields, our villages and rural homes, when contrasted with your old wilderness fireside. The stones that gave this town its name after you had left, the same old cove with its flowing tides, the same sun and moon and star lit heavens are there; but all else, how changed! Freedom to worship God is now written in the organic law of our land, and no slave can breathe the air of these United States. The land you came to settle under a monarchical form of government has broken its chains, and has become the "land of the free, and the home of the brave." The flickering, dissolving vapor that used to rise from Grandmother Palmer's tea kettle over at Wequetequock when she was preparing your morning and evening oblations has long since been utilized, and become the grand motive power of the civilized world. The winds that wafted the fleets of your day over the ocean have become a secondary power. Water power that moved the machinery of your time has lost its prestige, by being reduced to steam by the application of heat. The lightning's lurid flash that spangled through the rifted clouds, and gleamed around and through your forest home, has been bottled up and learned to go of errands. When you wished to send a letter to the Plymouth or old Bay colonies, it had to be done by a courier or post-rider, now the same information can travel by steam over iron rails, or if in a hurry you can have your thoughts put on a wire, and as quick as a flash of lightning they can be read by your descendants at Rehoboth and Charlestown, or flashed beneath the sea, telling your relatives in England that your descendants in America are having a grand re-union in Stonington to-day, and ere the benediction shall have closed these proceedings, receive their congratulations in reply. Well, Grandfather Palmer, perhaps you would like to know the part your descendants have acted in the grand drama of human events, since the grave clods closed over your remains? Taken as a whole they have worthily and well performed their part. The unyielding thirst for power in the church of England, that forced the dissenters of your day to cross the ocean to breathe an air untainted with usurped power ; in the years that followed, sought to break down and overthrow what of freedom the old charters contained. The struggle for power on the part of England, and for civil and religious liberty on the part of the colonies culminated in the war of the Revolution, 115 years after your departure. The little colony of Connecticut that you helped to settle performed prodigies of valor in that mighty struggle. Some of your descendants and their neighbors here rushed to Boston to assist the descendants of your friends in Charlestown and elsewhere, to beat back the cohorts of England, and there on a hill, upon the east side of which you built your first house, immortalized themselves in the battle of Bunker Hill. The colony of your loved Connecticut, with a population at that time of 238,000 inhabitants, sent to the battlefields of the Revolution 32,000 men. They were at Bunker Hill, at Newport, R. I., at Brooklyn, New York and White Plains. They were at Bemis Heights, and Saratoga. They were with Mad Anthony Wayne at the storming of Stony Point, and they suffered and starved at Valley Forge. They were at Brandywine and Monmouth, and finally at Yorktown, where the old British lion growled a reluctant consent that the colonies should be free and independent States. Perhaps, Grandfather Palmer, you may like to know if any of your descendants have been honored with promotions. Three of your sons were deacons in the old church here, and represented this town in the general court. Others down the ages have acted well their part. Some have chosen the profession of the law, of medicine and the ministry, and have risen to positions of eminence. Some of your blood has coursed the veins, of governors of Connecticut and Illinois, members of Congress, diplomatic servants and judges of our highest courts, State senators and representatives. When the last grand struggle for human rights prevaded this mighty nation from the circumference to the centre, your descendants and the colonies you helped to found earned a record of undying fame. Far away from your old home here, in one of the mighty States of the West some of your blood in its transmissions was coursing in the veins of a modest unassuming man. The Rebellion found him in the humbler walks of life; but the country's demand for a successful leader brought him to the front and elevated him to the position of lientenant-general of our armies, and to the presidency of the United States. And finally, Grandfather Palmer, we will take the liberty to congratulate you, and ourselves, too, that this mighty leader is your descendant and our distinguished relative. And now we will all unite in honoring the name of Ulysses S. Grant, the noblest, grandest soldier of the civilized world.

POEM

BY REV. A. G. PALMER, D. D., OF STONINGTON, CT.

I sing the hero who from England came
To inscribe upon this rock-bound coast his name,
And plant upon this barren soil the tree
Of civil and religious liberty.
By industry the wilderness to clear,
And carve out for himself a fortune here ;
Providing timely for the distant need
Of his large household, with parental heed
That when increased in numbers, more or less,
They might, through coming years, these lands possess.
Or hence, removing, find some richer soil
To stimulate and compensate their toil,
Spreading abroad, as now, on every side,
From the Atlantic to the Pacific's tide,
A stalwart, sturdy, vigorous, numerous clan,

Descendants from the loins of one brave man,
Walter Palmer by name, our grand old sire,
Puritan pioneer of Nottinghamshire.

And so, in sixteen hundred twenty-nine,
Begins the Anglo-Yankee Palmer line ;
Back of that date we have no means to go—
And if we had, we should not care to know
His English ancestry, or small or great,
Of lordly wealth, or poor and mean estate,
High born, low born, or of middle birth,
Merchant, mechanic, tiller of the earth—
It matters not to us—enough that we
Are branches of this old ancestral tree ;
The toughened fibre of a hardy stock,
Rooted amid the gravel, grit and rock
Of this old town, fruitful the years along,
Swelling a census twice six thousand strong ;
A goodly company, as all may see,
And worthy of so proud a pedigree.
In social, civil and religious life,
The rank and file of every righteous strife ;
Loyal in politics, and without guile,
Palmers in name and life—man's highest style.

I pause a moment here, simply to state,
Judge Wheeler favored sixteen twenty-eight,
At one time, as perhaps the the truer score,
That marks the Palmer epoch on this shore ;
Well, either way—we shall endorse his showing—
For what the Judge don't know is not worth knowing ;
I mean in genealogies and dates,
Births, marriages, and wills, and old estates ;
When born, when died, when married, this one, that,
Threading his winding pathway, to get at
The lineage of every stem and shoot
That ever sprang from Walter Palmer root ;
Gleaning from mouldy tome and dusty shelf
More about Walter than he knew himself.
The good old man, I dare say, never deemed
Himself a great man, never even dreamed
That in the nineteenth century, eighty-one,
From him would rise a portly judge and son,
In build and girth and brain, worthy to be
High priest and scribe of his long pedigree,

Able in rugged Anglo-Saxon prose
His history to search out and disclose,
By sharp analysis and acumen,
Both fact and fable with impartial pen,
A splendid proof of Darwin's famous plan,
Survival of the fittest, brute or man.

But these statistics—this and that and t'other—
To poets are an everlasting pother;
Just when you think you have the thing all right,
With words and phrases compact, wedged in tight,
And suited, by their harmony and jingle,
The ears of groundlings to delight and tingle,
Then some loose screw, of place or name or date,
Will work disorder, wild and desperate,
And with reckless, impious intrusion,
Tear into shreds your finely wrought illusion,
And tax your jaded and exhausted brain
To build your airy castles o'er again.

I don't believe old Homer could have written
His Iliad or Odyssey, if smitten
In his sublime poetical conceptions
By critical historical corrections;
I think the grand old singer would have faltered,
Had every third page needed to be altered
To meet some chronological decision
In genealogy, some last revision,
Cutting his lines in every shape and angle,
Mixing his numbers in a hopeless tangle.
All right for history; but he who sings
Must be allowed, sometimes, to stretch his wings,
And soar into the upper regions where,
It is reported, no staticians are.

Pardon this episode. Who could have thought
That such a crowd could be together brought
As, on this festal day, we proudly see,
Descendants of this brave old family.
Physicians, lawyers, clergymen and squires,
Downy-lipped scions and gray-headed sires;
Fair matrons, glowing with maternal pride,
Their fair daughters, blushing at their side:
With children full of fun and frolic free,
As Walter's dozen, less one, used to be.

Roaming the woods of Wequetequock all o'er,
Or wading knee-deep on the cove's low shore ;
At night, with childhood's weariness opprest,
Folded with prayerful tenderness to rest.

But to return, as scattering preachers say,
When they have drifted from their text away ;
As soon as Walter Palmer touched the shore
And looked New England's rising Athens o'er,
The hub and centre of the universe,
Where heresies, in embryo perverse,
E'en then were taking root, he left the place
And westward turned his honest English face ;
Passed on to Charlestown, just across the water,
And found a home there for himself and daughter—
For he was wifeless, and the young girl Grace,
For some years held the mother's vacant place.
But now, like most men of the widower sort,
He sought a wife and took Rebecca Short ;
For even our old hero found this his life
A lonely pilgrimage without a wife.

Pray, who a treasure ever lost as yet,
Without an effort to find it or get
A duplicate ? and with such earnest haste,
As well befits a sanctioned good taste ;
For who has laid one good wife in the earth
Knows best how much one like her may be worth.
So Walter Palmer, as he left behind
His early love in England, felt inclined,
Perhaps divinely moved, to seek another
Wife for himself, and for his child a mother.

But who Rebecca Short was, we don't know ;
We hope that genealogy will show
Though short by name, she was not short of brains ;
For in our Palmer arteries and veins,
Rebecca Short's blood courses strong and free,
In throbbing pulses of vitality ;
So that we know not, at this distant day,
Whether the Short or Palmer blood holds sway ;
For if, perchance, the Palmer was not strongest,
The Short infusion may hold out the longest ;
But the presumption is we are a mixture,
The Short and Palmer in an equal fixture,

Held in vital, permanent transfusion,
Two branthes in one stream, without confusion,
Together flowing onward to the sea
Of universal immortality.

Well, Walter found Rebecca in Charlestown,
Neatly attired in simple, homespun gown—
Perhaps at Shawmut, a suburb of that day,
But now a crowded avenue and way;
Its Indian name the land of flowers and beauty,
A fitting home for maiden love and duty—
Doing her household service timely well;
Bringing to market what she had to sell;
Chatting with Walter in his humble store,
Talking in confidence home matters o'er;
She, modesty itself, with downcast eyes,
Listening to his paternal, sage replies
To her inquiries, and with chastened air,
From underneath her shining braids of hair,
Flashing her beauty on his rugged face,
Its hard lines softened by her maiden grace;
Till words and smiles and blushes interblending,
Had then, as now, the same delicious ending—
A wedding and a little village party,
A simple marriage, rustic, honest, hearty,
The Puritanic ritual severe
In its simplicity and Godly fear;
Hands joined, and mutual pledges asked and given,
Of constancy, beneath the eye of Heaven;
The scriptures read, the prayer of blessing, then,
The benediction and the grave amen.

So Walter Palmer led his village bride
Homeward—young Grace in silence at his side,
With languid step and saddened, tearful eye,
Breathing a silent prayer that she might die;
For though a lost wife might allow another,
Alas, for her, there could be but one mother.
And though Rebecca Short might be all right,
And very sweet, as in her father's sight,
Yet how could she, her mother's eldest daughter,
Her mother in the churchyard, o'er the water,
Her spirit face, all sweetly undefiled,
Smiling in brightness o'er her weeping child,
To this young stranger-wife be reconciled?

But time is sorrow's healer and refiner,
And in due time Grace married Thomas Miner ;
And this old household into two was riven
By interblended griefs and joys from Heaven.

So true it is that sorrow's dark suspense
Oft heralds in some radiant providence ;
And that the surest way to brighten sorrow
Is from another light and joy to borrow ;
And that the sweetest way to heal a grief
Is in the balm of love to seek relief.

Ah, well, the prayer-book has it right, I trow—
As the beginning was, so is the now ;
Love is a light on night and cloud descending,
And so will ever be, " world without ending."

In the old church-yard, just across the tide
Of Wequetequock, sleep they, side by side ;
A huge, unchiseled stone covers the place
Where Thomas Miner rests, with his wife Grace.

So Walter Palmer lived the years in peace
At Charlestown, and of wealth had some increase.
Just what he did, of course we cannot know,
Or how his little into much did grow ;
Whether he tilled the earth, worked with his hands,
Or speculated lightly in new lands ;
Bought corner lots for less and sold for more,
And thus increased his capital and store ;
Dickered with Indians and gave them trash,
Gewgaws and beads for lands, in place of cash,
As in the Puritanic creed the might
To cheat an Indian made the thing all right ;
Or, if they might thereby from fear be freed,
To shoot an Indian was a saintly deed.
Were they not heathen, aliens from the Lord,
To be consumed by His avenging sword ?
Slaughtered before the open face of Heaven,
Fit only from their homes to be outdriven ;
As Perizite and Jebusite of old
Gave place to Israel, the chosen fold ;
Or, as our thinly-scattered western tribes
Before the surging and on-rushing tides

Of civil life are trampled in the dust,
To gratify the insatiate greed and lust
Of gold and power; so, at this early day,
The red men melted from their homes away.

But Walter Palmer, though in morals rude,
It may be, and in worldly matters shrewd,
And, with an eye to the main chance, and quick
To close a bargain tightly; yet no trick,
From Puritanic saintliness and grace,
In his transactions was allowed a place.
He kept his word, paid all his honest debts
The last farthing, with his small assets;
If aught was over that, with honest care,
He put aside for a wet day, with prayer.
No pious double-dealing on his name
Has left a blot, to cause his children shame;
And may his children to the latest day
His footsteps follow, in the same bright way.

In sixteen forty-three, from discontent,
Or hope of gain, no matter what intent,
He to Rehoboth came and pitched his tent,
Purchased new lands, organized a town,
And, as its chief man, gained fair renown,
Was sent up yearly to the general court,
As counselor of wise and grave report;
Was constable in sixteen fifty-two,
But, having worked the Seekonk problem through,
And gained by honest deal and interchanges
What could be made within the narrow ranges
Of a young trade that could not be extended,
He sagely thought his mission there was ended;
And so he pulled up stakes, sold out his chattel,
His block-house, lands, farming tools and cattle,
And once more moving with the setting sun,
By trail or sail, landed in Stonington,
At Wequetequock, upon the eastern shore,
And struck his pilgrim staff, to rove no more;
Built him a house, like the rude hut you see
Engraved upon our missive heraldy;
Made that his final home; there lived and died
Was buried there, and from thence glorified,
Where yet his ashes sleep, a sacred trust,
Waiting the resurrection of the just.

But we must hasten on our lengthened way,
Unsaid a thousand things we'd like to say;
Some dry and humorous, and some sedate,
The light and shade in mingled aggregate,
Customs and manners, which to our chaste sense
Of fitness might beseem to need defense;
But though grotesque and rude, they yet were free
From sham and shoddy and hypocrisy.

Better to work, they thought, a hard, cold soil,
With stalwart industry and patient toil,
And from reluctant nature conquer wealth,
At least a competence, with honest health
And a good conscience, than with godless pride
The higher places of the earth to ride;
Better content, with hard-earned moderate gains,
Than rapid increase, soiled with guilty stains;
Better the farmer's rustic, plodding life,
Than aristocracy, with waste and strife;
Better to hold the plough and drive the spade,
Than, in low, wanton idleness degrade
Your higher manhood, till your name shall rot
In infamy—a loathsome stain and blot—
Like many a modern swell, whose putrid breath
Is social poison, malaria and death.

So Walter Palmer thought, and stretched his line
North, from the little Narragansett's brine,
Full fifteen miles, until his purchase struck,
The wooded heights of old Pauchunganuc
Hill—not Pendleton—that name it never knew
Till late, and now but as a post-mark due
To local influences, a shallow game—
To cancel out an honored Indian name;
Let these old names be kept, and let them stand
The crude memorials of a people grand,
Even in their language, with its "tucks and nocks,'
As obdurate and stubborn as their rocks;
As guttural, too, as "honk" of goose or fowl
In Spring or Autumn, or the panther's growl;
No matter how obscure, we can checkmate them
As long as we have Trumbull to translate them;
We hope he'll give us a translation true,
Of Wequetequock and Pauchunganuc, too.

To this hill country, wooded region high,
Old Walter Palmer early turned his eye ;
His stalwart sons must have more land to till,
And so he sent them up to hold this hill.

With brawny arms and hands of royal brown
They felled the trees and cut the forests down ;
Tore out the roots and stumps, thrust in the plow,
And walled the fields in, as you see them now ;
Their houses, barns, and churches without steeple,
The rude, rough symbols of a sturdy people.

Hail ! old Pauchunganuc, land of my birth,
Thy airy heights o'ersweeping wide the sea,
To me the dearest spot on earth,
Home of a proud and noble ancestry ;
I never may forget, where'er I roam,
The beauties of my childhood's Highland home.

Ichabod Palmer, fourth from Walter down,
The tallest, strongest man of all the town ;
Who, when denied the use of boat or paddle,
With nothing but his trusty horse and saddle,
Dashed through the waves of Narragansett Bay,
And took from Newport Betty Noyes away,
Despite parental strategy and ire ;
I glory in the young man's blood and fire,
For you must know he was my great grandsire,
Lived on this hill, in old baronial pride,
Long years with Betty Noyes, his rescued bride,
And up there still they slumber side by side.
An incident of more dramatic glow
New England's history can nowhere show :
Which inspiration, through some genius yet,
In wealth of chaste and classic gold shall set.

The first religious service in the town,
Was held at Walter Palmer's, half way down
The narrow cove, wide opening to the bay,
The site of which remains unchanged to-day.
The sermon, rude and somewhat incomplete
In structure, doubtless, was yet very sweet,
And though from first to twenty-fifthly long,
Was orthodox and comforting and strong.

And so, in rustic style, life wore away—
Days, weeks, and months and years went flitting by,
The evening shade and morning twilight gray,
Darkened and lightened then as now the sky,
Six day's of toil, and Sabbath's quiet reign,
They rested, worshipped, and then toiled again.

Children were born, and infancy's glad smile,
With childhood's ringing laugh and sportive glee,
Boyhood and girlhood's bounding, joyous style,
And young folks brimming o'er with jollity,
Softening the staid severities of age,
Make this arcadian life a cheerful page.

Given the story of Ann Borodel,
Or of Rebecca Short, so rich and rare,
Or Betty Noyes, and let the poets tell
Of form and face and eyes and golden hair,
Of early buried loves across the ocean,
Of second loves, romantic with devotion ;
And Stonington will have its heroine,
Embalmed in light of poesy divine,
A face of girlhood, whose transcendant sheen,
Old Plymouth's beauty shall as far outshine ;
As our own Palmer girls excel in grace
Of form and classic comeliness of face.

Hail to this brave old town !   Old Britain's pride
Once cowered beneath her rude and rough defence ;
Her eighteen-pounders riddled Hardy's side,
And taught him that our boys had pluck and sense.
Leaving his anchor grappled in the bay,
He slunk between the night and morn away.

Hail to this rough old town, her ocean shore,
Bays, inlets, rivers, sparkling brooks and streams,
Her waves now breaking with a deafening roar
Upon the rocks, now flashing neath the beams
Of moon and star, while evening's freshening breeze
Floats up, with grateful coolness mid her trees !

Hail to the grand old town, long may she be
What she has been, and is, with rich increase,
And fruitfulness in full maturity,
Of social, civil and religious peace,

In all that makes men wise and great and good,
The highest culture of the Palmer blood !

For from this grand old stock has come a race
Of royal men in dignity and grace,
Of high renown and of distinguished worth,
Princes by right of culture, as of birth.

Among the noblest artists of this land
Is Palmer, whose creations chaste and grand,
In bronze and marble, to the latest age,
Will be his kindred's richest heritage ;
His Faith, a maiden gazing at the cross,
The world beneath her feet, as worthless dross,
With face aglow, and eye of love intent,
Of truth and purity the embodiment—
Who that has seen it, has not felt the thrill
Of art, the soul with ecstacy to fill ?
Who that has seen it, has not felt the power
Of art to intensify devotions hour?
Yet with so many garlands proudly won
His radiant, dazzling course seems but begun—
May Autumn's sere and ripening glories be
His crown of fame for immortality.

William Pitt Palmer, whose resplendent fame
As poet and banker we need but name;
Who, but for the infirmities of age,
Had with his presence graced to-day this stage,
And by his flowing numbers, chaste and terse,
Becharmed us with the rhythm of his verse ;
We'll wreathe his brow for generations late,
And crown him Palmer poet laureate.

Let these suffice.   They do but indicate
A brilliant galaxy, whose aggregate
Swells to a towering monument of fame,
Proud and enduring as the Palmer name.

Divines are here and statesmen eloquent,
And last and chief our soldier President,
Combining in himself the major key
Of Palmer force and Minor modesty.
The cool, courageous push and stubbornness,
That rebel dash was powerless to repress ;

That gave us Donaldson, mid snow and sleet,
And canceled from our arms the word defeat ;
And never faltered till the citadel
Of Southern anarchy at Richmond fell.
And Lee, with dignity of mein and word,
Gave up to U. S. Grant his vanquished sword.
And the old flag—the stars and stripes once more
Floated an undivided nation o'er ;
And Southern breezes nestled in each fold,
As trustingly as in the days of old ;
And kissed the shreds, all loyally and true,
As lovers reconciled are wont to do.

From the rough blasts that sweep our inland seas,
    And Minnesota's fertilizing snows,
To South Carolina's superheated breeze,
    And Georgian airs fragrant with orange blows.
He left his country, one from sea to sea,
The broad domain of man and liberty.

All hail the nation, from behind the cloud,
    That late enwrapped us in its sable fold,
The sun bright streaming through the rifted shroud,
    Pours down a wealth of flashing light and gold,
While mercy, with a sheltering hand and shield,
Covers our martyr President, Garfield.

Long may he live all bravely to dispense
    Its high and grave behests with pious care,
With an unshrinking trust in Providence,
    To guard against each deadly foe and snare ;
The nation consecrated by his blood,
Or North or South to loyalty and God.

And now to duty, what though life be brief,
    A fleeting cloud, a shade, the morning dew,
And generations fade as fades the leaf,
    Yet life is always young when just and true.
Our grand old sire gave God his highest powers,
Did his work well, like him let us do ours.

REV. A. G. PALMER, D. D.

(Brief Biography.)

Rev. A. G. Palmer, D. D., the pastor of the first Baptist Church, Stonington, Ct., was born in North Stonington, May 11th, 1813. His father, Luther Palmer, Esq., was an enterprising and thrifty farmer and a prominent man in the community. The early life of the son was devoted to farming in the Summer, and to study during the Winter in the common school. At the age of nine years he experienced religion, and this shaped his entire life. He made a public profession at the age of sixteen, and soon after began to preach and entered upon a course of classical study for the ministry. His first pastorate was at Westerly, R. I., beginning in 1837 and ending in 1843, six years of successful labor in the church, in that time increasing its membership from thirty to three hundred.

In 1843, he was settled at Stonington. After a very successful term of nine years he accepted a call from the First Baptist Church, Syracuse, N. Y., where he remained until 1855, when he received and accepted a call from the Baptist Church in Bridgeport, Ct. He labored there for three years, and in 1858 accepted a call from the Baptist Church at Wakefield, R. I., and in 1861 returned to Stonington, in response to an earnest call from the church where he had formerly labored. His pastorates have all been productive of great good, and have left their impress upon the churches with which he has labored. Dr. Palmer stands deservedly high in his profession, both as to character and ability. His action in speaking is easy, fervent and impressive, moving others by the intensity of his vivid convictions, thereby exerting a powerful influence over his audience. In all of his intercourse with his fellow citizens he sustains the character of a Christian gentleman, favoring every practical reform with unflinching devotion for the right. His ability and culture were early recognized by *Madison University*, which conferred upon him the honorary title of D. D.

Dr. Palmer has become distinguished as a poet, writing some very fine poems and memorial sonnets of exquisite tenderness and beauty. In his bi-centennial poem at the Old Road Church,

in 1874, alluding to the place and scenes of his childhood, he speaks of his old—old home as follows:

> "Hail! old Pauchunganuc, land of my birth,
>   Thy airy heights o'ersweeping wide the sea;
> To me thou art the dearest spot on earth,
>   Home of a proud and noble ancestry;
> I never may forget, where'er I roam,
>   The beauties of my childhood's Highland home."

Dr. Palmer descends from the Puritan, Walter Palmer, as follows:

Walter Palmer and wife, Rebecca Short; Gershom Palmer and wife, Anna Denison; Ichabod Palmer and wife, Hannah Palmer; Ichabod Palmer and wife, Elizabeth Noyes; Elias Sanford Palmer and wife, Phebe Palmer; Luther Palmer and wife, Sarah Kenyon; Rev. Albert Gallatin Palmer, D. D.

He thus stands connected with some of the most distinguished families of Connecticut and Rhode Island—from Capt. George Denison and Lady Ann Borodel, Mr. Thomas Stanton, the Interpreter General of New England, the Rev. James Noyes, Governor William Brenton and Governor Peleg Sanford, of Newport, and Joshua Kenyon, of Westerly, Rhode Island.

ADDRESS

BY HON. EPHRAIM WILLIAMS, OF STONINGTON, CT.

BATTLE OF STONINGTON.

Mr. President, Ladies and Gentlemen: It seems peculiarly appropriate that on this day, the 10th of August, so many descendants of Walter Palmer, one of the first settlers of this town, should meet together for pleasant intercourse, to become acquainted with each other as members of one great family, to visit the place where he lived and was buried, and to be brought nearer in thought to the difficulties and dangers encountered by those who crossed the ocean to make their abode in this country—then a wilderness, except here and there a spot scantily cultivated by the Indian—and contrast our town to-day, with its public roads and well-tilled fields, its pleasant villages, busy manufactories and manifold industries, with the time when your hardy ancestor settled in Stonington. And it is fitting that, as you trace the history of this town from that time down to the present, you shall call up a just pride that you are the descendants of one who filled a conspicuous place in the developments of its resources, and who, with others, in the forming of our town democracies, founded the principle of self-government, which resulted in the establishment of the civil and religious liberty we now possess. They came here to escape a strong government, and worship in their own way, and with good intent—not always gently or wisely impressed that way upon all—but they laid the foundation of their civil and religious polity, taken as a whole, broader than they dreamed, and their hatred of the form and oppressions of a kingly rule, their gropings, often dimly for the rights of man, their persecutions and retaliations for conscience sake, both alike too frequently cruel and unjust, worked on through successive generations, and out of their experiments and struggles and endurances our model republic arose. And a generation had hardly elapsed when the power from whom these colonies had wrested their independence, proclaimed that "Britannia ruled the waves," and their right to board our ships, and impress seamen into their service on suspicion that they owed allegiance to the crown ; and out of the contest, to maintain the sovereignty of our flag wherever it waved, whether on sea or on land, the incident to which I have been requested to call your attention arose. And so I think you should give more than a passing thought to this incident, as well as to the long train of events and actions preceding ; for the day which you have selected for the Re-Union of the Palmer Family is a day commemorative of brave deeds done on the 10th of August, 1814 ; and among the heroes who in that hastily constructed fort down by yonder breakwater, with only two or three guns, and poorly provided with the munitions of war, drove the English from our shores, the blood of Walter Palmer, in different channels of descent, bore nobly its part. In diverting your attention somewhat from the legitimate purposes for which you have assembled—namely, the well-deserved and proper glorification of the Palmer family, to the not less proper recognition of the day, as commemorative of the defence of Stonington on the 10th of August, 1814—I trust I shall be pardoned for intruding, and perhaps, adding to the general glorification, by giving some extracts of the occurrences on that memorial day, taken from an account that was furnished August 29th, 1814, for publication in the Connecticut *Gazette*, by the magistrates, warden and burgesses of the borough of Stonington:

On Tuesday afternoon of the 9th inst., anchored off our harbor, the frigate *Pactolus*, the *Terror*, a bomb ship, and the brig *Dispatch*, of twenty guns. A flag was discovered to leave the frigate and row towards the town. The impropriety of suffering them to come on shore was suggested, and a boat was immediately obtained. Captain Amos Palmer, William Lord, Esq., and S. A. Hough, of the detachment here, were selected, and the flag of the enemy met by ours, when we received the following unexpected and short notice:

"HIS BRITANNIC MAJESTY'S SHIP 'PACTOLUS,' }
9th of August, 1814, half past 5 o'clock P. M. }
Not wishing to destroy the unoffending inhabitants residing in the town of Stonington, one hour is given them, from the receipt of this, to remove out of the town.

F. M. HARDY,
Captain of H. B. M. Ship *Ramilies*.
For the inhabitants of the town of Stonington."

From the date of this communication, it will appear that Commodore Hardy was himself on board of the *Pactolus* to direct the attack, the *Ramilies* then lying at anchor at the west end of Fisher's Island. The people assembled in great numbers to hear what was the word from the enemy, when the above was read aloud. It was exclaimed from old and young, we will defend. And during the short hour granted us, expresses were sent to General Cushing, at New London, and to Colonel William Randall, of Stonington, commanding the Thirtieth Regiment of State militia. The detachment stationed here under Lieutenant Hough was embodied; Captain Potter, residing within the borough, gave orders to assemble all the officers and men under his command that could be immediately collected. The ammunition for our two eighteen-pounders and four-pounders was collected at the little breastwork erected by ourselves. The citizens of the borough assisted by two strangers from Massachuetts manned the guns. One course of discouragement, only, seemed to prevail, which was the deficiency of am-

munition.   Such guards of musketry as were in our power to
place, were stationed at different points on the shores.

About 8 o'clock in the evening they commenced by the fire
of a shell from the bomb ship, which we immediately returned
by a shot from our eighteen-pounder.   The attack from the
ship was immediately succeeded by one from three launches
and four barges surrounding the point, throwing rockets and
shot into the village.   We defended the town until about 11
o'clock, and had it not been for our spirited resistance, a landing,
no doubt, would have been effected.   Their shells and rockets
having been prevented from spreading the destruction intended,
they ceased firing them about 12 o'clock.   At daylight a fire
of rockets and shot from the launches and barges again commenced, which was spiritedly returned from our artillery taken
from the breastwork, in open view of the enemy, and exposed
to their shot on the end of the point ; and they were compelled
to recede, when our guns were taken back to the breastwork
or fort.   About 8 o'clock the brig *Dispatch* hauled within half
a mile of our breastwork and opened a well-directed and animated fire.   Her fire was returned with a spirit and courage
rarely to be equalled, and the brig was compelled to cut her
cable and retire out of the reach of our shot.   Our ammunition
having been expended, she kept up a constant fire for two hours
or more without having it in our power to return a shot—during which time we are confident, had there been a supply of
ammunition, she would have been taught the use and meaning
of her name.

WILLIAM LORD,
ALEXANDER G. SMITH,   } *Magistrates.*
JOSEPH SMITH, *Warden.*

AMOS PALMER,
AMOS DENISON,
GEORGE HUBBARD,   } *Burgesses.*
THOMAS ASH,
REUBEN CHESEBROUGH,

I also ask your attention to portions of a letter to the Secretary of War from Captain Amos Palmer, a lineal descendant of
Walter, chairman of the committee of citizens which had been
entrusted with the preparation for the defence, and noticed in
Pease and Nile's *Gazette*, as " distinguished for his integrity, his
republican principles and his patriotism," who died at Stonington, March 4, 1816, aged sixty-nine years :

STONINGTON BOROUGH, August 21, 1815.

To the Honorable William H. Crawford, Secretary of War :

SIR—The former Secretary of War put into my hands, as Chairman of the Committee of Defense, the two eighteen-pounders and all the munitions of war that were here belonging to the general government, to be used for the defense of the town. As there is no military office here, it becomes my duty to inform you of the use we have made of them. On the 9th of August, last year, the *Ramilies*, 74, the *Pactolus*, 44, the *Terror*, bomb ship, and the *Dispatch*, gun brig, anchored off the harbor. Commodore Hardy sent off a boat with a flag ; we met him with another from the shore, when the officer of the flag handed me a note from Commodore Hardy, informing that one hour was given the unoffending inhabitants before the town would be destroyed. We returned to the shore, where all the male inhabitants were collected, when I sent the note aboard ; they all exclaimed they would defend the place to the last extremity. We repaired to a small battery that we had hove up, nailed our colors to the flag-staff, others lined the shore with their muskets. At about seven in the evening they put off five barges and a large launch, carrying from thirty-two to nine pound carronade in their bows, opened fire from their ships, and sent their boats to land under cover of their fire. We let them come within small grape distance, when we opened upon them with our two eighteen-pounders with round and grape shot. They soon retreated out of grape distance and attempted a landing on the east side of the village. We dragged a six-pounder that we had mounted, from the fort, and met them with grape, and all our muskets opened fire on them, so that they were willing to retreat a second time. They continued their fire until eleven at night. The next morning at seven o'clock the brig *Dispatch* anchored within pistol-shot of our battery, and sent five barges and two large launches to land under cover of their whole fire (being joined by the *Nimrod*, 20-gun brig). We opened fire on them, when they retreated and came round the east side of the town. We dragged over one of our eighteen-pounders, put in it round shot and about fifty pounds of grape, and tore one of their barges into pieces. They retreated out of grape distance and we turned our fire upon the brig, and expended all our cartridges but five, which we reserved for the boats if they made another attempt to land. After the third express to New London some field ammunition arrived. We then turned our cannon on the brig and she soon cut her cable. The whole fleet then weighed and anchored nearly out of reach of shot, and continued there and the next

day to bombard the town.   They set the buildings on fire in
more than twenty places and we as often put them out.   In
the three days' bombardment they sent on shore sixty tons of
metal, and strange to say, wounded only one man, since dead.
Since peace the officers of the *Dispatch* brig have been on shore
here; they admit they had twenty-one killed and fifty badly
wounded, and that if we could have continued our fire any
longer they should have struck, for they were in a sinking condition, and the wind blew directly into the harbor; but while
we were waiting for our ammunition it changed to the north
and enabled them to get away.   All the shot suitable for the
cannon we have reserved, and have now more eighteen-pound
shot than was sent us by Government.   We have put the two
cannon in the arsenal, and housed all the munitions of war.

   Very respectfully, your obedient servant,

          AMOS PALMER.

  The *Gazette* also says: " The following is a list of the volunteers of those who so bravely stood the brunt of the attack
of Stonington Point:"

OF STONINGTON.

Capt. George Fellows,	Gurdon Trumbull,
Capt. William Potter,	Allen G. Smith,
Dr. William Lord,	Amos Denison, Jr.,
Lieut. H. G. Lewis,	·Stanton Gallup,
Ensign D. Frink,	Thomas Wilcox,
John Miner,	Luke Palmer,
Isaac Miner,	William G. Bush,
Asa Lee,	George Palmer.

OF MYSTIC.

Simeon Haley,	Jesse Deans,
Jeremiah Haley,	Deane Gallup,
Fred. Haley,	Jeremiah Holmes,
Frederick Denison,	Nathaniel Clift,
Ebenezer Denison,	Jedediah Reed,
Isaac Denison.	

OF GROTON.

Alfred White,	Ebenezer Morgan,
Frank Daniels,	Giles Morgan.

OF NEW LONDON.

Major Simeon Smith,   Capt. Noah Lester,
Major N. Frink,   (formerly of the army),
          Lambert Williams.

FROM MASSACHUSETTS.

Capt. Leonard and Mr. Dunham.

It is related that the first men that took station in the battery were four: William Lord, Asa Lee, George Fellows and Amos Denison, Jr. Just before six o'clock on the 9th, volunteers from Mystic—Jeremiah Holmes, Jeremiah Haley, Ebenezer Denison, and Nathaniel Clift—reached the place on foot, and ran immediately to help to operate the gun in the battery.

The battery being small but few could work in it, and it was operated, probably, by less than a dozen men at a time. It is said that the colors on the flag-staff were shot through nine times, and a fence near by was pierced by sixty-three balls.

I also give the muster roll of the 8th Company of Infantry under the command of Capt. William Potter in the 30th regiment of Connecticut militia in service of the United States, at Stonington, commanded by Lieut. Col. Wm. Randall, from the 9th of August, when last mustered, to the 27th of August, 1814:

NAME AND RANK.	COMMENCEMENT OF SERVICE.	EXPIRATION OF SERVICE.
Capt. William Potter,	Aug. 9,	Aug. 27.
Lieut. Horatio G. Sevin,	" 9,	" 27.
Ensign Daniel Finch,	" 9,	" 23.
Sergeants:		
Francis Amy,	" 19,	" 27.
Charles H. Smith,	" 9,	" 27.
Peleg Hancox,	" 22,	" 27.
Gurdon Trumbull,	" 9,	" 27.
Corporals:		
Azariah Stanton, Jr.,	" 16,	" 27.
Junia Chesebrough,	" 9,	" 27.
Joshua Swan, Jr.,	" 22,	" 27.
Privates:		
Phineas Wilcox,	" 9,	" 23.
Hamilton White,	" 9,	" 27.
Henry Wilcox,	" 9,	" 23.
Latham Wilcox,	" 9,	" 27.

Samuel Burtch,	Aug. 9,	Aug. 27.
Jonathan Palmer,	" 9,	" 27.
Andrew P. Stanton,	" 9,	" 27.
James Stanton,	" 9,	" 27.
Thomas Breed,	" 9,	" 17.
Amos Loper,	" 9,	" 20.
Samuel Bottum, Jr.,	" 9,	" 27.
Benjamin Merritt.	" 9,	" 15.
Elisha Chesebrough, Jr.,	" 9,	" 27.
Christopher Wheeler,	" 9,	" 23.
Amos Hancox,	" 9,	" 27.
Zebadian Palmer,	" 9,	" 27.
Nathaniel Waldron,	" 15,	" 27.
Thomas Spencer,	" 19,	" 27.
Nathaniel M. Pendleton,	" 20,	" 27.
Simon Carew,	" 22,	" 27.
Elisha Faxon, Jr.,	" 22,	" 27.
Ebenezer Halpin,	" 22,	" 23.
Asa Wilcox, Jr.,	" 22,	" 23.
Warren Palmer,	" 22,	" 27.
Joseph Bailey, Jr.,	" 9,	" 27.

(Waiter to Capt. William Potter.)

Nathaniel Lewis,	Aug. 9,	" 23.

(Waiter to Lieut. G. Lewis.)

Those under date of expiration of service, August 23, were ordered at that date for service at New London.

It was never known here how much the English suffered in killed and wounded. Captain Alexander S. Palmer told me last evening that in 1828, when on a sailing voyage to the Shetland Islands, he met an English naval officer, Captain Austin, who was a lieutenant on board the *Ramilies*, who told him that there were about forty killed on the barge, spoken of in Mr. Amos Palmer's letter as blown to pieces, and that one shot which entered the brig *Dispatch* swept between her decks and killed fourteen outright. My informant is one of three brothers, Nathaniel and Theodore, now deceased, who were accomplished ship-masters ; in fact, no. family in this country, or any other, ever produced three more able. Capt. Nathaniel, the eldest, was among the first explorers south of Cape Horn, and discovered the land now known as Palmer's land ; was the projector, and commanded the first clipper ship ever built, which was immediately followed by so many that our merchant marine at one time was the admiration of all nations; and the three brothers commanded some of the finest packet ships between New York and Liverpool, and afterwards renowned clippers in the East India trade. An account of their voyages and explorations, if fully written out, would read like a romance. I hope I shall be pardoned this digression, but I want to show you that the Palmers were bold cruisers on sea, as well as brave crusaders on land. It will thus be seen, ladies and gentlemen, that the defense of Stonington was an exploit of which you may feel proud, in that the blood inherited by so many, prominent in that affair, flows in your veins. A more brilliant engagement did not take place during the war of 1812, and nowhere was the loss and damage to the enemy so disproportionate to the harm they inflicted, for the popular ballad of that time said :

> " They killed a goose, they killed a hen,
> Three hogs they wounded in a pen ;
> But we bored their ships through and through,
> And killed and wounded of their crew
> So many, that they bade adieu
> To the gallant boys of Stonington."

The anniversary of that day has often been observed in a homely way—by processions, illuminations, firing of the historic old guns, and festivities suitable to the occasion—while the participants in that gallant defense were on the stage of action ; but they, with few exceptions, have overcome " the last enemy," and now sleep the sleep that knows no waking till the resurrection morning ; and familiy re-unions of this character, held on the commemorative day, will tend to keep alive in a social, quiet, but not less effective way, the memory of those patriots who fought bravely and successfully for their country and their homes ; and so many meeting together from various parts of the land who were before unknown to each other, though the offspring of one progenitor, will enlarge and strengthen the bond of friendship and family pride; patriotism, affection for kindred and veneration for the past, will be fostered and perpetuated ; and we shall all more truly feel that we are, indeed, members of one family, have a common heritage in our country's prosperity and partakers in her history. And you Palmers or pilgrims should bear in mind that you are but sojourners here, as all your fathers were, and that, as time rolls on, one after another of you will be numbered with the ancestors ; and that your posterities, when they meet, as I have no doubt they will, in pursuance of the custom you have this day inaugurated, will look back to the record you will have left, as you now are looking back to that of your ancestry. And may each of you, wherever you may lodge, whatever may be your position in life, do your duty well and live in the hearts of many generations of children, with whom your memory shall be as enduring and fragrant in good works as are to-day the virtues of those ancestors, whose memory and history you have now assembled to commemorate and perpetuate.

> " Soon you will cross the unknown sea
> And reach the heavenly haven, if pure you be ;
> Palmers and friends who have gone before,
> Bid kindly welcome to that peaceful shore ;
> So should we who here remain
> Toil on, in faith, 'that to die is gain.' "

IMPROMPTU ADDRESS,

BY DR. EUGENE PALMER.

To the call of the great State of Texas, the venerable Dr. Eugene Palmer responded as follows :

I fear that I shall not be able to make myself heard throughout this large pavilion, for nature has gifted me with a voice not strong enough even to blow my own trumpet ; and now you call on me to blow the trumpet for the great empire State of Texas. Already has Texas been twice called to the front, and twice been more ably represented in the cause of this Palmer Re-Union than any other State represented on the flag of the nation. I refer to that gifted daughter of song, the poetess, Mrs. Shindler, of Nacogdoches, who has given you a history of the most brilliant and distinguished branch of the Palmar family, which your genealogist had overlooked. Besides herself, this branch includes the Rev. Dr. Palmer of New Oleans, who,

if he were here to-day, that gifted orator would electrify this assembly from centre to circumference ; he would " make a rat-
tling among the dry bones."

Again, she has recited before you her beautiful original
poems, and told you something else that you did not know before, for you never believed that the Muses have sometimes
come down from the hill tops of Pernassus, to cull the rich
wild flowers that bloom on the prairies of Texas. Your secretary did not put down my name last evening among the speakers for to-day, and I am playing my role without a rehearsal.
Yesterday I sustained the role of two characters in the play—
both of them tramps—for in my haste to join the Stonington
boat my trunk was left, and having no means to make my toilet, I " came to the feast without a wedding garment." That
of the other tramp was the prodigal son, who had wandered to
a far country, and had come back to his birth-place ; but, unlike
that prodigal son, I had not wasted my substance in riotous living, but in my sympathies with a cause which I believed to be
just. " For where your treasure is, there will your heart be
also."

THE PALMERS' HYMN,

BY SARA A. PALMER, OF STONINGTON, CT.

A gathering clan to-day
From near and far away,
  We pilgrims haste
To give the honor due
To him, both strong and true,
Who built his home anew
  'Midst rocks and waste.

" God and my strong right arm
Shall shield me from all harm,"
  Our brave sire cried ;
" Across the trackless sea
I flee from tyranny,
To strike for liberty
  Whate'er betide."

Now we, his children, here
His memory revere
   With hearts aglow ;
As Palmers true and tried
We'll bravely stem the tide.
However deep and wide,
   Of wrong and woe,

A widely scattered band
We'll bear throughout the land
   Hearts pure within ;
Our glory e'er shall be
That all the world may see
" Who bears the palm must be
   Worthy to win !"

God of our father dear,
Bow down to us Thine ear,
   Accept our prayer ;
Thy mercies we implore,
On us Thy blessing pour,
Our name be evermore
   Thy hallowed care.

EVENING SERVICES.

PRAYER,

BY REV. E. BARNABAS PALMER, OF BOSTON.

Preserve, O Lord, within our heart of hearts, the memory of this auspicious day. May it lodge therein as a special token of Thy grace and favor. And as the " lines of influence " and ties of blood and kindred from all the past " intersect the present, and reach forward into all the future," may this external union of palm with palm form an inexhaustible font of tender feeling and sympathy. Bless Thou the hour, this moment now arrived, in which we in one rapture strive, with lip and heart, to tell our gratitude for Thy protecting care.

And now, what offering, what memorial can our sincerity

present, that would acceptable be to Thee, better than those trophies of the soul, achieved,

> " As Thy unerring precepts teach,
> Upon the internal conquests made by each,
> *Palmam qui meruit ferat,*
> Breathe Thou the bosom of this internal relation,
> With this day's vital undulation,
> That all who do this name inherit
> May conscious be of Thy moving spirit."

To us, it is a source of solemn joy ; to us, a hymn of prayer, and prayer of thanksgiving, that we inherit and enjoy a name consecrated by the triumphal entry of the blessed Jesus into Jerusalem ; a name associated with the hosannas that were sung, and palm branches that were spread before Him that came in the name of the Highest. A name achieved by our remote ancestral originals, when they returned from their long pilgrimage with the palm, bearing palm in the palm of their hands.

Gracious in Thy sight be this assembly, and service of the palmbearing branches—hallowed by its aim !

With emotions of devout reverence for Thee, with feelings of profound respect for the ancestral palm-tree, in whose name and under whose branches we are gathered in sun and shade, the banner of our joy

> " We now unfold and wait,
> That strength of love our souls may elevate."

IMPROMPTU REMARKS,

BY GEN. GEORGE W. PALMER, OF NEW YORK CITY.

On taking the chair the evening of the 10th, General George W. Palmer said in substance :

Palmers and kinsfolk : To say that I feel flattered and proud by being called upon to preside for a time over this great family gathering, is but a feeble expression of the sentiments I experience at this moment. Unexpected and undeserved as this honor is, I shall, nevertheless, treasure its pleasing memory in my heart of hearts through life, and leave the record of it as a rich legacy to my children.

From the East and the West, the North and the South, the Palmers and their relatives have gathered to the number of over three thousand, and to-night present a spectacle, as a family re-union, such as was never witnessed before in this or any other country. When a boy, at Christmas time, I remember the gatherings at my grandfather's house of his eleven living children, with many grandchildren, and I thought he was the greatest man on earth to be able to preside over so large a family. But now I am at the head of a larger table than anybody's grandfather ever presided over, and I am proud of it.

I must not detain you by even attempting to make a speech. You have been fed upon poetry and history and eloquence, and the feast is not yet over. Still it has occurred to me that before we separate for the night some business ought to be done and participated in by all the Palmers and their relations. At all events steps should be taken to perpetuate and nationalize these family re-unions, and I hope resolutions will be offered and and passed to that end. I await your further pleasure.

GEN. GEORGE W. PALMER.

(BRIEF BIOGRAPHY.)

Born in the town of Ripley, Chautauqua County, New York, June 7th, 1835. His parents were farmers, and his early education was only what could be obtained at a district school and close application at home. At the age of fifteen he commenced teaching school in his native town, and taught four consecutive Winters, in the meantime attending the Academy at Westfield, an adjoining town in the same county, during the Spring and Fall terms. He had prepared to enter Williams' College two years in advance, but illness prevented. On his recovery he commenced the study of law with Judge Marvin of his native county. He entered the Law University in 1855, was examined and admitted to practice law in all the Courts of the States in 1856, and in 1857, was graduated at the Law University at Albany, receiving the degree of L.L. B. He then continued practice in the town of Westfield, in partnership with Austin Smith, and was married September 1st, 1858, to Miss Sarah E. Keyes, the daughter of a prominent Baptist minister. He gained a considerable reputation as a lawyer and advocate. During the campaign of Abraham Lincoln, in 1860, he took a prominent place as a campaign speaker, and was captain of the first company, and commander of battalion of Wide-Awakes formed in that locality. The arduous labors of this canvass, added to his professional duties, again caused a serious illness.

In the Winter of 1861, he was appointed assistant clerk in the New York State Senate. Soon after Sumpter was fired upon, though still in poor health, he went to Washington and assisted in the defense of the bridges leading from Virginia to Washington. He was soon afterward appointed in the War Department, and for two years served in the Quartermaster-General's office under Secretaries of War Cameron and Stanton. He assisted in organizing the Provost Marshal's department, and soon after its organization was appointed Captain and Provost Marshal of the 31st District of New York. In this position, Secretary Stanton said of him : "I have one honest and able Provost Marshal in Captain Palmer." He held this position until the 1st of December, 1864, when he went to Albany with Governor Fenton, who made him his Military Secretary, which position he held until the Spring following, when he was appointed Commissary General of Ordnance of the State of New York, with the rank of Brigadier General ; and in the early part of 1868, he was also clothed with the duties of Quartermaster-General of the State, which position had formerly been held by Generals Edwin A. Merritt and Chester A. Arthur.

In January, 1869, he resumed the practice of his profession in the city of New York, but soon left it to assume the duties of Appraiser of the Port of New York, to which position he was appointed by the President and confirmed by the Senate. As Appraiser of the Port, Secretary Boutwell said of him that he was one of the best revenue officials in the Government.

In 1871, he again resumed the practice of his profession, but continued to take considerable interest, and actively participated in the National and State political contests, attending nearly all of the important Republican National and State conventions from the birth of that party. Early in 1879, he received the appointment of Deputy Collector of Customs at the Port of New York, in charge of the Law Department, which position he still holds.

COLLECTOR'S OFFICE, CUSTOM HOUSE, NEW YORK. {
7th Division—Law Department. {

The care of all suits brought against the Collector; the investigation of attempts to defraud the revenue ; the enforcement of Fines, Penalties, and Forfeitures, and all legal proceedings connected therewith ; the custody and sale of all goods seized by the Revenue Officers; the taking and cancellation of bonds, and the prosecution of those whose conditions have been violated ; the supervision of all Exports entitled to Drawback of Internal Revenue, and Customs duties on articles manufactured from foreign materials ; the ascertaining and certifying such duties ; the charge of all export entry-papers for the benefit of Drawback, and officers' returns thereon, and of Certificates in proof of the landing of such exports abroad ; the approval and registry of Powers of Attorney ; the custody of the archives and records ; the reception, recording, and disposal of all Protests and Appeals ; and the correspondence growing out of or connected with the above matters.

GEORGE W. WRIGHT, Chief Clerk.
GEORGE W. PALMER, Deputy Collector in Charge.

His genealogy will be particularly given in the second volume of this work, when published.

[Written for the Palmer Re-Union, in Stonington, Ct., and delivered on the evening of August 10th.]

MOTHER-TOWN.

BY REV. F. DENISON, OF PROVIDENCE, R. I.

I.

Whatever scenes of beauty we behold,
    Through viewing all the circle of the earth,
A grace unequalled and a charm untold
    Will bind us to the spot that gave us birth.

A mystic chord, undying in the breast,
    Is vibrant to the very name of home ;

A mother ever matchless stands confest,
    Her angel presence ours, where'er we roam.

So, Mother-Town, we reverent turn to thee
    Full-crowned with honors, won by Christian sires;
Thy templed hills thy home, by singing sea,
    Where, as of old, thou guarded virtue's fires.

II.

Endowed of Heaven, our fathers were the peers
    Of Britian's princes, the inheritors
Of kingly truths and rights ; unknowing fears
    Of men when flamed the fatherland with wars.

But full to hold their heritage from God,
    Commissioned by their faith the world to bless,
They turned, as exiles, from their loved abode
    To build for truth in this hoar wilderness.

Faith sped the axe and plow, the scythe and flail;
    Love sang to cradle, distaff, wheel and loom ;
The word of God, the chosen coat-of-mail
    To shield the bosom and adorn the home.

'Twas thus the Christian planting was begun
    By Stanton, Chesebrough, Palmer, Mason, Noyes,
Main, Miner, Gallup, Wheeler, Denison,
    And kindred souls, of whom the Lord made choice.

Of freedom's grand republic yet to be,
    Here was the opening promise and the type—
The humble town—league of equality—
    The germ prophetic of the cluster ripe.

Faith's drum-beat called the people to their prayer,
    O'er hearth-stones hung the ready, trusty swords ;
Charged firelocks sentinelled the pulpit stairs,
    And banners blazed with patriotic words.

III.

Hence spurned our Mother England's tax on tea,
    Swift stamped the Stamp Act underneath her feet ;
Set on her brow the cap of liberty,
    And vowed oppression's every step to meet.

Here, as from Boston's North Church, streamed the lights
    Along the hills to rally minute men ;
Heaven-leagued, defensive of unaliened rights,
    Here marched to battle Gideon's host again.

To Trenton, Valley Forge and Yorktown's plain,
    Our mother sent her "Sons of Liberty ;"
And braves to man our guns upon the main,
    Who fired their shots for right and victory.

The blood of Ledyard and his hero-band
    By traitor Arnold spilt on Groton Heights,
Refired her soul and nerved her hand,
    To do or die, to win our country's rights.

IV.

Alike prepared, when fell another blow
    Upon our sailors, striking down their right,
Her children rose to beard the lion-foe
    Again, and prove their manhood and their might.

From yonder waves the royal ships bore down,
    With great-mouthed, bull-dog boast and swelling jibs ;
But met such iron-thunder from this town,
    As sent them reeling back with splintered ribs.

Such was her Spartan purpose ne'er to yield,
    And such the telling, gallant victory won,
That e'en to-day, on England's battered shield,
    Are read the scars received at Stonington.

Within her bosom martyr children sleep,
    Wrapped in our country's fame as in her love ;
While others far-off fields of battle keep
    Their names, as stars, in freedom's banner wove.

V.

She finds fair writ on Scripture's radiant leaf,
    That harvest songs belong to those who plant ;
And hence she sings to-day our nation's chief—
    Her blood beats in the veins of General Grant.

Palmam qui meruit ferat—full she saith
   To him as victor both in field and state,
Repeating glad a grateful nation's breath,
   While still upon him highest honors wait.

And welcome now, as knightly pilgrims, come
   The Palmers, each with fitting palm in hand,
To bless with tribute their ancestral home,
   And hear anew their mother's high command.

Firm guardian of the common welfare still,
   With pulsing heart, by valley, crag and shore,
As faithful, loving mother ever will,
   She sits and counts her jewel children o'er.

VI.

Here let the Muse of History thoughtful pause,
   Here measure doctrines by the fruit they bear;
In justice's well-poised scale obtain the cause
   Why this once savage wild now blooms so fair.

The word of God, enthroned in human breasts,
   Transmits all things, e'en evil into good;
Pronounces just, beneficent behests,
   And builds the empire of our brotherhood.

The desert waste is cheered by Hermon's dew;
   The wilderness takes up redemption's strain;
The Rose of Sharon blooms where briars grew;
   And freedom's host swells out the grand refrain.

O, favored land elect, Heaven-blessed and free,
   Hold fast thy homes, thy churches, schools and laws—
Thy bulwark 'gainst home-bred conspiracy,
   And ages 'gainst malignant foreign wars.

VII.

In vision let another century glide,
   Our land by virtues, learning, arts combined,
Shall win new lustre and augment with pride,
   The peaceful trophies that exalt mankind.

Her temples and her halls of state she'll build
   On mountain ranges nearer to the sun ;
Her bounds, with cedars, palms and olives filled,
   From Arctic North to Tropic South shall run.

And in that opulent, abounding year,
   Supreme in majesty and wide renown,
The regent of this Western hemisphere,
   She'll not forget our worthy Mother-Town.

To be an actor on so vast a stage,
   To play in such grand scene a vital part,
May well our reverential thought engage,
   And with a pure devotion thrill the heart.

VIII.

Devout we gaze on monuments and urns,
   And spill the legends on the moss-rolled stones ;
Affection's tender flame within us burns ;
   The heart a tie unutterable owns.

Our honored ancestors here silent rest ;
   On every breeze endearing memories throng ;
The hills are with their thousand stories blest,
   And every vale repeats its hallowed song.

The man without a country and a home,
   How like a bird, smit by fierce tempest's sweep
At sea, mid angry clouds and hungry foam,
   To panting fall and perish in the deep.

O, Mother-Town, thou grandest sacred dust ;
   And, not in heartless words, this prayer is made ;
That, when is finished all our earthly trust,
   With father's ashes may our own be laid.

And then—that gathering in the bright beyond,
   That great re-union on the better shore,
Where life and love shall have perfected bond,
   And fellowships unfold forevermore.

IX.

Thus, kin and friends, fulfilling my small part,
  With yours, I lay my simple offering down,
Though less than yours in worth, not less in heart,
  A thankful tribute to our Mother-Town.

REV. FREDERIC DENISON.

(BRIEF BIOGRAPHY.)

Rev. Frederic Denison, son of Isaac and Levina (Fish) Denison, and great-grandson of Deacon Benadam and Bridget (Palmer) Gallup, was born in Stonington, Ct., Sept. 28, 1819: trained on a farm, in common schools and at Bacon Academy; learned the carpenter trade; became a school teacher; united with the Third (now Union) Baptist Church in Groton; was licensed to preach; studied in the Connecticut Literary Institution; graduated at Brown University in 1847; became pastor of First Baptist Church in Westerly, R. I., of Central Baptist Church in Norwich, Ct., of Central Falls Baptist Church in Rhode Island; entered the United States army as chaplain and served three years during the Rebellion; settled again as pastor in Westerly, in New Haven, Ct., in Woonsocket and in Providence, R. I.; married, January 12, 1848, Amy Randall Manton, daughter of Dr. Shadrach Manton of Providence, and has one daughter, Fredrica, living; has written various volumes of prose, history, biography and narratives, and small works of poetry; is a large contributor to periodicals, secular and religious; is corresponding member of the Rhode Island and Wisconsin Historical Societies; is now Historical Registrar of the Baptists of Rhode Island, and was a leading associate editor of the recent " Cyclopedia of Representative Men of Rhode Island."

PALMER FAMILIES.

ADDRESS BY NOYES F. PALMER,

OF JAMAICA, L. I., N. Y.

Mr. President: We are assembled to do honor and homage to the memory of Walter Palmer, a pilgrim from the Old World to the new, and the original ancestor of a long line of generations. Over two centuries ago, Walter Palmer made the Wequetequock Cove his abiding place, and now we, of the later generations, have returned to this ancestral spot, like pilgrims from afar, to view with our own eyes many places made sacred by the reminiscences of our grandfathers and mothers.

Our name, Palmer, it has been said, is "derived from pilgrimages, and is not last in the mists of antiquity. The crusaders, in their marches to Jerusalem in the Middle Ages, from the time of Peter the Hermit to the close of the fourteenth century, had many followers, who sought to see the tomb of Christ from sacred motives. Many of these pilgrims on their return wore palm leaves in their hats, or carried staves made from palm branches. They thus came to be called Palm-ers or bearers of the palm. Some were also distinguished by the scallop shell worn twisted in their hat band."

The name soon passed into literature. Shakespeare frequently uses the word: "My scepter for a Palmer's walking staff;" and also, "Where do the Palmers lodge, I do beseech you?"

In Spencer's Faerie Queene, he alludes to an aged pilgrim:

> " Him als accompanyd upon the Way,
> A comely Palmer, clad in black attire ;
> Of ripest years, and hairs all hoarie gray,
> That with a staff his feeble limbs did stire,
> Lest his long way, his aged limbs should tire."

Sir Walter Scott wrote :

> " I am a Palmer, as you see,
>   Which of my life much part have spent
> In many a far and fayre countrie,
>   As pilgrims do, of good intent."

In a work on "Our English Surnames," by Chas. W. Bardley, Esq., is an account of the derivation of the name Palmer, as follows: "The various religious wanderings of solitary recluses, though belonging to a system long faded from our English life, *find a perpetual epitaph in the directories of to-day.* Thus we have still our pilgrims, or 'peterins,' as the Normans termed them. We meet with Palmers any day in the streets of our large towns; names distinctly relating the manner in which their owners have derived their titles. *The Pilgrim* may have but visited the shrine of St. Thomas, of Canterbury. *The Palmer,* as his name proves, had, forlorn and weary, battled against all difficulties, and trod the path that led to the Holy Sepulchre,

> ' The faded palm branch in his hand,
> Showed pilgrim from the Holy Land.' "

The name Palmer has been associated with Palm and Palestine for ages, and has been engrafted into Holy Writ. The selection of palm branches by the pilgrims to the Holy Land had great significance; a characteristic of a palm tree is, that if bent or twisted out of shape, when released will regain its normal shape. So with truth crushed to earth, will rise again. The palm tree is mentioned in the Sacred Songs of Solomon: "This thy stature is like to a palm tree, and thy breasts to clusters of grapes. I said, I will go up to the palm tree, I will take hold of the boughs thereof."

In 92d Psalm, referring to the return of Babylonish captives to the Land of Promise, in 12th verse, we find: "The righteous shall flourish like the palm tree; he shall grow like a cedar in Lebanon."

When Jesus made his triumphal entry into Jerusalem, it is recorded in John xii: "When they heard that Jesus was coming to Jerusalem, took branches of palm trees and went forth to meet him, and cried, Hosanna! Blessed is the King of Israel that cometh in the name of the Lord."

Again, in John's Revalations, chapter vii, verse 9th: "After, I beheld, and lo! a great multitude, which no man could number, of all nations, and kindred, and people, and tongue, stood before the throne, and before the Lord, clothed with white robes and palms in their hands."

We therefore find in sacred and profane literature mention of palms and palm bearers.

In the Old World, the name Palmer applied to families of different paternity, and different nationalities, and only in modern times do we find it signifying any one family.

In ancient times there was even a difference between a Pilgrim and a Palmer. Bailey, in "Clark's Introduction to Heraldry," thus defines the difference: "A Pilgrim had some dwelling place, a Palmer none; a Pilgrim travelled to some certain place, the Palmer to all; the Pilgrim must go at his own charge, the Palmer must profess poverty whether real or wilful. The Pilgrim might give over his profession, but the Palmer might not."   .

That the name applied to many different families in Europe is evident from the fact, that Burke's "Encyclopedia of Heraldry" describes forty-five coats-of-arms, under the name of Palmer.

Not so with the family name in America. Here we have no coats-of-arms to confuse us and create caste in society. (Every Palmer in America wears his own "coat," rather than that of his grandfather.)

In America we have but a few Palmer ancestors, and we of to-day have made a journey, liken unto a pilgrimage, to pay respect to one of them—Walter Palmer, who came to America soon after the *Mayflower* pilgrims, and whose descendants are, perhaps, more numerous than that of any other pilgrim Palmer.

The intermarriages of Palmers have so commingled posterity that nearly all of the name are more or less related. Among the original stocks have been gathered from records:

1st. Wm. Palmer, who came from Nottinghamshire, England, in ship *Fortune*, second vessel after the *Mayflower*, in 1621. He sailed from Plymouth, England, and landed at Plymouth, Massachusetts Bay Colony; what was his abiding place is now known as Duxbury, Mass.

2d. Walter Palmer and Abraham Palmer, brothers, who came from Nottinghamshire, England, in 1629, along with John En-

dicott, in charge of "six ships with 400 persons, men, women
and children," landed at Charlestown, Massachusetts Bay Colony. Walter Palmer was one of the original founders of Charlestown, 1629, of Rehoboth, 1643, and of Southerton, now called
Stonington, 1653.

3d. Thomas Palmer, in ship *Expectation*, 1635 ; from Bradford, England, and the founder of the town of Rowley, Mass.

4th. John Palmer, in ship *Elizabeth*, 1634 or '35 ; settled in
Hingham, Mass.

I think Thomas and John (3 and 4) were brothers. Some of
his descendants on Long Island, N. Y., where John lived.

5th. Barnabas Palmer, from Belfast, Ireland, 1740; settled in
Rochester, N. H.

6th. Edward Palmer, from England to Boston, Nov. 12,
1746.

7th. Lieut. Wm. Palmer, made freeman at Yarmouth, June
7, 1638 ; settled on Long Island, and died there.

8th. Wm. Palmer, who went to Virginia. Descendants
throughout the South.

9th. John Palmer, in ship *Providence*, of Scarborough, England, in 1684 : settled in Pennsylvania, and from whom are descended vast numbers of Quaker Palmers.

10th. Joseph Palmer, from Higher Abbottsrow, Devonshire,
England, in ship *Wilmington*, to Boston, Mass., November 2d,
1746. Descendants in Massachusetts.

11th. Thomas Palmer, from Kelso, Scotland, 1790. Descendants in Philadelphia, Penn.

12th. Matthew Palmer, from Nottinghamshire, England, about
1720 landed in New York City. Descendants in Dutchess Co.,
N. Y. and Saratoga Co., N. Y.

13th. Capt. Wm. J. Palmer, from London, England, about
1812 ; settled in Galliopolis, Ohio.

There are some few later stocks, but whose descendants are
not as yet very numerous, so far as known.

The larger proportion of the Palmers of America are descended from four of these individuals—namely, Wm. Palmer,
of Duxbury, Mass.; Walter Palmer, of Stonington, Ct.; Thomas
Palmer, of Rowley, Mass.; John Palmer, of Hingham, Mass.

These four may be called the Palmer patriarchs of New England.

The intermarriages of Palmers have been so numerous, that all the living descendants are more or less mixed in their relationship to the ancient stocks, and it is no more than proper to say that a Re-Union of Palmers will embrace these different branches.

Tradition has transplanted from generation to generation many reminiscences, but one very important one is, that the Palmers are descended from three brothers. I presume this sprang from the brotherhood between Walter and Abraham, and from the many cotemporaneous Wm. Palmers, rather than from the fact that there really were three brothers. Records show two other brothers besides Walter and Abraham, that were original ancestors, but not brothers to Walter and Abraham ; their names were John and Thomas, who came from England about 1631 or '32; John settled on the Georges River in Maine, and Thomas in Newtown, Mass.

This Re-Union of the Palmer Family has special application to the direct lineal descendants of Walter Palmer, rather than to other stocks of the same name. We have already had a very able and interesting historical address by Judge Richard A. Wheeler, in regard to Walter, therefore it is not necessary for us to repeat.

But many are present who may ask the question, " Are we descendants of Walter Palmer?" We will give you from one of our books, called " Branches and Places," the name and place of residence of some *one* original ancestor who was a descendant of Walter, and whose descendants branched out of the localities where he and his children lived into various sections of the country. It must be remembered that this list of " Branches and Places " does not give the name of all the descendants who may have lived in these various localities, but rather the name of some *one* original ancestor, from whom there are still other branches and places connected therewith.

ALPHABETICAL ARRANGEMENT

OF PLACES WHERE SOME OF THE DESCENDANTS OF WALTER
PALMER HAVE LIVED.

ASHFORD, CT.: Gen. Nathan, Benjamin, Dr. Joseph. *Ansonia,
Ct.:* Albert L. *Andover, Ct.:* The Skinners, the Foxes.
Ackworth, Ct.: Philander. *Albany, N. Y.:* Chas. L. Ich-
abod, Luther M., Byron O. *Aroca, N. Y.:* Ira, S. H.
Auburn, N. Y.: Denison. *Agawam, N. Y.:* Samuel.
Ann Arbor, Mich.: Alonzo B., Russel D. *Athens, Ga.:*
Geo. H.

BRANFORD, CT.: William, Obadiah, Michael, Solomon, Benja-
min, John, Samuel, Stephen, Joseph, Abraham, Nathaniel,
Timothy (and over a thousand more). *Berlin, Ct.:* Col.
Chas. D. *Buckland, Ct.:* The Clarks. *Bridgewater, Ct.:*
Jonathan. *Brooklyn, N. Y.:* Dr. L. N., Wm. Pitt., the
Clarks, the Cutlers, James. *Bridgewater, N. Y.:* Jonathan,
the Lambs, Elias, Rev. Belia, David, Asa. *Brooklyn, Mich.:*
Priscilla, the Colgroves, the Randalls, the Austins, the
Ides, the Websters. *Bowery Bay, N. Y.:* Wm. E. *Bur-
lington, N. Y.:* Gen. Nathan, Stephen, William, Benjamin.
Brookfield, N. Y.: Gen. Noyes, Benjamin. *Brighton, N. Y.:*
The Barneses. *Berlin, N. Y.:* Gideon, Joseph B. *Boston,
Mass.:* Lewis M., Jonathan. *Bath, Me.:* Asa. *Benning-
ton, Vt.:* Seth. *Busti, N. Y.:* Whitman, Amos. *Buckland
Corners, N. Y.:* Sidney E. *Blackinton, Mass.:* David, Mary
B. *Buffalo, N. Y.:* The Wilguses, the Sheldons, the But-
lers, the Pecks. *Burlington, Ia.:* Luke. *Bronson, Fla.:*
The Simmons. *Batavia, Ill.:* Chas. A. *Brockport, N. Y.:*
Humphrey, Nathaniel. *Bethlehem, Ct.:* Sheldon, Samuel,
Isaac. *Brown Co., N. Y.:* Stephen. *Bradford, Pa.:* The
Weeds.

CHARLESTOWN, MASS.: Elihu, Nehemiah. *Coventry, Ct.:* Rev.
Eliott. *Columbus, Ct.:* The Littles. *Columbus, N. Y.:*
Elijah, Grant Billings. *Colchester, N. Y.:* Richard, Horace,
Seth, Hiram. *Canterbury, N. Y.:* James B. *Clockville,
N. Y.:* The Chapmans, the Randalls. *Columbus, O.:*
The Grows. *Columbus, N. Y.:* Benjamin, Asahael, Stephen,

Amos. *Cayuga, N. Y.:* Dr. Noyes. *Corning, N. Y.:* Olive,
Luther A. *Cardiff, N. Y.:* Avory F. *Castleton, N. Y.:*
James. *Chatham, N. Y.:* Ephraim. *Compton, N. Y.:* Sam-
uel. *Clarendon, Vt.:* David. *Chicago, Ill.:* Loomis T.,
Charles, the Durlands, Chas. T., Joseph, the Noyeses, the
Hilands, Herman C. *Castleton, Vt.:* David, Allen, the
Crarys. *Chattanooga, Tenn.:* Sidney. *Clarkson, N. Y.:*
Joel B., Russell. *Cincinnatus, N. Y.:* Charles. *Compton,
N. H.:* Dudley. *Chesterfield, Ct.:* Elisha C., Joshua. *Can-
astota, N. Y.:* Joseph, Hannah S. *Catskill, N. Y.:* Hiland.
Collingwood, N. Y.: Avory R. *Carbondale, Ill.:* Elihu J.
Cuba, N. Y.: The Medburys, Joseph. *Clarkson, N. Y.:*
Dea. Joel. *Covington, Ct.:* Christopher. *Coeymans Hol-
low, N. Y.:* William W. *Coxsackie, N. Y.:* Lewis, Jon-
athan B.

DANIELSONVILLE, CT.: Edwin L. *Dallas City, Pa.:* Amos T.
Decatur, Na.: Mary E. *Dover, N. J.:* Stephen J., Ezekiel,
Charles. *Dutchess Co., N. Y.:* Daniel, Aaron, Joseph.
Des Moines, Ill.: Albert S. *Delevan, Ill.:* O. B. *Danville,
Ill.:* Dr. Asa A., Judge Norman D., E. H. *Danesburgh, N.
Y.:* Caleb, Ira. *Dawkins Mills, O.:* Isaac. *Detroit, Mich.:*
Nathan H, Thomas, George T., Nehemiah, Nathan C.,
Friend. *Decatur, Ill.:* Ambrose W., the Ewings. *Delhi,
N. Y.:* Ezekiel, Joseph. Shubal, Urban. *Durand, Ill.:*
Geo. W.

EXETER. R. I.: Uriah, Amos. *Exeter, Ct.:* Ezra, Roswell, Rev.
Phineas, Rev. Gershom, the Havens, the Shermans, the
Whites. *Exeter, N. Y.:* Gen. Noyes, Elder Christopher,
Humphrey, Gershom, Michael, George, Abel. *East New
York, N. Y.:* Noyes G., George W. *Eau Clair, Wis.:*
Camillus Noyes. *Euclid, N. Y.:* Gideon, Nathaniel. *Ev-
ans Mills, N. Y.:* John R. *Eaton, N. Y.:* Ephraim. *East
Haddam, Ct.:* Edward, Levi. *East Killingly, Ct.:* The
Lewises. *East Hartford, Ct.:* The Atwoods, the Lewises, •
the Wilcoxs.

FAYETTEVILLE, CT.: Dr. Noyes. *Fayetteville, N. Y.:* Jerome,
Charles, Gilford, Denison. *Falls Village, Ct.:* Theodore H.
Fitchville, O.: Preston. *Fort Concho, Tex.:* Lieut. Geo.

H. *Fair Haven, Ct.:* Henry. *Fairfield, O.:* E. S. *Five Corners, N. Y.:* The Hunts.

GRISWOLD, CT.: Benjamin, Alvah, the Larkhams, the Wilcoxs, the Clarks, Asher, Amos F., the Holmes. *Greenville, Ct.:* Myron, Charles, Alfred, Chauncey. *Groton, Ct.:* Mary A. *Gorham, N. Y.:* James. *Galway, Ill.:* George Denison. *Great Barrington, Mass.:* Billings. *Green Springs, O.:* Ura H. *Green Co., N. Y.:* Jonathan, Gideon. *Grapeville, N. Y.:* Egbert, M. *Goshen, Ct.:* H. D., Robert, Addison. *Grand Rapids, Mich.:* The Walkers. *Gloversville, N. Y.:* T. R., Levi H. *Greenwich, Ct.:* Jonathan, Benjamin, Stephen. *Goshen, Ct.:* The Halls, Robert, Samuel, Joseph. *Guilford, Vt.:* Charles. *Greenville, N. Y.:* Gideon, Epenetus, Wm. R., Jonathan. *Geneva, N. Y.:* Levi.

HOPE VALLEY, R. I.: The Chapmans. *Hampden Junction, O.:* A. F. *Hebron, Ct.:* Horatio, Elliott, James. *Hartford, Ct.:* David, Josiah C. *Hopkinton, Ct.:* Lydia N. *Homer, N. Y.:* The Randalls, the Kinnes. *Havana, N. Y.:* Daniel, Zinney, John D.

JEWETT CITY, CT.: Lewis, Benj. W. *Jamaica, N. Y.:* Noyes F. *Jamestown, N. Y.:* John D. *Jackson, Mich.:* Geo. L. *Jackson, O.:* W. H. *Junction City, Kan.:* The Roses.

KALAMAZOO, MICH.: Dr. Geo. C. *Kawkins City, Kan.:* Albert J. *Kansas City, M. O.:* Albert W., S. C. *Keene, N. H.:* Charles. *Kenanee, Ill.:* Grove Noyes, Aaron.

LISBON, CT.: Benj. H. *Lakeville, Ct.:* Edward A. *Lenox, N. Y.:* Elijah, Elisha, Samuel, Joseph, Stephen W., Huldah, the Shermans, the Chapmans, the Randalls. *Leroy, N. Y.:* Elisha, Tyler, Rev. Roswell C., the Cooks. *Lyndonville, N. Y.:* Jas. M. *Lynn, Mass.:* Gershom, the Breeds. *Langdon, Mass.:* Benjamin. *Little Falls, N. Y.:* C. J. *Lebanon, Ct.:* Amos. *Litchfield, Ct.:* Elnathan, Samuel, Simeon. *Lockland, O.:* S. C. *Little Compton, R. I.:* Isaac, John, Job. *Lyons, Ia.:* The Kinskems. *Lincoln, Ill.:* Joseph. *Lockport, N. Y.:* Chas. N. *Lynn, Ct.:* Prudence, the Cadys. *Liberty, Mich.:* Benjamin. *Leoni, Mich.:* Frank, Theodore. *Logansport, Ill.:* Amos. *Lebanon, O.:* Clayton. *Lindley*

N. Y.: Leonard.   *Lafayette, N. Y.:* Denison.   *Lockport, Ill.:* Walter A.

MONTVILLE, CT.: Rev. Reuben, Gideon, Samuel, Elisha H., the Lambs, the Turners, the Landpheres, the Warners. *Mansfield, Ct.:* Dea. Amasa. *Mianus, Ct.:* Abraham. *Manliness, N. Y.:* Sandford. *Metrisstrip, N. Y.:* The Gallups. *Middletown, N. Y.:* B. G. *Montgomery, N. Y.:* Romeyn. *Mamaroneck, N. Y.:* Richard C. *Memphis, Tenn.:* William, Horace. *Minneapolis, Minn.:* The Woodwards. *Momence, Ill.:* The Randalls. *McAvory, Md.:* The Lewises. *Manchester, Mich.:* Rev. Wm. L., the Calhouns. *Memphis, Mich.:* The Ides. *Marietta, O.:* Jewett. *Middletown, R. I.:* Ziba. *Mobile, Ala.:* The Ensigns. *Mecca, O.:* Nathan. *Moscow, N. Y.:* Abel. *Madison, O.:* Isaac, Noyes, Walter, Erastus, Cullen, the Brooks. *Morgan Park, Ill.:* H. A. *Mystic River, Ct.:* The Langworthys. *Mewcayua, Ill.:* Albert. *Monmouth, Ill.:* William, Henry D. *Monononie, Wis.:* Stephen R. *Modena, N. Y.:* Samuel, "Debby." *Mystic Bridge, Ct.:* The Browns, the Moredocks, the Bromleys.

NEW LONDON, CT.: Solomon, Benjamin, the Lewises, the Weavers, the Newcombs. *New Briton, Ct:.* Henry F. *Norwich, Ct.:* William, Allen, Rev. Wm. S., Joseph, Arthur, Chas. H., Rev. Wm. B., John C., Jonathan, Leland, the Clarks, the Baileys. *Norwich Falls, Ct.:* Amos N., Abel. *Niantic, Ct.:* John B., Sybil A., Henry F. *North Branford, Ct.:* Joel, John, Albert H. *New York City, N. Y.:* Courtland, A. M., W. H., Lowell M., the Drapers (and many more). *Norvell, Mich.:* Stephen W., Huldah, Sylvanus B., Andrew J., Jno. J., the Austins, Joshua C., the Coles, William, the Randalls. *Napoleon, Mich.:* Martin, Harry M. *Napoleon, O.:* Hubbard, Elmer H. *New Leslie, N. Y.:* Benjamin. *Newtown, N. Y.:* Samuel. *Nine Partners, N. Y.:* Abraham, Rev. Henry, Rev. Asa, Rev. Eleazor. *New Marlborough, Mass.:* Henry, Nathan, Hattie L. *North Stonington, Ct.:* Stephen M., the Coutes. *North Bridgwater, N.Y.:* Asa, Chauncey. *Noank, Ct.:* Robert M., the Spicers. *North Bradford, Ct.:* Dea. Joel. *North East, Pa.:* The Noyeses,

the Sheffields. *New Orleans, La.:* Rev. B. M., B. F.
Newark, N. J.: F. A., Lydia, Wm. E., Thomas G.
New Leslie, Mich.: Benjamin. *North Thatford, Wis.:*
Henry. *Newbern, S. C.:* Gershom. *North Fayette, Me.:*
Henry K., Thos. F. *North Manchester, Ct.:* The Bissells.
Naragansett, R. I.: Ziber, Henry E., Warren. *Norfolk, Ct.:*
Elias, Silas A. *Norwichtown, Ct.:* The Shermans. *New
Milford, Ct.:* Arthur H.

ONEIDA, N. Y.: L. C., the Chapmans, the Gibbs, the Gallups.
Ottawa, Kan.: Hiram, Charles, Porter, Calvin. *Otis, Mass.;*
Lazarus, Calvin. *Otis, N. Y.:* Ransome. *Onion River,
Vt.:* Silas. *Otsego, N. Y.:* Joseph. *Orange, N. J.:* Jas. G.

PENDLETON HILL, CT.: Lieut. Ichabod, Stephen, Julius, Lu-
ther, Robert, Amos B., the Greens, the Chapmans, Row-
land. *Plainfield, Ct.:* Roswell, Walter, Henry C., Dr.
Isaac. *Portland, Ct.:* Rev. Elliott, Geo. S. *Preston, Ct.:*
Rev. Gershom, Rev. Reuben, Emma T., Jonathan, Joseph,
Jedediah, Jesse, Timothy. *Paris, N. Y.:* Amos, the Ran-
dalls. *Perryville, N. Y.:* Franklyn, the Maines, the Ran-
dalls. *Parma, N. Y.:* Samuel B., Cavlin B. *Providence,
R. I.:* Reginald, Samuel, William H., the Shermans, the
Havens, the Lewises, the Stantons, the Denisons. *Peacham,
Vt.:* Nathan. *Pecawonica, Ill.:* Russell, Roswell. *Pontiac,
Ill.:* Geo. R., the Randalls, the Thomases. *Philadelphia,
Pa.:* B. Frank, the Chesebroughs, the Simpsons, the Grants
(and hundreds more). *Pontiac, Mich.:* Charles H. *Paw
Paw, Ill.:* E. H., Amos. *Pompey, N. Y.:* Avery F. *Ports-
mouth, Va.:* Benjamin. *Panama, N. Y.:* Andrew J., C. S.
Plainfield, N. Y.: Vose. *Painesville, O.:* Noyes, Isaac,
Erastus. *Pequonic Bridge, Ct.:* The Brownes. *Perry, N.
Y.:* The Chapins. *Palmer, O.:* Joseph.

REHOBOTH, MASS.: Gershom, Jonas, William (and many later
generations). *Rochester, N. Y.:* Eunice, Azariah, Justus.
Richfield Springs, N. Y.: Esquire, Laton. *Racine, Wis.:*
Albert R. *Republic, O.:* Calvin G. *Roxbury, Mass.:* John.
Rutland, Vt.: The Burtons. *Romney, N. H.:* Dudley.
Rockford, Ill.: H. H. *Rutland Co., Vt.:* David, James.
Reedsburgh, Wis.: O. W. *Ransomeville, N. Y.:* Christo-

pher, Reuben, Gen. W. S. *Romeo, Mich.:* Amos. *Rockville, R. I.:* Josiah. *Rome, Ill.:* Ephraim. *Rochelle, Ill.:* John, Stephen. *Rome, N. Y.:* The Cadys, the Prescotts.

STONINGTON, CT.: Walter, Nehemiah, Dea. Gershom, Lieut. Joseph, Col. Jonathan, Benj., Moses, William, Denison, Andrew, Asa, Nathan, Dr. Nathan, Gen. Noyes, Benjamin, Gilbert, Polly, the Chesebroughs, the Chesebros', the Cheseboros, the Miners, the Stantons, the Denisons, the Hewitts, the Coates, the Sloans, Ichabod, Thomas, Rev. Christopher, Roswell, Geo., Elder Christopher, Zebulon, Luke, Noyes, Dr. Joseph, Samuel, Refus, Stephen, Asahael, David, Ensign, Moses, Eliphalet, Daniel, Israel, Amos, Henry, Saxton, Varnum Bates, Col. Elias S., Rev. A. G., Capt. Nat., Capt. Alexander S., the Wheelers, the Churchills, the Halls, the Williams (and thousands of others who migrated from Stonington to New York State, to Wisconsin, to Michigan, and various sections of the country). *Suffield, Ct.:* Rev. Thomas R. *Scotland, Ct.:* Wm. F., Ephraim, Rev. Levi, Stephen, Nathaniel, Nathan, the Lewises. *San Francisco, Cal.:* George, Chas. E. *Oakland, Cal.:* The Mathews. *Salamanca, N. Y.:* Wm. C. *Syracuse, N. Y.:* Stewart B., Jonathan, the Jordans, the Coates, the Saffords. *Sandwich, Ill.:* Alex. H. *S. Coventry, Ct.:* Asa. *Sheriville, O.:* Levi. *Stamford, Ct.:* Wm. C., Orrin, Jas. R., Abijah, the Minors. *S. Woodstock, Ct.:* Ira G. *Sutton, N. H.:* Rev. Christopher, Joseph. *Spencer, N. Y.:* Capt. Louis, Ezekiel, John H. *St. Clair, Mich.:* Titus. *S. Bryon, Wis.:* Alvah. *Savannah, Ga.:* Samuel, Herbert A. *Salem, Mass.:* Job. *Salem, Va.:* John H. *Stillwater, N. Y.:* George, Ashabel, Justina, Henry, Charles, Edward. *Spencerport, N. Y.:* Nelson. *Saratoga, N. Y.:* Josiah. *Sag Harbor, N. Y.:* Lucius. *Sharon, N. Y.:* Silas. *Seneca Falls, N. Y.:* Jefferson V., Wilbur. *Sharon, Mich.:* The Coles. *St. Johns, Mich.:* John O. *Springfield, Mass.:* Samuel. *Stockbridge, Mass.:* Henry Dwight, F. A., the Pitkins. *South Kingston, R. I.:* The Shermans, the Allens, Henry E. *Stonington, Ill.:* Elijah. *Spaulding, Ia.:* George G. *Spencer, N.*

Y.: Joseph, Christopher, J. H., Louis F. *Stedman, N. Y.:* Gen. Noyes, Andrew J.

TULLY, N. Y.: Prentice B., Andrew J.

UNIONVILLE, CT.: Emily A. *Utica, N. Y.:* Chauncey, Walter, A. J., Luther, the Abbotts. *Ulysses, Neb.:* The Smiths.

VOLUNTOWN, CT.: Nehemiah, Benjamin, Daniel, Elijah, Elisha, Joseph, Gershom, Rev. Jesse, Roswell, the Lewises, the Cases. *Vernon, Ct.:* Elliott. *Vernon, O.:* Gilbert. *Vermontville, Mich.:* The Harringtons. *Victor, N. Y.:* Dr. J. W., the Moffits.

WINDOM, CT.: Samuel, Rev. John, Rev. Gershom, Levi. *Waverly, N. Y.:* The Clarks. *Willetts, N. Y.:* Gershom· *Wyoming, N. Y.:* The Randalls, Amos. *Wethersfield, Ct.:* Isaac, John, Rev. Jesse. *Westbury, Ct.:* Walter. *West Hartford, Ct.:* Orlando. *Windsor, Ct.:* The Grants, the Minors. *Willimantic, Ct.:* Rev. Stephen. *Warsaw, R. I.:* Charles. *Westerly, R. I.:* Dr. Luther A., Rev. Reuben, Col. Elias S., Ichabod, Hiram, Denison, the Maines, the Perrins. *West Cornwall, Vt.:* Rev. Wm. S. *Westfield, Mass.:* Rev. Squire, Rev. Eldah, John C. *Walhalla, S. C.:* Jesse, B. *Washington, D. C.:* The Spencers, the Halls. *Woodstock, Ct.:* David, Gershom, Hezekiah, the De Lands, the Pellets. *Woodstock, Vt.:* Walter. *Waltham, Mass.:* The Banks. *Waitsfield, Mass.:* Wm. *Warren, O.:* E. A. *West Mecca, O.:* Nathaniel W. *West Cambridge, Mass.:* John. *Windsor, Ct.:* Nicholas. *West Winfield, N. Y.:* Vose, Walter. *Washington, O.:* F. M. *Watertown, N. Y.:* Reuben, Amasa. *Warren, N. Y.:* Urban, Abel, Shubal. *Worcester, Mass.:* The Baldwins. *White Salina, Wash. Ter.:* Cornelius J. *Ware House Point, Ct.:* Epaphroetus, F. E.

ZANESVILLE, O.: Eliakein.

[NOTE.—This memorandum of " Places where Descendants of Walter Palmer have Lived " is not complete. Since its preparation, just before the Re-Union, over twelve hundred records, letters, etc., have been received, which, when studied, will more than double the Palmer Records].

CELEBRATED PALMERS.

ARMY OFFICERS.

Among generals and army officers there have been:

Gen. Joseph Palmer, of Boston Tea Ship notoriety. An inmate friend of President John Quincy Adams, and who served during the Revolution.

Gen. Joseph Pease Palmer, of Guiliford, Vt., and Watertown, N. Y.; among whose descendants are the celebrated Hawthornes and Putnams of literary fame.

Gen. Nathan Palmer. Born in Stonington, Ct.; died in Burlington, Otsego Co., N. Y.

Gen. Noyes Palmer, of 1812. Died in Brookfield, N. Y., in 1858.

Gen. and President U. S. Grant. A descendant from Walter Palmer's daughter Grace.

Gen. J. Newton Palmer, of Washington, D. C.

Gen. W. S. Palmer, of Ransomeville, N. Y.

Gen. Geo. W. Palmer, of New York City, N. Y.

Gen. Jos. N. Palmer, New Haven, Ct.

Gen. W. H. Wessells, Litchfield, Ct.

Gen. Wm. J. Palmer, President of the Denver and Rio Grande Company.

Col. Thos. Palmer, Ulster Co., N. Y.

Col. Elias Sandford Palmer, Stonington, Ct.

Col. Chas. D. Palmer, Berlin, Ct.

Col. Edwin Palmer, Norwich, Ct.

Col. Geo. W. Palmer, Chicago, Ill.

Col. Jonathan Palmer, Stonington, Ct.

Capt. S. G. Palmer, Ripley, O.

Capt. Stephen W. Palmer, Lennox, N. Y.

Capt. Geo. W. Palmer, Durand, Ill.

First Lieut. Geo. H. Palmer, Fort Concho, Tex.

Lieut. Ichabod Palmer, Stonington, Ct.

Lieut. David Palmer, commission signed by Gov. Alden Bradford.

Lieut. Palmer Tilton, Baltimore, Md.

(And many more.)

CLERGYMEN.

DECEASED AND LIVING—ALPHABETICALLY.

A. M. Palmer, of Newark Conference.

A. R. Palmer, Collingwood, N. Y.

A. J. Palmer, of New York Conference.

Abel Palmer, Norwich, Ct.

Asa H. Palmer, Dutchess Co., N. Y.

A. G. Palmer, Stonington, Ct.

A. M. Palmer, Phillipsburgh, N. J.

A. F. Palmer, Cronomer Valley, N. Y.

Albert DeF. Palmer, Lawrence, Mass.

A. M. Palmer, New Milford, Ct.

Aaron Palmer, Poughkeepsie, N. Y.

Burton Palmer, Saratoga, Col.

B. M. Palmer, Charleston, S. C.

Benj. M. Palmer, New Orleans, La.

B. D. Palmer, Poughkeepsie, N. Y.

Benj. Wood Palmer, Upton, Mass.

Braman, Isaac, Georgetown, Mass.

Benj. D. Palmer, Mt. Horeb, N. J.

Charles Ray Palmer, Bridgewater, N. Y.

C. A. Lamb, Ypsillanti, Mich. Grandson of Rev. Reuben,
and still preaching in Michigan (1881), aged 83.

Chester Palmer. Died in 1856.

Christopher Palmer, Stonington, Ct. Died in 1805.

Charles Palmer, Meriden, Ct.

Cook, H., Essex Co., N. Y.

C. W. Palmer, Sandusky, O.

David Palmer, Vermont.

Denison, 'Fred., Providence, R. I.

David Palmer, Carlisle, Mass. A celebrated scholar and
writer of sacred songs.

David Palmer, of Townsend, Mass.

David Henry Palmer, Penn Yan, Penn.

Elliott Palmer, West Stafford, Ct.

Elisha Palmer. "The Blind Preacher."

Elliott Palmer, Portland, Ct.

Eleazer Palmer. Died in 1852.

Edmund Barnabas Palmer, Rochester, N. H.

Edward Palmer, South Carolina. Still preaching (1881), aged 95 years.

Edward Stanton Palmer, Fort Hill, Me.

Edward C. Palmer, Barnwell, S. C.

Elliott Palmer, Portland, Me.

Frank K. Palmer, Liberty, Mo.

Frederick K. Palmer, Clay Co., Miss. A missionary.

Fred. Palmer, Lonesdale, R. I.

F. G. Rossitter, Omra, Wis.

Frank Palmer, Norwich, Ct.

F. A. Palmer, Booth Bay, Me.

Frank Herbert Palmer, North Scituate, R. I.

Gershom Palmer, Exeter, R. I. Died in 1868, aged 94.

Gershom Palmer, Preston, Ct. Author of sacred songs.

Gurdon C. Noyes, Connecticut.

Geo. Rutledge Palmer, Illinois. Illinois M. E. Conf.

Henry Clay Trumbull, Connecticut.

Henry Palmer, Bradford, Orange Co., Vt.

Jesse Palmer, Wethersfield, N. Y.

John Palmer, Windham, Ct.

John Cotton Rossitter, Wisconsin.

Joseph P. Palmer, Norton, Mass.

John Palmer, Scotland, Ct.

L. E. Palmer, Almond, Wis.

Levi Palmer, Scotland, Ct.

Marcus Palmer, Lindonville, O. Died in 1880, aged 86.

Melvin Palmer, Fostoria, O.

Miner, Noyes W., Trenton, N. J.

Nelson Palmer, Albany, N. Y.

Reuben Palmer, Montville, Ct. Past 80 at death.

Ray Palmer, Newark, N. J.

Roswell Palmer, Exeter, R. I. Died in 1824.

Stephen Palmer, North Stonington, Ct.

Solomon Palmer, New York.

Streeter, Randall, Connecticut.

S. C. Palmer, Lockland, O.

Thomas R. Palmer, Suffield, Ct.

Urban D. Palmer, Warren, N. Y.

Wait Palmer, Stonington, Ct.
Wm. L. Palmer, Manchester, Mich.
Wm. B. Palmer, Jefferson City, Mo.
Wm. H. Palmer, Bridgwater, N. Y.
Wm. L. Palmer, Norwich, Ct.
Walter Palmer, New York City, N. Y.
Samuel Wood, Boneman, N. H.
Wm. B. Palmer, Norwich, Ct.

DOCTORS. (M. D. AND D. D.)

Asa Rice Palmer, Danville, Ct.
A. B. Palmer, Ann Arbor, Mich.   Professor.
C. Allen, Vernon, N. J.
A. H. Palmer, Brooklyn, Penn.
Arthur H. Palmer, New Milford, Ct.

Brayton, Chas. E., Stonington, Ct.
B. Frank Palmer, Philadelphia, Penn.   Inventor and manufacturer of artificial limbs.
Benjamin Palmer, Langdon, N. H.

C. A. Palmer, Princeton, Ill.
Charles Palmer, Fayetteville, N. Y.
Charles N. Palmer, Lockport, N. Y.
C. P. Palmer, Detroit, Mich.
Corydon Palmer, Warren, O.
C. Adelaide Palmer (Miss), Boston, Mass.

David Crary, Hartford, Ct.
~~Daloss~~ Palmer, New York City, N. Y.

E. L. Palmer, Noble, Ill.
Enos Palmer, Bennington, Vt.
Eugene Palmer, New York City, N. Y.
E. B. Palmer, Detroit, Mich.

Frederick Palmer, Boston, Mass.

George M. Palmer, New York City, N. Y.
George C. Palmer, Kalamazoo, Mich. Professor.
Gideon S. Palmer, Washington, D. C.
George B. Palmer, E. Hamilton, N. Y.
Gustavus Palmer, Waterville, Me.

H. C. Palmer, Brooklyn, N. Y.
Henry Palmer, Janesville, Wis.
Harris Palmer, Hubbartstown, Ct.
Henry Clay Palmer, Rome, N. Y.
H. C. Palmer, Albany, N. Y.

Isaac Palmer, Plainfield, Ct.
Isaac Palmer, N. Fayette, N. Y.
Ira F. Palmer, Onarga, Ill.
Ide, Henry H., Brooklyn, N. Y.
Irving Stanton, Baltic, Ct.
Isaac Palmer, N. Anson, Me.
Isaac Palmer, Meridan, O.

John K. Palmer, Boston, Mass.
Joseph Palmer, Stonington, Ct. Will dated 1790, and
from whom many Dr. Joseph Palmers are descended.
Joseph W. Palmer, Boston, Mass.
J. F. Palmer, Mobile, Ill.
Joseph Palmer, Ashford, Ct.
James G. Palmer, New Brunswick, N. J.
John Kingsley Palmer, Cambridge, Mass.
J. B. Noyes, Detroit, Mich.
J. W. Palmer, Victor, N. Y.
J. M. Rose, W. Whitfield, N. Y.
J. W. Palmer, Burnside, Penn.

Luther A. Palmer, Brooklyn, N. Y.
Lewis M. Palmer, Providence, R. I.
L. Curtis Palmer, Chicago, Ill.

Miner, O. E., Noank, Ct.

Nathan Palmer, Stonington, Ct. Born in 1711.
Noyes Palmer, Union Springs, N. Y. Died in 1863.

Nathan Palmer, New York City, N. Y.
N. C. Palmer, Norwich, Ct.
N. Palmer, Butternuts, N. Y.

Owen A. Palmer, W. Farmington, O.
Orrin Palmer, Beaver, Penn.

Samuel Palmer, Pound Ridge, N. Y.
Samuel Palmer, Holegates, O.
Stewart B. Palmer, Syracuse, N. Y.
Stanton, Geo. D., Stonington, Ct.

William H. Palmer, Providence, R. I.
Walter B., Utica, N. Y.

PROFESSORS IN LITERATURE AND ART.

Prof. Geo. H. Williams, Ann Arbor University, Mich.
Prof. A. B. Palmer, Ann Arbor University, Mich.
Prof. Daniel C. Eaton, Yale College, New Haven, Ct.
Prof. Jas. H. Palmer, Yonkers, N. Y.
Prof. Asaph Hall, Naval Observatory, Washington, D. C.
    The discoverer of the "Satellites of Mars."
Erastus Dow Palmer, the sculptor, Albany, N. Y.
Prof. Jos. Palmer, Fredonia Academy, Fredonia, N. Y.
Prof. Edward Palmer, Louisville, Ky.

PALMER DESCENDANTS THAT HAVE BEEN GOVERNORS OF STATES.

Gov. Wm. A. Palmer, of Vermont.
Gov. John M. Palmer, of Illinois.
Gov. Wm. T. Minor, of Stamford, Ct.
Gov. Pendleton, of Ohio.
Gov. L. B. Loomis, of New London, Ct.

JUDGES.

Judge Walter Palmer, of Windsor, Vt.
Judge William Palmer, of Gardner, Me.
Judge Gilbert Palmer, of Ohio.
Judge David Davis, of Illinois.
Judge Richard A. Wheeler, of Stonington, Ct.

Judge Norman D. Palmer, of Danville, Ill.
Judge Beriah Palmer, of Saratoga Co., N. Y.
Judge Daniel Palmer, of Stonington, Ct.
Judge William Palmer, of New Hampshire.

SEA CAPTAINS.

Capt. Nat. Palmer, of Stonington, Ct. Celebrated for having acquaintances in nearly every harbor on the globe.

Capt. Roswell Saltonstall Palmer, of Stonington; died in 1844. Celebrated during the War of 1812 as the Privateer Captain.

Capt. Amos Palmer, died in Stonington, 1876.

Capt. Nathan Palmer, born in Stonington, 1763.

Capt. Sandford Palmer, born in Stonington, and died in Oswego Co., N. Y., 1828.

Capt. Sandford Palmer, of Fayetteville, N. Y. Died in 1865.

Capt. Alex. S. Palmer, Stonington, Ct.

Capt. Wm. S. Palmer, Stonington, Ct.

Capt. Henry Palmer, Stonington, Ct.

Capt. Israel Palmer, Sterling, Mass.

Capt. David Palmer, Grafton, Vt.

Capt. Christopher, Stonington, Ct.

POETS.

Dr. John W. Palmer, of Baltimore, Md. The author of sacred songs.

Rev. Ray Palmer, of Newark, N. J. Author of " My Faith Looks up to Thee," and many other sacred hymns.

Wm. Pitt Palmer, of Brooklyn, N. Y.

Rev. A. G. Palmer, D. D., of Stonington, Ct.

B. Frank Palmer, LL. D., of Philadelphia, Penn.

Sara A. Palmer, Stonington, Ct.

Frank Averell Palmer, Stonington, Ct.

Rev. Fred. Denison, Providence, R. I.

INVENTORS AND DISCOVERERS.

Augustus H. Palmer, Utica, N. Y. Fire and Burglar Alarm.

John Palmer, who introduced the first Mail Coaches of Great

Britain, and which system has been extended into all civilized countries. His family received a pension from the English Government of $250,000, for improving the system of mail deliveries.

Chas. H. Palmer, of New York City. The inventor of the Gatling Revolving Cannon, now a standard weapon of warfare among various nations. The inventor of the Palmer Sewing Machine, and various mechanical contrivances.

Newtown W. Palmer, of New York City.

Moses G. Palmer.

Wm. Palmer, Hopkinton, R. I.

Noyes G. Palmer, East New York, N. Y. Inventor of a Rotary Engine, a Flying Machine, a Magazine Rifle, etc.

Hundreds of Palmer inventors could be enumerated. By reference to Patent Office reports, the name will be noticed in the various departments.

POLITICIANS.

John Palmer, Sheriff of Richmond Co., N. Y., in 1683 ; member of New York Government Council, and one of the original patentees of Brookhaven, N. Y., in 1686.

Col. Thos. Palmer, of Ulster Co., N. Y. Surrogate of Saratoga Co., 1873.

Thos. Palmer, Controller of New York City, in 1698.

Elisha Grow, son of Lois Palmer and Elisha Grow. Speaker of the House of Representatives, Washington, from Ohio.

Frank W. Palmer, the founder of the Chicago paper, "*Inter Ocean*,"

Geo. W. Palmer, Congressman, of New York City.

Lorin Palmer, one of Commissioners of Brooklyn Board of City Works, and Editor of *Union-Argus*.

Fred. A. Palmer, Auditor, Newark, N. J.

John C. Palmer, Speaker of the House, Connecticut.

Secretary of Interior, Usher, under Lincoln (a Palmer descendant).

J. L. Palmer, Little Rock, Ark.

Geo. W. Palmer, Tax Collector, New Lots, L. I., N. Y.

Thos. W. Palmer, Senator, Detroit, Mich.

WEALTHY PALMERS.

Potter Palmer, of Chicago, Ill.

Courtlandt Palmer, of New York City.

Chas. H. Palmer, of Pontiac, Mich.

Oliver H. Palmer, of Mutual Life Insurance Co., New York
City.

Francis A. Palmer, President of National Broadway Bank,
New York City.

Elisha H. Palmer, of Montville, Ct.

Chauncey Palmer, Utica, N. Y. Phœnix iron works.

NOTED PALMER WOMEN.

Mrs. Phebe Palmer, of New York City. Author of sacred songs,
and known as an evangelist who traveled over the world.
.   Her "meetings for holiness," held every Monday in New
York City, for a period of a quarter of a century, were attended by clergymen and laymen far and near.

Mrs. Phebe Palmer Randall was celebrated as a practicing
physician and surgeon.

Mrs. Henrietta Palmer, of Michigan, was a physician as well.

Mrs. Mary Dana Shindler, authoress of sacred songs, " Flee as
a Bird to your Mountains," " Sparkling and Bright," " I am
a Pilgrim and a Stranger," etc. Daughter of Rev. B. M.
Palmer.

Mrs. Jos. F. Knapp, daughter of the well-known Mrs. Phebe
Palmer. Sunday-school Superintendent, and composer of
music for the same.

Miss Charlotte Walker, the accomplished vocalist, New York
City.

Isabella Grant Meredith, of literary fame. (Mrs. Col. Meredith.)

PALMERS WHO LIVED TO ADVANCED YEARS.

Nehemiah, son of Walter, lived to be past 80. Rev. Gershom, to the ripe age of 94. Rev. Reuben, of Montville, 80 ;
Prudence, his wife, past 90. Dea. Stephen died in 1851, aged
82. Capt. Stephen W., and Huldah, his wife, passed sixty-four
years of married life together before his death in 1879, aged

84; she is still living (1881), aged 83. Thomas, of Hillsdale, N. Y., aged 93. Edwin lived to be 89, and his wife, Anna, to 93. Assenith Main was 92, and, if not deceased, is one of the oldest Palmers now living. Dr. Benjamin lived to be 80. Gershom, and his wife, Dolly, were husband and wife for sixty years, and both were past 80 at their death. Nathaniel, now living in Derry, N. H., is 88. Rev. C. A. Lamb is still preaching at the age of 83, in Michigan. Rev. Christopher lived to be 89, his wife, Debby, was aged 101 at her death. Rev. Edward, of Barnwell, S. C., is preaching at the ripe age of 93. Huldah P. Stafford, of Syracuse, N. Y., is living at the age of 97. Jared, of Thetford, Vt., living, aged 86. Ashabel, lives at Stillwater, N. Y., aged 88. O. B. Palmer lives at Delevan, Ill., aged 84. Barna died in Lisbon, N. Y., aged 95. Thomas, of Hillsdale, lived to be 93. Debby, of Moneda, N. Y., lived to be 93. Oliver, died in Grapeville, in 1877, aged 90. Amos, of Exeter, R. I., died 1820, aged 97. Thomas, of Dover, N. Y., died in 1830, aged 92. Capt. John Palmer died at Canterbury, N. H., October, 1846, aged 102 years and 5 months. Susan Kenny Palmer lived to be 102 years of age. Jonathan died in 1804, aged 104 years.

LARGE FAMILIES.

Walter Palmer, the original ancestor, had a family of twelve children.

Grace, his daughter, who married Thos. Miner, had a family of twelve.

Gershom Palmer and Ann Denison had but ten.

Three brothers—Jonathan, Daniel, and Nehemiah—had united families of twenty-nine children.

Mercy Palmer and John Breed kept up the " breed " by having ten children.

Dea. Joseph and Mary had eleven.

Nehemiah and Submit Palmer had ten.

Daniel and Mary but nine, while his brother Dr. Nathan Palmer and Phebe Billings had thirteen children.

Ichabod Palmer and " Betty Noyes " had a family of nine children, although Ichabod was only 47 at his death.

Rev. Gershom Palmer and Dolly Brown were blessed with eleven children.

His brother, " Dea. Joe.," and Elizabeth had twelve.

Denison and Marian had a family to provide for of eleven children.

Richard C. and Susan Palmer, of Mamaroneck, N. Y., during a married life of fifty-five years, were blessed with twelve children.

Alvah and Harriet Palmer were parents to thirteen children.

Rev. Reuben and Lucretia Palmer had a family of seventeen children, sixteen of whom grew up to mature years.

Elijah and Lucretia were blessed with ten.

One of the most prolific of Palmer families have been families of " Joseph " Palmer.

The first Joe. was son of Nehemiah (son of Walter), and this Joe. 1st was one of six; married Frances Prentice, and were parents to eight children ; among them Joseph 2d (or Dea. Joe.), his marriage with Mary Palmer produced eleven children ; among them Joe. 3d, who married Catherine Coates, and they were parents to twelve children ; among them Joe. 4th.   These Joe. Palmers have scattered the Palmer name throughont Connecticut, New York, Michigan, and Ohio.

David Palmer, of Stonington, had eleven children, whose descendants are a large proportion of the inhabitants of the State of Vermont.

Joseph Palmer and Susan Kenny were parents to ten children.   Nevertheless, he lived to be past eighty, and his widow lived to the remarkable age of one hundred and two.

Reuben Palmer and Lucretia Tyler were blessed with sixteen children, and neither died until past 80, while Lucretia outlived her husband some ten years, to the age of 91.

Lois Palmer, sister to Reuben, married Abel Palmer, and they had a family of thirteen children—both past 80 at death.

Col. Elias Sandford and Phebe Palmer were blessed with twelve children.

Amos Palmer and wife had the care and responsibility of sixteen children, and so well did they perform their parental duties that four out of ten boys became influential clergymen, and several others were physicians.

Roswell Palmer and three wives bore families of fifteen children.

Asher Palmer, of Griswold, Ct., had the care of sixteen children.

Luther Palmer had a family of thirteen, and so well did he provide for them that nine sons became either clergymen or physicians, second to but few. The poem delivered to-day was by one of these sons, the Rev. A. G. Palmer, of Stonington.

Gideon Palmer and Mercy Turner were parents to eleven children, one of whom is the worthy President of this Palmer Re-Union, Elisha H. Palmer, of Montville.

Lois Palmer and Elisha Grow brought up to manhood and womanhood a family of seventeen children, one of whom became Speaker of the House of Representatives.

Jas. Palmer and Agnes Boland were blessed with twelve children.

Stephen W. and Huldah Palmer had a family of twelve. Nine of whom are living whose united weight is 1945 pounds, or an average weight of 216 pounds each. The widow, Huldah, is living, aged 85, and has great-grandchildren aged 15 years.* Four of these heavy-weight Palmers were present at this gathering.

SEND RECORDS.

Let me take advantage of this occasion to ask all Palmers, or their maternal descendants, to send family records. Conceit must be excused when we add, send records of families; *for the Palmers are a prolific family.* Send biographical sketches; *for the Palmers are respected in society,* including Presidents of the United States, Secretaries in the Cabinets, Judges, Governors, Reverends, Doctors, Congressmen, etc. Send sketches of business prosperity, *for on the average the Palmers are well-to-do in this world's comforts.* Send photographs to be inserted in the record, *to let the younger generations see that their ancestors have been good-looking people.*

---

* NOTE.—See illustration of Chas. H. Palmer, N. G. P., etc., where appear living representatives of four generations—to wit.: Huldah, Noyes G., Noyes F., and Albert W.

ABOUT PUBLICATION OF RECORDS.

The voluminous character of the records will make it necessary to publish more than one book. *Volume No. 1., Palmer Record of Re-Union* held at Stonington, Ct., August 10th and 11th, 1881, consisting of the historical and biographical addresses delivered, with photographic illustrations of individuals, etc., and the account of the various proceedings, with brief sketches of individuals present on the occasion. *Volume No. 2, Palmer Genealogical Record,* of at least 10,000 descendants, giving families, relationship, dates, places and ages. *Volume No. 3, Palmer Biographical and Historical Record,* with photographic illustrations of individuals.

These various volumes will be duly announced by a prospectus of contents which will be mailed to all whose address we may have.

A work of this character is never actually completed, nor more than approximately correct in all its details, as its compilation is not one of personal researches alone, but a revision of letters, records, etc., sent by correspondents. Corrections are often beyond our knowledge, and errors are multiplied, subject to the corrections of older descendants having more accurate information than previous correspondents.

The publication of the Palmer Records *before* this Re-Union would have been a blunder, as from its publicity have sprung records all over the land. Letters to the number of over one thousand have been received during the last three months, and from these a mass of records are yet to be studied and arranged.

We have often been asked why this record was started, and when. It may not be out of place just here to make an explanation.

During a college vacation at Ann Arbor, Mich., in 1860, the writer passed three months with Grandmother Huldah Palmer, wife of Capt. Stephen W. Palmer, born in Stonington. Both these grandparents are descendants of Walter Palmer, in the following lines:

PATERNAL.	MATERNAL.	PATERNAL.	MATERNAL.
Stephen W.,	Stephen W.,	Huldah,	Huldah,
Stephen,	Prudence,	Elijah,	Lucretia,
Joseph,	Ichabod 3d,	Joseph 3d,	Gershom,
Dr. "Joe,"	Ichabod 2d,	Joseph 2d (Dea.),	Geo. ("Snip"),
Geo. ("Snip"),	Ichabod 1st,	Joseph 1st (Lieut.),	Gershom,
Gershom,	Gershom,	Nehemiah,	Walter.
Walter.	Walter.	Walter.	

Not only was Grandmother Huldah a Palmer before she married a Palmer, but her mother, Lucretia, was a Palmer before marriage to a Palmer ; and the same was true of Stephen W.'s mother, Prudence.

These marriages of Palmer women to Palmer men interlocked and confused relationship so much that we endeavored to find out some of these mysteries of genealogy. As a pastime for twenty years this work finally grew to be work and study. For twenty years this problem of relationship continued unsolved, and not until about four weeks before this Re-Union did its solution develop. A letter with records from Ashabel Palmer, an old gentleman aged 83, of Stillwater, N. Y., gave us the connecting link. We may add that this link joined to the Walter Palmer branch over two thousand descendants, among them our venerable President of this Re-Union, Elisha H. Palmer, of Montville. Another very important branch was discovered recently to be part of the Walter Palmer lineage, and are termed the Branford Palmers. This evidence embraces the pedigree of some twelve hundred descendants. It has long been a mystery whether Walter Palmer's son William ever married or had any descendants. Before the publication of Vol. 2, the Genealogical Records, I think the evidence will be developed that William *did* marry and had descendants, among them two sons—Michael, born about 1642, and Obadiah, born October, 1649 ; that these sons migrated from Stonington to Branford, Ct., about 1662, and are progenitors of the Palmers of that locality.

Now, before closing, please permit a few suggestions. Members of the family, please send for a regular printed blank to write family records upon. A systematic arrangement of records affords easy study.   All information not called for on a record blank, please send on a separate sheet, written in ink, on one side of the page, with a margin on the left of the paper, and do not forget to sign name and address at the last.   A few postage stamps will be a good hint that you want an answer, and will pay for it as well.

NOYES F. PALMER,

OF JAMAICA, L. I., N. Y.

(BRIEF BIOGRAPHY.)

Noyes F. Palmer is a descendant of the pilgrim, Walter Palmer, in several lines of pedigree, of which one is as follows :

1. Walter Palmer, born 1598, in England, married 2d, Rebekah Short.   Children—John 2, Grace 3, Jonas 4, William 5, Hannah 6, Elihu 7, Nehemiah 8, Moses 9, Benj. 10, Gershom 11, Rebekah 12, Elizabeth 13.

8. Nehemiah Palmer, married Hannah Stanton.   Children— Lieut. Joseph 16, Elihu 17, Jonathan 18, Daniel 19, Nehemiah 20, Hannah 21.

16. Lieut. Joseph Palmer, married Frances Prentice.   Children—Dea. Joseph. 35, Hannah 36, Benjamin 37, Sarah 38, Jonathan 39.

35. Dea. Joseph Palmer, married Mary Palmer.   Children— Sarah 58, Mary 59, Joseph 60, Francis 61, Amos 62, Moses 63, Hannah 64, Phœbe 65.

60. Joseph Palmer, married Catherine Coates.   Children— Joseph 92, William 93, Phebe 94, Capt. Amos 95, Phebe 96, Elijah 97, Elisha 98, Jonathan 99, Hannah 100, Benj. 101, David 102, Thomas 103.

97. Elijah Palmer, married Lucretia Palmer, and 2d, Miss Powell.   Children—Gershom 165, Dolly 166, Rebekah 167, Phebe 168, Joseph 169, Elisha 170, Lydia 171, Benj. 172, Jesse 173, Huldah 174.

174. Huldah Palmer, married Stephen W. Palmer.   Children —Chas. H. 352, Lucretia, 353, Sylvenus B. 354, Wm. L. 355,

N. O. PALMER.

BERTIE PALMER.

REV. W. L. PALMER.

STEPHEN M. PALMER.

CHARLES M. PALMER.

HULDAH PALMER.

GEO. W. PALMER.

SAIDEE PALMER.

NOTE? F. PALMER.

E. BIERSTADT N. T.

Noyes G. 356, Henrietta 357, Miraetta 358, Andrew 359, Priscilla 360, Martin 361, Geo. W. 362, John Jay 363.

356. Noyes G. Palmer, married 1st, Emeline E. Fink, 2d, Annie Forbell, 3d, Mrs. Willis Ackerman. Children by first, Noyes Fink 1885, William 1886, Julia 1887; by second, Huldah 1888; by third, Arthur Willis 1889.

1885. Noyes F. Palmer, born in Dunkirk, N. Y., June 30, 1845, married first, Rachel Tice, September 18, 1866; married second, Clara M. Johnson, Sept. 16, 1880. Children by first, Albert W. 2445, Saidee Emeline 2446; by second, William Walter 2447.

Noyes F. received usual common school education up to the age of fourteen. Attended Fredonia Academy, 1859 and 1860, preparatory to a course of studies as civil engineer at Ann Arbor University, Mich., completed in 1865. Has been identified with Cypress Hills Cemetery, L. I., N. Y., as Assistant Superintendent and Surveyor; with Cedar Lawn Cemetery, Paterson, N. J., as Superintendent and Surveyor for a number of years; and, at present Superintendent and Surveyor of the Maple Grove Cemetery, near Jamaica, L. I., N. Y.

CHAS. H. PALMER,

OF PONTIAC, MICH.

(BRIEF BIOGRAPHY.)

Chas. H. Palmer, Ex-Regent of the University of Michigan, and for several years Principal of the Romeo Branch of the same University, and previously Principal of the Fredonia Academy, Fredonia, Chautauqua Co., N. Y. A graduate of Union College, New York.

Mr. Chas. H. Palmer was born in Lenox, Madison Co., N. Y., June 4th, 1874, of parents Stephen W. and Huldah—the latter were both of Connecticut (Stonington and Voluntown), and are part of the Walter Palmer branch of the family.

Mr. Palmer has for a long period been connected with the copper, iron and railroad interests of Lake Superior.

ORIGINAL HYMN, SUNG AT THE RE-UNION.

BY REV. WM. L. PALMER, A. M.

"God forbid that I should glory, save in the cross of our Lord Jesus Christ."—
GAL. vi, 14.

I.

Yes, we'll rally round the cross, friends,
　　Round the sacred cross,
　Shouting the worthy name of Jesus;
We will count the world but loss, friends,
　　All the world but dross,
　Shouting the worthy name of Jesus.

　　CHORUS—Hosanna forever,
　　　　　The Saviour we praise,
　　　　　In loud swelling chorus
　　　　　　Our voices will raise;
　　　　　While we rally round the cross, friends,
　　　　　Around the sacred cross,
　　　　　Shouting the worthy name of Jesus.

II.

Look ye to the cross, friends,
　　Look ye now and live,
　Shouting the worthy name of Jesus;
Seek the wounded Christ, friends,
　　He'll your sins forgive,
　Shouting the worthy name of Jesus.

　　　　　　　　CHORUS—Hosanna, etc.

III.

Many loved have gone before, friends,
　　To the other shore,
　Shouting the worthy name of Jesus;
O'er the river now they wait, friends,
　　To see us safely o'er,
　Shouting the worthy name of Jesus.

　　　　　　　　CHORUS—Hosanna, etc.

IV.

Come and welcome to the cross, friends,
　　Join our sacred host,
　Shouting the worthy name of Jesus;

Christ will save if you believe, friends,
    And save the uttermost,
  Shouting the worthy name of Jesus.

        CHORUS—Hosanna, etc.

POEM FOR THE RE-UNION.

BY REV. WM. L. PALMER, A. M.

O, what joy now swells in each kindred heart,
    As we come from homes away—
Come back to the land of the loved and lost,
    Our tribute of love to pay.
With what joy do we greet returning sons,
    And clasp each welcoming hand,
As pilgrims we come to the dear, dear spot,
    A large and a happy band.

We sing the deeds of the honored and brave,
    Of those who have gone before,
Whose names are enrolled on fame's bright page,
    Who wait on the " evergreen shore."
What joy will burst on our raptured sight,
    To greet the friends passed away,
Have ever their smiles and their converse sweet,
    In homes of glorified day.

REV. WILLIAM LEDYARD PALMER,

OF MANCHESTER, MICH.

(BRIEF BIOGRAPHY.)

Rev. William Ledyard Palmer was born in Lenox, Madison Co., N. Y., January 21, 1820. His mother was Huldah Palmer, daughter of Lucretia Palmer, who was a daughter of Gershom Palmer, a brother of Dr. Joseph Palmer. William Ledyard Palmer's father was a son of Prudence Palmer, whose father was Ichabod Palmer, and a brother to Col. Elias Palmer. William Ledyard Palmer, was converted when eleven years old, and united with the Baptist Church in Brooklyn, Mich., on January 21, 1838. He removed from Lenox, N. Y., to Michigan with his father in September, 1836. He attended the academy in Fredonia, N. Y., of which his brother, Chas. H. Palmer, A. M., was then principal, in the Summers of 1839, '40 and '41, and followed teaching until the Spring of 1850. He then commenced preaching, and was licensed to preach by the Baptist Church, in Adrian, Mich. He was called to settle as pastor over the Baptist Church in Clockville, in the Summer of 1850, and was ordained at Clockville, in January, 1851. In the Fall of this year, he entered the senior class of the Academic Department of Madison University, Hamilton, N. Y., and graduated from the College Department in August, 1856. During a few months of the first of the year 1857 he supplied the pulpit of the Eighteenth Street Baptist Church, in Washington, D. C., and returning to Hamilton, he graduated from the Theological Department of Madison University, in August, 1859, receiving from the University the degree of A. M., and writing the hymn which was sung by the graduating class on the stage on the Commencement day. Mr. Palmer settled in Poultney, October, 1859, and remained with that church until the Summer of 1865. He commenced to labor in the Baptist Church in Cornwall, Vt., January, 1866, and remained there until January, 1870, when he accepted a call to the Baptist Church in Middletown Springs, Vt., where he remained until the death of his father, which took place at Norvell, Mich., May 24, 1879, when he preferred a settlement near his mother, and commenced labor with the Baptist Church, Manchester, Mich., August, 1879, where he now resides.

NOYES G. PALMER,

OF EAST NEW YORK, N. Y.

(BRIEF BIOGRAPHY.)

Noyes Grant Palmer was born February 24, 1822, in the town of Lenox, Madison Co., N. Y.

In 1836, his father moved from Lenox to Jackson Co., Mich., with a family of ten children, the subject of this sketch being one of them. Before Noyes G. was sixteen years old, he began teaching school, and continued to teach for part of each succeeding year, to get means to support himself while acquiring a classical education. His father " gave him his time," as the saying is, at the age of eighteen years, and he returned to the State of New York in 1840, and has resided therein ever since.

He commenced the study of law with Risley & Matteson, at Dunkirk, Chautauqua Co., in 1842, and soon after was directed to another profession. The part of the State in which he was located was literally swarming with law students, while there were very few civil engineers. He chose the latter profession and has followed it, with slight interruptions, to the present time.

We find him at two different periods of his life editor and proprietor of a newspaper. At another time, two-thirds owner of a large manufacturing establishment, in the western part of the State; and for the sale of their goods building a merchant boat on Lake Erie—he, as captain, taking it through the Erie and Beaver Canal to the Ohio river, trading from Pittsburg to Cairo, thereon; to Nashville, up the Cumberland, and from St. Louis to Natches, on the Mississippi. At another time, half owner of a free bank with fifty thousand dollars capital, in his native State.

In 1845, he prepared a prospectus of a plan for foretelling changes of the weather; which plan was identical with the system adopted by the U. S. Government since the Rebellion. In addition to the meteorological observation on land, he proposed stations at sea, that we might predict changes probable from that direction. In 1848, his proposals were submitted to Prof. Henry, of the Smithsonian Institute, and to Congress. His letters from Prof. Henry and Congressmen show that the then novel proposition was ahead of philosophers of that age.

In 1849, he settled down as Engineer and Superintendent of Cypress Hills Cemetery, on Long Island, and occupied the position for twenty-six years. His abilities and close attention to the lot proprietors gave that institution nearly all the success and popularity it ever had, and since his connection with it has been severed it has been going to ruin.

He is now located at East New York, Kings Co., N. Y., active and ready for any engineering the age may require.

GEORGE W. PALMER,

OF EAST NEW YORK, N. Y.

(BRIEF BIOGRAPHY,)

Geo. W. Palmer, seventh son of Stephen W. and Huldah Palmer, was born in Lenox, Madison Co., N. Y., Dec. 31, 1835, and was "an infant in arms" when the family moved to the State of Michigan, in 1836. He grew up in the latter State; was educated there; was a school teacher, a railroad agent, clerk and merchant there. Sold out and came back to the State of New York, A. D. 1860; settled in Kings Co., L. I., and has resided there to this date; soon after removing to Long Island, he engaged in school teaching again, and also became a successful insurance agent; was elected Collector of Taxes for the Town of New Lots, in 1869, and by strict attention and efficient performance of the duties of the office, has given such general satisfaction that the people re-elected him to the same office at every election thereto since.

HYMN FOR THE PALMER RE-UNION.

BY REV. A. G. PALMER, D. D.

(TUNE—"We are Tenting To-Night.")

We are tenting to-night on the old camp ground,
   As in the days of yore;
Our fathers met, their fires around,
   Upon this cold, bleak shore.

CHORUS.

Many are the hearts that are waiting to-night,
   Waiting on the golden strand;
Many are the voices calling us away
   To join their holy band.
Tenting to-night, tenting to-night,
   Tenting on the old camp ground.

We are tenting to-night on the old camp ground,
   From homes afar and near;
Our hearts are filled with peace profound,
   From olden memories dear.

                              Chorus.

We are tenting to-night on the old camp ground,
  Our souls with love aglow ;
Our grandsire's praises to resound,
  His sturdy virtues show.

                    Chorus.

We are tenting to-night on the old camp ground,
  Our voices full of cheer ;
Our songs shall through the air resound
  With notes of gladness clear.

                    Chorus.

We are tenting to-night on the old camp ground,
  We may not here remain ;
But, when another year comes round,
  We hope to meet again.

                    Chorus.

We are tenting to-night on the old camp ground,
  But soon our tenting's o'er ;
We'll meet the throne of light around
  Upon the radiant shore.

                    Chorus.

PROCEEDINGS.

SECOND DAY—AUGUST 11th.

The exercises on the 11th commenced as early as eight o'clock, not to say anything of the social gatherings in the hotels and various places even earlier. After a few preliminary matters were attended to, it was announced that the Palmers would make a pilgrimage to the old homestead and ancient burial ground of Walter Palmer. A press correspondent very aptly said :

" The Palmers then took an extra train of cars and carriages and moved on to Wequetequock, where, with great satisfaction, the pilgrims visited the site of Walter Palmer's house, securing relics—pieces of the front doorstep, bits of the chimney and sprigs from a tree—and then passed in procession to the ancient burying-ground 'where the rude forefathers sleep,' especially the remains of Walter Palmer, over which rests a long and massive native granite slab. Here hymns were sung, prayer was offered and a benediction was pronounced. These services were very touching and deeply impressive. The host then returned to the borough and re-entered the pavilion, where speeches were again in order, relieved by spirited singing. Dr. Stanton, of Stonington, responded to the name and families of Stanton ; the Rev. F. Denison, of Providence, R. I., responded for the Denisons ; the Rev. Amos Chesebrough responded for the Chesebroughs ; the Rev. E. B. Palmer, of New Jersey, replied for the Palmers ; Mrs. Mary Dana Shindler, of Texas, the famed poetess and singer, was introduced, and spoke happily and sang sweetly. The great audience joined her in singing 'Sparkling and Bright,' and also 'I'm a Pilgrim, I'm a Stranger.'

" Then came the dinner—a clam bake truly—got up by a true Rhode Islander ; and a feast it was.

"After dinner came family speeches, full of wit and wisdom, from the president, the Hon. E. H. Palmer; Benjamin F. Chapman, of New York; G. T. Palmer, of Arkansas; Irving H. Palmer, of New York; Dr. C. Palmer, of Ohio; the Rev. James S. Palmer, of Maine.

"Again Mrs. Shindler, of Texas, was called out, and spoke of the Palmers of the South, and then repeated her beautiful poem, ' Passing Under the Rod.'

"Speeches were then resumed—from Cornelius B. Palmer, of Sing Sing, N. Y.; the Rev. Wm. L. Palmer, of Michigan, who spoke and then sang an original song in the measure of the battle hymn. A choir of Palmers then sang 'America,' the whole assembly joining, and shaking the vast pavilion. Then Dr. A. G. Palmer led in another sacred song. Speeches were again called out—from E. H. Palmer, of Illinois, and Dr. Eugene Palmer, of Texas. Again came hymns and song. Next came a tasteful and pithy speech from Mrs. Isabella G. Meredith. Votes of thanks were passed to various generous and helpful citizens of Stonington. Francis A. Palmer, bank president, invited the vast Palmer tribe to meet next year in New York City, at his expense. All united in singing, ' There's a land that is fairer than day.' A general vote of thanks to assistants and speakers was passed, and prayer by the Rev. Wm. L. Palmer, and fitting words by the president, closed the first Palmer Re-Union. The singing of the beautiful hymn, 'Sweet Bye-and-Bye,' by the audience, was affecting; many an eye moistened, and one by one the singers' voices hushed through emotion. It was a moment long to be remembered by those present. After the benediction the assemblage separated, with the feeling that such scenes are productive of great good, and tend to the awakening of the finer feelings of man, and a fit preparation for that real separation that awaits us all."

There were many miscellaneous proceedings on the second day that were not especially noted, and are alluded to in the newspaper reports which appear hereafter. The various addresses, proceedings, etc., of the second day, with sketches of some of the individuals participating, follow.

THE PILGRIMAGE TO WEQUETEQUOCK COVE.

THE ANCESTRAL BURIAL GROUND, ETC.

Walter Palmer settled in Stonington, in 1653, on the borders of an inlet from the Sound, just above Stonington. This inlet runs back a mile or so, and was called after the Indian name Wequetequock. On either side of this inlet, or cove, land was level and fertile, and more easily developed. As the name Stonington implies, the country abounds in stones—not mere boulders, but solid large rock formations. Where these rock formations are few, there land has been cultivated. The enclo sures of farms are nearly always stone walls. It is not difficult to understand why Walter Palmer should have selected the low lands of the cove for his habitation. The old house stood with- in about one quarter of a mile from the head of the inlet, on a knoll. The old foundation stones are yet partly standing in the cellar hole, where hands placed them two and a quarter cen- turies before. No part of the building is standing. A rod or so from the house there is an immense rock that it would need a lad- der to surmount. Near the house stood the well, and from which water was drank on the occasion of the Re-Union. The burial ground is at the head of the cove, on the east side, and formerly extended down nearer to the edge than where its stone wall now marks its eastern line. Tradition says that an Indian died in the employ of Walter, and was buried on his land. From this burial grew the custom of using the grounds as a burial spot— now sacred to the memories of Palmer descendants all over the land. In 1828-'29, a stone wall was placed around the ground, which stands there yet, with steps and gate on the east side fronting towards the cove waters. Later, the east line was changed to grade a road on the east bank of the cove, and there- fore many graves were "shut out" and graded over. No records can be found of the burials, only as they may be deciphered from ye olde fashioned English nomenclature found among the headstones, many of which are passed all reading. There seems to have been a clustering of families in burying—the Stantons, the Miners, the Chesebroughs and the Palmers are grouped to- gether. This custom, perhaps, was continued until want of space surrounding each group made it necessary to go elsewhere. The exact burial spot of Walter Palmer is not fully known, as no inscription is found to corroborate any testimony. The grave.supposed to be his is located about the centre of the ground, and is covered with a huge, long, hog-back stone, to prevent wolves or evil-disposed persons from disturbing the grave. This stone is six feet eleven inches in length—which, testimony of old people say, was the statue of Walter Palmer. By the side of this stone is the legible headstone of Walter's favorite son, " Nehemiah Palmer, died February 17, 1717, aged 81 years." All of the inscriptions on these time-effaced grave-marks that we could find time to study out, are as follows :

Nehemiah Palmer, died Feb. 17th, 1717, aged 81 years.

Benj. Palmer, Capt., died April 10th, 1716, aged 74 years.

Rev. James Noyes, died Dec. 30th, 1712.*

Thomas Stanton, died April 11th, 1718, aged 80 years.

Robert Stanton, died Oct. 24th, 1724, aged 71 years.

Capt. Thomas Noyes, died June 26th, 1755, aged 76 years.

Elizabeth, wife of Thomas Noyes, died Oct. 23d, 1762, aged 77 years.

Dorothy, wife of Rev. James Noyes, died Jan. 19th, 1742, aged 91 years.

Joseph Palmer, Jr., died May 26th, 1760, aged 41 years.

Walter Palmer, died Nov. 1st, 1785, aged 69 years.

Mercy Palmer, died Dec. 25th, 1785, aged 71 years.

Walter Palmer, died Feb. 11th, 1726, aged 43 years.

Prudence, daughter of Ichabod Palmer, died Dec. 1st, 1716, aged 22 years.

Elias, son of Ichabod Palmer, died March 13th, 1738, aged 24 years.

Capt. Nathan Palmer, died Feb. 12th, 1791.

Sarah P., wife of Capt. Nathan Palmer, died Aug. 4, 1784, aged 40 years.

Dr. Nathan Palmer, died March 28th, 1795, aged 84 years.

Phebe, wife of Dr. Nathan Palmer, died April 3d, 1792, aged 78 years.

* NOTE.—One of the original incorporators of Yale College.

Hannah Palmer, died March 7th, 1834, aged 79 years; wife of Capt. Andrew Palmer.

Lemuel Palmer, died May 14th, 1850, aged 82 years.

Abigal, wife of Lemuel Palmer, died Jan. 22d, 1832, aged 54 years.

James Palmer, died June 20th, 1794, aged 74 years.

Hannah, wife of James Palmer, died Oct. 4th, 1814, aged 85 years.

John D. Palmer, died Jan. 6th, 1850, aged 47 years.

Zebediah Palmer, son to Noyes and Sarah Palmer, died Sept. 20th, 1790, aged 27 years.

Alan Palmer, son to Noyes and Sarah Palmer, died a prisoner in New York, in Jan., 1778, aged 19.

Capt. John Palmer, his brother, died Jan. 21st, 1778, aged 32 years.

Noyes Palmer, died Nov. 20th, 1783, aged 52 years.

Capt. Joseph Palmer, died Oct. 16th, 1822, aged 80 years.

Lydia, wife of Capt. Joseph Palmer, died Aug. 8th, 1801, aged 62 years.

Thomas Minor, died 1690, aged 83 years.

Many of these are not literal copies, as most of them are old style, with Scriptural verses and characters cut in the stone. Some show coats-of-arms, hour-glasses, angels' wings and head. Nearly all the grave-stones are old-fashioned slabs, imported from Wales and other localities nearer home. The peculiar bluestone headstones are least affected by time, while most of the later American marble stones are more decayed.

The area of about two acres within the burial ground is literally jam full of mounds, which one stumbles over in wending their way; no paths nor spaces to walk upon, and if there ever were any, they have long since been used for graves. Few interments have taken place within this ancestral city of the dead for a long period; so the spot may be said to have been neglected and disused for over a hundred years. On our first visit to this spot, some two months before the Re-Union, we found the area devoted to graves was one of the most desolate and woe-begone places our eye ever beheld—a mass of briars and weeds, that prevented any free access to the grounds.

A few days before the Re-Union some of this was cleared up. Perhaps it would not be unwise to suggest that a small fund be raised by Palmer descendants, the interest to be applied in some ordinary care of this ancestral graveyard.

SHORT ADDRESS,

BY HON. B. FRANKLIN CHAPMAN, OF ONEIDA, N. Y.

Mr. Chairman and Cousins—For by that endearing name I wish now and hereafter to call you, without counting the link in the chain that binds us to our great and noble progenitor, Walter Palmer. This is a fit and proper place for us to meet and organize the first Re-Union of the descendants of a worthy sire, so near to the old homestead, on the slope just above the waters of Wequetequock Cove, which we visited to-day, where nothing remains but the cellar wall, the old well, the large flat stone in front of the door, on which we were so delighted to stand, and on which our distinguished sire so often trod ; and in sight of the old well-preserved burying-ground of two hundred and fifty years ago, on more elevated ground, and half a mile away, and in which we saw no new-made graves within half a century in which we live.

Comparing them with to-day, what a contrast ! That old homestead, on its thousand acre farm, filled by the parents and a dozen children—a community by itself—a happy family, hearty, healthy, laborious and free from vice.

Look at the palatial residences amid the giddy allurements of to-day—houses occupied by the parents and a child or two, or none, and all run by servants. In warm weather fresh air is needed to breathe ; the house is closed ; family and servants at Long Branch, Coney Island, Saratoga, abroad in Europe, around the world on a pleasure trip ; the facilities for travel enable them to be continually on the " go." A continuing panorama is passing before our eyes ; a never-ending strain upon every muscle and nerve.

Look at the old "burying-ground" where Walter Palmer lies, and whose grave is covered over its entire length by a triangular stone, seven feet long and shaped like the roof of a house, to keep the wolves from digging down to and eating up his body. Contrast it with the cemeteries of to-day, with their expensive mausoleums and monuments piercing the very clouds.

Give me the humble cottage, with contentment and happiness. Give me the old burying-ground, with its simple mound and slab.

My friends, why this great concourse of people here to-day? Hundreds, nay, thousands of the descendants of Walter Palmer assembled here under these vast tents?

It is the love of home implanted in every human heart; the place of our birth, the home of our parents and grandparents; and distance often lends enchantment to the view. And natural history teaches us that this wonderful instinct to find the spot where life began pervades the whole animal kingdom; hence, the fish of the sea will flow through the ocean to the little streams where their life began; and birds will sweep through the air back to the place where they were born; and beasts of the forest will seek out and find their native birthplace.

We have come here because we could not help it; that tie of kindred, that instinct of nature planted in every living creature, led us cheerfully here, and we all rejoice at the opportunity of seeing and conversing with each other, and forming so many new and valuable acquaintances. For one, I can truthfully say that I have never spent two days of my life more happily and profitably.

Here we meet the child, the parents, the grandparents, coming from all parts of our Union; joy and gladness are seen in every face; mirth and song fills the air we breathe; and in the instructive and interesting historical and genealogical addresses delivered on this occasion, we rejoice to know that the descendants of Walter Palmer are not unknown to fame and history. The learned profession and the civil and military lists are filled with his descendants.

I hope to live and meet you again and again at future Re-Unions of the Palmers.

a constant and hard worker, enjoying, as he ever has, good health, blessed with a constitution capable of great endurance, endowed with a vigorous mind, entertaining and instructive in his conversation, interspersed with mirth and anecdote.

Amid all the tumults of life he has found time to devote to literary works; he has a model library, and for years has been accustomed to deliver popular lectures on various subjects, and among them, " Washington and its Defences," " Harper's Ferry," and especially his late and popular lecture on " Salem Witchcraft," which has been received with great favor throughout the country.

The Jackson *Citizen* (Mich.), in speaking of it, says : " Mr. Chapman is a lawyer of superior ability, and his word-pictures of that terrible delusion were as vivid as the closest acquaintance could make them. The audience seemed to be completely fascinated by his eloquence, and were swayed at his will as he described in graphic language those terrible scenes through which the people of Salem passed in that fated period.

[The foregoing biography is copied from the " History of Madison and Chenango Counties," pages 734, 735, by James H. Smith ; accompanied by a fine steel engraving ; 1880.]

FRANCIS A. PALMER,

OF NEW YORK CITY, N. Y.

(BRIEF BIOGRAPHY.)

The subject of our sketch was present at the Re-Union, with his family. His remarks, or impromptu address, was short, and not reported, and instead we give biographical sketch.

Palmer, Francis Ashbury, of New York City, President of the National Broadway Bank, was born in the town of Bedford, Westchester County, N. Y., on the 26th of November, 1812. His ancestors, who were from England, came to America in the early part of the seventeenth century, shortly after the arrival of the " pilgrim fathers," settled at Greenwich, Ct., at a place which was subsequently known as Palmers' Hill. They were respectable and sturdy people, with sincere religious convictions,

and taking up land in the New World, soon prospered. The
first mention of this family occurs in the records of the First
Congregational Church in Greenwich, as early as 1674, although
family tradition points to a much earlier date as that of its
arrival in New England.   During the Revolution, the Palmer
family were staunch patriots, and labored hard with their fellow-
colonists to achieve freedom and independence, several of them
serving in the Continental Army. At the close of the Revolutionary War, Stephen Palmer, the grandfather of the subject of this
sketch, removed from New England to New York, establishing
himself at Bedford, in Westchester County, where he built the
Palmer Homestead, of which the family still fondly retain possession.   Mr. Palmer passed his boyhood in his native place
and obtained his education at the old village academy, which
was then presided over by Prof. Samuel Holmes.   In 1831, he
came to the city of New York, and, entering the grocery business as a clerk, subsequently became proprietor of a store, and
finally became a prosperous merchant.   Perceiving the great
need existing in New York for a cheap method of transporting
passengers within the city limits, he invested a portion of his
capital in founding a line of omnibuses which, proving successful, led to the establishment of other lines, and eventually became a source of great profit.   On the 9th of August, 1849, Mr.
Palmer, in company with several other prominent business men,
organized the Broadway Bank, personally holding a large portion of the stock.   On the incorporation of the bank, Mr. Palmer was made president, and has since then held this responsible position, being to-day the senior bank president of the city.
Under his wise and careful management the Broadway Bank has
prospered, and has attained a status second to no other financial institution in the city.   It possesses to-day a capital of
$1,000,000, and is in a most flourishing condition.   He joined
with several others, and in 1851 founded the Broadway Savings
Bank, of which subsequently he became treasurer and vice-
president.   He has been a director in several other successful
financial institutions in this city.

More than fifty years ago, Mr. Palmer connected himself with
the Presbyterian Church in Bedford.   On the 22d of March,

1881, this congregation celebrated its two hundreth anniversary, which was attended, among others, by the living members of the Palmer family—most of them for several generations have received their religious training in its bosom. For many years Mr. Palmer has been a member of the Broadway Tabernacle Church (Congregational), presided over at the present time by the Rev. Dr. William M. Taylor. Mr. Palmer is a consistent temperance man, and during a long and active career has never used intoxicating beverages of any kind, and does not provide them at his table. To-day, in the full posession of health, with a clear intellect, a bright eye, and a degree of bodily vigor that would put to the blush many much younger men, he is a living example of the preservative power of habits of temperance and a well-occupied, useful life. His tastes are quiet and domestic, and his habits simple and unostentatious. He has never taken any active part in politics, but at the opening of the Civil War joined the Union Glee Club immediately upon its organization, and in common with the patriotic merchants of New York did all that was possible to strengthen the power of the Federal Government, and sustain its armies in the field. His interest in business affairs continued unabated, and he is present every day at his post of duty in the bank, carefully superintending the details of its large financial transactions and guarding with fidelity the interests of its stockholders.

IMPROMPTU ADDRESS,

BY EX-GOVERNOR WM. T. MINOR, OF STAMFORD, CT.

Mr. President—It has given me much pleasure to be present with you on this occasion, to join with you in commemorating the virtues and services of Walter Palmer, one of the first settlers of Stonington. While listening to the recital of those virtues and services, I have felt the Palmer blood coursing more rapidly through my veins, and have almost believed that an inch had been added to my stature.

But while according to Walter Palmer and the others of the Pilgrim Fathers all praise, that with their sturdy bravery and independence they came to this Western land and laid here the

foundations of empire, let us not forget to render the due meed
of praise to the wife of Walter Palmer, and the wives, mothers
and sisters of the other Pilgrim Fathers. The Pilgrim Mothers
ought not to be neglected and entirely passed by on such an
occasion as this. So far, I have not been able to find from the
addresses and proceedings here, that Walter Palmer had a
wife ; yet I know that he had, for his history informs us that
his daughter, Grace, married Thos. Minor, my first ancestor in
the United States, as a representative of the female portion of
the Palmer family. I propose to render to woman the honor
to which she is entitled.

The wife, mother 'and sister, equally with the husband,
father and brother, encountered all the perils of a long and
tempestuous passage across the stormy Atlantic, and with them
all the discomforts of an unhospitable climate, and a sterile,
rock-bound territory ; brave and unmurmuring, they guarded
their log cabin, in the absence of the men, against the attacks
of wild beasts, and themselves against the tomahawks and
scalping knives of the savage Indians. No hardship was encountered by the Pilgrim Fathers that was not, without complaint or murmur, shared by the Pilgrim Mothers.

It was by the training and example of the mothers that their
children was fitted to become founders of empire. No power
is more potent, no influence greater, than that of woman—
directly or indirectly she governs the world.

All honor, then, to the Pilgrim Mothers, as well as to the
Pilgrim Fathers! Together they laid the foundation, deep and
broad, of a Government which we believe and hope will last
forever.

Re-unions of this character and anniversaries of the first settlements of towns are always interesting socially. They are beneficial, besides—always on these occasions a great mass of facts,
resting mainly on tradition, are brought together and collated
by the local historian, and laid away for future use, when the
history of the State is to be written. We learn, too, of the first
settlers of our State, of their inner and public life. How they
selected a place in some convenient locality, which
was divided into home lots, on which the rude cabin,

strong enough to withstand hostile attacks, and compact enough to keep out the cold blasts of Winter, was erected ; and outside these home lots were the common fields, which, included in certain territorial limits, became the town.

We learn how they or their children again took up their line of march and formed new settlements and established new towns.

In our State, the first settlers formed our towns which, with us, performed the same duties and held the same relation to the State as counties in most of the other States of the Union. Our towns, as such, are represented in the town branch of the Legislature ; they levy all taxes, take care of their own poor, build and repair their highways, and educate their citizens. And, in my judgment, under this system, more of wisdom has ever been found, and less of peculation and dishonesty, than under the system in the other States which impose these duties on counties. From behind the ramparts of these municipalities the great principles of civil and religious liberty and popular education have been, now for more than two hundred years, successfully defended and maintained. Citizens of Connecticut, guard well these ramparts ; see to it that they are still preserved. Then shall our motto, " *Qui transtulit sustinet*," be true forever. .

HYMN.

BY FRANK AVERILL PALMER.

(Tune—" Battle Hymn of the Republic.")

We come to pay a tribute to the founder of our race,
To gallant Walter Palmer, stately Palm and full of grace ;
To reach the land of promise, toward these shores he set his face,
    His name is marching on.

        CHORUS —Glory, glory hallelujah,
            Glory, glory hallelujah,
            Glory, glory hallelujah,
            His name is marching on.

And now, in holy purpose, we are here from east and west,
From north and south, are gathered round his place of final rest,
To recount his many virtues, daring deeds and valor blest,
    His name is marching on.
                    Chorus.

He left his home and kindred, like the patriarch of old,
To gain our glorious heritage, of freedom's wealth untold,
And faith by far more precious than was Ophir's finest gold,
    His name is marching on.
                      Chorus.

Then hail, all hail, our grand-sire, for in him we claim a part.
May his memory ever flourish, and be green in every heart ;
His name be unforgotten till the last of kin depart,
    Then we'll all go marching on.

        CHORUS—Glory, glory hallelujah,
               Glory, glory hallelujah,
               Glory, glory hallelujah,
               Then we'll going marching on.

POEM.

WALTER PALMER'S HOMESTEAD.

No costly, sculptured walls were thine,
    No high-built, stately room,
Where gilded mirrors proudly shine,
    Amid their draperied gloom.

No pompous name has told thy praise,
    On fallen beauty decked ;
No child of song has woke thy lays,
    On famous pencil sketched.

No ; thine was but a simple frame,
    Well-reared by honest toil,
Beside this stream of Indian name,
    Where first was turned the soil.

An humble roof and simple stone,
    To mark an entrance there ;
Afar from other homes, and lone—
    Protected by God's care.

That brought this Palmer o'er deep seas
    And through the trackless wild ;
And blessed him well with goods increased.
    And many a happy child.

That made this desert bud and bloom,
　　And lightened every care;
In time they farther sought for room,
　　And planted homesteads there.

Till towns and states have circling grown,
　　As forest depths gave way;
His race, a legion, meet and own
　　And praise that power to-day.

August 11, 1881.　　　　　　　　　　　　　　S.

BRIEF REMARKS,

BY E. H. PALMER, OF DANVILLE, ILL.

This Re-Union is of double interest to me—it opens on a day which is the anniversary of a very important event in the history of my existence. Fifty-one years to-day I made another addition to the Palmer family, and I have never regretted the occurrence, and to-day am happy to meet so many of this extensive family.

Most of you were born and have lived among the rocks and hills of the East. I believe I am the only full-blooded sucker in the company,

My branch of the Palmers seemed to catch the pioneer spirit, first removing East and then West.

My father was born in South Coventry, Ct., in 1783, and died in Danville, Ill., in 1861, aged 79 years.

He was one of the early settlers of Eastern Illinois, moving there in 1825.

My father's younger brother also removed to this State at same time, and at time of overland emigration to Oregon, he took his three sons and three daughters to that far western State, where he left them, the first representatives of the Palmer family on the Pacific coast. Before leaving home to attend this meeting, I was accosted on the street by one of our citizens with the remark, "The original Palmers were, I understand, transported." I replied, "England done a good job for America." In looking over the list of the old stock, I find the names of Abel, Moses, Elisha, Elijah, Ichabod, Nathaniel, Hannah and Huldah, but no Cain or Jesebel. What do you think of that?

I am no speaker, but I would close by saying, Our great State of Illinois would welcome any and all of the Palmers—has a good and rich soil, which would bring forth an abundance under the hand of such a people. May this not be our last happy assembly.

BRIEF ADDRESS,

BY C. B. PALMER, OF SING SING, N. Y.

Mr. President, and my sisters, and my cousins, and my aunts—I put on my spectacles to view this grand spectacle. I see, Mr. President, where these Palmers have dined, "but where do they lodge, I beseech you?" I have the honor on this occasion to represent the Palmers in *Sing Sing* (laughter). My good friend, Noyes F., who has lived so long on Jamaica (I mean Jamaica Plains), has told you I am from outside the walls. I am pleased to say there are several very good Palmers outside the walls, but I have no personal knowledge of any inside (applause). The Palmers are a sharp set; they all go in under the name of Smith. I am glad to be present on this happy occasion. I regret that a circumstance so mournful has prevented General Grant from attending. I thought the General would be glad to see a man from Sing Sing. That's the reason I came. I went myself to see the *General* once, with the Army of the Tennessee.

Mr. President, are these modern Palmers that I see before me? Palmers without cowl or staff? Have they been on a pilgrimage to the shrine at Wequetequock? No longer, then, they side as Wilfred of Ivanhoe in the lists of Templeton. No longer cross lance with Lord Marmion on Flodden Field. They are children of a newer civilization. Monk Knights of a later crusade—a crusade as representatives of the principle of civil and religious liberty. Mr. President, it is not an unknown name. It was heard in the city of the Little Monk. It came up over the walls of Geneva; it echoed among the crags and peaks of Switzerland; it whistled amid the camp-fires of those soldiers that rallied around the standard of stern old Oliver ; it sounded as a death knell on the ear of the last of the house of Stuart as he stepped from Whitehall to a scaffold. *Lotuslike it crossed the broad Atlantic, on a Mayflower,* and planted itself deep with Carver and Standish at Plymouth, and Walter Palmer at We-quetequock.

Mr. President, since it has become generally known that I came from Sing Sing, I am surprised to find after two days hunting among all these Palmers, any one of them that owns relationship with me. I might say, in justification of my respectability, that I am a descendant of a line of Richard's father, grandfather, great-grandfather, dating back to 1770, when an ancestor bought four hundred acres of land in the manor of Courtland, Westchester Co., N. Y. What I want Noyes F. to do is to tell me where this ancestor came from—hardly from the poorhouse, as he would not have had six hundred pounds to pay for the land, as stated in the deed.

Like our friend Ex-Governor Minor, I am a ladies' man, and I would here speak a good word for them. The mothers of all these Palmers were women of another name and lineage ; and a cross blood has sometimes had good results. The neutral ground of the Revolution—good old Westchester—has been rendered famous not only in history, but by the magic pen of Fenimore Cooper. Tradition has, in connection with these scenes, the name of Elizabeth Hunter. She married a Palmer ; she was my great-grandmother.

Mr. President, time forbids my making any extended remarks, if I expect to get back to Sing Sing *before locking-up time.* I may, like my friend from Courtland, Judge Palmer, invite you all to come to *Sing Sing* (laughter). Thanking you for the courtesy of an invitation to address you, and for your courteous attention, I say good-bye.

CORNELIUS B. PALMER,

OF SING SING, N. Y.

(BRIEF BIOGRAPHY.)

Cornelius B. Palmer, of Sing Sing, N. Y., third son of Richard R. and Rachel Palmer, born in the Ninth Ward in the city of New York, July 1st, 1840. When about twelve years of age, his father retiring from business, removed to a country place in the vicinity of Sing Sing, N. Y., his former home, and that of his ancestry. The subject of this sketch attended the old academy at Canandaigua, N. Y., and subsequently prepared at Fort Edward Institute, N. Y., for Sophomore Class at College. Attended course at Law Department, Union University, and read law in office of N. H. Baker, District Attorney, Westchester Co.; was admitted to the bar, July 10th, 1861, ten days over twenty-one years of age. For seven years connected with the Internal Revenue successively as Clerk, Deputy Collector, and Acting Collector of Tenth Collection District, N. Y. Is now a practicing lawyer, having an office at Sing Sing. His grandparents all lived to a very old age. His grandmother, Catherine Doris, died in 1870, at the age of 92, leaving her surviving six children, fifty-three grandchildren, sixty-two great-grandchildren and one great-great-grandchild.

R. R. Palmer, His father, died suddenly in 1877, at the age of sixty-eight, while spending a Summer in the State of Maine. This branch of the family are presumably of Quaker origin.

SHORT ADDRESS,

BY JOSIAH LEE PALMER, OF LITTLE ROCK, ARK.

Mr. President—I am happy to be with you to-day as a member of the Palmer family, and I thank God that I am a Palmer, and a descendant of the great and noble Walter Palmer, in whose · name we have met in family re-union. I hope this pleasant Re-Union will be kept up annually as long as time shall last, and while I live you may rely upon seeing me. I trust this Re-Union will not adjourn until a sufficient amount is raised to

erect a monument over him. We are all proud to honor to-day
Walter Palmer. I have much more I would like to say upon
this occasion, but am too feeble.

JOSIAH LEE PALMER.

(BRIEF BIOGRAPHY.)

Josiah Lee Palmer was born in Galway, Saratoga Co., N. Y.,
May 11th, 1817. Married May 11th, 1847, to Sarah Eddy,
daughter of Dr. John Eddy, Lockport, N. Y.

Emigrated to Chicago, and engaged in mercantile business.
Came to Arkansas in 1859; was engaged in planting and hotel
business until after the war. In 1874, was appointed Assistant
Auditor of State, which place he still holds. For four years he
has been Acting Insurance Commissioner of State. He was
the first one to inaugurate the Christian Temperance Union
in that State, and held for three years the presidency of the
Union.

IMPROMPTU REMARKS,

BY REV. E. B. PALMER, D. D., OF BRIDGETON, N. J.

I am very glad that it has fallen to my lot to share in the
festivities of this great family gathering. The occasion is in_
deed one of great interest. For myself I wish to thank the
gentlemen of the committee, who have labored so perseveringly
amid so many discouragements, that they have brought us thus
together under circumstances so agreeable. And I can but
acknowledge my obligation to them in leading me to think a
little more closely of, and to appreciate a little more highly
the Palmer name.

It is often asked, "What is there in a name?" Sometimes
there is much of significancy, and then again but little. A
friend of mine was going up the Catskill Mountains, and a passenger was inquiring why the mountains were called the Cats-
kills. The stage-driver, somewhat annoyed at what seemed to
him a foolish question, replied, impatiently : "Why, everything
has to have a name ; you might just as well ask why the Hudson

came to be called the Hudson." Now, there are a great many names that seem to have no more reason for their existence, in fact, than the beautiful river that treads its way down that charming valley had, in the fancy of the ignorant stage-driver. It was needful that they should be called something, and that is about all can be said of it. There is often, however, a meaning in names that makes their study very suggestive.

The family name which we bear has an origin which speaks of two things most highly to be prized; for the name, Palmer, suggests two grand ideas—they are of *Reverence* and *Triumph*. Whatever may be our judgment of the Crusaders (and there is much in their history that we cannot approve), they did have boundless reverence for holy things and holy places. I have sometimes thought that we, in this age, might be their pupils with some degree of advantage. We live in times not over-stocked with this grace. It was reverence for the Holy Land, especially for the Holy Sepulchre of our crucified Lord, that gave the world the first Palmers. Then, too, that idea of triumph is a most exalted one. The bearer of the palm must needs be a victor. He must be a man of courage. He must love truth and bravely battle for it. He must know how to meet difficulties and master the situation. Yesterday, as we were making our way up to the old homestead and grove of our noble grand-sire, as I noted the huge stone fences enclosing the small fields, and saw about me enough remaining to build others equally great, as I observed the surface of this hard, unpromising soil, and imagined what it must have been more than two centuries ago, in its untamed state, with all the dangers of the primeval forests added thereto, I thought what a brave heart the "old patriarch" must have had in him. What magnificent courage it must have required to make a home and extort a living out of such surroundings.

Indeed, in a sense which we can hardly realize, the men of those times must have been brave men, and good old Walter must have been a veritable " palm-bearer" to have triumphed over such obstacles. I have also been somewhat surprised to see how the idea of the Palmer or palm-bearer links itself with our world's history, running on even to its close, mounting up

to the grandest and holiest triumph of the Redeemer's Kingdom. In the interesting genealogical account given us last
evening, our secretary alluded to that beautiful passage in the
Revelation which describes the entire throng of the redeemed
standing " before the Throne and before the Lamb, clothed
with white robes, and palms in their hands." Why, did you
ever think of it, the whole vast throng of the redeemed are to
be Palmers at last. All these Denisons and Minors and Chesebroughs, with those of all other names, sharing in the blessed
work of the Redeemer, are to come over to our family and rejoice in being palm-bearers—Palmers in the highest and best
sense, through the victory of the all-conquering Christ. It is
my prayer that this indeed may be the case with all in the joyous sense in which Christ gives the victory over sin in every
form.

May God grant that those of us who bear this noble name
may appreciate its worth, and catching the inspiration of its
birth, live to know the exalted triumph of which it is in origin
and history the symbol.

HOUR OF MY CHILDHOOD.

BY L. A. PALMER.

O home of my childhood, sweet memories of thee,
Come floating around like the breeze o'er the sea ;
And fresh to my mind each loved scene appears,
Not dimmed by the distance or faded by years.

The hills and the valleys, where once I was young,
The woodland and thicket where the nightingale sung ;
There the love of a father and mother I knew,
Kind brothers and sisters and friends that were true.

The old village church where we used to repair,
And worship our maker in accents of prayer ;
While each joined in singing sweet anthems of praise,
To him who preserved us and lengthened our days.

But time, the destroyer, has been on the track,
Has taken the loved ones, and ne'er brought them back :
Side by side in a churchyard where the last sunbeams play,
A father and mother lie mouldering away.

Those brothers and sisters, ah! the tale must be told,
Not one now remains on the homestead of old;
And the stranger treads carelessly, making his hay,
In the field by the brook where we once used to play.

But we look for a time to be gathered again,
In a world free from sorrow, temptation and pain;
Where sweet-sounding echoes shall fill all the place,
To Him who redeemed us and saved us by grace.

Honeoye Falls, N. Y., Sept. 10th, 1881.

RESPONSE FOR THE STANTON FAMILY.

BY DR. GEO. D. STANTON, OF STONINGTON, CT.

Mr. President, Ladies and Gentlemen—It would be exceedingly inappropriate for me, after the numerous, able and eloquent addresses with which you have been entertained during the past two days, to further tire your perhaps wearied patience with anything but a very brief response for the Stanton family, which I have been honored to represent on this occasion.

The Stantons, in common with the Denisons, Miners, and Chesebroughs, have become so interwoven by marriage with the descendants of Walter Palmer, that we cannot but feel a just pride in the fair fame of your family name, and we most heartily congratulate you for your enviable and honorable record—whether it be in the school of science, in the halls of legislation, on the field of battle, in the forum, and last, and by no means least, in the newspaper editor's sanctum sanctorum. We commend the laudable spirit which prompted your pilgrimage to your ancestral home, and we congratulate you on the unrivalled success which has crowned your praiseworthy enterprise.

As this is a Palmer Re-Union, you will not expect, nor will you care to hear anything concerning the history of Thomas Stanton, the Indian interpreter and pioneer associate of Walter Palmer; but this much I may state, that in his capacity as Indian interpreter for the colonies, and in his duties as mediator in the differences often occurring between the settlers and the natives he had, necessarily, frequent occasion to visit the habitations of the latter in this then rugged wilderness, by which he became familiar with the most desirable localities for settlements, and thus paved the way for those hardy pioneers. Stanton was first on the ground at Pawcatuck as an Indian trader, immediately followed by Chesebrough, and subsequently by Miner, Palmer, Denison and others. They wisely selected the rich meadow-lands adjoining the bays and coves of our coast, as suitable pasture fields for their herds and flocks, and it is not impossible that they may have had an eye to the " succulent and festive clam," for which we descendants have inherited an undisguised affection, and with which you have very properly decided to close this festive occasion.

Permit me again to congratulate you on your happy success in the union of hearts and of hands, and to wish you, one and all, a safe return to your respective homes.

REPORT OF TREASURER,

H. CLAY PALMER, OF STONINGTON, CT.

Dr.

1881. To cash paid as follows (bills):

August,	Treasurer's expenses to New York and Jamaica.................................	$20 00
June,	"Graphic," bill for invitations	50 00
July,	N. F. Palmer, postage bill to date.......	39 50
Aug. 10,	Bill of fireworks......................	65 00
"	Bill for clams (on acct. of caterer)........	27 00
"	Bill for calcium lights.	47 55
"	Schofield's bills, clams (for caterer)......	41 30
	Freight and express bills..............	46 32
	Anderson, on account of printing bill....	50 00
	Charles E. Randalls, on acct. of labor bill	56 15
	E. T. Palmer, bills as follows:	
	Atwood Mfg. Co., wood (for caterer) $5 00	
	Police $4, ice bill for caterer, $4..... 8 00	
	R. R. fares bill, for Noank Band.... 3 60	
	Bill for dinners " " " ... 5 60	
	Utter's printing bill .... 1 50——23 70	
	J. S. Anderson, balance on printing......	30 20
	Bills for empty boxes for seats.........	3 45
	Bill of S. O. Durgan, board for tent man.	8 00
	Bill of Thomas Capron, for use of boat...	3 00
	Chas. E. Randalls, bill of labor in full....	65 30

To C. P. Trumball's bill, express wagon...... $ 1 00
Thomas H. Hinckley, police duty two days
    and nights........................ 6 00
Orchestra leader Williams, of New York. 10 00
Palmer & Co., register book............ 2 25
Of labor 4 00
Noank Brass Band 53 60
Printing dinner tickets................ 2 00
Printing signs....................... 2 50
For team for hauling boards............ 3 00
N. H. Gates, for bill of lumber.......... 30 72
Telegraph bills...................... 5 06
"Graphic" bill, balance due on acct. N. F. P. 20 00
I. H. P., postage expenses to New York,
    Boston, and Providence............ 54 59
Badges, etc.......................... 3 75
Envelopes and postage stamps, N. F. P.. 21 85
Balance to account....................... 79

$797 58

1881.		CR.			
June,	By cash from E. H. Palmer................				$10 00
July 25,	"	"	"	to N. F. P......	50 00
" 21,	"	"	"	"	10 00
" 21,	"	"	"	"	10 00
" 21,	"	"	"	"	10 00
" 21,	"	"	"	"	10 00
Aug. 8,	Postal order from Peleg Noyes..........				1 00
" 8,	Cash from E. H. P....................				20 00
" 10,	" col'ct'd from Re-unionists by H. C. P.				110 75
" 10,	" " " C. D. Prescott.				230 33
" 10,	" " " N. F. P......				118 00
" 11,	" for dinner tickets by H. C. P..				62 50
" 11,	" " " " I. H. P..				61 00
" 12,	" " Col. G. W. Palmer, I. H. P.				5 00
" 12,	" " rent of tent, I. H. P.......				4 00
" 12,	" " Ed. T. Palmer, I. H. P.....				10 00
" 12,	" collected, A. M. Palmer, N. Y.....				25 00
" 12,	" " Dr. Eugene Palmer, Tex.				10 00
" 12,	" " William Butler, Boston..				5 00
" 12,	" " A friend				5 00
" 12,	" " A friend				5 00
" 12,	" " Asher Chapman				25 00

$797 58
By balance account........................ 79

NAMES OF CONTRIBUTORS.

F. A. Palmer, of New York City	$50	00
M. G. Palmer, Portland, Me	25	00
B. F. Chapman, Oneida, N. Y	10	00
B. R. Palmer, Oneida, N. Y	10	00
Robert Palmer, Noank, Ct	20	00
E. A. Palmer, Lansingburg, N. Y	2	00
Gidden Palmer	5	00
Luther Palmer, Brookfield, Mass	10	00
Peter A. Palmer, Lansingburg	5	00
Chas. L. Palmer, Albany, N. Y	5	00
Wm. A. Grant, Boston	5	00
Prof. D. L. Eaton, Yale College	5	00
Simeon Palmer, Boston	5	00
Mrs. Phœbe Palmer	5	00
Sarah N. Maise, Westerly	5	00
Allen Palmer	5	00
Miss F. Chesebro, Stonington	1	00
G. C. Morse	5	00
J. L. Palmer, Little Rock	5	00
A. B. Gardiner	1	00
H. H. Palmer, Portland	5	00
S. T. Palmer, Chicago	5	00
Wm. A. Woodward	1	00
Wm. H. Palmer, N. Y	5	00
R. P. Palmer	6	00
J. J. Palmer	2	00
C. H. Palmer, Norwich	2	00
H. J. Palmer	1	00
J. M. Languerthy	1	00
Nehemiah Palmer, Boston	5	00
J. E. Palmer, Mich	5	00
J. Palmer	1	00
A. M. Palmer	5	00
Alex. Palmer	1	00
Gen. G. W. Palmer	5	00
A. D. Palmer, Stonington	10	00
H. M. Palmer, Stonington	10	00
Noyes S. Palmer, Stonington	10	00
Courtland P. Palmer, N. Y	10	00
D. P. Chesebro	5	00
A. M. Palmer, N. Y	25	00
Asher Chapman	25	00
Dr. Eugene Palmer, Texas	10	00

Wm. Butler, Boston	$ 5	00
Two friends	10	00
Clarence P. Lewis	2	00
A lady	1	00
A. L. Lebanon	1	00
A. A. Muts	1	00
R. Wm. H. Palmer, Manchester	5	00
R. B. Palmer, Butternuts, N. Y	1	00
Two ladies	2	00
A. F. Chesebro, Philadelphia	3	00
Cornelius Palmer	5	00
E. H. Palmer	5	00
J. L. Hutchingson	1	00
B. H. Palmer	1	00
B. L. Palmer	2	00
B. G. Palmer	1	00
D. M. Palmer		25
J. R. Palmer	1	00
L. W. R	1	00
H. B. Palmer	1	00
A. W. Hewitt	1	00
H. L. Palmer	1	00
E. L. Palmer	1	00
Dr. J. F. Noyes	1	00
M. V. Palmer		50
W. C. Palmer	2	00
J. W. D	1	00
J. S. Palmer	5	00
A. Cook	1	00
F. W. Palmer	5	00
Bardick	1	00
G. W. Palmer	5	00
Chesebro	1	00
N. F. Palmer	5	00

H. CLAY PALMER.

(BRIEF BIOGRAPHY.)

H. Clay Palmer, Treasurer of the Re-Union, was born in Stonington, November 17, 1852; his father is Amos A. Palmer, a son of Allen Palmer, and a grandson of Noyes Palmer, who was born and resided in the same place; his mother was Emma Chesebro, daughter of Ezra Chesebro; her mother was Sally Palmer, daughter of Denison Palmer, of his native place; both branches of the family being direct descendants of Walter Palmer. After finishing his studies, he entered the office of Clifton A. Hall, one of the first architects of Providence, R. I., where he served his time perfecting himself as an architect, the profession he now follows. In 1878–'79 he was Tax Collector for the Town of Stonington, and has since been the Collector of the Borough and Ninth School District; of the latter he also served five years as its Clerk and Treasurer.

At the time of the Re-Union, August 10th, he was one of the five who first met to organize the first meeting, and was anxious and active in the *grand success* of the same.

CLOSING ADDRESS,

BY E. H. PALMER, PRESIDENT OF RE-UNION.

The last speaker on the afternoon of August 11th was President E. H. Palmer, and as he arose and for a moment remained silent, a hushed stillness pervaded the entire assemblage. The realization of the moment was pictured upon every countenance, and falteringly the speaker, in a subdued manner, spoke in substance as follows:

Friends—The hour that I have most dreaded, and to which I have almost shuddered when thinking of its approach, is at hand. From the inception of this grand Re-Union of the Palmer Family up to the present moment, I have looked only to its growth and progress from day to day. But now we are soon to separate, probably never to meet again. Some one of us, e'er another Re-Union will occur—some one of this assemblage, yes, perhaps many of you now before me—will have passed away. I, too, may be of that number, and never again have the pleasure of standing, as I do to-day (the head of this great family) in another Re-Union. The solemnity of this hour cannot be evaded. It is upon us, and we must meet it. To say good-bye to you all is to breathe a choking utterance. To think that many faces now before me, so bright and joyous for the past two days, so full of real hope and spirit, may never be gazed upon by me again, affects me to sadness. So, with thanks to you all for kindness and manifestations of friendship during our Re-Union, never to be forgotten, I will, in a spirit of hope for the future, bid you each and all good-bye.

POEM ON PALMER RE-UNION.

BY H. L. SPENCER, OF ST. JOHNS, N. B.

Where, where will be the birds that sing,
  A hundred years to come?
The flowers that now in beauty spring,
  A hundred years to come?
  The rosy cheek, the lofty brow,
  The hearts that beat so gaily now;
Where, where will be our hopes and fears,
Joys, pleasant smiles, and sorrow's tears,
  A hundred years to come?

Who'll press for gold this crowded street,
  A hundred years to come?
Who'll tread your aisles with willing feet,
  A hundred years to come?
  Pale, trembling age and firy youth,
  And childhood with its brow of truth;
The rich, the poor, on land and sea,
Where will the mighty millions be,
  A hundred years to come?

We all within our graves shall sleep,
  A hundred years to come!
No living soul for us will weep,
  A hundred years to come!
  But other men our lands will till,
  And others then our homes will fill;
And other birds will sing as gay,
And bright the sunshine as to day,
  A hundred years to come.

IRA H. PALMER.

(BRIEF BIOGRAPHY.)

Ira H. Palmer, the Corresponding Secretary of the late Palmer Re-Union, was born at Mystic Bridge, in the town of Stonington, Ct., April 18th, 1836, of parents Benjamin F. and Eliza Hart Palmer. At the age of twelve, he moved to the borough of Stonington, and became a clerk in the drug store of his brother, Franklin A. Palmer. He subsequently became the agent of the "Harnder Express Company," and for many years continued as such. Then follows some six years of banking and railroad experience.

In 1869, he became connected with an extensive quarry in Westerly, R. I., and during the last two years of his term was the manager.

The subject of our sketch built and managed a railroad connecting the quarries of Westerly with the Stonington Railroad.

Mr. Palmer is naturally of a quick turn of mind, very zealous, and hardly without a peer in the projecting of any new work. It has been remarked of him, that he is always "ten years in advance of the age."

In 1862, he purchased the well-known Wadawanuch Hotel, at Stonington, Ct. (then a Female Seminary), and opened it as a first-class hotel. For three years he managed it with practical assistants, and in 1865 sold it to its present owners.

Mr. Palmer managed the first steamer ever run to Watch Hill from Stonington—it was the *Dashing Wave*, owned by Capt. R. F. Loper, and run in connection with the Wadawanuch House.

His connection with the Palmer Re-Union is still fresh on the minds of all. From curiosity solely he attended the first meeting held at the Baptist Vestry, and was one of the five Palmers present. He at once grasped the idea of a Family Re-Union, and at that meeting infused spirit and encouragement into the four others present. Has been blessed with four sons, three of whom are living—the eldest, Arthur Trumbull Palmer, is in the wholesale department of Jordan, Marsh & Co., Boston, Mass.; the second, Henry Robinson Palmer, the well-known juvenile editor of the *Palmer Vidette;* Frank Trumbull Palmer being the youngest son.

Mr. Palmer, in addition to being a decendant of Walter Palmer, is by the maternal line a direct descendant of Roger Sherman, one of the signers of the Declaration of Independence; and to the Sherman side Mr. Palmer gives greatly the credit of any enterprise and tact he may possess.

SOCIAL MEETING.

After the proceedings on the evening of the last day were over, many wended their way homeward by trains, boats and carriages, so that the numbers became greatly reduced.

A social meeting took place at Palmer headquarters, " Brayton Hall," that was one of the most enjoyable occasions of the whole Re-Union services, and developed the fact that more real entertainment comes from a commingling socially than from public speaking, weary and tiresome to a large audience. At the social gathering individual introduction elicited for the first time real relationship, and a flood of reminiscences seemed to flow from groups of Palmers. Latent talent sprang up that had been dormant during the day services. The singing by Miss Lottie Walker, of New York City, was the finest musical entertainment of the whole Re-Union, and had this sweet singer appeared on the platform while the thousands could have listened to her trained voice, the enthusiasm would have been contagious, and well merited.

By this social meeting it soon became known that many eminent men and women had sat meekly listening at the services during the two days that ought to have been on the platform, while many on the platform would have enjoyed exchanging places with them. If these lines meet the eyes of many who thus humbly " hid their light under the bushel," they must receive the apology of the officers of the Re-Union that no slight was intended, and that only a want of social acquaintance prevented their occupying their proper position. The register list reveals many of these individuals.

1. MARY DANA SHINDLER.

2. MISS SARA PALMER.

3. ISABELLA GRANT MERIDITH

4. MRS. M. RYAN.

5. MRS. HENRY SMITH

6. MRS. PAUL S. PALMER.

7. MRS. ALDEN PALMER.

8. MRS. HENRY RHODES

9. MRS. M. B. WOOD

10. MRS. ABBIE A. P. WOODWARD.

11. MRS. C. A. PALMER BISSELL.

12. MRS. FULLER AYER CADY.

13. MISS MARTHA M. PALMER

14. FANNY CHESEBORO.

15. ELIZABETH PALMER ELMER

16. MRS. N. APPLEMAN

17. GEO. H. PALMER.

18. MRS. GEO. H. PALMER.

19. MRS. GEO. H. PALMER

20. MRS. GEO. H. PALMER

MISCELLANEOUS MATTERS.

[TO THE LADIES.—An apology is due to the Palmer ladies, whose efforts undoubtedly made the Re-Union a success. The interest first created in favor of the gathering emenated mostly through their influence and persuasion. The social meeting of the last evening developed this fact. Out of respect to their sex, a few allusions are made, accompanied by brief sketches and photographic illustration. Had more time been given to the preparation of this publication, a more extensive and appropriate showing would have been given to the part taken by the mothers of the Palmer decendants.]

MARY DANA SHINDLER.

The Re-Union proceedings were continuous in their character; for when not in regular order, as per programme, some other services were being held, and none were more interesting, nor more like a "Love Feast" than the singing of original hymns, etc., by Mary Dana Shindler, of Texas. So popular were these songs that the audience joined in, and the singing service was kept up spontaneously.

Mrs. Shindler is a daughter of the late Rev. Dr. B. M. Palmer, of Charleston, S. C.; born in 1810; married, in 1848, to Rev. Robert D. Shindler, who died in 1874. Mrs. Shindler resides with her son, Robert C. Shindler, in Nacogdoches, Tex.

Mrs. Shindler has contributed extensively in prose and poetry, and particularly in songs, to the various publications of the country for half a century. Among them have been published three musical works—"The Northern, Southern, and Western Harps;" a controversial work, entitled "Letters to Relatives and Friends;" a volume of poems, called "The Parted Family." Two works for seamen's libraries, published by the Harpers, and entitled "The Young Sailor," and

" Forecastle Tone ; " two song books, " The Temperance
Lyre," and the " Greenback Labor Song Book ; " a volume on
Spiritualism, entitled " A Southerner Among the Spirits," published recently by Colby & Rich, of Boston, Mass. ; and
several long serials which have appeared in the literary journals.

The old and familiar Sunday-School song, " I'm a Pilgrim,
and a Stranger," was sung by Mrs. Shindler very appropriately,
as she was a pilgrim and a stranger among the Re-Unionists ;
but many old people were present who joined in the singing of
a song familiar to them in younger days. The effect of hearing its author sing it was an inspiration of respect and veneration.

The following old but well-known poem by Mrs. Shindler is
published by request :

PASSING UNDER THE ROD.

" And I will cause you to pass under the rod, and I will bring you into the bond
of the covenant."—*Ezk. xx*, 37.

I saw the young Bride, in her beauty and pride,
    Bedeck'd in her snowy array,
And the bright flush of joy mantled high on her cheek,
    While the future look'd blooming and gay ;
And with woman's devotion she laid her fond heart,
    At the shrine of idolatrous love,
And she fasten'd her hopes to this perishing earth
    By the chain which her tenderness wove.
But I saw when those heart-strings were bleeding and torn,
    And the chain had been severed in two,
She had changed her white robes for the sables of grief
    And her bloom for the paleness of woe.
But the Healer was there, pouring balm on her heart,
    And wiping the tears from her eyes,
And he strengthen'd the chain he had broken in twain,
    And fasten'd it firm to the skies.
There had whisper'd a voice—'twas the voice of her God,
I love thee, I love thee—*pass under the rod !*

I saw the young Mother in tenderness bend
    O'er the couch of her slumbering boy,
And she kiss'd the soft lips as they murmured her name,
    While the dreamer lay smiling in joy.

Oh, sweet as a rose-bud encircled with dew,
    When its fragrance is flung on the air,
So fresh and so bright to that mother he seem'd
    As he lay in his innocence there.
But I saw when she gazed on the same lovely form,
    Pale as marble, and silent, and cold ;
But paler and colder her beautiful boy,
    And the tale of her sorrow was told.
But the Healer was there, who had stricken her heart,
    And taken her treasure away,
To allure her to Heaven he has placed it on high,
    And the mourner will sweetly obey.
There had whisper'd a voice, 'twas the voice of her God,
I love thee, I love thee—*pass under the rod !*

I saw the fond Brother with glances of love
    Gazing down on a gentle young girl,
And she hung on his arm while the whispering wind
    Freely played with each clustering curl.
Oh, he lov'd the soft tones of her silvery voice,
    Let her use it in sadness or glee,
And he clasp'd his brave arms round her delicate form
    As she sat on her brother's knee.
But I saw when he gazed on her death-stricken face
    And she breathed not a word in his ear,
And he clasp'd his brave arms round an icy-cold form,
    And he moisten'd her cheek with a tear.
But the Healer was there, and he said to him thus:
    "Grieve not for thy sister's short life,"
And he gave to his arms still another fair girl,
    And he made her his own cherish'd wife.
There had whisper'd a voice, 'twas the voice of his God,
I love thee, I love thee—*pass under the rod !*

I saw a proud father and mother who lean'd
    On the arms of a dear, gifted son,
And a star in the future grew bright to their gaze,
    As they saw the high place he had won ;
And the fast-coming evening of life promis'd fair,
    And its pathway grew smooth to their feet ;
And the starlight of love glimmer'd bright at the end,
    And the whispers of fancy were sweet.
But I saw when they stood bending low o'er the grave
    Where their hearts' dearest hope had been laid,
And the star had gone down in the darkness of night,
    And the joy from their bosoms had fled.

But the Healer was there, and his arms were around,
    And he led them with tenderest care,
And he show'd them a star in the bright upper world,
    'Twas *their star* shining brilliantly there!
They had each heard a voice, 'twas the voice of their God,
I love thee, I love thee—PASS UNDER THE ROD!

ISABELLA GRANT MEREDITH.

This lady took an active part in the exercises of the Re-Union, and her pithy and extemporaneous remarks from the platform being lost to the reporter, we append a brief sketch instead, and also, by permission of the authoress, the poem " Borodel."

The subject of this sketch is a descendant of Walter Palmer, through his daughter Grace Minor, and of Mathew Grant (1630), through his grandson, Josiah Grant, who moved from Windsor to Stonington, Ct., in 1695-'96, and in the same year married Rebecca, daughter of Ephraim, and granddaughter of Grace Minor.

Mrs. Meredith is the daughter of Julia Elizabeth Grant, and Joseph Clark Dowe, M. D., and the great-granddaughter of Minor Grant, M. D., who served as Army Surgeon under Washington in the Revolution.

She is a native of New England, having been born in Stafford, Tolland Co., Ct. While very young, her parents removed to Milwaukee, Wis., where all of her childhood and much of her youth were spent. Her playground was that " Beautiful Shore " which travelers have likened for lovliness to the Bay of Naples, and the great lake whose sapphire waters laved the strand was by turns her playmate and her teacher.

She began early to contribute stories, poems and articles to the press ; is the author of the " Papillon Papers," published in the New York *Evening Mail*; of " Sweet Briars," a volume first published serially in the *Christian Leader* ; of stories and poems which have appeared in the *Christian Union*, the *Old and New*, the *Galaxy, Scribner's,* and other magazines ; of the operatta " Bo-peep," etc.; etc. She has contributed New York correspondence for several journals under the signature of *Papillon*, and served editorally on the staff of a Washington, D. C., paper. Since her marriage, she has made her home principally in the Metropolis.

"BORODEL."

Daughter of Captain George Denison and Lady Anne Borodel ; born, 1657.

BY ISABELLA GRANT MEREDITH.

Two centuries have won largess
    Of August shine and April shower
And Winter's bleak and biting stress,
Since blossomed in the wilderness
    A maiden like a wilding flower,
Of whom the legends little tell
Save that her name was Borodel.

If she were fair they have not told,
    Of haughty mood, or winsome ways;
Or, if beneath her wimple's fold
Her tresses shone like threads of gold
    In plaits demure, or curly maze.
We only know a damosel
Once lived, whose name was Borodel.

And had she eyes of blue or brown?
    And were her lips of witching pout?
Did she glance side-long, and look down
And knit her brows in mimic frown,
    And gallants lure—their woes to flout?
Had she the triumphs of a belle,
Whom we must know as Borodel?

I wonder much how fared this maid
    In that wild home, in those rude days,
When painfully the fathers prayed,
And judged, and banished undismayed
    Their brethren to the desert's maze.
Did Calvin's doom of terror fell
Shake the sad soul of Borodel?

Clad, or in homespun, or brocade,
    With petticoat of paduasoy,
As maiden sweet, and matron staid,

I'm fain to think she ever made
　　Her household's best delight and joy.
It needs not musty scroll to tell
That leal was gentle Borodel.

And here she lived and loved apace,
　　The child of loyal Lady Anne ;
Here, meekly filled a daughter's place ;
Here, ruled her house with seemly grace,
　　As gentle dame and puritan ;
Till wended sadly up yon fell
The funeral train of Borodel.

Of late we thronged * in pious quest
　　Where tangled briars net the mounds;
From Texan pampas came the guest,
From the vast prairies of the West,
　　From Norombega's snow-wreath'd bounds
We sought her grave, ah, who may tell
Where slumbers Lady Borodel?

Two hundred years a-gone ! A faint,
　　Fair vision grows before my een
As of a non-conformist saint
In garb sad-colored, prim and quaint,
　　Dove-eyed, with still and holy mein ;
But, meek or proud, the old, old spell
Of silence thralls thee, Borodel.

I wot thy life was—woman's doom,
　　Something enjoyed, and much foreborne ;
Thy garland, braided shorn and bloom,
　　Thy chequer'd days half shine, half gloom,
　　Until death found thee overworn.
Brave heart and patient, rest thee well,
God's peace enfold thee, Borodel.

---

* Note.—This lady was an ancestress of many of the pilgrims from near and far
who met together at Stonington, Ct., August 10th, 1881, to celebrate the Palmer
Family Re-Union. Although, as the verses show, the writer has been able to gather
but few facts with regard to her history—even the place of her grave being unknown. One other date of interest has been gleaned from the *American Genealogist*—
namely, that of her marriage with Samuel Stanton, June 15th, 1680.

MISS SARA A. PALMER,

OF STONINGTON, CT.

Miss Sara A. Palmer is the only surviving daughter of Rev. Dr. Palmer, of Stonington, Ct. She is a young lady of many personal attractions and decided traits of character. Her kindly disposition, happy conversational powers, cultured and well-stored mind, make her an enjoyable companion, and win the profound respect and esteem of many chosen friends, not less from among the lowly than the refined classes of society. She is a very successful Sabbath-school teacher, and a genial auxiliary to her father in all parish and missionary work. Her abilities, as illustrated in poems furnished for various periodicals, and especially her hymn for the 10th of August, 1876, and for the grand Palmer Re-Union, 1881 (found in this volume), have the promise of a brightening literary future.

It is sufficient to say, that Miss Palmer is every way worthy of the grand old family to which she belongs, and is fully entitled to the place they have so proudly assigned her.

We cannot resist the temptation to digress from the scope of this volume, and therefore select one of Miss Sara's very able poems, in reference to a sad event contemporaneous almost with our happy Re-Union.

GARFIELD.

"Though dead, he speaketh."

As I sit in the little village church,
 Darkened with signs of woe,
To my heart comes faintly the preacher's voice,
 With its tremulous accents low ;
And I hear not the pleading words of prayer,
 That come through the falling tears ;
While the notes of song they strive to raise
 Fall on unheeding ears.

For my thoughts have flown to that distant grave
 By the lakeside in the West,
Where now they are laying our noble dead
 In his peaceful, final rest.
I think of the Nation bowed in grief,
 A million hearts as one,

A whole world shuddering at the thought
    Of this basest deed e'er done ;
Of our country, washed on every shore
    By a whelming wave of woe,
Baptized in sorrow, for what wise end
    No one but God may know.
And I pray that the Nation may be led,
    Through this way so dark and cold,
By "pillar of fire," or "pillar of cloud,"
    As was Israel of old.

Then suddenly the preacher's words
    Call back my wandering heart :
" Though dead, he speaketh yet," he saith,
    " And bids us act our part ;
His life so true and strong and brave,
    So full of godly trust,
So earnest in the cause of truth,
    So free from earthly rust,
Shall shine forever on our land,
    A glowing, guiding light,
To lead us on to nobler deeds,
    And bolder blows for right."

To God, who knows our every need,
    In silence, let us pray,
Unmurmuring while we tearful ask
    For strength to bear this day.

                                SARA A. PALMER.
Stonington, Sept. 26, 1881.

MRS. M. J. PITKIN,

OF STOCKBRIDGE, MASS.

Mrs. M. J. Pitkin, daughter of Paul S. and Hannah E. Palmer,
was a native of Stockbridge.   When nine years of age, her parents placed her under the watchful care and love of her uncle
and aunt, Mr. and Mrs. Henry Smith, of Stonington, to attend
the school of the Misses Sheffield and Stanton.   After three
years in this school she entered the Williams Academy, in Stockbridge, under the instruction of the loved teacher and poet, E.
W. B. Canning.   A few years later, her parents put her in the
care of her uncle and aunt, Mr. and Mrs. Wm. Pitt Palmer, of New

York, and through their advice attended the well-known school of Mrs. Mulligan and Miss Roberts, for one year. She then returned to her home, where she remained until after her marriage to James F. Pitkin, of New York City (son of Capt. John Pitkin, of East Hartford, a descendant of Governor Pitkin, of Connecticut), where she resided for fifteen years, until after the death of her husband, when she returned to the old homestead (in Stockbridge) " 'mid Berkshire Hills," where she now resides with her mother and brother.

MRS. HENRY SMITH.

Mrs. Henry Smith, of Stonington, oldest of the eight children of Lemuel and Abigail Davis Palmer (all of whom were born at their homestead within one mile of Walter Palmer's, at Wequetequock); born in September, 1797; named for her mother, familiarly known and loved as " dear Aunt Abbie." Was married in 1825 to Henry Smith (son of Col. Joseph Smith), one of nature's noblemen, kind, genial and refined. Mrs. Smith is an active member of the Congregational Church, is " never weary in well-doing," and a valued member of society. Her home for fifty-seven years, corner of Church and Main streets, and where she now resides with her daughter and her husband, Mr. and Mrs. C. S. Hull, is noted, as it always has been, for its unbounded hospitality.

MRS. PAUL S. PALMER.

Mrs. Paul S. Palmer, fourth child, born December 6th, 1804, was named Hannah Ells Palmer for her aunt, Mrs. Samuel Palmer, daughter of the beloved clergyman, " Priest Ells," of Stonington. Was married on February 15th, 1824, to her cousin, Paul S. Palmer, formerly of Stonington. From there she went to her beautiful home in the Berkshire Hills (known as the Judge Bacon place, and bought of him by Roswell S. P.), and where she has lived fifty-seven years. The mother of nine children, three only are living—W. H. Palmer, the eldest son, lives near her; M. V. Palmer Pitkin, and the youngest son, William Pitt

Palmer, who inherits the homestead, live with her there, and rise up daily to " call her blessed." Is a member of the Protestant Episcopal Church, and dearly loved by all. " Her standing in society second to none."

MRS. HENRY RHODES.

Mrs. Henry Rhodes, fifth child of Matilda B. Palmer; born 1806; was married in 1829 to Henry Woodbridge Rhodes, a merchant of Stonington (son of Simeon Rhodes). He left merchandise, and with his wife and four children went to live in Trenton, N. Y., where four youngest were born.

The mother of eight children, her home was proverbially one of love—the centre of all refinement, and people of marque in that region gathered around them. Four of her children are living, and settled in beautiful homes near her, where she can enjoy their society.

She is a member of Congregational Church, and altogether lovely.

MRS. ALDIN PALMER.

Mrs. Aldin Palmer, sixth child of Henry D. Palmer; born 1809; was married in 1832 to Maj. Aldin Palmer, son of Thomas Palmer and brother of Dr. Eugene P., of Texas (of Re-Union fame). She was the happy mother of eight children (seven are living), and the pleasures of their home are well known by many who were attracted to the " house on the hill " by the welcome they were sure to receive, and which always made the place and the hour warm. She is a member of the First Congregational Church in S.; charitable to the last degree, and an ornament to the society in which she moves.

FANNY CHESEBORO'.

The subject of this sketch, Miss Fanny Cheseboro', is the eldest of twin daughters, who were natives of Westerly, R. I.

In early infancy she was adopted by relatives—Mr. and Mrs. Joseph Cheseboro', of Stonington, Ct., where the first years of her childhood were spent. Later, the family removed to the old homestead, a farm of green meadows and rocky pastures in the vicinage of Wequetequock, originally owned by Mr. Cheseboro's great-grandfather, Dr. Nathan Palmer, who was the first regular physician in the town of Stonington.

Miss Cheseboro' was graduated at the State Normal School, at New Britian, Ct. She taught for several years in the public schools of Connecticut, and contributed occasional articles to the New York *Independent* and other periodicals of the day.

In 1864, she went to Boston and devoted herself for a season to the study of art, under Theodore Rabuske, a Polish gentleman, who was eminent in his profession.

Several years later, Miss Cheseboro' became a regular contributor to a journal published in Buffalo.

A season of ill-health supervening, forced her pen to lie idle, but within the last two years she has recovered sufficiently to be able to resume her active labors as a teacher and a writer.

On the maternal side (her own mother was Fanny Bliven, *nee* States) Miss Cheseboro' is descended from several of the early settlers of Stonington—being seventh in descent from William Chesebrough, the first settler of the town, through his son Elisha, who married a granddaughter of George Denison and Anne Borodel.

Her grandfather's mother, Esther (daughter of James Noyes and his wife, Margaret [Woodburn] Noyes), was a lineal descendant of Rev. James Noyes, the first settled minister of the town of Stonington.

Her claims to Palmer descent come through her grandmother, Fanny (Chesebrough) States, whose mother was Phebe Palmer, a daughter of Capt. Andrew Palmer, by his first marriage.

Capt. Palmer owned the " Mill House," as it was called—a large, low house adjoining the mill at the head of Wequetequock Cove.

He married for his second wife a sister of Lemuel Palmer, Esq., of Stonington.

Capt. Palmer was lost at sea.

MARIA PALMER WOOD.

(BRIEF ANCESTRY AND BIOGRAPHY.)

• John Palmer and Martha Brown, the oldest ancestors that we can refer to, lived at New City, Rockland Co., N. Y., as early as 1750, and tradition says that he came from Minefords (City Island) or vicinity, and was of English ancestry. John Palmer, Jr., born near New City, married Sarah Hubbard, born at Hakiat, dates unknown. John Palmer 3d, born Sept. 13, 1769, married Hannah Onderdonk, and moved to Warwick, Orange Co., N. Y., in 1807. Their children were David, Uriel, Anna, Sarah Maria, Rebecca, Hannah and Elizabeth. Maria Palmer was born Aug. 8th, 1809, and was married to James B. Wood on Dec. 18th, 1836. He continues to live near Warwick, and was seventy-two years old August 8th, 1881 ; has three sons living—Andrew, farmer, living at home ; Enos S., Principal of Valatia Graded School, Columbia Co., N. Y. ; and Charles, a farmer, residing near the village of Warwick, County of Orange, N. Y.

JAMES B. WOOD, JR.

(BRIEF ANCESTRY AND BIOGRAPHY.)

The Wood family are of English origin. Israel Wood, only son of the Earl of Warwick, came to America in company with the Duke of York, in 1664, and settled in town of Brookhaven, L. I. Married, and had three sons. Israel, the eldest, married a lady by the name of Oldfield, in Kings County, and settled in Flatbush ; built the first house on Brooklyn Heights, and mill at Red Hook. Had four sons and one daughter. Moved to Warwick, Orange Co. ; purchased several large tracts of land— drowned lands, Wickham's pond, and a large one near Warwick ; Settled upon this, and gave the part he occupied to his son Daniel, who married a Miss Schofield ; had eight sons and one daughter. His third son, John Wood, married Mary Benedict ; lived near Warwick ; had two sons. The eldest, James B. Wood, Jr., born Feb. 6th, 1810 ; farmer by occupation. Married Maria Palmer, December 18th, 1836 ; has three sons—Andrew, Enos S. (teacher), and Charles. Lives near Warwick ; has held public stations, and is nearly 72 years old.

LOIS NOYES APPELMAN.

(BRIEF BIOGRAPHY.)

Mrs. Appelman is a native of Stonington, Ct. When very
young she married Capt. Wm. H. Appelman, of Mystic, going
with him to California, *via* Cape Horn, in a clipper ship, commanded by Capt. Gardner, of Middle Haddam, Ct. The
young wife made her first home in a zinc house, in Sacramento.
In that city her eldest son was born, and the family passed
through strange experiences of flood and fire.

Eventually they removed to Mendocino, in the northern part
of the State, and some years later returned to Mystic, where she
has ever since resided.

Her two younger children were born in Connecticut. Some
time in the year 1878, her husband sailed in the vessel *Charles
Shearer*, bound for the South Shetland Islands, in pursuit of seal.
Capt. Appelman was accompanied by his eldest son, William,
and his nephew, Frederick Appelman. The son himself had
commanded a vessel for some years previous to this voyage with
his father. Capt. Appelman stopped at some island where they
expected to secure seal, and leaving a portion of his crew with
supplies for a certain time, went on, intending to stop on his way
back for the men and the fruit of their toil. That was the last
that was ever known of the vessel *Charles Shearer* and its last
accompanying crew. The sailors who were left behind managed
to subsist until the opportunity occurred for their return in another vessel.

The owners appealed to the Government, praying that a vessel might be sent to search for the missing vessel, as it was believed that there was a possibility of her being detained by the
ice, near the dangerous ground so often sought by adventurous
sealers.

The answer was, in substance, that the United States had at
that time no vessel which was properly equipped to make the
effort with any hope of success. Four years have passed away
since the *Charles Shearer* sailed, and no whisper of her fate
has reached the waiting wives and mothers at home.

Mrs. Appelman derives her Palmer descent from her grandmother, Eunice (Palmer) Stanton, a daughter of James and Hannah Palmer, of Stonington.

She has been prominent in the temperance movement, and was one of the delegates at the late convention in Washington, D. C.   Her father, the late Andrew Palmer Stanton, of Stonington, was a lineal descendant of the famous Interpreter General of colonial times, Thomas Stanton.

AUTOGRAPHS.

Among the mementoes of the Re-Union, are the signatures written upon cards and given to the writer as the Palmers passed in at the gate.   The crowds that flocked through the entrance to the grounds became so numerous that this autograph feature was abandoned, and the list is of but a small proportion of the many that passed in.   It is somewhat interesting, as showing various family representatives at the gathering.

In addition to this autograph list the writer has over eighteen hundred other signatures, received during a period of twenty years' correspondence with members of the family, in "Palmer Autograph Album."

A

Allen Palmer, Castleton, Vt.

Alex. Palmer, Stonington, Ct.

Alfred Palmer, Genesee, Ct.

A. G. Palmer, Rev. LL. D., Stonington, Ct.

Abel F. Palmer, Westerly, R. I.

Fred. J. Allen, Auburn, N. Y.

Amos N. Palmer, Norwich, Ct.

A. B. Palmer, Malden, Ct.

Mrs. Geo. P. Ash, Stonington, Ct.

Arabella Palmer, Salina, Ct.

Arthur W. Palmer, New York City, N. Y.

Mr. and Mrs. Amos S. Palmer, Hopkinton, R. I.

Alanson Palmer, Astoria, N. Y.

Thos. W. Avery, N. Stonington, Ct.

Miss Alida E. Palmer, Canterbury, Ct.

Mrs. Geo. A. Avery, N. Stonington, Ct.

Addie Palmer, Potter Hill, R. I.

Mrs. E. B. Abbe, Westfield, Mass.

Mr. and Mrs. Geo. A. Adee, New York City, N. Y.

A. S. Palmer, Danielsonville, Ct.

Mrs. Ella M. Palmer, Danielsonville, Ct.

A. E. Palmer, Flatbush, L. I. N. Y.

Sarah H. Alexander, Norwich, Ct.

Anna Palmer Ludington, Fair Haven, Ct.

A. P. Avery, Providence, R. I.

Katie E. Anderson, Stonington, Ct.

Benj. F. Ash, Stonington, Ct.

Alice L. Palmer, Canterbury, Ct.

A. H. Palmer, Dr., Brooklyn, Pa.

A. S. Palmer, Iroquois, Ill.

MISCELLANEOUS A (NO ADDRESS).—Mrs. Alden Palmer, Adaline and Geo. W. Smith, Alonzo A. Smith, A. D. Palmer, Louis N. Appelman, Abel Palmer, Allen S. Palmer, Arthur W. Palmer, Miss Katie Ash, Jonathan Allen, Miss Helen M. Awe, Nellie Adell, Elizabeth Avery, E. D. Avery, Mr. and Mrs. S. W. Ashley, Geo. W. Ashley, A. Palmer, Mrs. A. H. Palmer.

B

Byron R. Palmer, Fayetteville, N. Y.

William Palmer, Norwich, Ct.

Jas. B. Bales, Preston, Ct.

Lena Brown, Noank, Ct.

J. F. Billings, Morgantown, Kan.

Geo. Biglow, New Haven, Ct.

Margaret Brown, N. Stonington, Ct.

Nellie Brown, Noank, Ct.

Miss H. P. Babcock, Westerly, R. I.

Edith V. Babcock, Westerly, R. I.

Adelaide H. Brayton, Stonington, Ct.

Frances A. Brayton, Stonington, Ct.

Mrs. C. O. Bent, S. Gardiner, Mass.

V. R. Ball, Noank, Ct.

Dr. Chas. E. Brayton, Stonington, Ct.

Mr. and Mrs. John Burdick, Franklyn, Ct.

Mrs. Cornelia Palmer Bissell, N. Manchester, Ct.

Mrs. G. Brown, Noank, Ct.

Mr. and Mrs. B. H. Palmer, Greenville, Ct.

J. S. Bull, New York City, N. Y.

Herman Brown, N. Stonington, Ct.

Gilbert Billings, N. Stonington, Ct.

Betsey A. Palmer, Westerly, R. I.

Ellen Brown, N. Stonington, Ct.

Mrs. David Brown, Noank, Ct.

Sidney Bradford, London, Eng.

Atwood R. Brayton, Stonington, Ct.

A. G. Billings, Griswold, Ct.

Lottie P. Babcock, Westerly, R. I.

Geo. E. Brayton, Stonington, Ct.

Chas. S. Brown, N. Stonington, Ct.

H. Eugene Bolles, Boston, Mass.

Amanda Ball, Noank, Ct.

Maria S. Bromley, Rockland, Ct.

Lydia W. Brown, Mystic Bridge, Ct.

John D. Brown and family, Stonington, Ct.

Nelson A. Brown and family, N. Stonington, Ct.

J. E. Bush, New London, Ct.

Nellie Burdick, Potter Hill, R. I.

Calipha Brown, N. Stonington, Ct.

Mary L. Barber, Exeter, R. I.

W. O. Berjamin, New London, Ct.

Sarah P. Burdick, Ashaway, R. I.

H. E. Burdick, Ashaway, R. I.

Cornelia Brown, Jewett City, Ct.

Arthur Boardman, Lancaster, Pa.

Walter Boardman, Lancaster, Pa.

Wm. Brown, Noank, Ct.

Fred. Brown, Providence, R.I.

Wm. W. Butler, Saybrook, Ct.

Sarah T. Bell, Norwich, Ct.

Edwin J. Bates, Norwich, Ct.

Robert P. Bissell, N. Manchester, Ct.

Warden H. Benjamin, Westerly, R. I.

M. L. Browning, Uncasville, Ct.

Mrs. Abbie L. Bates, N. Stonington, Ct.

Mrs. and Mr. Geo. Burdick, Morgan, Ct

Mary E. Benjamin, New London, Ct.

Imogene Bales, Noank, Ct.

MISCELLANEOUS B (NO ADDRESS).—F. P. Babcock, Lizzie A. Babcock, N. P. Brown, Edith V. Babcock, B. Palmer and wife, Chas. Benjamin, Ollie Babcock, Harry H. Babcock, Mary Benjamin, Sarah A. Brayton, Mrs. William Bolles, Mr. and Mrs. C. W. Burdick, Mrs. E. E. Babcock, Georgia Birthiar, E. Benjamin, A. S. Burdick, Michael Burke, Cynthia B. Benjamin, Wm. C. Benjamin, Burrows S. Palmer, C. A. Babcock, Nellie G. Belliard, F. Belliard and wife, Mrs. S. M. Brayton, Carrie E. Bothune, Ammie L. Babcock, Ed. J. Brown, F. R. Brown, Smith Burrows, Mrs. M. D. Brown, Mrs. C. H. Babcock, Mrs. H. H. Brown, Lillie Brayton, B. G. Palmer, R. S. Bromley, Barkley Palmer, Jedediah Brown, Mrs. Smith Browning.

C

Charlotte M. Palmer, New York City, N. Y.

D. P. Chesebrough, Stonington, Ct.-

R. Emma Chesebrough, Philadelphia, Pa.

Mrs. E. A. P. Carpenter, Florida, N. Y.

Sarah B. Cook, Preston City, Ct.

Charles Palmer, Gloversville, N. Y.

John F. Chesebrough, Stonington, Ct.

Elias J. Palmer, S. Norwalk, Ct.

C. S. Palmer, Winstead, Ct.

Fannie D. Cranston, Norwich, Ct.

Chas. E. Caulkins, Preston, Ct.

Chas. Palmer, Newark, N. J.

L. Chesebrough and wife, Willimantic, Ct.

Mrs. Dyer L. Chesebrough, Norwich, Ct.

C. H. Palmer, Norwich, Ct.

Chas. L Palmer, W e b s t e r, Mass.

Chas. E. Chase, Mystic Bridge, Ct.

C. R. Palmer, Brooklyn, Pa.

Dr. Corydon, Palmer, Warren, Ohio.

C. A. Palmer, Rockville, R.I.

Dr. C. Palmer, Providence, R. I.

Mrs. Walter Chesebro', Noank, Ct.

Fanny Cheseboro, Stonington, Ct.

C. B. A. Palmer, Vernon, Vt.

Clark C. Palmer, Jewett City, Ct.

J. N. Crandall, St. Louis, Mo.

F. Chesebrough, Philadelphia, Pa.

Chas. L. Palmer, Albany, N.Y.

Chas. P. Palmer, Niantic R. I.

Chauncey W. Palmer, Greenville, Ohio.

Caleb W. Palmer, Troy, N.Y.

Mrs. Engene Chesebrough, Philadelphia, Pa.

Chas. W. Palmer, Norwich, Ct.

Nellie F. Cornell, Rochester, N. Y.

Clara H. Chase, Stonington, Ct.

E. B. Cox, Troy, N.Y.

C. S. Palmer, Norwich, Ct.

Adrin Cook, Norwich, Ct.

E. G. Cook, Norwich, Ct.

Ed. E. Chesebrough, Philadelphia, Pa.

Mrs. Clara R. Palmer, Noank, Ct.

Rev. A. S. Chesebrough, Durham, Ct.

C. B. Palmer, Sing Sing, N. Y.

C. J. Cook, Preston City, Ct.

Rebecca Comstock, Newport, R. I.

Calvin B. Palmer, Voluntown, Ct.

Jane E. Crandall, Stonington, Ct.

Arthur H. Chapan, Pendleton Hill, Ct.

Chas. W. Palmer, New Haven, Ct.

C. H. Palmer, Tarrytown, N. Y.

B. F. Chapman, Oneida, N. Y.

Chas. H. Palmer, Westerly, R. I.

C. R. Palmer, Brooklyn, Pa.

MISCELLANEOUS C (NO ADDRESS).—Mrs. J. P. Collins, Mrs. Geo. A. Chase, Lorenzo Crouch, Joseph G. Chesebro', Jessie Palmer Clayton, Edwin C. Chesebrough, Helena Chase, Gussie Chase, M. Carrington, Miss S. S. Cluster, Ellie C. Carrington, Mrs. Alfred Clark, Mrs. Austin, Mrs. Palmer, Joel S. Crouch, C. D. Palmer, Sarah J. Chaffee, Mrs. A. H. Chapman, Mary Agnes Crandall, Thos. Clark and son, Arthur D. Chase, P. H. L. Chesebrough, Mrs. Wm. F. Clark, Mr. and Mrs. Chas. B. Palmer and daughter, Lillie W. Carrington, Ada L. Crandall.

D

Chas. M. Davis, Stonington, Ct.

Hattie Davis, Boston, Mass,

Mrs. Chas. Davis, Boston, Mass.

W. J. Dickinson, Norwich, Ct.

A. P. Davis, Jewett City, Ct.

Mrs. M. L. P. Downing, Providence, R. I.

G. M. Downing, Providence, R. I.

Chas. Davison, Norwich, Ct.

David P. Palmer, New Haven, Ct.

Sarah A. Davison, Mystic Bridge, Ct.

Dwight Palmer, Stonington, Ill.

Darrance Palmer, Stonington, Ct.

Dr. Deloss Palmer and wife, New York City, N. Y.

Mrs. J. A. Douglass, Niantic, R. I.

Rev. F. Denison, Providence, R. I.

W. C. Dewey, Palmer, Mass.

Mrs. E. A. P. Davis, Jewett City, Ct.

Ella Douglass, Niantic, R. I.

L. P. DeLand, N. Brookfield, Mass.

MISCELLANEOUS D (NO ADDRESS).—David Palmer, Walter H. Davis, Nellie Davis, Thos. Davis, A. B. Davis, Denison Palmer, A. M. Davis, Rev. A. Darrow, Chas. H. J. Douglass, Nathan N. Denison, S. H. Dewey, Dwight A. Palmer, Fred. A. Davis, Y. M. Dickson.

E

Ellen J. Palmer, Branford, Ct.

Mrs. Emily J. Palmer, Jewett City, Ct.

Elmer E. Palmer, Gilbertsville, N. Y.

Mrs. Elizabeth Easton, Boston, Mass.

Eugene A. Palmer, Belmont, N. Y.

Ella E. Palmer, Rockville, R. I.

Emily E. Palmer, Potter Hill, R. I.

Dr. E. Palmer, Houston, Tex.

Fidelia Palmer Eaton, Fayetteville, N. Y.

Mary E. Easton, Boston, Mass.

Edwin E. Palmer, Mystic, Ct.

Rev. Elliott Palmer, Portland, Ct.

Edwin Palmer, Norwich, Ct.

Mrs. E. H. Palmer, Montville, Ct.

E. A. Palmer, Montville, Ct.

E. P. Palmer Turner, Norwich, Ct.

S. L. Edwards, Westerly, R. I.

Rev. E. B. Palmer and wife, Boston, Mass.

S. J. Edwards, Westerly, R. I.

Hattie Palmer Edwards, Westerly, R. I.

Emma H. Palmer, Richmond, Va.

Rev. E. B. Palmer, Bridgeton, N. J.

Emma E. Palmer, Winsted, Ct.

Emma C. Palmer, New London, Ct.

Prof. Daniel C. Eaton, New Haven, Ct.

Eugene J. Palmer, Rockville, R. I.

Etta Palmer, Potter Hill, Ct.

MISCELLANEOUS E (NO ADDRESS).—Emma Palmer, Robert Eldred, Eunice Palmer, Eugene Palmer, E. Palmer, E. L. Palmer, Mrs. Eunice Ward Palmer.

F

Miss Frank E. Palmer, Canterbury, Ct.

Fletcher Rateneur, Thetford, Vt.

Flora Palmer, Niantic, R. I.

Frank A. Palmer, Westerly, R. I.

Frank H. Palmer, Brooklyn, N. Y.

Maria L. Faxon, Stonington, Ct.

James D. Fish, New York City, N. Y.

Samuel Fletcher, Thetford, Vt.

Miss Fannie Palmer, Branford, Ct.

Miss Fannie Palmer, New York City, N. Y.

James B. Fowler, New York City, N. Y.

Frank A. Palmer, Newark, N. J.

Mr. and Mrs. Thos. C. Forsythe, Mystic, Ct.

Friend Palmer, Detroit, Mich.

MISCELLANEOUS F (NO ADDRESS).—Frances M. Palmer, L. D. Fairbrother, Mrs. F. C. Palmer, Frank L. Palmer, Frank Palmer, Juliet S. Fenney, F. N. Palmer.

H

Henry S. Palmer, Rockville, Ct.

Ray G. Haling, Fitchburgh, Me.

R. R. Hoes, New Rochelle, N. Y.

Bessie Hancox, Stonington, Ct.

Geo. L. Hunt, Hoboken, N. J.

John Hood, Stonington, Ct.

Edward Havens, Providence, R. I.

Mrs. L. T. Hakes, Norwich, Ct.

Mrs. E. S. Henry, Rockville, Ct.

John Hutchins, Fayetteville N. Y.

Geo. E. Hanron, New London, Ct.

P. Hopkins, Noose Neck Hill, R. I.

Mrs. C. F. Hull, Providence, R. I.

N. W. Howell, Jr., Brooklyn, N. Y.

W. H. Hobart, Stonington, Ct.

Mrs. Bertrand Healy, N. Hartford, Ct.

Mary E. Hill, Norwich, Ct.

Lewis E. Hill, Norwich, Ct.

Fred. L. Hill, Norwich, Ct.

C. E. Hammond, Stonington, Ct.

John Hammond, Stonington, Ct.

Fred. F. Huntley, Lynn, Ct.

Martha E. Huntley, Lynn, Ct.

Mary T. Howard, Norwich, Ct.

C. F. Howard, Norwich, Ct.

Mrs. Thos. H. Hinckley, Stonington, Ct.

Miss H. Hinckley, Stonington, Ct.

C. H. Hinckes, Stonington, Ct.

C. W. Hinckes, Stonington, Ct.

Annie E. Hoey, Brooklyn, N. Y.

Jas. B. Hoey, Brooklyn, N. Y.

L. W. Hayes, Stonington, Ct.

C. A. Hewett, Stonington, Ct.

Chas. E. Hewett, N. Stonington, Ct.

Mrs. Denison Hewett, N. Stonington, Ct.

Annie M. Hewett, Norwich, Ct.

Mrs. and Mr. E. A. Hewett, Norwich, Ct.

Kate A. N. Hewett, Stonington, Ct,

Fannie D. Hewett, Stonington, Ct.

Geo. Hewett, Unionville, Ct.

Maggie H. Hewett, N. Stonington, Ct.

Dudley R. Hewett, Stonington, Ct.

Jennie M. Hewett, N. Stonington, Ct.

Amos G. Hewett, N. Stonington, Ct.

Denison Hewett, N. Stonington, Ct.

Hattie R. Palmer, Westerly, R. I.

Horace Palmer, Westerly, R. I.

Henry Clay Palmer, Greenville, Ct.

Hannah Palmer, Plainfield, Ct.

H. J. Palmer, Norwich, Ct.

H. G. Palmer, Stonington, Ct.

H. Clay Palmer, Stonington, Ct.

Harriet E. Palmer, Westerly, R. I.

Mr. and Mrs. Henry Palmer, Greenville, Ct.

H. F. Palmer, Norwich, Ct.

H. W. Palmer, New York City, N. Y.

H. H. Palmer, Rockford, Ill.

Henry L. Palmer, Brooklyn, N. Y.

Henry R. Palmer, Stonington, Ct.

H. W. Palmer, N. Danville, Vt.

Henrietta Palmer, Potter Hill, R. I.

Helen Palmer, Amherst, Mass.

Henry C. Palmer, Potter Hill, R. I.

Henry C. H. Palmer, Sing Sing, N. Y.

Mr. and Mrs. Henry C. Palmer, Fair Haven, Ct.

H. C. Palmer, Mystic, Ct.

Mrs. H. J. Palmer, Nowich, Ct.

Hannah Palmer, Mystic, Ct.

Miss Hannah Palmer, Mystic, Ct.

Howard S. Palmer, Mystic, Ct.

MISCELLANEOUS H (NO ADDRESS).—John P. Hoxie, Mrs. J. H. Hunter, Miss Maria Hautor, A. C. Hand, Frank Hawkins, Miss Fanny Haley, Chas. E. Holmes, Mrs. J. Holmes, Mrs. John Hill, C. O. B. Hammond, Louisa A. Hewett, Alden Hewett, Richard B. Hewitt, Mary E. Hewitt, Mrs. Lucy A. Hewitt, Mr. and Mrs. G. L. Hewitt, E. Hewitt and family, Mrs. H. M. Palmer, H. T. Palmer, Henry Palmer.

I

Ida Palmer, Norwich, Ct.

MISCELLANEOUS I (NO ADDRESS).—Isabella Palmer, Mrs. Ira Palmer, Ida H. Palmer, Irving H. Palmer.

J

J. B. Palmer, N. Stonington, Ct.

John S. Palmer, Stonington, Ct.

John M. Palmer, Rockville, R. I.

James B. Palmer, Canterbury, Ct.

James M. Palmer, Cambridge, Mass.

J. Cathburt Palmer, Brooklyn, E. D., N. Y.

John H. Palmer, Brooklyn, E. D., N. Y.

Julia W. Palmer, Pendleton Hill, Ct.

J. L. Palmer, Little Rock, Ark.

John Palmer, Norwich, Ct.

Joseph Palmer, Potter Hill, R. I.

Josiah Palmer, Rockville, R. I.

Mrs. Josiah Palmer, Rockville, R. I.

Mrs. J. J. Palmer, Norwich, Ct.

Jay Palmer, East New York, N. Y.

Josiah Palmer, Brooklyn, N. Y.

J. D. Palmer, Jersey City, N. J.

Mrs. John B. Palmer, Providence, R. I.

Mrs. James Palmer, Jewett City, Ct.

Mrs. John M. Palmer, Rockville, N. J.

Joseph R. Palmer, New Jersey, N. J.

J. Albert Palmer, N. Cranford, Ct.

Justus Palmer, Brooklyn, N. Y.

J. S. Palmer, Providence, R. I.

J. J. Palmer, Norwich, Ct.

J. P. Palmer, Boston, Mass.

Julius Palmer, Providence, R. I.

Mrs. J. M. Langsworth, Mystic, Ct.

MISCELLANEOUS J (NO ADDRESS).—Mrs. J. C. Palmer, Jennie Palmer, Col. Jeremiah Palmer, Dr. Jas. L. Palmer, Joseph C. Palmer, John J. Palmer.

L

Lucy G. Palmer, Plainfield, Ct.

Libbie Palmer, Niantic, R. I.

Lucian W. Palmer, Providence, R. I.

L. M. Palmer, Spencerport, N. Y.

Louis N. B. Palmer, Norwich, Ct.

Dr. L. A. Palmer, Westerly, R. I.

Mrs. Dr. L. A. Palmer, Westerly, R. I.

L. H. Palmer, Gloversville, N. Y.

L. N. Palmer, Brooklyn, N. Y.

Lewis A. Palmer, Boston, Mass.

Lizzie Palmer, Hopkinton, R .I.

Lizzie Palmer, Potter Hill, R. I.

Lucy W. Palmer, Stonington, Ct.

Louisa S. Palmer, Norwich, Ct.

Lavinia S. Palmer, New London, Ct.

L. A. Palmer, New York, N. Y.

Mrs. Wm. A. Lewis, New York, N. Y.

Mrs. Wm. H. Larkham, Canterbury, Ct.

Mrs. Carrie E. Larkham, Canterbury, Ct.
W. H. Larkham, Canterbury, Ct.
Mrs. B. F. Latham, Noank, Ct.
B. F. Latham, Noank, Ct.
Russell Lewis, Norwich, Ct.
A. N. Lewis, Westerly, R. I.

Rev. R. M. Luther, Philadelphia, Pa.
Lucy C. Palmer, A m h e r s t, Mass.
Mr. and Mrs. E. A. Lyons, Jewett City, Ct.
Lorin Palmer, B r o o k l y n, N. Y.

MISCELLANEOUS L (NO ADDRESS).—Lizzie M. Palmer, F. B. Loomis, Mr. and Mrs. Robert Lewis, Jas. M. Lee, Mary Palmer Lee, R. F. Loper, Jr., Dr. B. K. Land, Elizabeth Palmer Loper, F. Loper, Jr., Alex. Palmer Loper, Cornelia J. Lee, Mrs. Russell Lewis, Lucy A. Palmer, Mrs. L. W. Palmer, Effie L. Lamb, E. Lamb, Lizzie Lamb and family, M. P. Lewis, E. A. Landphere, Lucy A. Landphere, Francis Landphere.

M

Col. J. H. Meredith and wife, New York City, N. Y.
Isabella Grant Meredith, New York City, N. Y.
Rev. H. H. Mead (no address).

N

Noyes Grant Palmer, E a s t New York, N. Y.
Dr. N. Palmer, New York City, N. Y.
Nehemiah Palmer, Unionville, Ct.
Nellie Palmer, Canterbury, Ct.
N. B. Palmer, Woodville, R. I.
N. G. Palmer, Lebanon, Ct.
Nelson Palmer, Spencerport, N. Y.

Nellie M. Palmer, Mystic, Ct.
Nettie H. Palmer, Hopkinton City, R. I.
Chas. S. Noyes, Stonington, Ct.
Mrs. S. Noyes, Stonington, Ct.
Harriet E. Noyes, M y s t i c Bridge, Ct.
Dr. Jas. F. Noyes, Detroit, Mich.
Jas. Newcomb, New London, Ct.

MISCELLANEOUS N (NO ADDRESS).—Mr. and Mrs. Nathan Palmer, Nellie Palmer, Noyes S. Palmer.

O

O. Palmer, Stamford, Ct.

Mrs. Oscar Palmer and son (no address).

P

Mr. and Mrs. C. D. Prescott, Rome, N. Y.

J. F. Pomeroy, Newark, N. J.

Asa Perkins, Groton, Ct.

Dr. Thos. Wells Perry, Providence, R. I.

Mrs. Phebe Palmer, Pendleton Hill, Ct.

Peter A. Palmer, Lansingburgh, N. Y.

Peter P. Palmer, R. I.

Miss Phebe Palmer, Pendleton Hill, Ct.

P. G. Palmer, Niantic, R. I.

Harry Palmer Powers, Pittsford, Vt.

MISCELLANEOUS P (NO ADDRESS).—S. L. Pelletts, Miss A. P. Pelletts, Mrs. Stephen C. Parker, James Parker, L. H. Potter, L. S. Prosser, Bessie Perry.

R

Robert L. Palmer, Bridgeport, Ct.

Robert Palmer, Jr., and wife, Noank, Ct.

R. T. Palmer, New London, Ct.

Robbie Palmer, Niantic, R. I.

T. B. Robinson, Fayetteville, N. Y.

Sophie P. Robinson, Fayetteville, N. Y.

Mr. and Mrs. Ray, Scotland, Ct.

L. Reafield, New York City, N. Y.

A. J. Rice, Norwich, Ct.

Ella J. Rice, Norwich, Ct.

Mr. and Mrs. D. T. Richards, Preston, Ct.

Sabina L. Rockwell, Groton, Ct.

Robert S. Renz, Bridgeport, Ct.

Robert J. Palmer, Norwich, Ct.

Henry S. Richmond, Brooklyn, Ct.

E. P. Randall, Bridgeport, Ct.

MISCELLANEOUS R (NO ADDRESS).—C. D. Rice, R. Heber Palmer, Dr. Jas. M. Rose, B. A. Palmer Rose, Robert Palmer, R. B. Palmer, R. P. Palmer, David F. Roach, Mary Palmer Rogers, Lizzie C. Rice, Winset Rogers, Mrs. D. T. Richards, Mrs. O. P. Ricker.

S

S. L. Palmer, Levena, Ill.

Stephen Palmer, Pleasantville, N. Y.

Simeon Palmer, Boston, Mass.

Stephen Palmer, Manchester, N. Y.

S. E. Palmer, Potter Hill, R. I.

Sabra DeBell Palmer, Amherst, Mass.

Samuel F. Palmer, Plainfield, Ct.

Simeon Palmer, Stonington, Ct.

Sarah A. Palmer, Stonington, Ct.

Susan Palmer, Hopkinston City, R. I.

S. Palmer, Rockford, Ill.

Sarah H. Palmer, Jewett City, Ct.

Samuel K. Stedman, Westerly, R. I.

Hattie M. Stedman, Westerly, R. I.

Cornelia E. Sesson, Binghampton, N. Y.

Lucy Swinburne, Newport, R. I.

Alice H. Spicer, Noank, Ct.

Mrs. S. A. Saunders, Greenville, Ct.

Gracie Spencer, Mystic Bridge, Ct.

Mrs. H. P. Spencer, · Mystic Bridge, Ct.

Miss Lena W. Stetson, Greenwich, Ct.

Dr. Geo. D. Stanton, Stonington, Ct.

Mrs. A. P. Stanton, Stonington, Ct.

Wm. C. Stanton, Westerly, R. I.

Edna G. Stetson, Greenville, Ct.

Mrs. H. W. Stetson, Greenville, Ct.

Mrs. Hannah Smith, Stonington, Ct.

Joseph E. Smith, Stonington, Ct.

B. A. Smith, Jewett City, Ct.

Mary Smith, Stonington, Ct.

Charlotte A. Smith, Stonington, Ct.

Mrs. D. H. Smith, Stonington, Ct.

Mrs. Geo. Sherman, Norwichtown, Ct.

Peleg A. Sherman, Providence, R. I.

Mary Dana Shindler, Texas.

MISCELLANEOUS S (NO ADDRESS).—Miss Mary Stanton, Miss Jennie Slack, Mrs. F. Stanton, Mrs. Chas. T. Stanton, Grace Stanton, Henry L. Stanton, T. J. Sawyer, Louisa C. Sawyer, Mrs. T. J. Sawyer, Anna Sawyer, Henlen F. Sawyer, Mrs. Statts, D. W. Stevens, Mrs. Levi Spicer, Silas Spicer, Miss Spicer, A. L. Story, Mrs. A. L. Story, James Palmer Story, Welcome A. Smith, Mary A. Smith, Joseph Smith, James Smith, Sarah Palmer, Sarah E. Palmer, Mrs. Samuel Palmer, Susie A. Palmer.

T

Mr. and Mrs. W. E. Turner, Brooklyn, N. Y.

Lida Palmer Turner, Norwich, Ct.

M. C. Palmer, Norwich, Ct.

William Turner, New York City, N. Y.

Mrs. John Turner, Norwich, Ct.

Mrs. H. Tuttle, E. Marion, L. I.

Lila Thompson, N. Stonington, Ct.

Samuel Thompson, N. Stonington, Ct.

Nellie Thompson, N. Stonington, Ct.

Fannie Thompson, N. Stonington, Ct.

Theodore Palmer, Falls Village, Ct.

Mrs. Geo. E. Tripp, E. Mystic Bridge, Ct.

Geo. Tuttle, E. Marion, L. I.

J. A. Thurber, Syracuse, N. Y.

Mrs. E. C. Palmer Thurber, Syracuse, N. Y.

Theodore J. Palmer, Hackensack, N. J.

H. Clay Trumbull, Philadelphia, Pa.

J. Hammond Trumbull, Hartford, Ct.

M. B. Trumbull, Stonington, Ct.

Mrs. H. Clay Trumbull, Philadelphia, Pa.

Isaac Tourtelots, Norwich, Ct.

MISCELLANEOUS T (NO ADDRESS).—Geo. A. Thompson, T. R. Palmer, J. R. Taylor, John Taylor, Lucy A. Tabor, Mrs. Towne.

V

Vashti H. Palmer, Boston, Mass.

Mrs. J. A. P. Van Velsor, Greenpoint, N. Y.

Miss J. A. P. Van Velsor, Greenpoint, N. Y.

E. W. Vars.

W

Wm. A. Wadsworth, Unionville, Ct.

Wm. D. Palmer, New York City, N. Y.

Walter Palmer, Philadelphia, Pa.

Wm. F. Palmer, E. Haddam, Ct.

Wm. C. Palmer, Stamford, Ct.

Walter L. Palmer, Plainfield, Ct.

Wm. H. Palmer, Brooklyn, N. Y.

Wm. R. Palmer, New York City, N. Y.

Wm. R. Palmer, Boston, Mass.

Mrs. R. Palmer, Boston, Mass.

Mr. and Mrs. Wm. P. Palmer, Colchester, Ct.

Mrs. Wm. H. Palmer, Stonington, Ct.

Wm. L. Palmer, New York City, N. Y.

Wm. Wells, Westerly, R. I.

E. H. Wells, Woodstock, Ct.

Robert T. Walker, Rome, N.Y.

Rev. W. C. Walker, Andover, Ct.

Walter Palmer, Hoboken, N. J.

Miss Margaret Walker, New York City, N. Y.

Miss Jessie Walker, Rome, N. Y.

Julia A. Weaver, New London, Ct.

Frank A. Weaver, New London, Ct.

Stephen S. Wray, New York City, N. Y.

Mrs. B. F. William, Mystic Bridge, Ct.

D. P. William, Manchester, Ct.

S. M. William, Groton, Ct.

Mrs. Allen M. Wheeler, N. Stonington, Ct.

Allen U. Palmer, Stonington, Ct.

Mrs. Ephraim Wheeler, N. Stonington, Ct.

Mrs. Alice S. Wheeler, Boston, Mass.

Richard A. Wheeler, Stonington, Ct.

Mrs. Richard A. Wheeler, Stonington, Ct.

Delia A. Wheeler, Stonington, Ct.

Mr. and Mrs. Ezra Wheeler, Stonington, Ct.

Hattie A. Wheeler, Stonington, Ct.

Benj. P. Wheeler, Stonington, Ct.

L. W. Wessells, Litchfield, Ct.

Mrs. W. Wessells, Litchfield, Ct.

Jennie A. Wolf, Mystic Bridge, Ct.

Miss M. A. Whiteley, Norwich, Ct.

Wm. H. Palmer, Genesee, N. Y.

Rev. Wm. L. Palmer, Manchester, Mich.

MISCELLANEOUS W (NO ADDRESS).—Mrs. Williams, Willie H. Williams, Mrs. John A. Williams, Mrs. C. P. Williams, John P. Williams, Mrs. M. P. Williams, J. H. Wilcox and wife, Lucy Palmer Wheeler, Emily Wheeler, Robt. Wheeler, W. W. Palmer, Mrs. C. B. Wilcox, W. A. Wadsworth, Eva Whitler, M. A. Wells, A. J. Wiley, E. A. Palmer Wadsworth, Grace Wheeler, Mrs. Henry Ward, H. B. Ward, S. L. Ward, Edward D. Ward, W. L. Palmer, W. E. Palmer, W. H. Palmer and wife, Walter Palmer, W. M. Palmer, W. W. Palmer, Wm. L. Palmer, Walter Palmer, Jr.

Y and Z

Sallie P. York.

Clayton Palmer Zerk.

Mrs. Lydia Zerk.

Wm. C. Zerk.

REGISTER LIST

AT THE PALMER HEADQUARTERS.

Perhaps the most interesting feature, to a disinterested person, was the collection of Palmers about the register in Brayton Hall (the use of which apartment was kindly tendered the Re-Unionists by Dr. Brayton). Here people from all parts of the Union gathered in squads in the pursuit of familiar names and in search of old-time acquaintances. Brayton Hall was the scene of many a happy meeting on both days.

C. B. Palmer, Sing Sing, N. Y.; W. H. Palmer, Brooklyn, N. Y.; Robert L. Palmer, Sing Sing, N. Y.; C. H. Palmer, Tarrytown, N. Y.; Geo. E. Palmer, Tarrytown, N. Y.; Mrs. Mary Dana Shindler, Nacogdoches, Tex.; Mrs John S. Bull, New York; Stephen Wray, New York; L. H. Palmer, Gloversville, N. Y.; Charles Palmer, Gloversville, N. Y.; Guy C. Palmer, New Hartford, N. Y.; Geo. W. Palmer, N. Bridgewater, N. Y.; T. B. Palmer, Butternuts, N. Y.; Dr. N. Palmer, Butternuts, N. Y.; Orrin Palmer, Stamford, Ct.; David P. Palmer, New Haven, Ct.; Chas. J. Palmer, S. Norwalk, Ct.; Halsey S. Palmer, Gilbertsville, Ct.; Elaner Palmer, Gilbertsville, Ct.; James G. Palmer, New Brunswick, N. J.; Clara M. Palmer, New Brunswick, N. J.; Gen. Geo. W. Palmer, New York, N. Y.; Mrs. Sarah E. Palmer, New York, N. Y.; Col. and Mrs. T. J. Meredith, New York, N. Y.; Wm. Chauncey Palmer, Stamford, Ct.; Joseph Palmer, Potter Hill, R. I.; Henrietta Palmer, Potter Hill, R. I.; Samuel E. Palmer, Potter Hill, R. I.; Addie Palmer, Potter Hill. R. I.; Etta Palmer, Potter Hill, R. I.; George C. Palmer, Potter Hill, R. I.; Henry C. Palmer, Potter Hill, R. I.; Emily E. Palmer, Potter Hill, R. I.; Lizzie A. Palmer, Potter Hill, R. I.; Daniel M. Palmer, Potter Hill, R. I.; Nellie J. Burdick, Potter Hill, R. I.; Robert Walker, Rome, N. Y.; Jessie Walker, Fairfield, N. Y.; Charlotte Walker, New York, N. Y.; Margaret Walker, New York, N. Y.; Wm. H. Palmer, New Haven, Ct.; George M. Palmer, Elyria, O.; Geo. L. Palmer and wife, Potter Hill, R. I.; Lydia S. Palmer, Potter Hill, R. I.; John Palmer, Warwick, R. I.; Mrs. C. A. Palmer Bissell, N. Manchester, Ct.; Robt. Palmer Bissell, N. Manchester, Ct.; Mrs. C. A. Palmer Carpenter, Florida, N. Y.; Mrs. C. L. Palmer Smith, Potter Hill, R. I.; Miss Sadie F. Carpenter, Florida, N. Y.; Mrs. J. A. Palmer Van Valsor, Brooklyn, N. Y.; Miss Van Valsor, Brooklyn, N. Y.; Arthur W. Palmer, New York, N. Y.; Mrs. J. A. Clayton, Brooklyn, N. Y.; Willie F. Cornell, Rochester, N. Y.; Nellie F. Bullard, North Hamlin, N. Y.; J. S. Palmer, Providence, R. I.; Julius Palmer, Providence, R. I.; B. R. Palmer, Fayetteville, N. Y.; Mrs. Franklin Eaton, Fayetteville, N. Y.; Mrs. Sophie Robinson, Fayetteville, N. Y.; T. B. Robinson, Fayetteville, N. Y.; J. N. Hutchins, Fayetteville, N. Y.; Jas. N. Hutchins, Fayetteville, N. Y.; Lauren Redfield, New York, N. Y.; Ray Greene Huling, Fitchburg, Mass.; Geo. W. Palmer, New York, N. Y.; Rev. Dr. N. W. Miner, Trenton, N. J.; Mrs. Dr. N. W. Miner, Trenton, N. J.; Miss Kate E. Miner, Trenton, N. J.; Dr. L. M. Palmer, R. I. Hospital, Providence, R. I.; Edward Havens, Providence, R. I.; Caleb W. Palmer, Troy, N. Y.; Alanson Palmer, Astoria, N. Y.; E. R. Palmer, New Brunswick, N. J.; Wilbur M. Palmer, Flatbush, L. I.; Dr. J. B. Noyes, Detroit, Mich.; A. E. Palmer, *Tribune*, Flatbush, L. I.; P. A. Sherman, Providence, R. I.; S. K. Stedman, Westerly, R. I.; Lorin Palmer, *Brooklyn Argus*, Brooklyn, N. Y.; Mary Palmer, Brooklyn, N. Y.; Sophia Palmer, Brooklyn, N. Y.; Henry Palmer, Brooklyn, N. Y.; Chas. H. Palmer, Westerly,

R. I.; Justus Palmer, Brooklyn, N. Y.; G. G. Palmer, Richmond,
Va.; Emma H. Palmer, Richmond, Va.; Henry C. H. Palmer,
Sing Sing, N. Y.; Stephen Palmer, Pleasantville, N. Y.; Joseph
Cutler and wife, Brooklyn, N. Y.; Eliza T. P. Prescott, Rome,
N. Y.; Fidelia W. P. Cady, Syracuse, N. Y.; O. D. Prescott,
Rome, N. Y.; A. C. Burdick, Ashaway, R. I.; J. R. Palmer,
New Brunswick, N. J.; E. B. Palmer, Bridgeton, N. J.; H. H.
Palmer, Rockford, Ill.; S. D. Palmer, Rockford, Ill.; Louise S.
Prosser, Providence, R. I.; Sarah P. Burdick, Ashaway, R. I.;
Dr. A. H. Palmer, Brooklyn, Pa.; Gideon Palmer, New York
City, N. Y.; Mary L. Barber, Exeter, R. I.; W. H. Palmer,
Cortland, N. Y.; J. T. Palmer, Rockville, R. I.; Benj. G. Palmer,
Middletown, N. Y.; Jay Palmer, East New York, L. I.; L. R.
Case, wife and child, Norwich, Ct.; Rev. W. C. Walker and
wife, Andover, Ct.; Theodore H. Palmer, Falls Village, Ct.
Calvin I. Cook and wife, Preston, Ct.; Ansel C. Marshall, Am-
herst, Mass.; Lucy C. P. Marshall, Amherst, Mass.; Marvin L.
P. Downing, Providence, R. I.; Josiah Palmer, Brooklyn, N. Y.;
Noyes G. Palmer, New York City, N. Y.; C. A. Gray and
wife, Potter Hill, R. I.; Wm. H. Palmer, Catskill, N. Y.;
Elizabeth Palmer, Catskill, N. Y.; Sabra De B. Palmer, Am-
herst, Mass.; Helen Palmer, Amherst, Mass.; Mrs. E. C.
Abbe, Westfield, Mass.; W. H. Palmer, Le Roy, N. Y.;
Nelson Palmer, Spencerport, N. Y.; L. M. Palmer, Spencerport,
N. Y.; H. L. P. Spencer, Dover, Del.; Henry W. Palmer, N.
Danville, Vt.; E. H. Palmer, Danville, Ill.; Rev. Elliott Palmer,
Portland, Ct.; Louisa P. Chapin, Perry, N. Y.; Wm. Ledyard
Palmer, Manchester, Mich.; Mrs. Lucy L. Ward, Mystic Bridge,
Ct.; L. W. Wessells, Litchfield, Ct.; Mary M. Wessells, Litch-
field, Ct.; Pardon Hopkins, Moose Neck, R. I.; Edwin C. Chese-
bro, Philadelphia, Pa.; Samuel Fletcher, Thetford, Vt.; Kath-
erine Fletcher, Thetford, Vt.; W. D. Palmer, Stonington, Ct.;
C. S. Palmer, Stoneham, Mass.; Robert E. Green, Westmore-
land, N. H.; Walter Palmer, West Winfield, N. Y.; Miss Alice
Palmer, Mitchell, N. Y.; Miss H. Maria Palmer, Woodville,
R. I.; Betsey A. Palmer, Woodville, R. I.; Mrs. I. M. Palmer,
Rockville, R. I.; I. M. Palmer, Rockville, R. I.; D. R. Hewitt,
Stonington, Ct.; G. M. Palmer, Portland, Me.; Miss Fannie D.
Hewitt, Stonington, Ct.; N. B. Palmer, Hopkinton, R. I.; Amos
S. Palmer and wife, Hopkinton, R. I.; Ada E. Palmer, Hopkin-
ton, R. I.; Susan E. Palmer, Hopkinton, R. I.; Nettie H. Pal-
mer, Hopkinton, R. I.; Lizzie S. Palmer, Hopkinton, R. I.;
Mary S. Palmer, Hopkinton, R. I.; Alex. S. Palmer, Stonington,
Ct.; Moses H. Main, Hope Valley, R. I.; Mrs. M. H. Main,
Hope Valley, R. I.; Silas E. Main, Hope Valley, R. I.; Chas.

A. Palmer, Rockville, R. I.; Joseph Smith, Potter Hill, R. I.; Sarah B. Cook, Preston City, Ct.; Wm. C. York and wife, N. Stonington, Ct.; C. P. York, N. Stonington, Ct.; Wm. T. Miner and wife, Watch Hill, R. I.; C. W. Miner, Watch Hill, R. I.; Emma C. Miner, Watch Hill, R. I.; Mrs. Arthur Palmer, Brooklyn, Pa.; P. G. Palmer, Niantic, R. I.; Libbie Palmer, Niantic, R. I.; May E. Palmer, Niantic, R. I.; Flora Palmer, Niantic, R. I.; Robbie Palmer, Niantic, R. I.; Charlie Palmer, Niantic, R. I.; Mrs. John Collins, Stonington, Ct.; Mrs. Asher Chapman, Pendleton Hill, Ct.; Mrs. E. E. Babcock, Westerly, R. I.; Mrs. C. W. Burdick, Stonington, Ct.; Mrs. John F. Chesebro, Stonington, Ct.; Mrs. Frank Chesebro, Stonington, Ct.; Hannie Babcock, Westerly, R. I.; Lottie P. Babcock, Westerly, R. I.; Denison Palmer, Stonington, Ct.; Hettie I. Palmer, Stonington, Ct.; Albert M. Palmer, Stonington, Ct.; Lula Palmer, Stonington, Ct.; Frederic Palmer, Stonington, Ct.; Nannie Palmer, Stonington, Ct.; M. L. Browning, Waterford, Ct.; Simeon Palmer, Boston, Mass.; Mrs. Geo. Hewitt, Waterford, Ct.; Caroline E. Palmer, Stonington, Ct.; James McLee, Bay City, Mich.; Mary L. McLee, Bay City, Mich.; Howie McLee, Bay City, Mich.; Frank McLee, Bay City, Mich.; Caroline E. Hammond, Stonington, Ct.; Walter W. Hammond, Stonington, Ct.; W. W. Hammond, Bay City, Mich.; Joseph H. Palmer, Stonington, Ct.; Frank E. Hammond, Stonington, Ct.; Carrie E. Hammond, Stonington, Ct.; Charles O. B. Hammond, Stonington, Ct.; Louis E. Hammond, Bay City, Mich.; E. M. Palmer, Mystic, Ct.; Fred. E. Palmer, Mystic, Ct.; H. S. Palmer, Mystic, Ct.; Nellie M. Palmer, Mystic, Ct.; Wm. W. Palmer, Mystic, Ct.; Mary E. Palmer, Mystic, Ct.; Howard Palmer, Mystic, Ct.; Horace Palmer, Mystic, Ct.; W. L. Palmer, Cromwell, R. I.; Nathan Palmer, wife and son, Cromwell, R. I.; W. E. Palmer, wife and family, Cromwell, R. I.; Eli Hewitt and wife, Windham, Ct.: Mary A. Hewitt, Windham, Ct.; G. D. Hewitt and wife, Norwich, Ct.: J. H. Wilcox and wife, New London, Ct.; Miss C. B. Wilcox, New London, Ct.; F. Williams and wife, Mystic Bridge, Ct.; Miss H. E. Noyes, Mystic Bridge, Ct.; N. S. Noyes, Mystic Bridge, Ct.; Walter Boardman, Lancaster, Pa.; Arthur Boardman, Lancaster, Pa.; Arthur Billings, Griswold, Ct.; J. A. Billings, Morgantown, Kan.; Mrs. Alice S. Wheeler, Boston, Mass.; Samuel Palmer, Springfield, Mass.; Nettie F. Palmer, Springfield, Mass.; Stephen Palmer, Manchester, Mass.; E. M. Miner, Groton, Ct.; Sabrina L. Rockwell, Groton, Ct.; Mrs. Walter I. Chesebro, Noank, Ct.; Addie E. Spicer, Noank, Ct.; Alice H. Spicer, Noank, Ct.; James M. Palmer, Cambridge, Mass.; Jonathan P. Palmer, Boston, Mass.; Louis A. Palmer, Boston, Mass.; Ezra

Wheeler, N. Stonington, Ct.; Hattie A. Wheeler, N. Stonington, Ct.; Mary H. Wheeler, N. Stonington, Ct.; Mrs. Elizabeth Easton, Boston, Mass.; Miss M. Lizzie Easton, Boston, Mass.; Nannie J. Moredoc, Mystic Bridge, Ct.; Abbie M. Moredoc, Mystic Bridge, Ct.; Mary Healy, Hartford, Ct.; Mrs. John B. Palmer, Providence, R. I.; Miss Laila B. Palmer, Providence, R. I.; Mrs. John B. Palmer, Providence, R. I.; Miss Lucy A. Palmer, Providence, R. I.; Daniel Cady Eaton, New Haven, Ct.; Henry L. Douglass, Westerly, R. I.; C. H. J. Douglass, Ann Arbor, Mich.; Henry Palmer and wife, Fair Haven, Ct.; Annie P. Ludington, Fair Haven, Ct.; George Palmer, Branford, Ct.; Ellen J. Palmer, Branford, Ct.; Fannie Palmer, Branford, Ct.; Allen P. Palmer, Castleton, Vt.; H. P. Powers, Littleford, Vt.; L. W. Palmer, Providence, R. I.; Miss Jennie C. Palmer, Providence, R. I.; Ira A. Thurbur, Syracuse, N. Y.; Mrs. E. C. Thurbur, Syracuse, N. Y.; C. L. Palmer, Webster, Mass.; Maria P. Hull, Providence, R. I.; Adelaide H. Lambertson, Goshen, Ct.; J. A. Palmer, N. Branford, Ct.; Mrs. H. M. P. Russell, New Haven, Ct.; Mrs. M. E. Huntley, Old Lyme, Ct.; Walter Potter Palmer and wife, Plainfield, Ct.; Samuel Palmer and wife, Plainfield, Ct.; Samuel F. Palmer, Plainfield, Ct.; Susie A. Palmer, Plainfield, Ct.; George A. Palmer, Plainfield, Ct.; Walter L. Palmer, Plainfield, Ct.; Ella F. Palmer, Plainfield, Ct.; Lydia C. Dorrance, Plainfield, Ct.; Henry Dorrance, Plainfield, Ct.; Col. Edwin Palmer, Norwich, Ct.; Rev. Frank Palmer, Norwich, Ct.; C. L. Brown and wife, N. Stonington, Ct.; Fannie Chesebro, Stonington, Ct.; J. L. Palmer, Little Rock, Ark.; Gilbert Billings, N. Stonington, Ct.; Mary A. Billings, N. Stonington, Ct.; Abbie L. Cutts, N. Stonington, Ct.; Miss Denison Harnott, N. Stonington, Ct.; Sarah M. Main, N. Stonington, Ct.; Rebecca Comstock, Newport, R. I.; Lucy Sanborne, Newport, R. I.; Mrs. Vashti H. Palmer, Boston, Mass.; Mrs. George Sherman, Norwichtown, Ct.; Charles Wilberforce Denison, a grandson of Joseph Palmer, Norwichtown, Ct.; John P. Williams and wife, N. Stonington, Ct.; Allen Wheeler and wife, N. Stonington, Ct.; Delia Wheeler, N. Stonington, Ct.; Geo. W. Palmer, Galesburg, Ill.; A. G. Palmer, East Haddam, Ct.; Matilda S. Palmer, East Haddam, Ct.; Wm. F. Palmer, East Haddam, Ct.; Dr. Wm. H. Palmer, wife and children, Providence, R. I.; Wm. R. Palmer and wife, Gt. Barrington, Mass.; Mrs. Nancy P. Gray, Potter Hill, R. I.; Mrs. S. P. Sisson, Potter Hill, R. I.; Mrs. A. P. Mowry, Providence, R. I.; Phebe Palmer, Pendleton Hill, Ct.; Julia W. Palmer, Pendleton Hill, Ct.; J. P. Potter, Westerly, R. I.; Amelia Potter, Westerly, R. I.; Sarah P. York, Wellesville, N. Y.; J. C. Palmer, Brooklyn, N. Y.;

Gertrude E. Palmer, Brooklyn, N. Y.; S. L. Palmer, Seneca, Ill.; K. E. Palmer, Wataga, Ill.; Denison Hewitt, N. Stonington, Ct.; Mrs. J. A. Williams, New Britain, Ct.; Fremont D. Palmer, Norwich, Ct.; Mrs. Cynthice Benjamin, Mystic River, Ct.; Wm. C. Benjamin and wife, Mystic River, Ct.; Geo. D. Palmer, Griswold, Ct.; Mrs. Clark W. Reynolds, Jewett City, Ct.; Edwin Benjamin, Preston, Ct.; Mary E. Benjamin, Preston, Ct.; C. W. Palmer, New Haven, Ct.; W. V. Gould and wife, Norwich, Ct.; Mrs. W. F. Clark, Brooklyn, N. Y.; M. I. Lewis, Norwich, Ct.; C. J. Lewis, Norwich, Ct.; James L. Case, Norwich, Ct.; Sarah C. Case, Norwich, Ct.; R. P. Palmer and wife, Pauchnegeruc Hill, Ct.; Sarah Palmer, Pauchnegeruc Hill, Ct.; Jettie R. Palmer, Pauchnegeruc Hill, Ct.; Silas Spicer, Noank, Ct.; F. A. Palmer, Newark, N. J.; E. A. Palmer, Belmont, N. Y.; A. A. Smith, Lebanon, Ct.; Maria S. Bromley, Rockville, Ct.; Lydia M. Brown, Mystic Bridge, Ct.; Maro V. Palmer, Windsor Locks, Ct.; Geo. W. Palmer, Pawtucket, R. I.; Weeden H. Berry, Westerly, R. I.; Mrs. Delia A. Berry, Westerly, R. I.; Hattie E. Berry, Westerly, R. I.; Saxton Berry, Westerly, R. I.; Leman Berry, Westerly, R. I.; Mrs. C. Crandall Walker, Rome, N. Y.; Mrs. C. M. Robinson, Auburn, N. Y.; W. O. Benjamin, New London, Ct.; Mary E. Benjamin, New London, Ct.; Dr. Delos Palmer, New York, N. Y.; Dr. Eugene Palmer, New York, N. Y.; Corydon Palmer, D. D. S., Warren, O.; Calvin B. Palmer, Voluntown, Ct.; A. S. Palmer and wife, Onarga, Ill.; C. J. Palmer and wife, Seneca Falls, N. Y.; Herbert I. Palmer and wife, Norwich, Ct.; Mrs. J. C. Palmer, Norwich, Ct.; C. M. Davis, Stonington, Ct.; Fred. I. Allen, Auburn, N. Y.; A. B. Palmer and wife, Malden, Mass.; Miss G. Nowlin, Brooklyn, N. Y.; Miss M. Clark, Lyme, Ct.; Mrs. Lizzie Lamb, Noank, Ct.; Mrs. Carrie Latham, Noank, Ct.; Thomas Clark, North Stonington, Ct.; Wilford A. Clark, North Stonington, Ct.; Amos G. Hewitt, North Stonington, Ct.; C. E. Hewitt, North Stonington, Ct.; Grant M. Hewitt, Lowell, Mass.; Mrs. D. O. Allen, Lynn, Mass.; Fred. Denison, Providence, R. I.; A. R. M. Denison, Providence, R. I.; Fred. Denison, Providence, R. I.; Emily D. Noyes, Mystic Bridge, Ct.; Henry B. Noyes, Mystic Bridge, Ct.; Ellen M. Noyes, Mystic Bridge, Ct.; H. B. Noyes, Jr., Mystic Bridge, Ct.; N. P. Palmer, Thompsonville, Ct.; Lewis A. Palmer, Boston, Mass.; M. G. Palmer, Portland, Me.; C. H. Babcock, Westerly, R. I.; A. H. Babcock, Westerly, R. I.; Annie L. Babcock, Westerly, R. I.; Edith V. Babcock, Westerly, R. I.; Henry H. Babcock, Westerly, R. I.; Mrs. W. R. Wells, Ashaway, R. I.; Mrs. J. P. Spicer, Noank, Ct.; Frank A. Weaver, New London, Ct.; Julia E. Weaver, New London, Ct.; Mary Benjamin, New London,

Ct.; H. F. Palmer and wife, Norwich, Ct.; George S. Palmer and wife, Montville, Ct.; F. C. Palmer and wife, Montville, Ct.; E. L. Palmer and wife, Montville, Ct.; E. A. Palmer and wife, Montville, Ct.; E. H. Palmer and wife, Montville, Ct.; Mrs. J. S. Latimer, Montville, Ct.; Mrs. Alice M. Mitchell, Montville, Ct.; Noyes F. Palmer, Jamaica, L. I.; Ira H. Palmer, Stonington, Ct.; Rev. Dr. A. G. Palmer, Stonington, Ct.; Judge R. A. Wheeler, Stonington, Ct.; Rev. Fred. Denison, Providence, R. I.; B. F. Chapman, Oneida, N. Y.; Charles R. Palmer, Noank, Ct.; Wm. H Palmer, Mamaroneck, Ct.; E. A. Stillman, Westerly, R. I.; Mrs. E. A. Stillman, Westerly, R. I.; Miss Sadie S. Stillman, Westerly, R. I.; T. J. Palmer, Hackensack, N. J.; Frank L. Palmer, New London, Ct.; I. E. Palmer, Middletown, Ct.; W. W. Butler, Boston, Mass.; Lottie E. Palmer, Sing Sing, N. Y.; Mamie Grant, Sing Sing, N. Y; James Newcombe, New London, Ct.; Wm. A. Wadsworth, Unionville, Ct.; Mrs. E. A. P. Wadsworth, Unionville, Ct.; Mrs. J. F. Bushnell, Saybrook, Ct.; Mrs. E. H. Palmer, New York, N. Y.; Cornelia P. Bolles, Boston, Mass.; Emerson P. Turner, Norwich, Ct.; Col. Geo. W. Palmer, Chicago, Ill.; W. C. Dewy, Palmer, Mass.; F. C. Palmer and wife, Palmer, Mass.; Lida P. Turner, Norwich, Ct.; Vinnie S. Palmer, New London, Ct.; H. Palmer, East Greenwich, R. I.; Annie J. Palmer, New York City, N. Y.; Tyler R. Palmer, Worcester, Ct.; John E. Bushnell, Old Saybrook, Ct.; Arabella P. Latimer, Montville, Ct.; A. L. Spicer, Noank, Ct.; Chas. R. Palmer, Noank, Ct.; L. N. Palmer, Jr., Brooklyn, Mass.; Wendell E. Turner and wife, Brooklyn, N. Y.; Miss Jeannette P. Stanton, Monson, Mass.; H. Clay Palmer, Monson, Mass.; Minnie Palmer, Stockbridge, Mass.; H. P. Palmer and wife, Catskill, N. Y.; Wm. S. Palmer, Catskill, N. Y.; Priscella Palmer, Catskill, N. Y.; Susette Palmer, Catskill, N. Y.; Byron Palmer, Leeds, N. Y.; Simpson Palmer, Leeds, N. Y.; Atwood R. Brayton, Stonington, Ct.; Mrs. A. R. Brayton, Stonington, Ct.; Sarah A. Brayton, Stonington, Ct.; Frances A. Brayton, Stonington, Ct.; H. Adelaide Brayton, Stonington, Ct.; Atwood W. Brayton, Stonington, Ct.; George E. Brayton, Stonington, Ct.; Mrs. E. Brayton, Stonington, Ct.; Edward B. Cox, Troy, N. Y.; Emily Dickinson, Troy. N. Y.; Dr. Chas. E. Brayton, Stonington, Ct.; M. Lilian Brayton, Stonington, Ct.; Simeon Palmer and wife, Stonington, Ct.; Chas. O. B. Palmer and wife, Stonington, Ct.; John Hammond and wife, Stonington, Ct.; Joseph Hammond, Stonington, Ct.; Frank Hammond, Stonington, Ct.; Carrie Hammond, Stonington, Ct.; Walter Hammond and wife, Stonington, Ct.; A. Allen Palmer, Stonington, Ct.; John Palmer, Stonington, Ct.; Clarence Palmer, Stonington, Ct.; Capt.

A. S. Palmer, Stonington, Ct.; Alexander Palmer, Jr., Stonington, Ct.; Capt. Wm. L. Palmer, Stonington, Ct.; T. D. Palmer and wife, Stonington, Ct.; R. F. Loper and wife, Stonington, Ct.; Wm. Letchford, New Orleans, La.; Nathan Palmer, Stonington, Ct.; Denison Palmer, Stonington, Ct.; Grove White and wife, Stonington, Ct.; Rev. A. C. Palmer and wife, Stonington, Ct.; Emma Palmer, Stonington, Ct.; Sarah Palmer, Stonington, Ct.; Dr. G. D. Stanton and wife, Stonington, Ct.; James E. Palmer, Wequetequock Cove, Ct.; J. W. Bradford, Voluntown, Ct.; Mrs. Margaret Collins, Stonington, Ct.; Mrs. Emma Chesebro, Stonington, Ct.; Capt. J. E. Smith, Stonington, Ct.; Nathan G. Smith, Stonington, Ct.; Mrs. C. York, Stonington, Ct.; Mrs. John F. Trumbull, Stonington, Ct.; Mrs. B. F. Palmer, Stonington, Ct.; Mrs. Maria Faxon, Stonington, Ct.; Mrs. Lucy Woodbridge, Stonington, Ct.; Mrs. Maria Faxon, Stonington, Ct.; Geo. W. Mathews and wife, Stonington, Ct.; Miss Caddie Smith, Stonington, Ct.; Miss Minnie Trumbull, Stonington, Ct.; Chas. P. Palmer and wife, Stonington, Ct.; Courtland Palmer, New York City, N. Y.; Ex-Lieut. Gov. F. B. Loomis, New London, Ct.; Frank H. Palmer, Brooklyn, N. Y.; Robert Palmer, Bozrah, Ct.

THE PALM-TREE.

BY JOHN G. WHITTIER.

Is it the palm, the cocoa-palm,
On the Indian sea, by the isles of balm,
Or is it a ship in the breezeless calm?

A ship whose keel is of palm beneath,
Whose ribs of palm have a palm-bark sheath,
And a rudder of palm it steereth with.

Branches of palm are its spars and rails,
Fibres of palm are its woven sails,
And the rope is of palm that idly trails!

What does the good ship bear so well?
The cocoanut with its stony shell,
And the milky sap of its inner cell.

What are its jars, so smooth and fine,
But hollowed nuts, filled with oil and wine,
And the cabbage that ripens under the Line?

Who smokes his nargileh cool and calm?
The master, whose cunning and skill could charm
Cargo and ship from the bounteous palm.

In the cabin he sits on a palm-mat soft,
From a beaker of palm his drink is quaffed,
And a palm-thatch shields from the sun aloft!

His dress is woven of palmy strands, ·
And he holds a palm-leaf scroll in his hands,
Traced with the Prophet's wise commands!

The turban folded about his head
Was daintily wrought of the palm-leaf braid,
And the fan that cools him of palm was made.

Of threads of palm was the carpet spun
Whereon he kneels when the day is done,
And the foreheads of Islam are bowed as one.

To him the palm is a gift divine,
Wherein all uses of man combine—
House and raiment, and food and wine!

And, in the hour of his great release,
His need of the palm shall only cease
With the shroud wherein he lieth in peace.

" Allah il Allah !" he sings his psalm,
On the Indian sea, by the isles of balm ;
" Thanks to Allah who gives the palm !"

CAPT. ALEXANDER S. PALMER,

OF STONINGTON, CT.

Capt. Alexander S. Palmer was born at the site of his present
home (called Pine Point) at Stonington, January 26th, 1806.
When an infant his parents moved into the borough of Stonington, and there he remained until June 21st, 1821, when he started
on his first voyage in the brig *Alabama Packet*, Capt. Wm. A.
Fanning, bound on a sealing voyage to the South Shetlands.
His education was confined to the common schools.   After leaving school he was placed in a lawyer's office, but could not stand
the confinement.

After coming home in the *Alabama Packet*, made two coasting voyages to Philadelphia in the schooner *Alonzo*, Capt. R. F. Loper; then sailed to the West Indies in the brig *Thetis*, Capt. Savage. On return, went to Carthagena in the schooner *Cadet*, Capt. N. B. Palmer, July 5th, 1824. From Carthagena sailed to Chagris, carrying part of General Bolivar's army, who was assisting the Peruvians drive out the Spanish from Chagris; carried Spanish prisoners to St. Gago, Cuba. On the return voyage to New York, November, 1824, was wrecked at Long Branch; schooner a total loss. Then made seven voyages in the brig *Tampico*, Capt. N. B. Palmer, to the Spanish Main; 1826, he took command of the brig *Tampico*, and made two voyages. Then commanded respectively, the schooner *Penguin*, Sept. 5th, 1827, and ship *Charles Adams*, Sept 1st, 1831, on whaling and sealing voyages to Cape Horn, South Shetland and Falkland Islands; sailed from Stonington. Next commanded ship *Louisville* (1834), on voyages to New Orleans and Liverpool; sailed from New York. Next commanded ship *Shakespeare* (1838), from New York to New Orleans; then ship *Garrick* (1839 and 1840), from New York to Liverpool; also ship *Southerner* (1841). Then commanded ship *Hoqua* (1845), from New York to China, being the second ship to enter the port of Shanghai, after this port was opened to commerce. He brought to this country the first Shanghai fowl. His last voyage, in 1847, was made to Liverpool from New York, in ship *Southerner*. Was married in June, 1837, to Priscilla Denison Dixon, daughter of the Hon. Nathan F. Dixon. His first vote was cast for General Jackson, at his first election. Always has been a democrat in politics; has represented the town and district, as representative and senator, five times —namely: Representative, in years of 1857, 1858 and 1875; senator, in years of 1876 and 1877.

A PALMER PILOT—"CAPTAIN NAT."

BY REV. F. DENISON.

Of Palmers famous on the sea,
The wide world owns Nathaniel B.—
In story and familiar chat
For euphony styled "Captain Nat."—

Pure-blooded son of Stonington,
In seamanship excelled by none,
Of ardent, broad and sunny soul,
Bold sealman nigh the southern pole ;
Polite, prompt, generous and brave,
The very man to rule the wave.

Far voyaging he struck the strand
Now blazed on charts as Palmer Land—
Vast rocks and bergs—alive with seal,
And swore his crew to ne'er reveal
The wild, storm-lashed Antarctic shore,
That they of furs might gain the more.

He sped his keel, and speedy made
In sealing trips a thriving trade ;
But once while on the island's rim,
He spied on the horizon's brim
A ship-of-war, with pennants free,
On bearing to the coast alee,
Slow beating up by tack and tack,
And feeling out the dangerous track.

From jutting crag high on the strand
He sharp surveyed, with glass in hand,
The laboring ship until he found
That she was on discovery bound,
Intent possessive right to claim
In some far foreign sovereign's name.

He read old Russia's yellow field,
With horseman on its crimson shield,
From main-top waving in the clouds,
And sailors watching from the shrouds,
And knew the Russian officer
With all on board were now astir,
Prepared, with bunting spread to suit,
To fire a national salute,
And take possession of the isle
In ceremonious, royal style,
And win a badge of heraldry
By this their grand discovery.

He slyly then his anchor tripped,
Out from his rocky harbor slipped,
Each man of his brave crew on deck

Obedient to his word and beck,
And bearing down upon the ship,
With speaking-trumpet at his lip,
Cried, " Ho ! do you a port prefer,
And wish to have a pilot, sir ?"

How quick that ship was brought in stays,
And faded out the flag displays ;
How sore, chopfallen and chagrined,
As veering off before the wind,
The Russian magnate, while he bowed
To Captain Nat., vehement vowed :
" I'd like to see that earthly bound
That Yankee Palmers never found."

August, 1881.

COL. JONATHAN PALMER.
(BRIEF BIOGRAPHY.)

Col. Jonathan Palmer, deceased, of the third generation, was a gentleman of considerable distinction; not only as a military man, in which he was very active, but as a citizen he was very popular, holding during his lifetime some very important Government positions. His commission, as Collector of the Port of Stonington, dated at Philadelphia, A. D. 1791, signed by George Washington, President, and Thomas Jefferson, Secretary of State ; also his commission as Naval Officer of Stonington, signed by Mathew Griswold, Governor of the State of Connecticut, and his commission from Timothy Pickering, Postmaster-General, as Postmaster of Stonington, dated at Philadelphia, A. D. 1792. He was highly esteemed, not only by his own citizens but by those who occupied high places in the land. He died at the age of sixty-four, loved and respected by the entire community.

CAPT. JONATHAN PALMER.

Jonathan Palmer, son of Col. Jonathan, of the fourth generation, and the last of the name, was born at Stonington, in 1793. After obtaining an education, he taught school at Westerly, R. I., for a short time, after which he established himself in business at that place. During this period the attack was made on

Stonington by the British fleet, in 1814, in which he took a very active part in defence of his native town. He was the man who, when the British shot down the flag, climbed the pole and nailed it fast in the face of the combined fire of the fleet; he also brought a keg of powder that had been hidden in a garden some distance off, which was used with good effect in driving off the fleet. His mother, during this time, was engaged in making cartridges of her carpets and flannel skirts in the old mansion at the upper end of the town. You will see from this that he came from fighting stock, and strongly inherited the patriotic feeling of his parents. For some years he was engaged in a seafaring life; at one time he had charge of a fleet of three vessels on a sealing voyage to the South Seas. After this he engaged in shipping produce to Philadelphia, and finally settled there as a merchant, about 1826. Mr. Palmer's career as a merchant was a long and successful one. At one time he was largely engaged in the shipping business between Philadelphia and Boston, being the proprietor of a line of barks doing business between the two cities and other ports of the country. He remained in business for over half a century, and retired at a good old age with a name untarnished, and with the good will and affection of all who knew him.

DR. CHAS. E. BRAYTON,

OF STONINGTON, CT.

Though not a Palmer by name, yet as a descendant he participated in the Re-Union, and was one of those to whom many thanks are due for his efforts to entertain the "Re-Unionists." The headquarters were at Brayton Hall, which he freely gave for the purpose.

Charles E. Brayton was born in Stonington, Ct., February 11th, 1851; son of Atwood R. and Sally M. Davis Brayton, the tenth child. Was educated at the common and private schools of the town, and also in Providence; began the study of medicine with Dr. Wm. Hyde, in 1868, at Stonington, and graduated in March, 1873, at College of Physicians and Surgeons, New York City. Began practice with Dr. Hyde in

April, 1873, and succeeded (at his death, September 25, 1873,) to his practice, and has been engaged in a good practice since that time. In August, 1880, commenced the building, Brayton Hall.

LUCIEN W. PALMER,

OF PROVIDENCE, R. I.

Lucien Webster Palmer, Superintendent N. Y. & N. E. R. R., was born in Castleton, Vt., Sept. 1st, 1839.

His father, Allan Palmer, was a farmer in good circumstances. His mother, Ruth Webster, was a sister of the late Horace Webster, LL.D., President of the New York Free College for over a quarter of a century. His father and mother were both well educated, and the parents of six children—three sons and three daughters.

Two of the sons died at an early age, leaving the subject of this brief sketch as the only surviving son. His education was received at Castleton Seminary. Having no taste for the life of a farmer, he set out in 1861 to make his own way in the world. Going to Springfield, Mass., he first commenced work in the United States Armory, but disliking the favoritism practiced by many of the subordinate officers in that institution, he went to Providence, R. I. Here he worked in the Armory of the Providence Tool Company for about three years, preparing himself for a better position by spending his evenings in study. He went through a commercial college, taking up various branches that might be of use to him. At the expiration of this time he accepted a position as book-keeper in a wholesale house, where he remained one year.

Having made the acquaintance of the manager of the Providence and Worcester Railroad, he was offered a position as clerk in his office, which he accepted. In this position he was entrusted with many important duties, which he discharged with such ability and fidelity that his promotion was rapid. He was soon appointed freight agent of the road and placed in full charge of that department. The position was a difficult one, in which several men had been unsuccessful. This was an opportunity to succeed where others had failed, and bringing to the business all the energy at his command, he soon had the department thoroughly organized.

The ability and economy with which he managed this business caused him to receive an offer of the position of Superintendent of the Passumpsic Railroad, in 1872. Soon after taking this position it became apparent that the fractious and erratic disposition of the president of the road would cause much annoyance, and after some months spent in ineffectual efforts to ascertain what general policy the president intended to pursue, he decided to follow such a course as would be creditable to himself, whether satisfactory to the president or not. Knowing this would not harmonize matters, although sustained by the board of directors, he tendered his resignation, to take effect at the close of the year.

Immediately on learning this the managers of the Providence, & Worcester Railroad sent to know if he would return to his old position as freight agent, at an increase of salary. Accepting this offer he returned to his former position, but in a few months he was sought out by the late General Burnside as a fitting man to adjust some serious difficulties upon the Cairo & Vincennes Railroad, of which he was president.

This being a temporary service he obtained leave of absence for two months, and started upon the difficult mission. The required service was so well performed that some six weeks after, when General Burnside reached Cairo, he desired him to take the office of General Superintendent of the road.

At this time a lawsuit had been commenced, to place the road in the hands of receivers, and after some hesitation the offer was accepted upon the representation that there was no possible chance for the suit to succeed. It did succeed, however, and at the expiration of about two years he found himself out of business. Returning to Providence he was soon offered and accepted a position in the freight department of the New York & New England Railroad, as contracting agent, where he remained until by consolidation the road required other superintendents, when he was appointed superintendent of the Providence division, where he still remains.

In the year 1863 he was married to Jennie C. Greene, a direct descendant from the same family as Gen. Nathaniel Greene, and has two sons—Harry L., aged sixteen years, and Ernest W., aged ten years.

JAMES G. PALMER, D. D. S.,

OF NEW BRUNSWICK, N. J.

· Dr. James G. Palmer, a very efficient co-worker at the Re-Union, was born at Mt. Horeb, Somerset Co., N. J., November 15th, 1850. His father, Benjamin D., was a Methodist Episcopal minister, and owing to the itinerant system of that Church, his place of abode was frequently changing. As a consequence, James attended school in various parts of the State.

When about sixteen years of age, he became imbued with the desire to become a dentist, and soon entered the office of Dr. S. R. Osmun, of Hackettstown, N. J. From there he went to New York City, where he entered the office of Dr. R. M. Streeter, then of 22 West 35th street, with whom he remained about four years. During this time he matriculated at the Medical Department, N. Y. University, but subsequently graduated from the Pennsylvania College of Dental Surgery, in Philadelphia.

In 1876 he located in New Brunswick, N. J., where, as the junior partner of the firm of Hull & Palmer, he is conducting successfully a large practice.

WM. PITT PALMER.

This worthy son of Berkshire Hills, Mass., was prevented by sickness from attending the Re-Union, and occupying the chosen position among the poets on that occasion. It is no more than proper that some notice be taken of his absence; for, had he been present, he would have received a large share of the notice of the pilgrim Palmers at the Re-Union.

Wm. Pitt is a direct descendant from Walter in the paternal line, as follows: 1st. Walter; 2d. Nehemiah; 3d. Justice Daniel;

4th. Dr. Nathan; 5th. Andrew; 6th. Roswell Saltonstall; 7th. Wm. Pitt Palmer.

Wm Pitt Palmer, son of Roswell S. and Desire Palmer, was born in that part of the Old Stockbridge Mission (called South Lee in the present century), on Feb. 22, 1805. He was a farmer boy until fifteen, when he was sent to the academy of the Rev. Jared Curtis, and thence to Williams College, where he graduated, A. B., Sept., 1828. At his father's desire he entered the law office of Sedgwick & Field, New York, but ultimately yielded to his own preference of a profession, and became a pupil of Prof. Joseph M. Smith, M. D., New York. He was not long after induced to become a professor himself in a famous high school on the Hudson. After some years he was prevailed upon to return to the city and join an old and paternal friend in the "ranks of business." For well-nigh a half century he remained therein, to the satisfaction of all his just wishes and expectations, until the infirmities of age at length dismissed him from the desk to the easy-chair. As was natural, the change seems to have been as agreeable as it was necessary, his only regret being that it did not take place earlier than at three score and fifteen years, so that he might have better and longer enjoyed the blessings of a happy home. In his retirement he still keeps his pen from resting, and last year published a volume of poems—"Echoes of Half a Century"—which a great critic confidently declared "will live." Be that as it may, some of them have been widely popular—such as "Light," "The Smack in School," "Dame Salisbury's Pudding," "Loves Second Sight," etc.—and seem to possess a promising vitality. We insert a few poems:

"ARE YOU 'ROUND YET?"

Still, still around, though faint and slow,
　With weary feet and shoulders galled
Yet loth to leave my task and go
　The long, dark way before I'm called.

Like Æsop's hoary fagot slave,
　Who cried for Death to end his pain,
I too, if heard, should humbly crave
　His help to lift my pack again.

With sands so few, and cares so prest,
    I fain recall what Pascal said :
There will be time enough for rest,
    When the green turf is o'er me spread.

Well, yes, my friend, I'm still around,
    In spite of fortune's cruel blows ;
The weed, you know, oft holds its ground,
    In presence even of the rose !

Death seems to spurn or quite forget,
    At times, the meanest thing that crawls ;
The while his dart strikes down the pet
    Adonis of imperial halls.

Your blurted question doubtless grew
    From wonder, bluntly unconcealed,
That earth had not yet snatched from view
    This laggard to the Potter's field.

Am *I* to quarrel with the fate
    That spares me, howsoe'er abhorred,
And, with my own hand, antedate
    The severing of " the silver cord ?"

I'm always fain my friend to please
    In aught that conscience may condone ;
But life is *life*, and its surcease
    The All-disposer leaves to none.

If I had made myself, be sure
    Some traits of worth should stand so clear,
That even *you* might still endure,
    Perhaps, my longer presence here :

For you should see me give their due
    To friend and foe, whate'er it be ;
And inly feel my debt to you
    Was always less than yours to me.

But let that pass—the world is wide,
    With room for all and courses meet—
The broad highroad for flaunting pride,
    The close, shy path for humble feet :

So we may go our several ways,
    Good strangers, near or far apart ;
For though the sky be full of days,
    Not one shall bring us heart to heart.

To you I leave the shining goal
  So often won with honor wrecked
I fail, yet failing, will console
  My loss with unlost self-respect.

And so my simple faith shall rest
  In this fond hope, as aye before;
That some, though few, who knew me best,
  Will sigh, when I am "'round no more."

ENVOY.

Friend! though to careless, common sight,
A kind word, like the widow's mite,
    Seem but a worthless thing;
In all the social marts of love
Its purchase-power is worlds above
    The coffers of a king!

WONDER.

FROM THE GERMAN OF NOVALIS.

The mead took on a tender green,
Faint bloom about the hedge was seen
And every day new plants appear;
The air was soft, the sky so clear!
I knew not how my eyes were spelled,
Nor how that was which I beheld.

And aye the grove more shadowy grew,
As birds their vernal homes renew:
Whence stole to me, from all sides round,
Their descant of melodious sound;
I knew not how my ears were spelled,
Nor how that was which I beheld.

Now gushed and revelled everywhere,
Life, color, music, dulcet air;
And all in such sweet union met,
That each, the while, seemed lovlier yet ·
I knew not how my sense was spelled,
Nor how that was which I beheld.

Then mused I, is 't a soul awakes,
Which all things thus so vital makes;
And *will* its presence manifest
In thousand forms by Flora drest?
I knew not how my sense was spelled,
Nor how that was which I beheld.

* A new creation it must be !
  Loose dust becomes a blade, a tree,
  The tree a beast, the beast a man
  Complete in action, shape and plan ;
  I knew not how my sense was spelled,
  Nor how that was which I beheld.

As thus I stood in wildered thought,
  With pulsing bosom passion-fraught,
  A charming maiden near me stole,
  And captive took my sense and soul ;
  I knew not how my heart was spelled,
  Not how that was which I beheld.

The greenwood veiled us from the day ;
  It is the Spring ! Love's own sweet May !
  And *now* I saw, in this new birth,
  That men become as gods on earth ;
  And well I knew, each doubt dispelled,
  How all was so as I beheld !

LOVE'S SECOND-SIGHT.†

Far through the dim, lone vistas of the night,
  As eye to eye, thy form and face appear,
Love's inward vision needs no outward light,
  No magic glass to bring the absent near.

Seas roll between us. Lo, the palm-tree throws
  Its shadow southward from yon moonlit hill ;
And stars that never on my boyhood rose,
  Are round me now, and yet I see thee still !

Alone thou sighest on the beaconed steep,
  While sports thy sister by the waves alone ;
Why dost thou gaze so fondly o'er the deep ?
  Ah, blush not, love, the tender truth to own !

I see thee sink upon thy bended knees,
  Yet not as one who bows in mute despair ;
Nor need I listen to the tell-tale breeze,
  To learn whose name is oftenest in thy prayer.

Thy cheek is wet—was that a falling gem
  From the pearled braid that binds thy golden curls ?

---

* NOTE.—Written before Darwin was born.
 † Supposed soliloquy of a young sailor of the North, looking homeward, or rather *loveward*, from far Southern seas.—WM. PITT PALMER.

No, never shone from jewelled diadem
    A gem so bright as beauty's liquid pearls.

Thou turn'st away—though fair the moonlit main,
    No sail appears, thy yearning heart to thrill;
One long, last gaze, and on the night again
    Thy casement closes, yet I see thee still !

On thy sweet face, as in a magic glass,
    I see the shapes that haunt thy slumbering eyes ;
What smiles of joy, when Hope's gay visions pass !
    What pictured woe, when Fear's dark phantoms rise !

Why dost thou wake, while yet the East is dark,
    To hold sad commune with the wind and surge ?
T'was but a *dream* that wrecked thy lover's bark ,
    Only a dream that sang his ocean dirge !

Even now that bark, before the homeward gale,
    Flies like a bird that seeks her callow nest ;
Soon shall thine eyes behold its furling sail,
    Soon thy fond bosom to my own be prest !

I could not fail to hold my course aright,
    Though every orb were quenched in yon blue sea ;
Love's inward vision needs no outward light,
    Star of my soul, no cynosure but thee !

WILBUR MERTON PALMER.

Wilbur Merton Palmer, of the city staff of the New York *Tribune*, was born in Winterton, Sullivan Co., N. Y., October 6, 1850. He is the second son of Daniel W. Palmer, a farmer. Upon leaving the public school, he prepared for college at the Hudson River Institute, Claverack, N. Y., of which the Rev. Dr. Fleck was principal. Graduating here, in 1869, he entered Wesleyan University, at Middletown, Ct., as a freshman, in the same year. Both before and in his college course he spent considerable time in teaching school. He was graduated with the degree of Bachelor of Arts at Wesleyan, in 1873, and received the degree of Master of Arts three years later. Upon leaving college he resumed teaching, intending to follow it as a profession. In successive years he was principal of graded and high

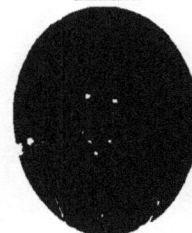

schools at Richville, N. Y., Scarsdale, N. Y., and Southington, Ct. After two years' service in the latter town he resigned teaching, in 1878, and turned his attention to journalism. He joined the city staff of the *Tribune*, with which his brother, Mr. A. E. Palmer, was connected, and has since been in the service of that newspaper. His home is in Flatbush, L. I.

ARCHIE EMERSON PALMER.

Mr. Archie Emerson Palmer, whose portrait is presented to the readers of this volume, is at present a member of the editorial staff of the New York *Tribune*. He is twenty-nine years of age, having been born on the 13th day of January, 1853. He is the youngest son of Mr. Daniel W. Palmer, of Flatbush, L. I., and his native place was Winterton, Sullivan Co., N. Y., a small hamlet on the line of the New York, Ontario and Western Railroad. His early years were spent on his father's farm, and he attended district schools where very good facilities for obtaining an education were furnished. At the beginning of 1868, when just entering his fifteenth year, he accompanied his older brother, Wilbur M. (a sketch of whom appears herewith), to the Hudson River Institute, at Claverack, Columbia County, N. Y. He continued to attend this institution during the greater part of the two following years, and left it at the close of the Spring term, in 1870, after completing his preparation for college. In the Fall of that year he entered Wesleyan University, at Middletown, Ct., where his brother (previously mentioned) had already been matriculated. The subject of this sketch was a painstaking and faithful student throughout his college course, giving especial attention to the classics. He was graduated as third in a class of thirty-six. While in college he took two prizes in Greek, and prizes in Mental Philosophy, Geology and Moral Science. He was a member of the Greek Letter Society, Alpha Delta Phi, and also of the Phi Beta Kappa. In his senior year in college he taught in the higher department of the graded school in Haddam, Ct., a village a few miles from Middletown. He was graduated as Bachelor of Arts, and three years later received the degree of

Master of Arts. Before leaving college, Mr. Palmer had decided upon journalism as his profession, and on Oct. 9, 1874,
he joined the city staff of the *Tribune* as a reporter. He remained connected with that journal in this capacity —being for
the greater part of the time in charge of the Brooklyn department—until May 29, 1880, when he was promoted to be the
assistant night city editor, which position he still holds. Mr.
Palmer was married on Sept. 26, 1876, to Miss Mattie Leavens,
the oldest daughter of Mr. John Leavens, of Brooklyn, by
whom he had one son, born on August 20, 1877. Mrs. Palmer
died on January 9, 1880, after a three-months' illness. On
October 12, 1881, Mr. Palmer was married to Mrs. Rebecca L.
Trall, of Brooklyn. His only child, Bert Leavens Palmer,
died January 24, 1882. Mr. Palmer's present address is No.
280 Monroe Street, Brooklyn.

JUDGE RICHARD A. WHEELER

(BRIEF BIOGRAPHY.)

Judge Richard A. Wheeler, the subject of the following notice, was born Jan. 29, 1817. He is the son of Richard Wheeler
and Mary Hewitt Wheeler.

His mother was from one of the best families of North Stonington. His father was an industrious, thrifty farmer, and so
his boyhood was under the discipline of the typical " New England home," which has furnished some of the best specimens
of American manhood.

The period of his minority was divided between the industries of the farm during the Spring, Summer and Autumn, and
the educational culture of the common school for the Winter.

The range of studies in these "seminaries" at that time was
very limited—Webster's Spelling Book, Daboll's Arithmetic,
Morse's Geography, Murray's English Grammar, and Murray's
English Reader, being the exclusive text books.

But the teaching and discipline were often severe, and the
scholarship had a corresponding value of thoroughness and
solidity for all practical ends. Judge Wheeler's industrious use
and improvement of the common school is seen in the fact that

this rudimental education has been equal to all the varied positions of responsibility he has, during his opening and ripening
manhood, filled with so much credit to himself, with honor to his
town, and to the full satisfaction of his friends and fellow-
citizens.

Early called to important civil trusts, he has attained to a
degree of legal culture that gives to his counsel great weight
and value, and often render his rulings decisive and final.

In genealogical lore Judge Wheeler has no rival, and few, if
any, equals. His researches here are thorough and fearless, dis-
pelling many a beautiful tradition, but fixing the plain, prosaic
truth by figures and data that will not lie.

His discourse at the late Palmer Re-Union, at Stonington—a
masterly grouping of events, scattered over a period of two hundred and fifty years—held the attention of a large and promiscuous crowd to its close.

Judge Wheeler has been twice married—first to Miss Frances
Mary Avery, of North Stonington, Jan. 12, 1843, and second to
Miss Lucy A. Noyes, of Stonington, Nov. 5, 1856.

He is descended from the following New England families—
Wheeler, Park, Thompson, Payson, Tilestone, Elliott, Burrows,
Culver, Latham, Hubbard, Gore, Draper, Denison, Prentiss,
Gallup, Lake, Stanton, Burch, Fanning, Burd, Chaplin, Hewitt,
Lord, Borodel, Short, Palmer, and others.

In 1838, when twenty-one years old, he was chosen one of the
Society Committee of the Road Church, and has held that office
for forty-three years, to the present time.

He was chosen Selectman in 1847 and '48 ; Representative to
the Legislature, 1851 ; Sheriff of New London County, 1860 ;
re-elected in 1863, '66 and '69, and holding the office until 1872,
when he declined re-election.

In the Spring of 1864, he was chosen Judge of Probate, and
by successive re-elections has held the office until the present
time.

During the Spring of 1881, he was unanimously chosen President of the Groton Monument Association, in Connecticut, which
office he held during the reconstruction of the monument and
improvements upon the surrounding grounds. He was one of

the Vice-Presidents of the Groton Heights Centennial Committee, Chairman of the Historical Committee thereof, a member of the Committee of Admission of Members; also one of the Committee of the New London County Historical Society, and a member of the Committee of Reception during the celebration on the 6th of September, 1881.

Judge Wheeler has written the History of the First Congregational Church of Stonington, a book of 300 pages; also an historical sketch of the three first Congregational Churches in New London County, a historical sketch of the Pequot Indians, and a sketch of the Mystic Valley.

Judge Wheeler also wrote the history of the towns of Stonington and North Stonington, for the New London County History, recently published.

He has collected a large amount of genealogical material of some twelve to fifteen of the earliest families of the town of Stonington, for future publication.

The above are the principal events of Judge Wheeler's active and varied life. He has a fine physique, an open countenance, pleasing address, and genial manners. Besides, he has an inexhaustible fund of genealogical anecdote, can tell a good story of olden or modern times, and excite and enjoy an honest, hearty laugh.

The proverb, " a prophet is not without honor save in his own country," is not applicable to Judge Wheeler, for nowhere is he more popular than among his own town men, and by none more highly esteemed than by his own immediate neighbors.— *From New London County History.*

ADDRESS,

BY B. FRANK PALMER, OF PHILADELPHIA, PA.

[This gentleman had been expected to deliver an address at the Re-Union, and made preparation for the same, but was prevented coming by circumstances beyond his control. We prevailed upon him to send us the substance of his intended address, and he kindly sent them.|

PHILADELPHIA, August 9, 1881.

Hon. E. H. Palmer, Pres't, Noyes F. Palmer, Esq., and Ira H. Palmer, Esq., Committee of Invitation of the Palmer Family Re-Union, August 10, 1881 :

Gentlemen—When you first invited me to the festivities of the Re-Union, I was in doubt as to my having any claim to a seat among the six thousand Palmers found in the line of the honored and honorable Walter, whose "ship came in" to Charlestown, Mass., from Nottinghamshire, England, in 1629.

Not liking to appear by an act of your courtesy only, if I had no right there, I spent a few moments in writing to Noyes F., the family historiographer, asking a few questions ; and his reply to them, just received, leaves me in no doubt as to the direct line.

John Palmer was the father of Joseph 2d ; Benjamin was the son of Joseph, and the father of Benjamin Franklin (or B. Frank).

Joseph was a small boy when (in 1767) the family removed to New Hampshire, where he was found aiding, with his little hands, in forming the first " Palmers' Lodge " in the " vast wilderness," when the fathers pitched their " camp " in the now beautiful and noted vale of Camptown, or Campton. Joseph there married one of the best of Christian women, Martha Taylor. They lived a quiet, useful life ; and the records of Campton show them to have been among the most esteemed of the intelligent citizens. They rest in the Campton Cemetery, near the beautiful spot from which, in a long lifetime,

" Their sober wishes never learned to stray—
Where, during a period of more than 'three score and ten,'
Along the cool, sequestered vale of life,
They kept the noiseless tenor of their way."

There Benjamin was born, in 1790. With a fair education (finished at the Holmes Plymouth Academy), Benjamin, when a young man, taught throughout Grafton County, district and singing schools in the Winter, and engaged generally from Spring to Fall in the pursuit of a farmer, in the beautiful valley about the confluence of the Pemigewasset and Beebe's rivers. A little distance from there runs the Palmer brook, along which I first went fishing. Artists now seek a poetical nook in our old terraced homestead, to sketch the grandest of mountain views, looking through Thornton towards Franconia.

Benjamin Palmer married Abigail Goodwin, and was the father of seven children, six of whom (four sons and two daughters) are now living, the youngest being fifty-three. Benjamin Franklin (the third son), you may count as a poor specimen of this Palmer family, who, at your request, presents here such thoughts as arise on the moment and demand expression. They are epitomized in a few sentences and rhymes, some of which were prepared by request, for the first centennial celebration of the town of Campton, N. H., Sept. 12, 1867; but seem suited to the first Re-Union of the living thousands of the ancient Palmer line, now first assembled in solid phalanx since the return of Peter the Hermit from Jerusalem with his victorious Christian army, bearing palms and singing psalms, in the eleventh century. No person is the better for having a good family line, and none can safely boast of family name who has not added to its lustre. Such need not. But we cannot wish to repudiate a good name fairly won and inherited—the only legacy of a knightly and a Christian ancestry, whose heroic deeds illumined it through a period of near two hundred years, during eight crusades to the Holy Land; for the great crusader, Peter, inflicted the first great blow upon the intolerant infidels, rescued the Holy Sepulchre, and opened the highway to Christian liberty.

All that was gained by the pilgrim, Peter, and the Pilgrim Fathers, has been saved by his and their followers in the Old World and the New. May this liberty never suffer in the charge of their descendants.

Of Walter Palmer and his Puritan band it may be said :

" We read their history in a Nation's eyes."

The intelligent forefathers displayed better than Royal arms; and the ancient Palmer demesne, stretching from Wequetequock harbor to the crest of Mt. Washington, now presents a family shield on which our ancient motto is written in living lines, more potential than heraldic blazonry—*Palmam qui meruit ferat.*

Descended in a more than Royal line—
Ye pilgrim sons, your hopes, your joys are mine;
Let others boast heraldric fame and birth—
Sons of the great who subsidize the earth;
But ye may boast (and none dispute your claim)
An ancestry whose *deeds* transcend a name;
Whose earnest life-work gives example great,
On the broad battle-grounds of CHURCH and STATE.

*   *   *   *   *   *

Our Fathers' faith caught Liberty's first beam,
Which o'er world-conflicts shed its fitful gleam,
And through Time's vistas led the onward way
Of heaven-born freedom, to this glorious day.
Triumph of faith sublime in souls intense—
Unseen till angel voices called them hence—
As we seeing the record, clear and bright,
Their blazon glories in lines of lustrous light.

*   *   *   *   *   *

Guard well the shrines where sleep the patriot sires—
Whose great example my rapt strain inspires;
And monumental bust ye need not raise,
Nor lettered pomp to consecrate their praise.
The Spartan youth heard—starting for the field—
" Bring back or be brought on an honored shield; "
The Pilgrim Matron to her heroes said,
"Come with the honored living, or the honored dead!"

*   *   *   *   *   *

And thus they came—when ceased war's thunder-peal
That caused the pillars of the State to reel;
When great Ulysses, of our ancient line,
Returned victorious in the cause divine!
Sheathing his sword he said—" Let us have peace,"
Let love fraternal in our land increase;
Their memory shall th' admiring world embalm—
Then—" Let him who has won it bear the palm."

AN APOSTROPHE TO LIBERTY.

O how shall the muse, unaccustomed, indite
    A strain that befits so exalted a theme?
The " Nine " with charmed fingers an epic might write,
    Yet tell not the bliss of our goddess's dream.
With tremulous heart, and with faltering hand,
    I waken the harp-string to Liberty's sound—
Its numbers have thrilled where wave answers to strand,
    And mountain to valley re-echoes them round!

The bard and the druid have swept o'er its chord—
    The prophet and priest have bent over its tone—
The psalmist hath tuned it to Faith's cheering word,
    And felt " hands of fire " directing his own.
Old Jura hath listened, red Sinai hath spoken,
    And Palestine wakes at the Crusader's touch ;
Greece, Sparta and Rome have, in phalanx unbroken,
    Marched forth to the music the soul loves so much!

It rings in sweet strains, to Germania's praise—
    O'er Poland and Hungary murmurs its sigh—
Old Gallia flames with the fierce *Marseillaise*,
    And " God save the queen " rings through Albion's sky !
I list to the strain that down Avon has rolled
    As Ocean's loud billows call back from afar—
I hear the lone exile, as, weary and cold,
    He strikes to the numbers of " Erin go bragh ; "

I hear Caledonia, vocal with strains,
    As Abbotsford answers to Ettrick's wild hill ;
And Erin, through all of her sorrows, retains
    " The harp that through Tara's Halls " ever shall thrill !
I sigh for the rapturous music that rolled
    Along the sweet banks of the pure gurgling Ayr—
For the harp, like the *heart*, of the poet is cold,
    And his eye rests no more on that " lingering star. "

But now the New World feels the vibrations grand,
    That master-hands wake round the Puritan's Shrine ;
And the refluent wave, from Columbia's strand
    Bears treasures as rich as the waifs of Lang Syne !
Her songs bless the land, and their life-cheering strains
    Have given new heart-beats of hope o'er the wave ;
Then while Freedom wakes, or our Country remains,
    " The Star Spangled Banner " shall lead on the brave !

Her sons, 'midst the joys of the Orient may roam,
　And linger wher'er the " old Genii " have trod ;
But the heart's inner chord still shall murmur " Sweet Home,"
　And the pilgrim-foot haste to press Liberty's sod.
Poor Howard Payne sounded the key-note sublime—
　And lo! what a chorus of joy shakes the skies ;
Like holy bells ringing their joyfulest chime
　The pæans of freedom and glory arise!

Potential New England—the pride of the land—
　The nursery of Empire is trusted to thee !
The cradle of Liberty rocks by the strand—
　These, these are your shrines, O ye sons of the free !
Then guard ye the rock and the hallowed sod,
　On which your brave fathers—a prayer-loving band—
First stepped from the Mayflower, worshipping God,
　For freedom they found and preserved in the land !

My Country ! I view with a heart full of pride,
　The fame of thy sons and the vastness of thee ;
Thy golden gate opes to Pacific's broad tide—
　Thy sons to the pole plough the disc of the sea ;
And long as that gray shaft in grandeur sublime
　Shall tower o'er the graves where the patriots sleep ;
Their names shall be traced on the pillar of Time,
　Where'er Freedom's angel her vigil shall keep !

And thou in each *science* and art shalt excel—
　Thus " good will toward man " o'er the earth will increase ;
And where'er thy sails of the triumph shall tell,
　The angel of mercy will often say—" peace."
Sail on ! let the starry flag kiss every sky !
　Great ark of the Nations, thou'rt leading the van—
Sail on ! where'er mortals for liberty sigh—
　Bear *hope* to the down-trodden—*Freedom to man !*

THE FAMILY FEATURE.

BY H. EUGENE BOLLES, OF BOSTON, MASS.

　Every well hath its spout,
　And the truth will leak out ;
And our secret is known far and near ;
　So, the Tribes all around
　From the lakes to the sound,
Are on hand for our free lunch and beer.

The ravenous Bear—
Over head in his lair—
Grunts across to the Dog in the sky.
Even comets* appear,
And, with shy look and queer,
Whisk around us like fish round a fly.

Hark! hear that uproar
Joneses make at the door!
Smiths, like rain, stand outside there and rap;
Just as if we could rent
The North Pole for our tent,†
And keep the Atlantic on tap.

To get in, many clans
Will resort to low plans;
The *Smiths forge* our family armor;
And the children of Jones,
Having polished his bones,
Try to palm off his ghost for a Palmer.

And some will rely
On their blue Palmer eye;
And some, of their curling sun-beams;
Trust them not, for alas!
The best eyes may be glass,
And that curl may not grow where it streams.

Then come to our aid,
Lovely muse! from thy shade,
And distinguish our own from the rest.
"There is only one way,"
So I hear the muse say,
And sing this infallible test.

"All family creatures
Have family features—
The impress of nature's own hand—
As each tonic or bark
Has its private trade-mark,
And each whiskey is known by its brand."

---

* NOTE.—Two comets were in sight at the time of the Re-Union.

† The dinner was served in a large tent.

"Some are told everywhere,
By the blush on their hair;
Some by the nose, *a la* Roman or Greek;
And some are so plain
They don't have to explain,
Except when your own eyes are weak."

" Does he act very shy,
And grin his reply,
And feel *unimportant and meek ?*
Then put him right out!
He's a fraud, without doubt,
For a Palmer is known by his *cheek.*

RESPONSIVE LETTER FROM

JUDGE R. A. WHEELER.

PALMERS AND GRANTS.

Rev. P. C. Headley, in his life and campaigns of Gen. Grant, says that he " is of Scotch descent. More than a century ago his ancestor came to the shores of America, then comparatively a wilderness, and settled in Pennsylvania, while a brother who emigrated with him went on to Canada. By honest industry our hardy pioneer supported his growing family upon his forest girdled clearing, until the Revolutionary war called him to its fields of strife. After bravely following the flag of the rising republic he returned with the dawn of peace to his home in Westmoreland County, Pennsylvania." This statement is very far from being correct. Gen. Grant is a direct descendant of Matthew Grant, who was one of the original company who came in the Mary and John to Dorchester, Mass., in 1630. He came to Windsor, Ct., among the very earliest settlers of that town, where he became an active and prominent man, and rendered important service to the then new settlement. He continued to reside at Windsor, until his death, which took place December 16th, 1861.

1. Matthew Grant married Priscilla ——, November 16th, 1625. By the marriage there were four children, viz.: (2) Priscilla, (3) Samuel, (4) Tahan, and (5) John. Samuel Grant,

No. 3, born Nov. 12th, 1631, married Mary Porter May 27th, 1658. Their children were (6) Samuel, (7) John, (8) Matthew, (9) Josiah, (10) Nathaniel, (11) Mary, (12) Sarah, (13) Abigail. Samuel Grant, No. 6, born April 20th, 1659, married first Hannah Filley, Dec. 6th, 1683, by whom he had one child, (14) Hannah, who died young. Her mother died April 18th, 1686. He married for his second wife Grace Miner, April 11th, 1688. She was the daughter of John and Elizabeth (Booth) Miner, and granddaughter of Grace (Palmer) Miner, of Stonington, Ct. Grace Palmer was the daughter of Walter Palmer, and was married to Thomas Miner, April 23d, 1633. Samuel Grant, No. 6, had by his second wife, Grace Miner, eight children, viz.: (15) Hannah, (16) Samuel, (17) Noah, (18) Abigail, (19) Ephraim, (20) Grace, (21) David, and (22) Ebenezer. Noah Grant, No. 17, born Dec. 16th, 1692, married Martha Huntington, of Norwich, Ct., June 12th, 1717. They had four children, viz : (23) Noah, (24) Adoniram, (25) Solomon, and (26) Martha. Noah Grant, No. 23, born July 12th, 1718, married Susannah Delano, Nov. 8th, 1746. They had two sons, viz.: (27) Noah, (28) Peter. Noah Grant, No. 27, born June 20th, 1748, and married for his first wife Mrs. Anna Richardson, by whom he had two sons, (29) Peter, and (30) Solomon. After the death of his first wife, this Noah Grant, No. 29, moved to Pennsylvania from Coventry, Ct., about 1787, where he married Rachael Kelly in 1791. By this marriage there were seven children, viz.: (31) Susan, (32) Jesse Root, (33) Margaret, (34) Noah, (35) John, (36) Roswell, and (37) Rachael. Jesse Root Grant, No. 32, born in January, 1794, married Hannah Simpson, June 24th, 1821. She was born near Philadelphia, and moved with her father to Ohio, where she was married. Their children are Gen. Ulysses Simpson Grant, born April 27th, 1822, Samuel, Clara, Virginia, Orvil L., and Mary Frances Grant. Matthew Grant, his son Samuel, and grandson Samuel Grant, lived and died in the ancient town of Windsor. Noah Grant, son of Samuel Grant No. 6, was born in the same township, and lived there until the town of Tolland was formed from a part of Windsor, when he became an inhabitant of the new town. Noah Grant, No. 24, removed to the adjoining town of Coventry about 1750 ;

and he and his brother Solomon joined the expedition against Crown Point in 1755 and were both killed the same year. Noah Grant, No. 27, served with distinction in the army of the Revolution, and after the close of the war went to Pennsylvania to reside. This is doubtless the ancestor of Gen. Grant, to whom Mr. Headley alludes as coming to America more than a century ago, and whose brother went on to Canada, which was wide of the mark. The direct line of descent of Gen. Grant from Walter Palmer, of Stonington, is as follows:

1. Walter Palmer and first wife ——; 2. Grace Palmer and husband Thomas Miner; 3. John Miner and wife Elizabeth Booth; 4. Grace Miner and husband Samuel Grant; 5. Noah Grant and wife Martha Huntington; 6. Noah Grant and wife Susannah Delano; 7. Noah Grant and wife Rachael Kelly; 8. Jesse Root Grant and wife Hannah Simpson; 6. Gen. U. S. Grant.

RICHARD A. WHEELER.

Stonington, May 14, 1881.

RESPONSIVE LETTER FROM

COURTLAND N. PALMER,

OF NEW YORK CITY.

I am proud of possessing this name, a name we should all feel honored in bearing, and a name we must all in our daily walk and conversation, strive to honor more as time waves on.

I well remember the account my father gave of his early struggles; how, as a boy, renouncing his little patrimony in favor of his needier sisters, he took passage by sloop to New York, since railroads then were a thing of the future. Employed by his brother Amos as a clerk in his hardware store, he rose by hard work and long work, through prudence and economy, until he was the head and master of his own warehouse, resulting finally in the formation of a partnership controlling the largest hardware trade between the South and the North. Failing in the crisis of 1837, he gathered what he could save from the wreck of his business. This he invested in New York real estate, he being one of the earliest citizens of the Metropolis of the New World, to perceive its coming growth and greatness.

Such was my father, a fine type of the American man of energy, self-reliance, honesty and commercial foresight.

I remember one day boasting to an aunt on my mother's side, of my pride in my father as a self-made man. She shrugged her shoulders and remarked : I do not wish to detract from the tribute you render to your father, but be assured that your gentle blood comes from your Knickerbocker descent through your Suydam mother. I had at that time taken but little interest in my genealogical tree on either side, but the good lady, my aunt, promised to send me the printed annals of her family, on the perusal of which I discovered that my maternal grandparent of some two hundred years ago was a worthy blacksmith.

Well, I am glad he was a blacksmith, instead of some pirate freebooter in the times of William the Conqueror, but I am also glad that this Re-Union proves to me that my descent on my father's side, from Walter Palmer in 1629, is at least as ancient and honorable as on that of my mother.

But as old Ben Johnson wrote :

> " Titles are marks of honest men and wise ;
> The fool or knave who wears a title lies ;
> Those who on noble ancestry enlarge,
> Their *debt* produce instead of their *discharge*."

This is the point. As the French motto has it, " Noblesse oblige." By the records and traditions of the past of our great family we are bound to carry the name on to still higher glory. We are the descendants of the past, but the parents of the future.

Those who can read the signs of the times, read in them that wonderful changes are pending in politics, science and religion. Old things are passing away and all things are becoming new. Let us as a family stand in the van of this onward-marching civilization, and welcome the morning breeze from the mountain tops, and hail the rising sun of a new epoch. As Tennyson says,

> " Ring out the days of sloth and crime,
> Ring in the Christ that is to be."

And thus it is and thus only, in the words of George Eliot, that we shall " join the choir invisible of those immortal dead who live again in minds made better by their presence ;" thus it is that we shall have done our share in passing down to the children Palmers to come, the tendencies of a new, a happier, and a better era.

RESPONSIVE LETTER FROM

PROF. DANIEL C. EATON,

OF NEW HAVEN, CT.

I had some other friends in Stonington, and gave them part of my time, and I had to leave the meeting before it was ended to take my train.

I was much interested in Mr. Wheeler's paper on Walter Palmer, and consider it a wonderfully fine production.

I will add a few items in relation to Prudence Palmer, who was a daughter of Jonathan and Mercy Palmer, and was born March 31, 1719. She married Ebenezer Cady, born at Canterbury, April 19, 1714. They had a family of seven sons and one daughter, mostly born at Lyme. About 1764 they removed to Canaan, Columbia Co., N. Y., where Mr. Cady died in 1779, his wife surviving him several years. It is recorded of the sons that most of them served in the war of the Revolution. Their descendants reside mostly in Columbia Co., and along the valley of the Mohawk, though many are scattered in distant places. Among the more conspicuous descendants were Judge Daniel Cady, of the Court of Appeals of New York, and Brevet Major-General Amos B. Eaton, Commissary General of the U. S. Army, from 1864 to 1874.

[Written for the Palmer Gathering, at Stonington, Ct., August 10 and 11, 1881.]

THE PALMER.

BY SIMEON PALMER, BOSTON, MASS.

In the dim past of shadows and of dreams,
Of loathsome superstitions, nameless crimes—
The age of boor and serf, where lurid flames,
Rank with the blood of martyrs, hide the beams
Of the dimmed sun : roaming from land to land
A homeless beggar, bearing in his hand
A branch of palm—seeking from shrine to shrine
If, haply, he may find his Mecca, Palestine ;

Behold our ancestor! A holy man,
As they accounted holiness. In skins,
Like John, he clothed himself ; but then his pan-
Taloons were wisps of straw wound round his shins.*
In faith abounding, innocent of work,
Hating a Jew e'en as a Jew hates pork ;
He of the *world to come* had firmest hope,
But, *in this sphere*, took no account of soap.

His washing, it was figurative ; blood
Was his chief cleanser ; and a frequent dish—
For famine stinted his supply of food—
Was boiled, or raw, or roasted human flesh.
He knew no prattle of a chlid, no wife ;
His daily prayer was for eternal life,
And to escape the clutches of the evil
One whom he knew as Satan, or the Devil.

To mortify his flesh was his delight,
The ripened product of the age of faith—
Knowing no wrong and ignorant of right,
Obedience was his motto, unto death ;
Or to the priest, or to the powers that be.
His God the slaughtered Lamb of Calvary.
Upon the darkness of his mental night
No reason dawned, no science shed its light.

But, in the baleful shadow of the cross
That casts athwart the Universe its gloom,

---

* NOTE.—For an account of the wretched condition of the masses, in Europe in the age of " faith," see Dr. J.W. Draper's "Conflict between Religion and Science."

Counting all earthly treasures but as dross,
He took his cheerless journey to the tomb ;
The tomb, as he believed, for all below,
The yawning portal to eternal woe.
His way beset with goblin and with ghost,
And spirits of the damned forever lost.

A wanderer, through long and weary years
Seeking a Saviour's tomb in Palestine,
He found refinement, manners ; found ideas,
And the keen blade of courteous Saladin ;
And reason vanquished faith.   No more he'll roam
Bearing his palm branch, seeking Jesus' tomb ;
No more, for life to come, will barter joys
Of earth ; he has his home, his wife, his boys !

He sings no longer of a " shining shore "
On neighboring planet, or on distant star,
A grander music is the Atlantic's roar,
Breaking in foam upon the harbor bar ;
And dearer far than shining shore, or shrine
Of saint or fabled God in Palestine,
The homestead, where the boundless prairie waves
Its wealth of green, and stacks its golden sheaves.

Or where the fisher's cot looks out to sea,
Watching the offing for the home-bound sail,
And the white lighthouse sends its welcome ray
To cheer the sailor when the threatening gale
Moans in the rigging, and the fog-bell tolls
Its mournful requiem o'er departed souls.
Whatever is his lot ; or if he be
Fameless, or honored with the *fleur de lis*.*

While he is free and owner of the soil
He tills with his own hand, no blighting dread
Of famine haunts him ; happy in his toil
That those he loves are by his labor fed,
The phantoms of his age of faith are gone.
No goblin haunts his path, nor churchyards yawn
With graves of gibbering ghosts, nor death-watch check
His fleeting moments with their hurried tick.

NOTE.—* I am told that the right to engrave the *"fleur de lis"* upon his coat of
arms was, for some public service, conferred upon a member of the Palmer family
by Henry IV.

He knows his rights, he is a man, is free.
This earth, it is his heritage, his own.
He bows to no one, save in courtesy;
Yields no obedience to priest or throne,
But only to the laws himself has made ;
And as the poet Halleck truly said,
" He never kneels except it be to pray,
Nor even then *except in his own way.*"

Pity our ancestors, that in the night
That lowered o'er Europe for a thousand years,
Through the dark clouds there shone no ray of light
From the deep firmament of blazing stars,
Nor knew they that behind the clouds there shone;
Brighter than star or the eternal sun,
An orb of light, in whose celestial ray
Their children's children should be ever free!

Honor our ancestors! That we are free
From loathsome superstition's foul embrace ;
That we have equal right and liberty
Each to enjoy his heritage in peace;
That we are sovereign and not subjects, make
Aud unmake laws and rulers, for *our* sake ;
That we call no man master, and our vote
Is humbly sought for by our men of note
(With hat in hand, and with exceeding grace
Of manner, like *all* servants out of place).

We owe to those who gave their lives that we
Might know no shackles on our limbs, our lips
No padlock, and our quivering flesh no stripes.
And that we value this rich legacy.
Ye hosts of the innumerable dead,
If, haply, ye be gathered overhead,
Dear spirits of our fathers! hear our vow :
That when our children, as we're gathered now,

Shall stand here when a hundred years have fled,
Through no neglect of ours shall they have lost
The sacred rights that we inherited ;
But as we now, with honest pride may boast,
The virtues of our fathers, they shall show
No stain on our escutcheon, and shall know
Our cherished motto in their day fulfilled :
" Freedom for man, for woman, and for child ! "

Literature of the Press after the Re-Union.

[New York *Tribune*, August 11th.]

PALMER FAMILY RE-UNION.

LARGE GATHERING AT STONINGTON—THE DESCENDANTS OF
WALTER PALMER MEET NEAR THE OLD HOMESTEAD—
OTHER BRANCHES OF THE FAMILY REPRESENTED — A
QUIET NEW-ENGLAND TOWN THRONGED WITH VISITORS—
SPEECHES, POEMS AND OTHER EXERCISES—THE GATHER-
ING SUCCESSFUL.

STONINGTON, Ct., Aug. 10.—The visitor to this staid New
England town would be fully justified in addressing any one
whom he might meet in the street to-day as " Mr. Palmer."
The street urchins salute every passer with this title, and when
one of a crowd of corner loungers near the post-office called out
" Mr. Palmer!" this morning, not less than fifteen men turned
toward the speaker. The Stonington brought a hundred members of the family last night, and the trains this morning were
all crowded. " Palmer lemonade " is for sale on the street corners, and the boot blacks will give you a " Palmer shine" for no
more than the usual fee. The hotels and boarding-houses are
crowded, and many persons slept last night on cots in the parlor of the Hotel Wadawanuck. To-night it is expected that
cots will be put up in the hotel hall and office, and perhaps on
the broad veranda. One quotation from Shakespeare, " Where
do the Palmers lodge, I beseech you?" has often been on the
lips of the committee which has charge of entertaining visitors.

All this is on account of the Re-Union of the Palmer family,
which began to-day, and will be continued through to-morrow.
This date was chosen because August 10, is the anniversary of
the battle of Stonington, the principal event in the history of
this quiet borough. Stonington's glory departed with the decline of the whale fishery business. Time was when thirty
whalers were sent out from here each year. Every family had
both a personal and pecuniary interest in this business, and
Stonington flourished and its people grew rich. But that era
of prosperity passed. Later, visions of popularity as a summer
resort dawned upon the people, but Stonington was over-
shadowed by the nearness of Watch Hill, distant only a five

miles' sail. This Re-Union was started by the Connecticut descendants of Walter Palmer, who settled in Stonington in 1653, and died here eight years later ; but much of its success is due to the efforts of Mr. Noyes F. Palmer, of Jamaica, L. I., who has collected a large number of facts in connection with the genealogy of the various branches of the family. Mr. E. H. Palmer, of Montville, Ct., is the president of the Re-Union, Mr. A. S. Palmer, Jr., the secretary of record, Mr. H. Clay Palmer, the treasurer, and Mr. Ira H. Palmer, the corresponding secretary. Mr. Noyes F. Palmer, has served as the Committee on Invitation, and has sent out over 3000 invitations.

The headquarters of the Re-Union are at Brayton Hall, just across the street from the shaded lawn of the Wadawanuck. A register has been kept here, and at three o'clock this afternoon about 400 names had been put down. These, however, do not represent more than one third the Palmers who are here. Among the names on the register are the following : General George W. Palmer and wife, Col. and Mrs. J. T. Meredith, A. W. Palmer, Lauren Redfield, Gideon Palmer, Dr. Corydon Palmer, Dr. Delos Palmer, Dr. Eugene Palmer, and Stephen Wray, of New York; W. H. Palmer, Mrs. J. A Palmer Van Valsor, Miss J. A. Palmer, Mrs. J. A. Palmer Clayton, Lorin Palmer, wife and two daughters, Justus Palmer, Joseph Cutter and wife, and Josiah Palmer, of Brooklyn ; George W. Palmer, of East New York ; Alanson Palmer, of Astoria ; Dr. James G. Palmer and wife, of New Brunswick, N. J.; and Jay Palmer, of East New York. Some names are registered from as distant points as Illinois and Texas.

A large tent with open sides has been erected in the western part of the town near the railway station, and only a few blocks from the hotel Wadawanuck, and here the public exercises were held to-day. Seats were provided for over a thousand persons, and all were occupied before the exercises began. It was not until 11:20 A. M. that the Hon. E. H. Palmer rapped upon the desk and called the meeting to order. Upon the platform was seated a good number of ladies and gentlemen all presumably bearing the name of Palmer, or descendants of persons bearing that name. Among them were the following : the Rev. A. G. Palmer, D. D., of Stonington ; Mr. Ira H. Palmer, of Stonington ; ex-Governor W. T. Minor, of Stamford ; ex-Lieutenant-Governor F. B. Loomis, of New London ; State Senator Alexander S. Palmer, of Stonington ; the Rev. Dr. E. B. Palmer, of Bridgeton, N. J.; the Rev. C. B. Minor, of Trenton, N. J.; and Dr. Corydon Palmer : Judge R. A. Wheeler, of Stonington ; Mr. Noyes F. Palmer ; Mr. Francis A. Palmer, of

New York; Mr. Lorin Palmer, of Brooklyn, and Mr. L. W. Palmer, of Providence.

After music by the Norwich City Band a prayer was offered by the Rev. Dr. E. B. Palmer. The chairman then introduced the Rev. Dr. A. G. Palmer, the father of Mr. A. M. Palmer, the well-known manager of the Union Square Theatre, who made an address of welcome. He said that great credit was due to Mr. Elisha H. Palmer, of Montville, who had been chiefly instrumental in arranging the Re-Union, and hoped that one result of the Re-Union would be the permanent organization of the family. An address was also made by President E. H. Palmer. He was in the best of humor and was frequently applauded.

There was a good deal of disappointment at the absence of General Grant, who is a direct descendant of Walter Palmer's oldest daughter, and who had promised to be present a part of one day at least. Arrangements had been made for a special train to bring him from New York to Stonington. He was compelled to be absent, however, on account of the death of his brother. On Monday Mr. Ira H. Palmer received the following dispatch in response to one which he sent to the ex-President on Saturday:

NEW YORK, August 8.

TO IRA H. PALMER:

Domestic reasons will prevent my attending the Palmer Re-Union.

U. S. GRANT.

This dispatch was read by Ira H. Palmer just before the close of the morning exercises. As the audience was dispersing, a bright little paper called *The Palmer Vidette*, found many buyers. It is announced as published monthly by Henry R. Palmer, a boy of thirteen, a son of Mr. Ira H. Palmer. It is devoted exclusively to the interests of the Palmer family. This number which is said to be "Volume 1, No. 1," contains a full report of the address delivered by the Rev. Dr. Palmer this morning.

The afternoon exercises were even more largely attended than those of this morning. They began with the playing of "Home, Sweet Home," by the band. Then came an interesting historical address by Judge R. A. Wheeler. This was devoted mainly to an account of the life of Walter Palmer, whose origin is somewhat involved in obscurity. He came from Nottinghamshire, England, to Charlestown, Mass., in 1629, under a patent from the Plymouth Council. He was a widower with five children—Grace, William, John, Jonah, and Elizabeth. In Charlestown he married Rebecca Short, of Boston. There

he remained until 1643, when he went to Rehoboth, in the
Plymouth Colony.   In 1653 he came to Stonington (then called
Pawcatuck), where he lived during the rest of his life.   He died
November 10, 1661.   While in Rehoboth he represented that
town in the Colonial Court for two years.   After he came to
Stonington he took an active and prominent part in the affairs
of the town.   By his second wife he had seven children—Han-
nah, Elihu, Nehemiah, Moses, Benjamin, Gershem and Rebecca.
Judge Wheeler's address was listened to with close attention.

After music a poem was read by the Rev. Dr. A. G. Palmer,
who reviewed the deeds of the family at considerable length.
This was followed by an address on " Palmer Families " by Mr.
Noyes F. Palmer, who spoke of various branches of the family
and of what has been accomplished by their members.

A poem by the Rev. Frederick Denison, of Providence,
opened the evening exercises, aud afterwards there were several short speeches by non-resident descendants of Walter Palmer.
The gathering partook somewhat of the character of an experience meeting, and everybody was kept in the best of humor by
the semi-personal character of some of the remarks.   A display of
fireworks closed the first day of the Re-Union.   This was witnessed by a great throng of people.   The most interesting
pieces were those in honor of Washington, President Garfield,
and others, and they were received with applause.

To-morrow morning there will be an excursion by train to
the Wequetequock Dry Bridge, and thence the descendants of
the original Palmers will march to the site of the Walter Palmer
homestead and to the old Wequetequock Burying Ground,
where Walter Palmer was buried.   After the return of the excursion train there will be a clambake on the Re-Union grounds
here.

[New York *Tribune*, Second Day.]

THE PALMER GATHERING.

THE RE-UNION AT STONINGTON A SUCCESS—A CROWD ALMOST
TOO GREAT TO BE ACCOMMODATED, BUT EVERYBODY CON-
TENTED AND HAPPY—TAKING A TRIP TO THE SITE OF
WALTER PALMER'S HOMESTEAD AND THE SPOT WHERE
THE ANCESTOR OF THE FAMILY IS BURIED—AN OLD-FASH-
IONED CLAM BAKE IN THE BIG TENT—HOW THE VISITORS
WENT HOME.

STONINGTON, CT., August 12.—Members of the numerous
Palmer family continued to arrive in Stonington in large num-

bers yesterday morning. The weather has been delightful for the last few days, and this has been no small element in the success of the Re-Union. That it has been a complete success is the opinion of nearly everyone of the thousands who have participated in it. Of course there are two or three growlers, who not being descendants of Walter Palmer, think that one branch of the family has been glorified to the exclusion of descendants of other Palmers who came to this country a few years after—and, in one case a few years before—the arrival of Walter. Wednesday was a busy day, and yesterday was equally so. Those who were fortunate enough to get good beds at night slept soundly. There has been considerable complaint about the management of the Hotel Wadawanuck. Persons who engaged rooms there several days ago, found upon their arrival Tuesday and Wednesday that the rooms which they expected had not been reserved. Then the force of cooks and waiters was entirely inadequate. The service in the dining-room was very slow, and some persons after waiting an hour or more were compelled to abandon the attempt to get a meal. The hotel proprietor seemed to fail wholly in endeavoring to comprehend the situation, and was as much surprised by the influx of guests, which he had had every reason to look for, as the steady-going people of Stonington have been by the crowds that have thronged the streets of their borough during the last few days.

The crowd which gathered to see the fireworks Wednesday night was probably the largest that Stonington ever boasted of, and there was no hitch or failure in setting off the various pieces. The final one was a memorial of Walter Palmer. This contained a figure which may be supposed to represent Walter Palmer, with his name and the dates " 1653—1881." It was heartily applauded. At the evening meeting a few remarks were made by Mr. Francis A. Palmer, of the Broadway National Bank, New York, who a year or two ago purchased a church in Thirty-fourth street in order to establish a free church " for the people," and who more recently had a quarrel with the pastor whom he had engaged, the Rev. George J. Mingins. Mr. Palmer said at the close of his short speech that if a re-union of the family should be held in New York City he would see that all the visitors were entertained. It is probable that this offer will be accepted at no distant day.

Yesterday morning about half-past 9 more than five hundred members of the family went by special train to view the site of the house in which their principal ancestor lived during a part of his residence in Pawcatuck (Stonington), and also the ancient

Wequetequock Burying Ground, where he was buried. These are situated about two and a half miles from the center of the borough. A number also went out by carriage, and a few walked. The burying ground is situated on a slope at the head of Wequetequock Cove, a few rods from where the Anguilla Riverlet flows into the Cove. Walter Palmer's estate, embracing about 1,200 acres, lay on the east side of the cove, and extended from its upper end down to the ocean. The burying ground was set apart by him and originally bordered upon the Cove. Now, however, a road runs along the shore and is divided from the burial plot by a substantial stone fence. It is not an absolute certainty that Walter Palmer and his wife Rebekah are buried here ; but it is believed that his bones (or what may remain of them) lie under a huge "hog back" stone. This stone is said to have been described in Walter's will, with the request that it be placed over his grave. There is no inscription or mark whatever upon the stone, which is 6 feet 11 inches in length—the reputed height of Walter Palmer, whose weight was 300 pounds—and must weigh at least half a ton. One reason why this is believed to be the grave of this ancestral Palmer is that a stone marking the burial spot of his son Nehemiah stands alongside of the stone already described. Another of Walter Palmer's children, his oldest daughter, Grace, who married Thomas Minor, is also buried a rod or two away, together with her husband. A flat stone covers the common grave, bearing the figures " 1690." His son, Elihu, who died in 1665, is buried here, and the first wife of his son Gershem. The inscription upon the rude, lichen-covered stone which marks Nehemiah Palmer's grave is as follows :

Here lyeth ye body
of Nehemiah Palmer
Esqr. Dyed Feb'ry
the 17, 1717, in
the 81st year of
his age.

The burying ground is surrounded by a stone wall, which is dilapidated in parts. It has been much neglected, and evidently has been allowed to grow up to weeds and briars. These had recently been cut, but had not been raked up this morning, and many were the complaints of the ladies to whose skirts the briars clung with much persistence. After spending some time in viewing the interesting features of the ground the visitors gathered together around Walter Palmer's grave. Here two hymns written for the occasion were sung, and a prayer was offered and the benediction pronounced by the Rev. Dr. A. G. Palmer.

On their way to the burying-ground most of the visitors stopped to see the site of the old homestead. This is a few rods from the road, and·marks the site of the second occupied by the original Walter. It is only a short distance from the Wequetequock Cove, which was the only highway to the sea two centuries ago. The cellar walls are in a dilapidated condition and are overgrown with weeds and thorns. A group of balm-of-Gilead trees stands near the spot. Nearly everyone carried away some relics in the shape of stones or walking-sticks or flowers. A few steps from the house in the direction of the Cove, is an old well at which Walter Palmer doubtless many times quenched his thirst when weary with toiling in the rocky fields of which much of his farm consisted. A pole and pail and a couple of glasses were provided here and all had an opportunity to drink from the clear, cold water.

The party returned to Stonington about noon, and then there were a number of addresses in the tent by the representatives of various branches of the family.

After the speeches had been concluded a clambake was served in the large tent. About 500 persons sat down at four large tables, and clams and clamshells were soon rapidly disappearing—the latter being tossed under the table. This practically concluded the exercises of the re-union, although there was some speech-making afterward. The late afternoon and evening trains in both directions were crowded, and there was a large quota of Palmers who started for New York. The moon was shining in an unclouded sky, and the first hours of the trip promised to be very enjoyable. After the clambake and before the hour when the Narragansett started, a considerable number went over to Watch Hill and had a sea-bath. The sail is very delightful, and when wind and tide are favorable the trip can be made in twenty minutes.

[New York *Times*, August 11, 1881.]

A TOWN FULL OF PALMERS.

THE NOTABLE FAMILY RE-UNION AT STONINGTON—DESCENDANTS OF WALTER AND WILLIAM PALMER FILLING THE PLACE AND THE ADJACENT HAMLETS—WHAT WAS DONE YESTERDAY.

Justly proud of its part in the bitter War of 1812, the village of Stonington, Ct., has never failed to celebrate the anniversary of that 10th of August when off its coast the brave, undisciplined Continental cannonaders put to rout the heavy ships of Britain. The day is always a gala one, more generally observed and more enthusiastically hailed by local patriots than even Independence Day itself. And yesterday the old town surpassed every celebration recorded in the past. Never were its streets so filled, never did strangers so abound, and never was patriotic sentiment so earnestly displayed. The orders of the day were of greater scope than usual, embracing exercises in honor of that stern, conscientious old Puritan, Walter Palmer, the colleague of John Endicott and the virtuous founder of Stonington more than two and a quarter centuries ago. The descendants of this man and of his kinsman, William Palmer, the first Pilgrim of the family name who reached America, as well as the descendants of divers other Palmers of ante-Revolutionary times, endeavored yesterday to do justice on so appropriate an occasion to memories long honored too modestly.

When Walter Palmer died, in 1661, twelve children survived him ; now there are not less than 6,000 citizens of his adopted land who claim him as progenitor. These 6,000 persons were largely represented in Stonington yesterday. For more than a week past they had been gathering. Every train brought them in force, and the boats from New York during the past several days have received fully two-thirds of their patronage from this one source. The hotels were all filled with Palmers, and Palmers overran the private boarding-houses of the quiet town, and, indeed, the reign of Palmer extended even into the neighboring hamlets, accommodations being practically exhausted in Stonington before many more than half. of the guests had been provided for. A family re-union on such a scale was never before attempted in New England. But its success renders certain the early gathering of the clans of Noyes and Stanton and Minor and Denison and Chesebrough, and a half-hundred others who have reason for pride in historic ancestors, and whose numbers are become almost countless.

Stonington is a pretty town, with its cozy cottages, broad lawns, and fresh-faced maidens. It boasts two or three hotels more or less distant from first-class establishments. Liquid refreshments stronger than coffee are not served, and one of the Palmer family who so far forgot himself yesterday afternoon as to ask for a seltzer lemonade, almost completely stupefied the amiable clerk, and subjected himself to a severe reprimand on account of the terrible viciousness of his appetite. Bunting streaming from every building, and the inhabitants were out en masse to bid cordial greeting to their guests. On the streets everything was " Palmer." " Palmer avenue " stared the pedes-

trians in the face from black-lettered signboards; " Palmer bit-
ters " were advertised at the village drug store; a " Palmer
Base-ball Club " played against another ragamuffin nine at the
depot; " Palmer lemonade " was dispensed on the street corners, and the one bootblack of the place vociferously yelled :
" Here's where ye git yer Palmer shine." The visitors during
the early part of the day scattered about the town and learned
of its historic attractions. The two old 18-pound guns that
did duty on that eventful 10th of August, 67 years ago, were
chief among the subjects of inspection. They stand down near
the ocean, bright with new paint, with their lips kissing, and
their wooden wagons only a little less well preserved than in 1814.
Up the street, a walk of a minute or two, is kept the banner
that floated over the brave patriots of the " Point " in the historic fight. It is sadly tattered, and relic-hunters have had
good chance to despoil its folds. The State Historical Society
has vainly endeavored to have the borough transfer its title to
the flag, and there is room to fear that the lack of effort to secure proper preservation may in the future be regretted. On
the same street, and only a little distance removed from the
house where the flag hangs, is the home of Miss Mary Howe,
who, as a child of 14, witnessed the engagement of Yankee
valor against British power; and she probably. is better able to
relate the story of that engagement than any other person now
living. On the corner of the avenue in front of her residence
stands a granite monument surmounted by one of the heavy
shells thrown into the town by the English cannon. It is in-
scribed as follows:

> In Memory of
> GEORGE HOWE FELLOWES,
> Who Nailed the Flag to the Mast.

Tender memories of this hero are cherished in Stonington.
A shell struck down the American flag, whereupon the brave
young Fellowes, in the thickest of the fight, caught up the
fallen banner and coolly nailed it to the mast.

The morning had more than half passed before the family, in
all its strength, gathered upon the tented grounds in the upper
part of the village, within a stone's throw of the depot. A score
or so of cozy canvas tents were grouped about the canvas pavilion set apart for the public meetings. Beyond stretched a beautiful lawn sloping down to a miniature lake. The small tents were
all occupied for the most part by Palmer families from New
York, bent on " roughing it." One of the tents served as a

newspaper office, yesterday being the honored day of birth of the *Palmer Vidette*, a journal " devoted to the interests of the Palmers all over creation." Its founder is Henry Robinson Palmer, a lad about 13 years old, residing in Stonington. He is well supported, there being much pride aroused in the fact that the Palmers can claim the youngest editor in the country. The paper is to be published monthly and will print no news except such as is directly connected with the Palmer family; nor will advertisements be accepted from persons outside the same circle. The leading article of the first issue advocates the adoption of August 10 as " Palmers' Day," to be celebrated annually. Prominent place is also given to the following start-ling announcement : •

" James E. Palmer, of Wequetequock, is the man who introduced Pekin ducks into this country."

Not a few well-known names belong to the line of Palmer. Gen. John M. Palmer, ex-Governor of Illinois, is a direct de-scendant of Walter, and this honor he shares with Gen. George • W. Palmer of this city ; Erastus D. Palmer, the sculptor ; the Rev. Dr. Ray Palmer, author of " My faith looks up to Thee " and other popular hymns ; F. W. Palmer, who established the Chicago *Inter-Ocean* ; A. M. Palmer, of the Union Square Theatre ; Dr. J.'W. Palmer, the Baltimore author ; ex-Gov. W. T. Minor, of Stamford ; ex-Lieut.-Gov. F. B. Loomis, of New London ; Capt. Aleck Palmer, of Stonington ; United States Senator David Davis, of Illinois, and a host of others. But the crowning glory of all, in the Palmer view, is the relation borne by Gen. Grant, who in the eighth generation is descended from Walter " as straight as a string." When Walter Palmer came to New England he brought with him five children by a wife who had died. These children were Grace, William, John, Jo-nah, and Elizabeth. Grace married Thomas Minor, the head of the great Minor (and Miner) family of the Eastern States. From that union descended Gen. Grant. Weeks ago the Re-union having become assured, a pressing invitation was sent to the General to be present. He replied that he should be " very glad to attend if in any wise it was possible. The palace car " Palmer " was chartered to carry him in a special train to Stonington, and every arrangement had been made by those in charge to render the distinguished guest's stay among his kith and kin one of marked pleasure. All the forenoon yester-day the great majority of those present in the village were earn-est in their expectation of the ex-President. Every train ar-riving at the depot was besieged by crowds, who did not attempt to disavow their disappointment at the non-appearance of the one anticipated. At 11 o'clock the formal morning session of the Re-union opened and Gen. Grant had not yet come. On every face was written anxiety and every lip was ready to question, " Do you really think he will come?" Finally Mr. Ira H. Palmer, who has had charge of the 4,700 invitations issued, announced that he was in receipt of a dispatch from Gen. Grant. There was an instant hush. He read :

Domestic reasons prevent my attending the Palmer Family Re-union.
U. S. GRANT.

Continuing the morning session, Rev. E. B. Palmer, of Bridgeton, N. J., said a prayer in behalf of the large family gathered under such novel circumstances. The address of welcome was delivered by the Rev. A. G. Palmer, Pastor of the First Baptist Church of Stonington. Following this address there was music by the Palmer Brass Band, each member of which boasts descent from the founder of Stonington or his Puritan brothers. The music was good, and so was the address by the Hon. E. H. Palmer, President of the day. In an intermission of two hours, fortunate visitors secured dinner. Some there were, however, not of the fortunate. The afternoon exercises began at 2 o'clock, with an elaborate sketch of Walter Palmer, and his movements from a date prior to his landing in New England up till the time of his death, in 1661. This address was made by Judge R. A. Wheeler, one of the first of Connecticut's local historians, and it was supplemented by a historical poem by the Rev. A. G. Palmer, recounting the achievements of those of the Palmer name. Noyes F. Palmer, of Jamaica, L. I., presented the story of the " Palmer Families," closely tracing the genealogy of the various branches of the family. A review by ex-Warden Williams of the battle of Stonington closed the afternoon exercises. In the evening there were oratory and song and fire-works. To-day an excursion is to be made, each Palmer carrying a palm leaf, to Walter Palmer's original homestead site, and thence to the ancient Wequetequock burying-ground, where is the grave of the famous old Puritan and his twelve children. The Re-union register bears the names of the following New- Yorkers: Gen. George W. Palmer and wife, Dr. N. Palmer, Mrs. John S. Brull, Stephen Wray, Col. J. T. Meredith and wife, Charlotte Walker, Margaret Palmer, A. W. Palmer, Lauren Redfield, Gideon Palmer. The Brooklyn registrations were W. H. Palmer, Mrs. J. A. Palmer Van Valsor, Miss J. A. Palmer Clayton, Lorin Palmer and wife, May Palmer, Sophia Palmer, Justus Palmer, Joseph Cutler and wife, Josiah

Palmer, Henry L. Palmer, George W. Palmer, and Jay Palmer represented East New York, and W. M. Palmer and Archie Palmer were present from Flatbush, with Alonson Parker, of Astoria. The Rev. R. Randall Hoes was a prominent guest, as also was Mrs. Mary Dana Shindler, aged 71, of Texas. She is a descendant of Walter, and is well known in literary circles as the author of "Flee as a bird to yon mountain," "I am a pilgrim and a stranger," and other hymns. The Palmer present from the furthest point west was J. L. Palmer, of Little Rock, Ark.

[From Brooklyn *Union-Argus*, August 11.]

PALMERS ALL.

WALTER PALMER'S DESCENDANTS AT STONINGTON—A RE-
MARKABLE RE-UNION—THE TOWN OVERRUN BY THE
FAMILY—HOSPITALITY OF THE RESIDENTS—THE EXER-
CISES—A STROLL THROUGH THE TOWN—PILGRIMAGE
TO-DAY TO THE GRAVE OF THE OLD PURITAN.

STONINGTON, Conn., August 10.—This is the only time and place where the size and capacity of the big Rockaway Hotel would be appreciated. From last evening until now the poor hotel clerk of the Wadawanuck House has grown feeble in repeating "rooms all taken." The town is fairly overrun with Palmers who are pulling the door bells of the private houses and begging for a night's lodging. To the credit of the Stonington people, though they be not, perhaps, invited to the jubilee, with few exceptions throw wide their doors to the weary travel-stained descendants of the ancient Walter P. If that stately pilgrim is looking on to-day, he must smile to see how his descendants have for the first time become veritable Pilgrims and all in a lump, so to speak. Many people will be forced to go out of town for the night to Watch Hill, Westley, Mystic, New London, or, perhaps worse, to the steamer *Frances*, which lies moored to the dock to receive the overplus, and it must be confessed in not a condition to suit the most fastidious. In fact, Stonington seems to have been taken possession of by a surprise party, and is consequently wholly unable to cope with the incoming crowds.

The exercises, which began this morning about eleven o'clock, were held in a large tent a few rods back of the Wadawanuck House, capable of holding over 1,200 people. It was fairly bulged out by the attendance of to-day, and it is not safe to predict its tension to-morrow. A score or so smaller tents are grouped around the big one. One of the tents serves as a news-paper office, to-day being the day of birth of the *Palmer Vidette*, a journal "devoted to the interests of the Palmers all over creation." Its founder is Henry Robinson Palmer, a lad but 13 years old, residing in Stonington. He is well supported, there being much pride aroused in the fact that the Palmers can claim the youngest editor in the country. The paper is to be published monthly, and will print no news except such as is directly connected with the Palmer family ; nor will advertise-ments be accepted from persons outside the same circle. The leading article of the first issue advocates the adoption of August 10 as " Palmers' Day," to be celebrated annually.

Very interesting indeed were the exercises. Rev. Dr. A. G. Palmer, in his address of welcome, served to engender a family feeling in the following fitting words :

" We welcome you to the old town, as rugged in its history as in its rocks and hills ; and in its more marked epochs as sub-lime and grand as the storm-driven waves that dash and break upon the rocky shore. It is the soil that Walter Palmer and his compeers, the Chesebroughs, the Minors, the Stantons, the Noyeses, and others broke up from a wilderness state and made homes thereupon. You are here from every part of the land, especially from the West, to which many of the Palmers from this town early removed, and laid the foundation for that golden prosperity in wealth and liberal culture, and also in social and religious relations, for which the family is now as distinguished as any other family in the land, as records will show."

If any man living can tell " where the Palmers lodge," that man is Mr. Noyes F. Palmer, of Jamaica, L. I., whose admira-ble address on " Palmer Families " I sent you yesterday. So long were most of the addresses and papers that this evening the speeches were limited to five minutes each.

The headquarters for registry at Brayton Hall contains seve-ral hundred names at present writing, and the cry is " still they come." A stroll through the town revealed a genuine local interest in the combined celebration of the Battle of Stoning-ton and the family re-union. Flags and bunting are seen at the corners of every street, while the ancient bombs, mounted on corner posts, which were thrown from the ship *Terror* on Au-gust 10, 1814, and the two antiquated cannon at the south end of the town, muzzle to muzzle, serve to remind the Palmer tribe strongly of an animated time during that 10th of August long ago. Stonington is a very cool town despite its low level. It is located on a rocky peninsular, so that the breezes blow across it from both sides unobstructedly.

The scenes on the street are very amusing to the new comer. The fresh arrival is hailed by the rustic gamin with "Hello, Palmer," and the unwary arrival turns his head instanter, as does everyone who does not think twice, and the laughter is audible at the involuntary "give away." People are here on a double purpose—to have a good time, and find out who they are if they can. Men don't stop for an introduction, but begin right away to plough up their family trees and compare roots, and for the most part the would-be blood relations find themselves only seven or eight generations apart. There are all kinds of Palmers represented—the sun-bronzed farmers with fists like leather, and well-dressed merchants with unsoiled palm, while the ladies, too, are as widely divergent as Newport and New Utrecht. Despite the inconveniences experienced in lack of accommodations, the Re-union will prove of itself an event long to be remembered for its gathering of so many of a large family who have never before in the long run of years met and saw what manner of people they were. Taken altogether, they show their good stock, good breeding, and, more than all, good humor, and a disposition to take things easy, and not fret because everything don't happen to run on a smooth basis.

General Grant, who is a descendant, and had accepted an invitation to be present, telegraphed this morning to Ira H. Palmer that "domestic reasons would prevent his attending the Re-union." This is a great disappointment to everyone. The palace car "Palmer" had been chartered to bring him in a special train to Stonington, and every arrangement had been made by those in charge to render the distinguished guest's stay among his kith and kin one of marked pleasure.

The programme for to-morrow includes an excursion to Wequetequock Dry Bridge, marching with music of "Battle Hymn of the Republic" to Walter Palmer's homestead site, thence to the ancient Wequetequock burying-ground, where appropriate services will be held. On the return there will be an old-fashioned clam-bake, weather permitting.

[From New York *Herald*, August 11.]

PROLIFIC PALMER.

TWO THOUSAND DESCENDANTS OF THE OLD, ORIGINAL WALTER VISIT THE HOMESTEAD AND OVERRUN STONINGTON—SINGING HIS PRAISES AND THEIR OWN IN PROSE AND VERSE.

STONINGTON, August 10, 1881.—The Palmers are a prolific family. Of the assemblage of two thousand, at the family re-union to-day, all are direct descendants of sturdy Walter Palmer, who came from Nottinghamshire, England, in 1663, and settled near this place. A part of the old homestead and the burial ground in which he and his children lie are to be the objects of a pilgrimage by the Palmers to-morrow to Wequetequock Cove, a mile and a half east of Stonington. To-day the exercises were devoted to sounding the praises of the Palmers in prose and poem. Flags are flying on all the public and many private buildings, and there is a general attempt at decoration. The hotels are overflowing, and many have sought quarters in adjacent villages. A large tent was erected on the sweeping lawn of the famous old Loper mansion, near the depot, and there were numerous smaller tents and booths in the shade of trees. General Grant was expected, but early in the day he telegraphed that the funeral of his brother Orvil would prevent his attendance.

Among the prominent members of the great Palmer family present were President Palmer, of the Broadway National Bank; George W. Palmer, of New York; Alderman Palmer, of Brooklyn; Chauncey F. Palmer, of Utica; Noyes F. Palmer, of Jamaica, L. I., author of the Palmer Genealogy; ex-Governor Minor. of Stamford; Professor Eaton, of Yale; Professor Asaph Hall, of Washington, D. C.; Rev. E. B. Palmer, of Bridgeton, N. J.; Lorin Palmer, of the Brooklyn *Union-Argus*, and many others. All of the Eastern and Middle States are represented largely, and a score or more of Palmers are here from Western cities.

The programmes of to-day's exercises bear the inscription, " Palmam qui meruit ferat," and every Palmer on the ground was decorated with a red badge. This forenoon the Rev. Dr. Palmer, of Stonington, delivered an address of welcome. This afternoon Judge Ralph Wheeler, of New London, gave an historical address, and Mr. Ephraim Williams, of Stonington, an address on the defence of Stonington against the British in 1813, to-day being the anniversary. A poem of an historical character was read by the Rev. Dr. Palmer, of Stonington. This evening there were impromptu speeches and an address on Palmer families by Noyes F. Palmer, and at a later hour there was a fine pyrotechnic display with several set pieces. To-morrow the principal event will be the visit to the ancient Palmer homestead, but there will also be exercises extending into the evening.

[From *The Day*, New London, Conn.]

PROLIFIC WALTER.

FIFTEEN HUNDRED OF HIS DESCENDANTS OVERRUN STONINGTON—A MAMMOTH RE-UNION—ELABORATE OBSERVANCES, WEDNESDAY AND THURSDAY—PALMER PROGENY PRESENT.

" Is this where you live, Cap'n? Be you a Palmer?" were the words that fell on the ear as a reporter of this paper strolled past the Wadawanuck Hotel, at Stonington, Wednesday morning. The speaker was an urchin about six years old who had one of the crimson Re-union badges of the Palmers pinned upon his breast, nearly covering his entire jacket front. The crowds of visitors had but just commenced to roll into the place. It was not until after dinner that the people began to assemble in earnest. The cheerful, breezy old town of Stonington and the shipping in the harbor was gaily decked with bunting of all colors out of courtesy to the Palmers, and in respect to the memory of those who fought so bravely the battle of Stonington Point in 1814. The New York boats and the trains East and West were well filled with pilgrims. Street venders shouted themselves hoarse with Palmer cards, Re-union cigars, Palmer lemonade, Palmer ice cream, Palmer double-jointed peanuts, and Palmer Jackson balls and candy. The man with the magic mouse, the lifting machine and the blower, were each in their individual glory. Everybody seemed to grow in good humor as the jam on the streets increased. Long before the afternoon services began it was evident that there were not sufficient accommodations for one-half the visitors, and considerable fault-finding was the result. When it is considered, however, that the weight of the arrangements fell on the shoulders of two or three men, one wonders how they could have done as well as they did. But the fact remained that " feed and lodgin'," as one of the Palmers expressed it, " wuz mighty sca'ce," as the day progressed. Several wearied with long journeys from distant States arrived weak, weary and dusty, to find that having sought and found the Palmer Mecca, the next object of their research must needs be a boarding place. But the distresses of the masses meant dollars to the ears of hotel men and restaurateurs. Food commanded fabulous figures. Ham sandwiches melted away like the morning dew at a York shilling apiece, ice cream went at twenty cents per dish, and where it was possible to get a hotel dinner, $1.25 was the ruling price. On Thursday, the crowd was not so large, hence the people were more fairly used, but during both days the hotels at Westerly, Watch Hill, Mystic, and in the borough and also the steamer *Francis*, at the wharf, were filled to overflowing. The quotation which the Palmers have taken from Shakespeare: "Where do the Palmers lodge, I beseech you?" had a thoroughly truthful as well as a poetical application, Wednesday night.

The morning had more than half passed before the Palmer family, in all its strength, gathered upon the tented grounds on Loper Park, in the upper part of the village. A score or more of cozy canvas tents were grouped about the canvas pavilion, set apart for the public meetings. Beyond stretched a beautiful lawn, sloping down to a miniature lake. The small tents were all occupied for the most part by Palmer families from New York, bent on "roughing it." One of the tents served as a newspaper office, being the honored place of birth of the *Palmer Vidette*, a journal "devoted to the interests of the Palmers all over creation." Its founder is Henry Robinson Palmer, a lad but thirteen years old, residing in Stonington, and a son of Ira H. Palmer. He is well supported, there being much pride aroused in the fact that the Palmers can claim the youngest editor in the country.

The Palmer Re-union was started by the Connecticut descendants of Walter Palmer, who settled in Stonington in 1653, and died eight years later; but much of its success is due to the efforts of Noyes F. Palmer, of Jamaica, L. I., who has collected a large number of facts in connection with the genealogy of the various branches of the family. E. H. Palmer, of Montville, was the President of the Re-union, A. S. Palmer, Jr., the Secretary of Record, H. Clay Palmer, Treasurer, and Ira H. Palmer, Corresponding Secretary. Noyes F. Palmer served as the Committee on Invitation, and sent out over four thousand invitations. Not a few well-known names belong to the line of Palmer. Gen. John M. Palmer, ex-Governor of Illinois, is a direct descendant of Walter, and this honor he shares with Gen. George W. Palmer, of New York; Erastus D. Palmer, the sculptor; Rev. Dr. Ray Palmer, author of "My faith looks up to thee," and other popular hymns; F. W. Palmer, who established the Chicago *Inter-Ocean;* A. M. Palmer, of the Union Square Theatre; Dr. J. W. Palmer, the Baltimore author; ex-Gov. W. T. Minor, of Stamford; ex-Lieut. Gov. F. B. Loomis, of New London; Capt. Aleck Palmer, of Stonington; United States Senator David Davis, of Illinois, and a host of others. But the crowning glory of all, in the Palmer view, is the relation borne by Gen. Grant, who in the eighth generation is descended from Walter "as straight as a string."

At 11.20 the exercises in the tent were begun by music by the Noank Brass Band, after which President E. H. Palmer called the assemblage to order and prayer was offered by the Rev. E. B. Palmer, of Bridgeton, N. J.   An eloquent and cordial address of welcome was delivered by Rev. A. G. Palmer, D. D., of Stonington, in which he described the small beginnings of the movement for a Re-union, paying due honor to the grit and energy which had been displayed by Hon. E. H. Palmer in pushing the matter to a vigorous success.   Hon. E. H. Palmer followed in a brief impromptu address, saying that he felt prouder to be President of the Palmer Re-union than he would to be President of the United States.

The afternoon observances were much more largely attended than those of the morning.   They began with the playing of "Home, Sweet Home," by the Band.   Then came an interesting historical address by Judge R. A. Wheeler.   This was devoted mainly to an account of the life of Walter Palmer, whose origin is somewhat involved in obscurity.   He came from Nottinghamshire, England, to Charlestown, Mass., in 1629, under a patent from the Plymouth Council.   He was a widower with five children—Grace, William, John, Jonah, and Elizabeth.   In Charlestown he married Rebecca Short, of Boston.   There he remained until 1643, when he went to Rehoboth, in the Plymouth Colony.   In 1653 he came to Stonington (then called Pawcatuck), where he lived during the rest of his life.   He died November 10, 1661.   While in Rehoboth he represented that town in the Colonial Court for two years.   After he came to Stonington he took an active and prominent part in the affairs of the town.   By his second wife he had seven children—Hannah, Elihu, Nehemiah, Moses, Benjamin, Gershom, and Rebecca. Judge Wheeler's address was listened to with close attention.

A collection amounting to over $450 was then taken in a few moments to aid in defraying the expenses of the Re-union, which were over $900.   The hat was passed again with good success, Thursday.   After music, a poem was read by Rev. Dr. A. G. Palmer, who reviewed the deeds of the Palmer family at considerable length.   This was followed by an address on "Palmer Families" by Noyes F. Palmer, who spoke of what has been accomplished by its members.

A stirring poem by Rev. Frederick Denison, of Providence, opened the evening exercises, and afterward there were several short speeches by non-resident descendants of Walter Palmer. A fine display of fire-works closed the first day of the Re-union. This was witnessed by a great throng of people from Norwich, New London and neighboring towns.   The most interesting pieces were those in honor of Washington, President Garfield, Grant, Bigelow, Walter Palmer and others, and they were received with applause.

On Thursday morning an excursion train was run to Wequetequock dry bridge, where the family marched to the " Battle Hymn of the Republic " to Walter Palmer's Homestead, and thence to the ancient Wequetequock burying ground, where appropriate services were held.   Remarks and responses by descendants of ancestral families of Stonington were in order as soon as the pilgrims returned from the excursion, which was not till late.   The next exercise was the " including " of an old-fashioned clam bake on the Re-union grounds.   A tent meeting and a general good time prolonged the exercises of the evening to a late hour.

Hundreds of the Palmers still linger about Stonington, seemingly loth to leave the place.   It is certain that a family re-union on such a scale was never before attempted in New England.   But its success renders sure the early gathering of the clans of Noyes and Minor and Denison and Chesebrough, and a half hundred others who have reason for pride in historic ancestors, and whose numbers are become almost countless.

[From the *Commercial Advertiser*, Aug. 11.]

THE Palmers very properly asserted themselves at Stonington. Yesterday the descendants of " worthy Walter Palmer," the first settler of the old Connecticut town, met and remembered him and his in prose, in verse, and in a royal good time, interwoven with music and feasting.   The occasion was one that will be remembered by thousands who know the worth and wisdom of the Palmer blood as mingled in the progress of the country since Connecticut was a colony.   The absence of General Grant, who is a direct descendant of "worthy Walter," on account of recent domestic affliction, was the only disappointment of the hour.   The celebration continues to-day, when, like the pilgrims of old, the families of the original settler will march in procession to the ancient homestead and to the "God's acre," in which their ancestors lie, to think of them with honor as they rest from their labors.

[From the *Sun.*]

THE Palmers, who this week made their long-contemplated family pilgrimage to Stonington, the resting place of the first Palmer who ever journeyed to this country, certainly turned out in force.   So many of a kind filled the city, and overflowed through the suburbs. They came from all parts of the United States—for these Palmers are sturdy travelers. It was a woman of the Palmer stock who wrote " I'm a pilgrim " and " Flee as a bird to you mountain." Family re-unions are contagious ; and now that the Palmers have successfully had theirs, we shall hear that others are going to do likewise.

LIEUT. GEO. H. PALMER,

OF FORT CONCHO, TEXAS.

[Brief Biography.]

Geo. H. Palmer is a descendant of Walter Palmer—viz. : Walter, Gershom, Ichabod, Ichabod, Jr., Elias Sandford, Elias S., Jr., Noyes, Geo. W., Geo. H. His father, Geo. W., was captain in the United States Army (calvary service), during the Rebellion. His ancestor, Elias S., was a colonel in the army, and his ancestor, Noyes, was Major-General ; so the family may be called a military one.

Geo. H. went into the volunteer service from Illinois in April, 1861, and served until the end of the war as captain. During the last year of the Rebellion he had command of a picked company of mounted men, and was engaged in fighting guerillas in Kentucky and Tennessee. Since the war he has been in the Regular Army, and served on the plains and in the Southern States. His present rank is first lieutenant. He was born at Leonardsville, Madison County, N. Y., April 16, 1841 ; married Estelle J. Hoban, at Utica, N. Y., and have children— Geo. G., Mary Estelle, Ruth, H. Bruce, Edwin A.

[From Anderson's Stonington Directory.]

HISTORICAL SKETCH OF STONINGTON.

The claim of the Anglo race to the territory now embraced in Connecticut, originated in the discoveries of Sebastian Cabot in 1497, while he was in the employment of King Henry the Seventh of England.

No apparent effort was made on the part of that Government to profit by Cabot's discoveries for more than a century, nor until 1606, when King James the First granted a Charter to Thomas Hanham and others, which included our State in its boundaries. But no permanent settlement took place under that Charter in Connecticut. Soon after the pilgrims left England for America, and before their arrival at Plymouth—to wit : on the 3d day of November, 1620—King James the First, by letters patent under the Great Seal of England, incorporated forty noblemen, knights and gentlemen by the name of the Council established at Plymouth in the County of Devon, for the planting, ruling and governing New England in America. The territory included in the patent extended from the 40th to the 48th degree of north latitude, and east and west from sea to sea. It was ordained by this patent that the country embraced in its boundaries should be called New England in America, and by that name have continuance forever. In 1629 the Council of Plymouth granted to its President, Robert, Earl of Warwick, the territory granted by him in March, 1631, to William Viscount Say and Seal and others as used for Connecticut ; which grant the noble earl had confirmed to him by Charles the First. The territory now embraced in the town of Stonington was included in all the foregoing discoveries, grants, patents and charters. The Colony of Massachusetts having provided men and munitions of war for the conquest of the Pequot Indians in 1637, claimed an interest by right of conquest in all the lands held by the Pequots upon their overthrow, and preferred her claims to the Commissioners of United Colonies in 1646. Connecticut claimed all of it by patent, purchase and conquest. The Commissioners held that unless Massachusetts could show better title she could not sustain her claims. This decision did not end the controversy, for during the next year (1647), the matter of jurisdiction was again brought by Massachusetts to the attention of the Commissioners, who again decided in favor of Connecticut.

The first English settlement in Eastern Connecticut took place at the Nameaug, now New London, in 1645-6. The

boundaries of that township extended four miles east and
west of the Pequot River (Thames), and six miles from the
sea northwardly.   The first settlement in what is now Stonington took place in 1649.   William Chesebrough located himself
at Wequetequock in the fall of that year.   He was soon followed
by Thomas Stanton and Walter Palmer.   The forest homes of
Chesebrough, Stanton and Palmer were outside the recognized
jurisdiction of any township.   He was summoned before the
magistrates of Connecticut to give an account of his solitary life,
in 1649-50.   He did not respond before 1651, when he appeared at Hartford, and after satisfying the magistrate of his
good intentions he made an arrangement with the deputies of
Pequot to become an inhabitant of that town if they would confirm to him the lands he occupied at Wequetequock.   So in order to give the town of Pequot jurisdiction over Mr. Chesebrough's new home in the wilderness, the General Court extended the boundaries of that town eastward to Pawcatuck
River.   After this Mr. Chesebrough's land was confirmed to
him by the town of Pequot, soon after 1650.   The name of
Mystic and Pawcatuck was applied to the territory lying between the Mystic and Pawcatuck Rivers ; and under this name
the inhabitants sought to become a township of themselves in
1674.   This object was frustrated by the opposition of the inhabitants of the Western part of the plantation, who outvoted
them in town meeting when the matter came up for consideration.   But notwithstanding the opposition that they encountered, they still continued to agitate the question of dividing
the town of Pequot on the line of the Mystic River.   But all
their efforts in that direction were unavailing.   The Connecticut General Court *would not* allow them to form a new township.   So remembering the claims of Massachusetts based on
the right·of conquest, some of the planters in October, 1657,
addressed a letter to the Massachusetts General Court, asking
to be taken under that Government, and allowed the privilege
of a township.   In May, 1658, they presented another petition
to that Court, asking again for corporate powers.   The Court
declined to take any action, suggesting, however, a reference of
the matter to the Commissioners of the United Colonies, meantime advising the planters to order their own affairs peaceably,
and of *common agreedent* until some provision be made in their
behalf.   Following out this suggestion of the Massachusetts
Court, the planters assembled on the 30th day of June, 1658,
and formed a compact, called by them " the association of Pawcatuck people."   Massachusetts sympathizing with these planters, and knowing the condition of affairs, esteemed it a good

time to renew, and did renew her claim to a portion of the conquered Pequot territory, and brought the matter again before
the Commissioners of the United Colonies, and this time successfully, for in September, 1658, they rendered their decision,
which was that all of the said conquered territory west of the
Mystic River should belong to Connecticut, and all east of it
should belong to Massachusetts. Immediately after this decision became known to the planters, they petitioned the Massachusetts General Court for corporate powers, which were granted
them, on the 19th day of October, 1658, in these words : " In
answer to the petition of the inhabitants of Mystic and Pawcatuck, the Court judgeth it meet to grant that the English plantation between Mystic and Pawcatuck be named Southington,
and belong to the County of Suffolk, and order that all prudential affairs thereof be managed by Capt. George Denison, Robert Park, William Chesebrough, Thomas Stanton, Walter Palmer and Thomas Miner, till the Court take further order."
Connecticut remonstrated but yielded reluctantly to the decision in the premises. The town of Southerntown remained
under the jurisdiction of Massachusetts till after the restoration
of the monarchy in England, when King Charles II. granted
a new charter to Connecticut in 1662, placing Southerntown
in the limits of our State. Massachusetts gave up all claim to
our territory, and Connecticut again asserted jurisdiction, when
the General in 1665 changed the name of the town to Mystic.
In the year 1667 the General Court again changed the name to
that of Stonington. At first these changes in the jurisdiction
and names of the township produced contention and litigation
which lasted for years, but finally subsided, and the town increased in population and wealth. That portion of the old
town of Southerntown now embraced in the limits of the borough of Stonington, was included in the Chesebrough land
grants, and remained a pasture until 1750, when a new highway
was laid out, from the town square northwardly to Preston.
Previous to this the business of the town had been transacted
at Pawcatuck, Tangwonk, Agreement Hill, and Mystic. But almost immediately after this highway was established, business
centered here, and the population increased very rapidly, so
that by 1770, the village contained about five hundred inhabitants. The first meeting house was built in 1787, and the money to pay for the same was raised by a lottery. The village
was bombarded during the Revolutionary War, and again more
formidably during the last war with England. The borough
was organized under a charter obtained of the General Assembly in 1801.

1662.

WALTER PALMER'S WILL.

Vnto my sonne *John*, a yoake of three yeare old steares, and a horse; to my dau. *Grace* 20ˢ; to all my Grand Children 20ₛ a piece—To my sonne *Jonas*, halfe the planting Lott at yᵉ new meadow River, by Seaconck & yᵉ Lott betweene *John Butter-worths*, according to the fouer score pound Estate, & the use of halfe yᵉ housing & halfe of the whole Farme for fouer yeares— To my sonne *William*, the other halfe of yᵉ same farme at Sea-conck foreuer, and to take *Robert Martine* or some othᵣ skill full man & to devide the houseing & the whole farme in two equall pᵣts & to take his owne & dispose of it as he pleaseth— I giue him, also, a Mare with her foale, two redd oxen, a pair of Steares of three yeare old a piece, fouer Cowes & a Muskett with all such things as are his owne allready—The other halfe of the farme at Seaconcke I give to my Sonne *Gersham*, for ever, after the tearme of fouer yeares—all the rest of my Land goods, and chattell vndisposed I leave vnto my wife, whome with my sonne *Elihu*, I make my full executor, to pay my debts, bring vp my Children & pay them theire portions as my Lands and Estate will beare; but, in case my wife marry againe, before my Children are brought vp & their portions payd, then, my three sonnes, Elihu, Nehemiah, & Moses to enter vpon the farme & Estate, and pay vnto their mother, 10£ pr annum during hir life & yᵉ Land & Estate duely valued to be equally distributed among my Children,—Elyhu, Nehemiah, Moses, Benjamin, Gersham, Hannah, & Rebecca, with Consideration of the tenn pound yearely to be payd to theire mother out of yᵉ Land— But if my wife pay their portions, according to her discretion & my three sonnes Elihu, Nehemiah, & Moses Possesse the Land, they shall give £20 a piece out of the Land to my sonne Benjamine, besides his mothers portion, in 3 years after they are possesst of the Farme.

WALTER PALMER.

In the prnce of
William Cheesbrough,
Samˡˡ Cheesbrough,
Nathaniell Cheesbrough.

Memorandum.—If Elihu, Nehemiah, or Moses decease before they have any years, Benjamine is to succede in theire pᵗ of yᵉ Farme & give to my dau. Elizabeth, two Cowes—I give my Executoʳs a yeares time for payment of these Legacies.

Testified to, by three witnesses, on oath, before George Deni-son, Commissʳ.

Approved by the Court on Petition of Lieut. Richard Cooke, in behalfe of ye Widow Palmer, relict of Walter and Elihu, theire sonne, on the oathes of Wm., Samuell & Nathanll Chees-brough, 11 May 1662.

Inventory of the Goods & Chattells of Walter Palmer, now deceased, at Southertowne, in the Countie of Suffolke, as it was taken the Last of Mrch 1662 by William Chesbrooke & Thomas Stanton of the same towne.

Amt £1644.05s.

One horse valued at £12, added by Elihu Palmer, as Execu-tor who deposed, 13 May 1662.

—[*From the Records of Suffolk Co., Mass.*]

THE INVENTORY OF WALTER PALMER.

An inventarie of the goodes & chatels of walter Palmer Now deceased at Sothertwn in the Cowntie of Suffolke as it was ta-ken the Last of March 1662 by William Chisbroh & Thomas Stanton of the same towne.

4 horses at	£45	00	00
5 mares at	66	00	00
4 cowltes at	30	00	00
halfe a hors	06	00	00
19 yeerlings at	38	00	00
19 too yer owldes at	76	00	00
18 two yeer & vantag at	90	00	00
4 Steeres & a bull at	29	00	00
8 Oxen at	64	00	00
23 Cowes at	115	00	00
80 Sheepe at	44	00	00
wvn bull not seen at	03	00	00
4 fatting hogs at	08	00	00
3 younger hogs at	1	10	00
4 more swine at	4	05	00
20lb of fetheres at	1	00	00
50lb of wool at	2	10	00
9 gwnes 4 foling Peeses at	15	00	00
3 sordes at	01	10	00
4 beds of furnyture at	14	00	00
3 beds of furnyture at	25	00	00
4 Chiestes & yt in them	12	00	00
Pewter bras & other goods	20	00	00
1 tabell & forme at	01	10	00

plowgeares & Castes at £30 00 00
Lumber and toolles ,......................... 22 00 00
his apparell at............................... 12 00 00
Corne & haye at.............................. 55 00 00
Provision in the hows at...................... 25 00 00
1 boat at 07 00 00
goods at New London, Seaconk & the duch....... 120 00 00
howsing and Landes 661 00 00

  Totalis 1644 05 00

    WILLM CHESEBROUGH.
    THO. STANTON.
one horse more Added at 12£ at Seacuncckc virte.

[On the back of the inventory is the following :]

13 may, 1662, at Generall Court, Elihu Palmer deposed as
executor to his late father Palmer's will, deposed yt hauing
added to this Inventory one horse at twelve pounds, is a true
Inventory of his late father's Estate to his best knowledge that
when he knowes more he will discover it.

    EDWARD RAWSON, Secrety.

THE WALTER PALMER FARM AT WEQUETE-
QUOCK COVE.

This farm contains 231 acres, and is that portion of Walter
Palmer's immense tract which he gave to his son Nehemiah,
and upon which he built his house (now standing), and where
he reared his family, the names of whom are given in another
column.   On this " Walter Palmer farm " is the ancient burying-
ground, in which repose the dust of the early settlers (of Stonington) and of their children ; also it is the very spot where
Walter first built his log-house as a temporary abode, on his
arrival from Rehoboth (the excavation in the side hill can still
be seen), consequently it is historic ground, and probably more
so than any other of the original Palmer territory.

The northern edge of the farm borders on the old mill pond
and Anguilla brook, and at the head of the pond traces can be
seen of the old saw-mill dam built by Walter and others.   The
grist mill, built some 220 years ago, is still in operation, and its
appearance is the best evidence of its antiquity.

The Stonington and Providence Railroad runs across the
southern portion of the farm, and at that point is the tank-

house of the Railroad Co. supplied by water from a reservoir on the farm. Until within a few years all trains on the Stonington Railroad stopped there to "water." From the railroad track up the hill to the farm-house is only 600 feet.

The farm is admirably adapted to grazing purposes, and many years ago it was purchased by a Mr. Baldwin for ten thousand dollars, and since that time it has been known as the "Baldwin farm."

But a little while ago it was offered for sale, and Ira H. Palmer, of Stonington, seeing with others the desirability of securing and retaining the large property, with its historic associations, in the Palmer family, entered into negotiations for it, which were concluded in the early part of this month. The farm is now tenanted and will continue to be; improvements will gradually be made, and the descendants (who are very numerous) of Nehemiah Palmer, son of Walter, when they visit Stonington, will *particularly* be interested in this part of Walter's domain. Although the house now standing has been oft times repaired, yet it is of the original shape and style as built by Nehemiah. The Re-unionists to Stonington last summer did not have this property pointed out to them, consequently knew nothing of its associations. We trust Walter's descendants will know more of it in the future.—*From* "*Vidette.*"

IN MEMORIAM.

During the interval of the Re-union, and the publication of this volume, there have been deaths of some of the family. Such as we have learned of we insert a brief biography of.

[From the *American Grocer*, December 8, 1881.]

JAMES WOOLSEY PALMER.

The subject of this sketch, who died at his late residence, 213 Washington street, Jersey City, on Monday, the 5th inst., after a month's illness, was for forty-three years a resident of Jersey City, and for forty-two years a wholesale grocer in New York City. The deceased was born near Paterson, N. J., on the 2d January, 1810, and was the son of Captain James M. W. Palmer, of the ship *Marshall*, and grandson of Brigade-Major Thomas Palmer, of the British Army, and Esther Woolsey, his wife, whose brother was the father of President Theodore D.

Woolsey, of Yale College. Mr. Palmer came to New York when a boy, and in 1832 became a clerk for the old wholesale grocery house of Clark & Tallmadge, which firm he left in 1834 to become, at the age of 24 years, one of the firm of Beam, Lyon & Palmer, wholesale grocers. In 1837 Mr. Beam retired from business with a competence. when Mr. Palmer associated himself with Mr. Samuel J. Berry, under the firm name of Berry & Palmer, and so continued under that firm name for 28 years, until 1865, when Mr. Berry also retired from business. Mr. Palmer then concluded to continue the business under the firm name of James W. Palmer & Sons, taking into partnership his sons, James W. Palmer, Jr., now of the firm of H. K. & F. B. Thurber & Co., and David W. Palmer, who during the war was an Assistant Adjutant-General in General Sherman's army, but died March, 22, 1873, widely known and highly respected. In 1876, the senior member of the firm retired from active business, and since then has occupied his time in attending to the affairs of the George M. Woolsey estate, of which, as executor and trustee, he has had the management for the past thirty years. In early life Mr. Palmer was a very active member of the old Whig party, especially during the campaigns of Clay and Harrison, but of late years he has taken no special interest in any political organization. On December 6, 1841, at its first meeting, he was elected an incorporator and trustee of the Provident Institution for Savings of Jersey City; on December 2, 1850, he was elected a Vice-President, and on January 15, 1851, a member of the Board of Investment, of which he was for many years the Chairman. In fact, so highly were his services appreciated that, in 1867, he was presented with a service of silver plate for his faithful labors, rendered gratuitously, as a member of the Board of Investment. After twenty-six years' service as Vice-President and member of the Investment Committee, he resigned, December, 1876. He was again elected Vice-President in December, 1879, which office he held at the time of his death, having served the Institution faithfully, wisely and gratuitously for 37 years. In all the relations of life he was faithful and conscientious, and although he only sought the friendship of those whose friendship was worth having, he was a warm friend to the needy and afflicted who came to him for comfort, assistance or advice. He was a kind father, a wise counsellor, a good citizen and an honest man. His funeral took place from his late residence on Wednesday afternoon, 7th inst. The remains will be taken to Goshen, N. Y., to be buried by the side of his wife and children.

REV. MARCUS PALMER,

OF FITCHVILLE, OHIO.

PALMER—Feb. 15, 1881, Rev. Marcus Palmer, in his eighty-sixth year.

The following is an abstract of a memorial discourse, preached by Rev. J. H. Walter, at the funeral services held at Olena, Huron County, on the 15th, the remains being conveyed to the family burial-ground at Fitchville.

The same discourse was preached in the Presbyterian Church in that place, the Sunday previous.

The deceased was a native of Greenwich, Fairfield County, Conn.; born the 24th of April, 1795. He was the seventh in age of a family of fourteen, two younger brothers yet living at Fitchville.

At the age of nineteen he united with the Congregational Church, and on the death of the father, the family removed to Huron County, Ohio. The deceased remained East with a brother, a physician, and studied medicine and graduated at the Medical College in New York City. In 1820 he was recommended by Dr. Gardner Spring, pastor of the Brick Presbyterian Church, New York, to the United Foreign Missionary Society, as a suitable person for a physician among the Indians west of the Mississippi. The appointment was made and accepted, and Dr. Palmer set out from New York for Philadelphia, in one of the first steamboats ever built. Thence in company with about eight persons for the same mission, he crossed the Allegheny mountains with one of the long wagon-trains, to Pittsburg; thence by flat-boats down the Ohio and Mississippi rivers to the mouth of the Arkansas, and up that river by poles and bushwhacking, to Little Rock; thence to the Union Mission, now in Southern Kansas, among the Osage Indians.

Here his work began, amid the difficulties and sufferings which attended the removal of the Indians westward.

In 1824 Dr. Palmer was married to Miss Clarissa Johnson, then having care of the Mission School, and who, after twelve years, died on her way East, and was buried at Granville, Ohio.

HULDAH PALMER,

WIDOW OF STEPHEN W. PALMER.

"GRANDMOTHER."

At the close of our volume, we are pained to note the close of Grandmother Palmer's earthly career.

She was a remarkable woman in many ways. In physique

large and portly, weighing in usual health 240 pounds, and seldom ill—the mother of twelve children, all but two grown up to manhood and womanhood, and whose average weight was 216 pounds. She was a *home* mother, and during the period of a quarter of a century, left her house to visit her neighbor's but two or three times. I doubt if she beheld a locomotive more than two or three times, though hearing the whistle daily. She had a wonderful memory, and her mind was a store-house of information, which she kept daily refreshed by reading and study. She was strong-minded to that extent that few politicians in her neighborhood could out-talk her on the topics of the day. Four of her sons became active representatives in the Democratic party, in the various sections where they lived; but mother's advice and counsel was always held in high esteem by them.

We have given, on page 136, a brief-mention that " Palmer Records " emanated from her influence, when we passed a three months' vacation with Grandmother. We outlined what Bible records she had, and by gradual study she gave us the pedigree of over four hundred Palmers. This was the nucleus upon which was built the Record, now containing the lineage of over 10,000 Palmers. She took an active interest in the work, and wrote hundreds of letters in a hand-writing almost like print—writing the letters slow and in the shape of type, rather than script penmanship. In one of her letters she writes: " I joined the Church in Lenox, in 1819, a firm believer in Christ, as all my connections were, and most of them were members of the Baptist Church. Near my birth-place were high ledges of huge rocks, which mother said were rent asunder when Christ was crucified, which, in our infancy, created no little interest for the great God of Heaven and Earth. And the teachings of a Christian mother, endowed with a mother's kind heart, stamped the minds of her children impressions that will endure like the rock of ages."

On page 138 will be noticed one of the lines of descent of Grandmother from Walter, and on page 137 another; and on page 139 her likeness, with that of her husband Stephen W., her four sons, Chas. W., Wm. L., Noyes G. and Geo. W., with that of her grandson, Noyes F., and two of her *great*-grandchildren, Albert W. and Saidee E.

Our great regret is that she did not live to see some of the Record in print—a fond hope of hers for years.

Grandmother Huldah was born December 28th, 1797, and died January 30th, 1882, aged 84 years and 1 month.

STEPHEN W. PALMER,

OF NORVELL, JACKSON COUNTY, MICH.

Grandfather Stephen W. Palmer was born at Stonington, on November 22d, 1793, and lived there until about 1810, and moved into New York State—Lenox, Madison County. At the age of twenty, he married Huldah Palmer, who was "sweet sixteen" at that time. He joined the Masonic Fraternity in 1814; held important offices, and finally received the degree of Royal Arch. and took several honorary signs; held a captain's commission in the Militia; was called out in 1815, just before the War of 1812 closed, and for services received a bounty of 160 acres; moved to this land, situated near Napoleon, Jackson County, Mich., in 1836; was elected Postmaster and Justice of the Peace several times. He was a man of strong convictions, stern and decided; he had a marked influence in any matter requiring deliberation and judgment. His avocation as farmer was in the line of stock-cattle breeding, and in which he became known all over the State as owning the best breed of Durham cattle.

He died March 23d, 1879, aged 86 years. His likeness appears on page 139.

CULLEN PALMER,

OF MADISON, OHIO.

PALMER—In Madison, August 28th, 1881, after a painful and protracted illness of over a year, Mr. Cullen Palmer, aged 69 years.

The deceased was one of Madison's most respected and influential citizens. Having lived in Madison during the past 40 years, he aided materially in the upbuilding of the town and society, and won to himself many friends and acquaintances. He was born in Concord, Ohio, in 1812, was a son of Dr. Isaac Palmer, of that place, and a descendant of Walter Palmer, who came from Nottinghamshire, England, with the pilgrims, and settled in 1653 in Stonington, Conn. While living in Concord, the deceased, in company with Mr. Robert Murray, now of Mentor, bought and sold cattle quite extensively, buying them in that vicinity and driving them overland in large droves across the Allegheny Blue Ridge mountains to Philadelphia, where they were sold—the hardship and enterprise of the business being far different than now, when the herds of cattle are transported by rail. While living in Madison, he devoted his energies to farming, buying and selling cattle for the Buffalo and home market. At the age of 52, soon after the death of his son, he united with the Congregational Church. During his sickness he bore his suffering with patience, and died trusting in Christ's mercy and his atoning blood. He leaves a wife, three sons and a daughter, who deeply mourn his loss.

REV. GEORGE PALMER WILLIAMS,

OF ANN ARBOR, MICH.

WILLIAMS—Rev. George Palmer Williams, LL.D., for forty years professor in Michigan University, died Sept. 4, 1881, at Ann Arbor, of general debility.

Dr. Williams was a native of Woodstock, Vt., having been born April 13, 1802, and was a brother of the late Hon. Norman Williams, and whose mother was a daughter of Gershom Palmer. He graduated at Burlington in 1825, and afterward at Andover Theological Seminary, and in 1827 went west and became a tutor in Kenyon College, Gambier, O. From 1831 to 1834 he was a professor of languages in the Western University of Pennsylvania at Pittsburg, and from 1834 to 1837 again at Kenyon College. In 1837 he received the first appointment to the place of instructor made by the board of regents of the Michigan University as principal of the Pontiac branch. July 22, 1841, he received the first appointment in the department of ancient languages to a professorship in the University proper. This position, however, he did not accept, but instead that of mathematics and natural sciences. In 1854 the department of physics was otherwise provided for, leaving him only mathematics. This, in 1863, he exchanged for physics, with which department he was connected as emeritus professor. Astronomy, though not nominally in his professorship, he taught until 1844, and great enthusiasm in the calculation of eclipses was annually awakened among the students. At the age of 45 he entered the ministry. He served at one time for more than a year as rector of St. Andrews Church, Ann Arbor, and by the donation of his salary relieved the church from debt. In 1827 he married Elizabeth Edson, of Randolph, Vt., who died in 1850. In 1852 he married Mrs. Jane Richards. Some years ago the Alumni of Michigan University conceived the idea of raising an endowment fund, and the total amount subscribed was $27,374.46, the interest on which was paid Dr. Williams.

WILLIAM BROWN PALMER, of Covington, Wyoming Co., N. Y., died January 31, 1882. Was the oldest son of Uzziel and " Nabby " Palmer, and was born in Stonington, May 10, 1795. Was a direct descendant from Rev. Wales Palmer. He moved to New York State when a young man.

WALTER PALMER, of Winfield, N. Y., died at that place January, 1882. He was one of the most prominent citizens of the locality, and connected with the National Bank of Winfield.

MRS. HARRIET N. PALMER, of Norwich, Conn., and wife of Col. Edwin Palmer, died October 31, 1881.

GEO. W. PALMER, of Union Park, Conn., died November, 1881. He was for over twenty years Treasurer of the Middlesex Horse Railroad in Boston, Mass. His amiability and strict business habits won for him a high standing in society. The funeral was attended by the Handel and Hayden Musical Society, who furnished sacred music on the occasion. The remains were buried in Brandon, Conn.

CAPT. GIDEON H. PALMER, of Newport, R. I., died in March, 1881, much respected and esteemed.

WILLIAM WALTER PALMER (No. 2,447, page 139) died February 5, 1882, aged 1 year, 5 months and 4 days, infant son of Noyes F. and Clara M. Palmer. This little fellow had something to do with the Re-union. He used to play around the room, and scatter the invitations being written to the Palmers. He used to spoil some of them, too, and blot them, as he sat upon our knee, when we were writing, and with his chubby hand reach out and try to help. He had something to do in putting sunshine in this book when we were weary in the task—a romp on the floor brought back our spirits. He used to help us by spilling the ink, breaking off the end of our lead pencils, and creep over our desk on the top of papers. In short, he was company to us in many ways. Now he is in company with angels in heaven, and we in sorrow and sadness.

MRS. PAUL S. PALMER.

[Likeness No. 6, page 177 ; Biography, page 185.]

PALMER.—At Stockbridge, March 13, Mrs. Hannah Palmer, aged 77 years.

"Dear, good Mrs. Palmer!" is the exclamation universally following the mention of the decease of this excellent lady, by

our citizens. No woman has better deserved such testimony,
and no monument that may rise above her place of rest can
better commemorate her. No community can spare such members without sorrow, and a feeling of impoverishment. Mrs.
Palmer was born in Stonington, Ct., in the year 1804. Her
bright and joyous girlhood ripened into the tempered vivacity
which she brought with her to her adopted residence here, and
radiated like sunshine from her home to all who were blessed
with her acquaintance. In 1824, she married Mr. Paul S. Palmer, moved to this town and commenced a life-long career of
love and usefulness. The family residence on the upland north
of our village became proverbial for good cheer, hospitality and
happiness. Her husband was an intelligent, courteous and independent farmer, preaching by his own example the " dignity
of labor." When Lord Morpeth visited our town in 1842, for
larger knowledge of the modes of American life, he was taken
to Mr. Palmer's as a place affording a most favorable specimen
of the American farmer and domestic management. Nor did
it fail of proper appreciation, of which the genial, lady-like mis-
tress came in for a full share. Mrs. Palmer was the soul of
sympathy and helpfulness. Her charity knew no sectarianism,
and "the blessing of Him that was ready to perish" was always hers. The victims of misfortune found in her an invalu-
able ally. All children loved her as a mother. Her words of
kindness and deeds of beneficence brought cheer to the dis-
tressed ; her hand was ever efficacious to smooth the pillow of
pain, and the remedials suggested by her rich experience often
proved more efficacious than those of the physician. There
could be no despondency when and where she was present. To
her last days she could equally well entertain those of her own
age and the gayest of the young. The natural sedateness of
years was remarkably tempered by an inborn cheerfulness
which prompted her, not to withdraw from social pleasures, but
rather to promote them by a geniality which made her presence
agreeable to old and young. Her well-stored mind, large experience and interesting conversational powers rendered her a
model guest and hostess. The death of her husband, in 1875,
dampened but could not subdue her inherent cheerfulness, while
it brightened the Christian faith which dominated all her fac-
ulties and enhanced her sympathy toward general humanity.
A son and a widowed daughter, Mrs. Mary Palmer Pitkin, remained in her stricken home, whose loving devotion to her in
her increasing years, augmented by that of another son's family,
occupying the adjoining farm (three only surviving of nine
children), and numerous grandchildren, all of whom almost

worshipped her, rendered life still desirable and happy. Here, finally, after a brief illness, death overtook her, in full possession of her mental powers, though at the ripe age of 77 years, and closed her eyes on earth to be opened on the glories of the better land. Such a life in any community is a golden example and a benediction, and the loss of it can only be recompensed by the assurance of eternal reward to the one who lived it.

> "She set as sets the morning star, that goes
> Not down behind the darkened west, nor hides
> Obscured among the tempests of the sky,
> But melts away into the light of Heaven."

Stockbridge, March 25, 1882.

Extract from a sermon preached by the Rev. Arthur Lawrence, rector of St. Paul's Church, in Stockbridge, March 19th.

"We have laid this week out of our sight one of the sweetest and best of our number—one who for more than fifty years has been the centre and the sunlight of that best of all things on earth—a Christian home—one whose clear wisdom, whose gentle nature, whose loving heart have drawn to her the tender respect and tender affection of every one she knew. Was the tender smile which was ever on her lips inconsistent with an humble spirit? Was the cheerfulness with which she welcomed those who turned to her—and never in vain—for sympathy or greetiug out of keeping with a heart that had been sanctified by suffering and acquainted with grief?

APPENDIX.

⁙

[After the "business minutes" of the Re-union had been published in this volume it was discovered by the Secretary that several records had been omitted, and we insert, to keep the record complete.

PALMER RE-UNION, Stonington, Conn., Aug. 10, 1881.

[Part of omitted Minutes, page 20.]

At a mass meeting of the "Palmer Re-union," held on the evening of this date, in the large tent on the Re-union grounds (Loper lot), Gen. Geo. W. Palmer, of New York, Acting Chairman. Hon. C. D. Prescott, of Rome, N. Y., then moved:

That whereas, the officers having charge of this grand Re-union have demonstrated their fitness for the respective offices they hold, and their eminent ability to plan and successfully carry out another re-union.

Resolved, That such officers be and they hereby are elected and continued as the officers of the "Palmer Re-union Organization" now formed, to hold until the next re-union, with full power to determine the time when and the place where the same shall be held, and to do all acts and things necessary and proper with reference thereto.

The above motion being seconded, was carried unanimously.

The thanks of the Re-union was voted separately to Hon. E.H. Palmer as President, Ira H. Palmer as Corresponding Secretary, and Noyes F. Palmer as Committee on Invitation, for their indefatigable efforts in arranging and planning so effectively the interests of the Re-union.

Adjourned to mass meeting, August 11th, same place.

From the Record.

(Attest),   IRA H. PALMER,
                                                          Acting Clerk.

PALMER RE-UNION, Stonington, Aug. 11, 1881.

* * * * By those assembled at this time, and as the representative body of the " Palmer Re-union," the following was passed unanimously, Hon. E. H. Palmer, Chairman :

Voted, That the " Palmer Re-union " does now adjourn, subject to the call of the President.

(Attest),   IRA H. PALMER,
                                              Acting Clerk.

[In addition, the proceedings of the business meetings, preliminary to the *second* Re-union is also inserted. Efforts have been made to perfect a " *Palmer Re-union Association* " that will perpetuate re-unions from time to time, and will provide ways and means for the expenses.]

MINUTES OF FIRST MEETING

FOR PERMANENT ORGANIZATION

OF THE

PALMER RE-UNION ASSOCIATION,

November 28th, 1881, at 237 Broadway (Broadway National Bank), New York City.

Meeting held pursuant to call of President of Re-union—E. H. Palmer.

PRESENT—E. H. Palmer, Montville, Ct.; Gen. Geo. W. Palmer, New York City; Francis A. Palmer, Esq., New York City; Lorin Palmer, Esq., Brooklyn, N. Y.; Courtlandt Palmer, Esq., New York City; James U. Palmer, Esq., Brooklyn, N. Y.; B. Frank Chapman, Esq., Oneida, N. Y.; Noyes F. Palmer, Jamaica, N. Y., and others.

On motion of Francis A. Palmer, Esq.,

Voted, That E. H. Palmer, the President of the late Palmer Re-union, be called upon to preside.

On motion of Gen. Geo. W. Palmer,

Voted, That Noyes F. Palmer be Secretary *pro tem.*

After general discussion as to the objects of the meeting, on motion of Courtlandt Palmer, Esq., it was

Voted, That a permanent organization, for the purpose of perpetuating Palmer Family Re-unions, and for social and literary intercourse, be formed under the name of PALMER RE-UNION ASSOCIATION.

On motion of Gen. Geo. W. Palmer, it was

Voted, That E. H. Palmer, of Montville, Conn., be President of the Association.

On motion of Lorin Palmer, Esq., it was

Voted, That Gen. Geo. W. Palmer, of New York City, be First Vice-President of the Association.

On motion of Noyes F. Palmer, it was

Voted, That Rev. A. G. Palmer, D. D., of Stonington, Conn., be Second Vice-President of the Association.

On motion of Courtlandt Palmer, Esq., it was

Voted, That Francis A. Palmer, Esq., of New York City, be Treasurer of the Association.

On motion of Gen. Geo. W. Palmer, it was

Voted, That Noyes F. Palmer, of Jamaica, N. Y., be Secretary of the Association.

On motion of Lorin Palmer, it was

Voted, That the five officers (President, First Vice-President, Second Vice-President, Treasurer, and Secretary) be an Executive Committee, with power to appoint sub-committees.

After general discussion as to the basis of control of the said Association, on motion of Courtlandt Palmer, it was

Voted, That the Executive Committee prepare a certificate of membership to issue to members of the family (paternal or maternal) descendants; that said certificate not to stipulate that it is obligatory for the recipient to pay for the same, but that the requirements necessary to obtain a certificate be set forth in the By-Laws of the Association, and not appear in the certificate.

On motion of Gen. Geo. W. Palmer, it was

Voted, That the Executive Committee prepare a set of By-Laws, and report at the next meeting, said meeting to be called by the Secretary when the Executive Committee are prepared to report.

On motion of Lorin Palmer, it was

Voted, That Vice-Presidents be elected to represent different branches of the family in various sections, and that the Secretary prepare a list of the same, and report at the next meeting for approval.

On motion of E. H. Palmer, it was

Voted, An expression of thanks to F. A. Palmer, Esq., for his courtesy in allowing the Association a temporary place of meeting.

On motion of Lorin Palmer, it was

Voted, To adjourn, subject to call of the Secretary.

[NOTE.—The minutes were amended by a subsequent meeting held at St. Paul's Evangelical Church, April 6, 1882. At the latter meeting the report of Committee on Constitution, By-Laws, etc., was made and adopted.]

———

PALMER RE-UNION, Stonington, Conn., Jan., 1882.

Notice is hereby given that a business meeting of the " Palmer Re-union " will be held at Brayton Hall, January 30th, at 7:30 o'clock, for the consideration of, and the acting upon measures appearing necessary—to create additional offices, if desired, and to fill the same.   By order of

E. H. PALMER,

President.

IRA H. PALMER,
    Cor. Sec'y and Acting Sec'y of Record.

[NOTE.—The proceedings of this informal meeting of January 3, 1882, were superseded by the action of the Re-union meeting held at St. Paul's Evangelical Church, New York City, April 6, 1882.]

PALMER RE-UNION ASSOCIATION.

CALL FOR MEETING.

[From Brooklyn Union-Argus, April 1, 2, 3, 4 and 5, 1882, New York Tribune, April 5, 1882, and other papers.]

PALMER FAMILY—SECOND RE-UNION—BUSINESS MEETING. —A meeting of the members of the family, and officers of the late Re-union, is to be held in New York City, on the first Thursday in April (6th), at St. Paul's Evangelical Church, corner Thirty-fourth street and Eighth avenue, at 8 P. M.; the object of the meeting being to discuss the advisability of holding stated re-unions and to perfect a permanent association to perpetuate the same. All members of the family (ladies as well) are particularly requested to attend and participate in this business meeting. You are specially invited to be present.

(Signed)   ELISHA H. PALMER, Montville, Conn.,
                                    President of Re-union.

[From Stonington Mirror, March 25, 1882.]

PALMER RE-UNION.—There will be a meeting of the Palmer Re-union, in New York City, at St. Paul's Evangelical Church, April 6th, at 3 o'clock P. M., for the consideration and transaction of business appearing necessary at that time.

By order of   E. H. PALMER, President.
I. H. PALMER, Acting Secretary of Record.
Stonington, Conn., March 22, 1882.

MINUTES.

NEW YORK, ST. PAUL'S EVANGELICAL CHURCH,
    250 W. Thirty-fourth street, April 6, 1882.

Pursuant to published call, this meeting was held.

Elisha H. Palmer, of Montville, Conn., President of Re-union, in the chair: Ira H. Palmer, of Stonington, Conn., Corresponding Secretary of Re-Union, Clerk.

On motion of Rev. A. G. Palmer, of Stonington, Conn.,

Voted, That the Clerk read the call for the meeting.

The Clerk read the same.

The Chair directed the Clerk to read the minutes of the previous meeting, held at Stonington, Conn., January 30, 1882; and the same was read.

Upon motion of Noyes F. Palmer, of Jamaica,

Voted, That the minutes of the previous meeting be super-seded by the deliberations of the present meeting.

The Chair then made a few remarks, and called upon Gen. Geo. W. Palmer, of New York City, who made an explanation in regard to the necessity of having a permanent association formed to assist the officers of the late Re-union in any future meeting of this character; that the motion adopted at the close of the late Re-union stipulated that the officers may do such acts as are necessary to promote re-unions, and have proper regulations made to accomplish the same.

Therefore, on motion of Benj. F. Chapman, of Oneida, N. Y.,

Voted, That the Palmer Re-union Association be formed.

Proposed Constitution and By-Laws of the Palmer Re-union Association read by Gen. Geo. W. Palmer, and upon his motion, seconded by Rev. A. G. Palmer,

Voted, That the same be adopted as a whole.

On motion of Benj. F. Chapman, of Oneida, N. Y.,

Voted, That the date of August and November meetings be left to the discretion of the Board of Officers.

On motion of Prof. Joseph H. Palmer, of Yonkers, N. Y.,

Voted, That there be no restrictions as to the age of appli-cants for certificate of membership.

Amendments adopted, and the Constitution and By-Laws, as a whole.

On motion of Gen. Geo. W. Palmer,

Voted, That the officers of the Palmer Re-union Association be chosen.

On motion of Gen. Geo. W. Palmer,

Voted, As President, Elisha H. Palmer, of Montville, Conn.

Voted, As First Vice-President, Rev. A. G. Palmer, of Ston-ington, Conn.

On motion of Noyes F. Palmer,

Voted, As Second Vice-President, Gen. Geo. W. Palmer, of New York City.

On motion of E. H. Palmer,

Voted, As Third Vice-President, Robert Palmer, of Noank, Conn.

Voted, As Treasurer, Francis A. Palmer, of New York City.

Voted, As Chaplain, Rev. E. B. Palmer, D. D., of Bridgeton, N. J.

Voted, As Recording Secretary, Noyes F. Palmer, of Jamaica, N. Y.

Voted, As Corresponding Secretary, Ira H. Palmer, of Stonington, Conn.

Voted, As Grand Marshal, F. C. Palmer, of Montville, Conn.

The questions of Life Membership and Honorary Membership were discussed, and deferred until the next Re-union.

Dr. Corydon Palmer made an explanation in reference to coat-of-arms, and exhibited a large painting of one of the emblems.   Matter referred to Committee on Certificate.

Committee on Certificate appointed by Chair—Gen. Geo. W. Palmer and Noyes F. Palmer—with power to print in pamphlet form the Constitution and By-Laws, and have prepared a suitable form of Certificate of Membership, and to do such other acts as are necessary to perfect the Association.

Literary Committee appointed by the Chair, with power to increase their number : Rev. A. G. Palmer, of Stonington, Conn., Chairman ; Mrs. Isabella Grant Meredith, of New York City ; Miss Sara A. Palmer, of Stonington, Conn. ; Mrs. Mary Palmer Pitkin, of Stockbridge, Mass. ; Arch. M. Palmer, of New York City ; Prof. Joseph H. Palmer, of Yonkers, N. Y. ; C. B. Palmer, of Sing Sing, N. Y. ; Noyes F. Palmer, of Jamaica, N. Y. ; Frank H. Palmer, of Brooklyn, N. Y.

Rev. A. G. Palmer, D. D., of Stonington, made a very happy address to the Palmer Family, welcoming them to meet at Stonington, at their next Re-union.

Whereupon, it was

Voted, To hold another Re-union at Stonington the coming Summer.

Upon motion of Gen. Geo. W. Palmer,

Voted, Thanks to the hospitality of Francis A. Palmer in tendering to the Palmers the use of the edifice in which the meeting was held.

Adjourned subject to call of the President.

CONSTITUTION.

ARTICLE I.

Of the Name of the Association.

SECTION 1. The name of the Association shall be "THE PALMER RE-UNION ASSOCIATION," and its object shall be the perpetuation of the re-union of the Palmers and their paternal and maternal kindred through the Palmer lineage ; to collect and preserve information respecting the history of the family, and to promote social and literary intercourse among its members. •

ARTICLE II.

Of Members.

SEC. 1. Any descendent, paternal or maternal, of the Palmer lineage, of good moral character and in respectable standing in society, shall be eligible as a member.

§ 2. Each member shall, immediately upon admission, sign the Roll of Membership (in person or by proxy) with full name and residence, which will entitle him or her to a voice in the proceedings of any meeting ; but members shall not be entitled to vote upon any question unless they shall hold certificates of membership, in their own name, in the form prescribed.

§ 3. Certificate members shall not be held liable for any greater amount than the sum voluntarily pledged by them to the Association ; nor shall they be liable for any dues, assessments, or any indebtedness of the Association.

§ 4. In case any indebtedness is created, by reason of the non-payment of pledged funds, a statement thereof shall immediately be prepared by the Treasurer and sent to each certificate member, with the *pro rata* amount necessary to be contributed by each, to maintain the integrity of the Association.

ARTICLE III.

Of the Officers of the Association.

SEC. 1. The officers of the Association shall be a President, a First, a Second and a Third Vice-President, a Chaplain, a Treasurer, a Grand Marshal, a Corresponding Secretary, and a Recording Secretary, who shall be elected by the certificate members at the close of each Re-union of the Association, at which time they shall be installed and hold thier offices until their successors are duly elected and qualified.

§ 2. The election shall be by ballot in person or by proxy, and a plurality of votes shall constitute a choice.

§ 3. The officers named in Section 1 of this Article shall constitute an Executive Committee, to be styled the "*Board of Officers.*"

§ 4. The President shall, when he is present, preside at all meetings of the Association, preserve order, put the question, and declare the decision. He, in conjunction with one of the Vice-Presidents, may call special meetings of the Association when they shall judge proper, and he shall call them when required by the Board of Officers, or when requested in writing by any nine members holding certificates, specifying in such request the object for which such meeting is desired. He shall appoint the time and place of all meetings, and shall sign orders on the Treasury from the Board of Officers, of which Board he shall be President.

§ 5. The Vice-Presidents shall assist the President in presiding at the meetings. The duties specified in the preceding section shall, in case of the inability to act of the President, by reason of his absence or sickness, devolve on the first Vice-President, and, in the absence or sickness of both, on the Second Vice-President; and so on, according to rank—only that, in regard to signing orders on the Treasurer, each shall have equal powers with the President.

§ 6. The Treasurer shall have the custody of the money and other property of the Association. He shall keep regular accounts of receipts and disbursements in suitable books provided for that purpose, which shall be open at all reasonable times to the inspection of the members. He shall enter on his books each sum paid by him in consequenee of the recommendation or order of the Board of Officers, and preserve vouchers for all disbursements. He shall present a full report at each Re-union meeting of the financial condition of the Association, and at such other times as the Board of Officers may direct.

§ 7. The Chaplain shall perform the religious duties at the meetings of the Association, and shall by his counsel and advice promote harmony and good will among the members.

§ 8. It shall be the duty of the Grand Marshal to supervise the details of the Re-unions of the Association, and he shall be *ex officio* a member of each and every general and special committee.

§ 9. The Corresponding Secretary shall have general supervision over the correspondence of the Association; give notice of all meetings, whether stated or special, and publish the same in the newspapers when so directed by the Board of Officers; in the absence of the Recording Secretary to act in that capacity, and make memorandum of all the proceedings, and forward the same to the Recording Secretary.

§ 10. The Recording Secretary to assist the Corresponding Secretary, and in the absence of the Corresponding Secretary to act in that capacity. He shall keep a roll of the members of the Association, and have custody of all the journals, records and papers of the Association, and make entry therein of all proceedings of the Association; and also act as Secretary of the Board of Officers.

§ 11. The Board of Officers shall meet whenever they deem it expedient and the interests of the Association require. Special meetings may be called by either of the Secretaries under the direction of the President, or of the Vice-President acting in his stead, or of any three members of the Board of Officers. In addition to the general management and supervision of the affairs of the Association hereby delegated to them, the Board of Officers shall execute all such business as may from time to time be committed to them by any law or resolve of the Association, and they shall report their proceedings at every Re-union of the Association; but they shall not create any indebtedness not provided for by the funds of the Association or the funds pledged by certificate members. The presence of at least five members shall be necessary for the transaction of business.

§ 12. In case of the death, resignation, or disability of the President (see Sec. 5, Art. III). As to other vacancies (see By-Laws.

ARTICLE IV.

Of Committees.

SEC. 1. The Board of Officers shall constitute the Finance Committee and have charge of all the funds of the Association. All funds and money belonging to the Association shall stand in the name of the "THE PALMER RE-UNION ASSOCIATION." No money shall be disbursed except upon order of said Board to the Treasurer, signed by the President, and countersigned by the Recording Secretary.

§ 2. There shall be appointed at each Re-union meeting when the officers of the Association are elected, a Committee of Installment, consisting of two certificate members, who shall present and install the officers elected for the ensuing term.

§ 3. All committees (special, as well as standing) whose appointment is not otherwise directed by the Constitution or By-Laws, or a resolution of the Association, shall be nominated by the President, and confirmed by the Board of Officers.

ARTICLE V.

Of Meetings.

SEC. 1. As the natural object of this Association will be greatly promoted by social intercourse among its members, the Board of Officers may, whenever in their judgment it is deemed expedient, appoint a time and place for the holding of a Re-union meeting, and a two-thirds vote shall be necessary for such action. But the General Re-Union of the Association and Palmer descendants shall take place at least once in five (5) years—the first having been in 1881, the second to be 1886, the third 1891, etc.—at Stonington, Conn., in the month of August, it being desirable that they be held on the 10th and 11th, but the Board shall have power to fix any other days in August for such Re-union.

§ 2. Special meetings may be called as provided in Section 4, Article 2, of this Constitution. Special meetings shall be competent for the transaction of any business which may come before them, except such business as by this Constitution or the By-Laws may be confined to Re-union meetings.

§ 3. All business meetings of the Association shall be held at such hour and place as the President, or person acting as President for the time being, shall appoint.

§ 4. A quorum for the dispatch of business, except in cases where a larger number may be required for any special act by any Article of the Constitution, shall consist of such number of members as shall be prescribed by the By-Laws, but any number of members present at the time appointed for a stated meeting may, from time to time, adjourn such stated meeting.

ARTICLE VI.

Of the Funds, etc.

SEC. 1. The funds of the Association shall be under the control of the Board of Officers, who shall have power to determine of the necessity of raising funds for the Association, and shall direct the manner of collecting the same; and if a surplus of funds be created at any time, such surplus shall remain in the Treasury of the Association, credited against future *pro rata* subscriptions of the members who may have contributed to such surplus.

ARTICLE VII.

On the Mode of Altering the Constitution of the Association.

SEC. 1. No alteration, appeal or amendment of any part of this Constitution shall take place unless the proposition for such alteration, repeal or amendment shall have been made at a previous stated meeting ; and such proposition shall not take effect unless there are present at least seventy-five members, three-fourths of whom shall vote in the affirmative, and the votes on such question shall be recorded by the Secretary, if required by five members present.

§ 2. The By-Laws of this Association may be altered, repealed or amended, either at a stated meeting or a special meeting, when called, for the object of making such alteration, such object being expressed in the notice of said special meeting. The proposition for such alteration, repeal or amendment must have been made at a previous meeting.

BY-LAWS.

SEC. 1. The business meetings of the Association shall be held on the date of the Re-union, and immediately before the Re-union exercises commence, or they shall be held in November in each year, upon such day as fixed by the Board of Officers.

§ 2. The Corresponding or Recording Secretary shall give at least ten days' notice, through the mails, to all members, of the time and place of all meetings, whether special or stated, and shall issue all invitations wherever Re-unions may be called by the Board of Officers.

§ 3. At special meetings, the consent of two-thirds of the members present shall be necessary to constitute a vote.

§ 4. Fifteen members shall be necessary to constitute a quorum, except in cases where a larger number may be required by the Constitution or By-Laws for any special act.

§ 5. At each meeting of the Association, immediately after the presiding officer shall have taken the chair, the minutes of the previous meeting shall be read by the Secretary, and passed upon by the Association. The next business in order shall be reports of officers and committes ; then new business. The same order shall obtain at each meeting of the Board of Officers.

§ 6. Any member having observations to make or resolutions to propose, shall rise in his place and address the Chair; and all resolutions shall be submitted in writing and handed to the Secretary, and shall be by him entered on the minutes.

§ 7. Certificates of membership, in form approved by the Board of Officers, shall be prepared by the Recording Secretary, signed by the President and the Treasurer, or any Vice-President, and countersigned and sealed by the Recording Secretary, and when issued shall not be transferable.

§ 8. Whenever any question arises touching the eligibility of an applicant for membership, the same shall be submitted to and decided by the Board of Officers.

§ 9. A seal bearing such device and legend as may be approved by the Board of Officers shall be provided for the Association, and until the same shall be prepared a common seal is hereby adopted.

§ 10. A fee of one dollar shall be collected for each certificate of membership issued, and paid into the General Fund of the Association.

§ 11. The Recording Secretary, upon application to him, shall send to each descendant (paternal or maternal) of the Palmer lineage, a certificate of membership, and a copy of the Constitution and By-Laws.

§ 12. All bills for stationery, postage, etc., shall be paid by the Treasurer, on proper order, and when, in the judgment of the Board of Officers, the services of any officer of the Association deserve special compensation, the same shall be voted and paid.

§ 13. No topic connected with the party politics of the day or religious beliefs, shall ever be discussed at the meetings of the Association.

§ 14. The Board of Officers shall appoint District Secretaries in such localities as are necessary to assist them.

§ 15. The Board of Officers shall appoint such non-resident Vice-Presidents as deemed expedient.

[NOTE.—At the next meeting of the Board of Officers of the Palmer Re-union Association will be adopted a form of certificates, to be issued to the family, also a list of non-resident Vice-Presidents, and of District Secretaries. Thereafter a pamphlet containing the Constitution, By-laws, List of Officers, etc. will be issued to all Palmer descendants, paternal or maternal, whose address the Recording Secretary may have.]

[NOTE.—This publication has been delayed to incorporate the foregoing matter in relation to Palmer Re-Union Association, and thus keep up a unity of records between the first and subsequent Re-unions. It is hoped that patient subscribers will accept this excuse for long delay.]

CONTENTS.

C

D

E

ERRATA.

Page 12, 20th line from bottom of page, for "Soper" read "Loper."

" 17, 6th " "correspounding" read "corresponding."

" 71, read " No. 1 " Grace.

" 72, " " No. 2 " William.

" 112, 10th line from top, for "last" read "lost."

" 127, for "Doctors (M. D. and D. D.)" read " M. D. and D. D. S."

" 139, 5th line from bottom for " 1874 " read " 1814."

" 222, (5) Ashabel, should be Rev. Gershom, of Exeter, R. I.

" 177, (9) should be Mrs. J. B. Wood.

" 222, (17) " J. B. Wood.

" 235, " Courtland N.," read "Courtlandt."

" 270, 7th line from bottom, "Chas. W.," read "Chas. H."

[The writer will appreciate receiving from readers of this volume any corrections of errors discovered by them.]

SUPPLEMENT TO VOLUME NO. 1

—OF—

PALMER RECORDS.

ADDRESSES~+~POEMS~+~PROCEEDINGS

OF THE

Second Palmer Family Re-Union,

HELD AT

STONINGTON, CONN., AUGUST 10, 11 & 12, 1882,

THE

ANCESTRAL HOME OF WALTER PALMER, THE PILGRIM OF 1629.

UNDER THE AUSPICES OF THE

PALMER RE-UNION ASSOCIATION.

EDITED BY

NOYES F. PALMER, Recording Secretary.

JAMAICA, L. I., N. Y., Lock Box 420.

L 17 : 2

PRICE, $1.00.

PALMER RE-UNION ASSOCIATION.

BOARD OF OFFICERS.

1882.

President.

ELISHA H. PALMER.   -   Montville, Conn.

First Vice-President.

Rev. A. G. PALMER. D. D.,   -   Stonington, Conn.

Second Vice-President.

Gen. GEO. W. PALMER,   New York, N. Y.

Third Vice-President.

ROBERT PALMER,   Noank, Conn.

Treasurer.

FRANCIS A. PALMER, -   -   New York, N. Y.

Chaplain.

Rev. E. B. PALMER,   -   Bridgeton, N. J.

Grand Marshal.

F. C. PALMER.   -   -   Montville, Conn.

Corresponding Secretary.

IRA H. PALMER.   Stonington, Conn.

Recording Secretary.

NOYES F. PALMER.   Jamaica, N. Y.

Non-resident Vice-Presidents

Amos N. Palmer, Norwich Falls, Conn.; Andrew Palmer, Janesville, Wis.; Asa A. Palmer, Gorham, Mass.; Ashabel Palmer, Stillwater, N. Y.; Alex. S. Palmer, Capt., Stonington, Conn.; A. M. Palmer, New York City, N. Y.; A. G. Palmer, Terre Haute, Ind.; A. B. Palmer, Dr., Ann Arbor, Mich.; A. J. Palmer, Rev., New York City, N. Y.; Amos Allen Palmer, Stonington, Conn.; Albert Palmer, Rev., Boston, Mass.; Alanson L. Palmer, Auburn, N. Y.; B. Frank Palmer, L.L. D., Philadelphia, Pa.; Chapman, Asher H., Pendleton Hill, Conn.; Chas. Palmer, Albany, N. Y.; Chas. H. Palmer, 418 W. 77th st., New York City, N. Y.; Chas. Ray Palmer, Rev. Dr., Bridgeport, Conn.; Clark, Wm. F. Brooklyn, N. Y.; Courtlandt Palmer, New York City, N. Y.; Chas. H. Palmer, Pontiac Mich.; C. A. Palmer, Dr., Princeton, Ill.; Chauncey Palmer, Utica, N. Y.; Chesebrough, E. C., Market st. wharf, Philadelphia, Pa.; C. T. H. Palmer, Oakland, Cal.; Corydon Palmer, Dr., Warren, Ohio. Daloss Palmer, N. Y. City; David C. Palmer, Reading, Pa.; Dixon, C. P., New York City, N. Y.; Elliott Palmer, Rev., Portland, Conn.; Eaton, Prof. Daniel C., New Haven, Conn.; E. H. Palmer, Danville, Ill.; Edwin Palmer, Col., Norwich, Conn., Edward Palmer, Rev., Barnwell, S. C.; Erastus D. Palmer, Albany, N. Y.; Edwin B. Palmer, Chicago, Ill.; Friend Palmer, Detroit, Mich.; Gideon Palmer, New York City, N. Y.; Geo. C. Palmer, Dr., Kalamazoo, Mich.; Geo. W. Palmer, Plattsburgh, N. Y.; Geo. W. Palmer, East New York, N. Y.; Henry W. Palmer, Southfield, Mass.; Irving H. Palmer, Courtlandt, N. Y.; Israel Palmer, Ripley, Chaut. Co., N. Y.; J. Woolsey Palmer, New York City, N. Y.; James Palmer, Rev., Cambridge, Mass.; Josiah Palmer, Greenpoint, N. Y.; Jewett Palmer, Marietta, Ohio ; Joseph H. Palmer, Prof., Yonkers, N. Y.; John M. Palmer (Ex.-G.), Quincy, Ill.; Jas. U. Palmer, Brooklyn, N. Y.; James E. Palmer, Stonington, Conn.; John C. Palmer, Norwich, Conn.; J. H. Trumbull, Hartford, Conn.; Lorin Palmer, Brooklyn, N. Y.; Lamb, Rev. C. A., Ypsillanti, Mich.; Lowell M. Palmer, New York City, N. Y.; Loomis T. Palmer, Chicago, Ill.; Lucian W. Palmer, Providence, R. I.; L. N. Palmer, Dr.,

Brooklyn, N. Y.; Minor, Wm. T. (Ex. G.), Stamford, Conn.;
Noyes G. Palmer, East New York, N. Y.; O. A. Palmer, Dr.,
W. Farmington, Ohio ; Oliver H. Palmer, New York City,
N. Y.; Peter A. Palmer, Lansingburgh, N. Y.; Potter Palmer,
Chicago, Ill.; Robert N. Palmer, Poughkeepsie, N. Y.; R. P.
Palmer, N. Stonington, Conn.; Solon Palmer, New York City,
N. Y.; S. B. Palmer, Syracuse, N. Y.; Stanton, Dr. Geo. D.,
Stonington, Conn.; S. C. Palmer, Rev., Lockland, Ohio ; Thos.
R. Palmer, Rev., Suffield, Conn.; Thos. W. Palmer, Chicago,
Ill.; Thos. W. Palmer, Stonington, Conn.; Wm. Palmer, North-
east, Erie Co., Pa.; Wm. L. Palmer, Stonington, Conn.; Wheel-
er, R. A., Judge, Stonington, Conn.; Wessels, L. W., Gen.,
Litchfield, Conn.; Wm. Pitt Palmer, Brooklyn, N. Y.; Wm. L.
Palmer, Rev., Manchester, Mich.; Williams, Ephraim, Stoning-
ton, Conn.; Walker, Robert J., Oneida, N. Y.; Wood, J. B.,
Warwick, N. Y.; Wm. H. Palmer, Catskill, N. Y.

District Secretaries.

Allen Palmer, Castleton, Vt.; Appelman, Mrs. Lois N., Mys-
tic Bridge, Conn.; Ada R. Palmer, Chicopee Fall, Mass.; A. H.
Palmer, Starkboro. Vt.; A. P. Palmer, Hazardville, Conn.;
Albert Palmer, N. Branford, Conn.; Albert W. Palmer, Kansas
City, Mo.; A. Craig Palmer, Albany, N. Y.; Arch. M. Palmer,
New York City, N. Y.; Bissell, Mrs. C. P., N. Manchester,
Conn.; Benj. Palmer, Danville, Miss.; Barnebas, Palmer, Roch-
ester, N. H.; B. D. Palmer, Poughkeepsie, N. Y.; B. P. Palmer,
Boston, Mass.; Bolles, Eugene, Boston, Mass.; Case, Miss Fan-
nie M., Norwichtown, Conn.; C. L. Palmer, Chicago, Ill.; C. B.
Palmer, Sing Sing, N. Y.; Chester Palmer, Willoughby Lake,
Ohio ; Charles L. Palmer, Webster, Mass.; C. Albert Palmer,
Philadelphia, Pa.; Chas. H. Palmer, La Crosse, Wis.; C. M.
Palmer, Editor, Minneapolis, Minn.; Chapman, B. Frank, Onei-
da, N. Y.; C. W. Palmer, New Haven, Conn.; C. T. Palmer,
Faribault, Minn.; Delia Palmer, Milan, Ohio ; David Palmer,
Bridgewater, N. Y.; E. H. Palmer, Barlow, Ohio ; Ensign,
Henry P., Mobile, Ill.; E. L. Palmer, Danielsonville, Conn.; F.
B. Palmer, Prof., Fredonia, N. Y.; Frank Palmer, Norwich,

Conn.; Frank H. Palmer, Brooklyn, N. Y.; Geo. H. Palmer, New Bedford, Conn.; Geo. Palmer, Branford, Conn.; Gidley Palmer, Grooms Corner, N. Y.; Geo. S. Palmer, Detroit, Mich.; Geo. Palmer, Ashtabula, Ohio; Havens, Edward, Providence, R. I.; H. G. Palmer, Riverside, Iowa; H. H. Palmer, Rockford, Ill.; H. F. Palmer, Norwich, Conn.; H. Beatrice Palmer, Fayetteville, N. Y.; Isabella Grant Meredith, New York City, N. Y.; J. P. Palmer, Rockville, R. I.; J. Alonzo Palmer, New York City, N. Y.; J. Wm. Palmer, Washington, D. C.; J. G. Palmer, New Brunswick, N. J.; L. M. Palmer, Mrs., Albany, N. Y.; Lynda Palmer, New York City, N. Y.; M. D. Palmer, Jamestown, N. Y.; M. G. Palmer, Portland, Me.; Mary Amanda Palmer, Carlisle, Mass.; N. B. Palmer, Pittsburgh, Pa.; Preston Palmer, Fitchville, Ohio; Pitkin, Mrs. M. P., Stockbridge, Mass.; Prescott, C. D., Rome, N. Y.; Powers, Harvey P., Sutherland Falls, Vt.; Robinson, Edwin, Brooklyn, Conn.; Reuben T. Palmer, New London, Conn.; Sabra DeB. Palmer, Amherst, Mass.; Shindler, Mary Dana, Nacogdoches, Texas; Simon Palmer, Boston, Mass.; Timothy R. Palmer, N. Branford, Conn.; Ura H. Palmer, Green Springs, Ohio; Van Velsor, Mrs., Green point, E. D., N. Y.; Woodward, Abbie, E. A., Minneapolis Minn.; Walter, Palmer, Plainfield, Conn.; Wm. Palmer, Monmouth, Ill.; Wilber M. Palmer, New York City, N. Y.; W. R. Palmer, Stamford, Conn.

INTRODUCTION.

This supplement will contain principally the Addresses, Poems and proceedings in brief of the Second Re-Union of the Palmer family, held August 10, 11, 12, 1882, at the same ancestral homestead, Stonington, Conn.

Vol. No. 1 was published last year, and was a memorial volume of the First Re-Union, held at the same place, in August, 1881, consisted of 296 pages, with 74 artotype illustrations, with addresses, poems, genealogical, historical and biographical data pertaining to individuals participating in the First Re-Union.

It would be a repetition to make this supplement as extensive as the memorial volume of the First Re-Union, not to say anything of the extra expense and labor involved. It seems to us more appropriate to reproduce only the proceedings, addresses and poems in an economical publication, that more may subscribe for it.

The first Re-Union was a novelty and was largely attended, surpassing the expectations of the most enthusiastic. The second Re-Union lacked this novelty, but was more of a Palmer Re-Union and more of a social success than the first, though not so largely attended by the public generally.

The second Re-Union was held under the auspices of the Palmer Re-Union Association, duly organized, with appropriate Constitution and By-Laws, and proper officers, resident and non-resident. The main object of holding a second Re-Union so soon after the first was to ratify this organization. The foundation of the association is a *Certificate of Membership* granted at a nominal fee to any Palmer descendent, maternal or paternal, and upon which certificates an election of officers can take place to fill vacancies, and thus perpetuate the Re-Union management under the provisions of the Constitution and By-Laws. This organization was duly ratified at the second Re-Union. The Constitution provides that the general re-unions shall take place in Stonington, Ct., at least once in five years, in August. The first having been in 1881, the next general Re-Union to be in 1886, etc., etc. Auxiliary re-unions may be held at such time and place as the Board of Directors may determine. A copy of the Association pamphlet, containing the Constitution, By-Laws, etc., will be mailed by application of a Palmer descendent to the Rec. Secty. It is very much desired on the part of the officers of the association that their efforts to place the association in the front ranks of gatherings of this character will be duly co-operated with by members of the family by their procuring a certificate of membership.

The Address and Poems. It is hardly necessary to allude, by way of introduction, to the addresses and poems delivered at the second Re-Union, for they are of such a literary character that little else seemed necessary in this publication. It is to be regretted, though, that some of the extemporaneous remarks were last to record, particularly that of Stiles T. Stanton, who, in behalf of the borough authorities of Stonington, gave a hearty welcome to the Palmer Re-Unionsts from various sections of the land. It is also to be regretted that, for want of opportunity, the addresses of several well-known Palmers were missed, particularly that of N. B. Palmer, Esq., of Pittsburgh, Pa., and Loomis T. Palmer, of Chicago, Ill. We opine that like others of note, they were so much interested in the ceremonies they forgot to appear on the platform at the time. The fact that there was no lack of speakers is an evidecne of the interest created in the subject and the success of the Re-Union.

The Tent, Grounds and Accommodations. The large tent seated about one thousand people. and was the scene of a continual service for two days and evenings, and the third day until past noon. The caterer's Tent, under the capable management of Mr. Chaffee, assisted by H. F. Palmer and J. J. Palmer, of Norwich, afforded all the refreshments required, at reasonable rates—two very desirable advantages to be secured in such a gathering and quite an improvement over the managemont of the first Re-Union. Other tents were located on the grounds for the accommodation of President E. H. Palmer, the

Recording Secretary, Noyes F. Palmer, assisted by his son, Albert W., and other tents in abundance for those who could not find other accommodations. The Hotel Wadawanuck, located in Stonington, under the management of C. A. Lindsay, was all that first-class guests could ask for, and the hospitality of the residents of Stonington, in affording private lodgings, was no less a credit to them, and a means of accommodation to the kindred of many of them.

The Rail Roads and Steamboats. Under the judicious management of the President, assisted by H. F. Palmer, of Norwich, and Lucian W. Palmer (Supt. of the N. Y. N. E. R. R.), excursion tickets were secured at lower rates and the best of facilities given in return. The grounds being located adjacent to the Stonington depot, where trains came and went almost hourly from the East and West. The Stonington line of steamboats, under the Presidency of Mr. Babcock, afforded great advantages to the Re-Unionists, and the association management, by a system of excursion tickets at lower rates and also a rebate to the association. The spirit of co-operation manifested by the railroad and steamboat companies and hotel managements of Stonington and connecting therewith, conduced largely to the success of these Re-Union gatherings.

The Loan and Relic Exhibition, under the management of Isabella Grant Meredith, of N. Y. City, and Miss Emma W. Palmer, of Stonington, was a new feature introduced at this Re-Union. Nevertheless it was well received and interesting. It was held at the same old headquarters, tendered by Dr. Chas. E. Brayton. A description of the articles on exhibition, by the Secretary, Miss Emma W. Palmer, of Stonington, will be found in this supplement.

The Concert by the Palmer Band of Whitfield, N. H., under the directorship of its leader, Frank H. Palmer, assisted by several well-known Palmer artists, was one of the great surprises to the Palmers. That the concert was interesting and highly appreciated was manifested by the large attendance for a whole evening.

The pilgrimage to the old Wequetequock Cove, where lived

and died and was buried Walter Palmer, the original ancestor of 1629, was a repetition of last year's excursion, by R. R. and by carriage, and otherwise, " horse, foot and dragoon." Relic hunters abounded, and so did the relics, even down to the bullrushes of the swamp, now termed " Palmer Cat Tails."

The Sojourn of Palmers to Watch Hill, Pawcatuck, Panchunganuc and other favorite resorts adjacent to Stonington left no lack of amusement and afforded no little pecuniary advantage to the places in question and to the commoncarriers thereto.

The Fire Works, though not as elaborate as at the first Re-Union, were very fine, and a great crowd from the country around flocked to witness the display. An early shower ere the culminating pieces dampened the display and cooled the enthusiasm of the event very much. This reminds us of a saying of the President in a letter to us: "*I have arranged for everything but the weather.*"

In conclusion of this introduction : Some may read these lines who will remark : " Of what consequence are these Re-Unions ?" We answer, perhaps of little consequence to any but Palmers or their kindred. To doubt that such gatherings have any latent influence in society would be to deny the benign influence of *Parentage* and *Home*—the nursery of mankind.

That the Palmer Re-Union has become so popular in the family is no doubt owing to the fact that so many of the name can trace their lineage from the tenth generation of 1882, back to the first ancestor of 1629. While the first ancestor from England to America, Walter Palmer, may not have been as celebrated as *George Washington, Daniel Webster* or *Thomas Jefferson*, nevertheless, the sacred memories that cling around *Mt. Vernon, Mansfield* and *Monticello*, the homes of Washington, Webster and Jefferson, are no more held in reverence with their descendants than is *Stonington* to the descendants of *Walter Palmer*. A strange fact coupled with this thought is that while the descendants of the latter now number at least six thousand, very few, *if any*, of the same name live, of the three most distinguished statesmen of America.

THE PRESS—SECOND RE-UNION.

[FROE THE NATION (NEW YORK CITY) JUNE 1, 1882.]

The Palmer family is to meet again at Stonington this Summer. Last year the gathering was almost impromptu; now there is a Palmer Re-Union Association, with a full list of officers including a Treasurer, a Chaplain, and a Grand Marshal. The membership is open to any respectable descendant, "paternal or maternal," of the Palmer lineage, and there is nothing in the constitution to prevent the collateral descendants, of either sex, from being chosen to direct the Association ; but the present Board is wholly male and Palmer. The permanence of the spirit of re-union is greatly favored by the charms of Stonington and its vicinity as a seaside resort. The Western branches, who naturally seek the salt water in the heat of summer, will doubtless time their flight to Newport, Westerly, Watch Hill, or New London, so as to have a share in the Palmer hand-shaking and picnicking. Moreover, the proceedings of last year have all been set down in a book of some 300 pages (Jamaica, L. I., N. Y.: Noyes F. Palmer), where also are to be found artotype illustrations of places and persons—a veritable portrait-gallery— brief biographies, much genealogical information, and even a necrology of Palmers deceased since the first meeting. There is an "alphabetical arrangement of places where some of the descendants of Walter Palmer have lived,"and a list of "celebrated Palmers," classified by occupation—as, General Grant among the Army officers, Senator David Davis among the judges, General John M. Palmer and Senator Pendleton among State governors; Professor D. C. Eaton, the sculptor Palmer, the maker of Palmer's artificial limbs, the inventor of the Gatling gun, ex-Speake Galasha Grow—the wealthy, the long-lived, the large-family Palmers (twelve children was the example of the founder, Walter Palmer) and so forth. Grandmother Palmer" passed away in January. She was the ultimate cause of the Records, though her own habits were so far unsocial or ungaddish that

" during the period of a quarter of a century she left her house
to visit her neighbors but two or three times." Her grandson
doubts" if she beheld a locomotive more than two or three times,
though hearing the whistle daily." She was brought up in the
Baptist faith. "Near my birthplace," wrote this old lady, "were
high ledges of huge rocks, which mother said were rent asunder
when Christ was crucified, which in our infancy [*circa* 1800] created no little interest for the great God of Heaven and Earth."
There is much else that is curious and instructive in this volume.

[FROM THE NEW LONDON DAY, AUG. 9.]

One of the notable events of this section during the present
week will be the Palmer re-union, which is to be held at Stonington commencing on Thursday and continuing for three days.
The re-union last year far surpassed the expectations of its pro-
jectors. It was largely attended and successful in every respect.
That of the present year, however, promises to throw it completely in the shade. During the last twelve months the officers of the reunion association have made arrangements on a
most complete and elaborate scale for the approaching meeting,
and the responses that have been received from Palmers all
over the country warrant the belief that the family gathering
of the present week will far surpass any event of the kind that
has ever transpired in the United States. The large attendance
that is promised will tax to the utmost not only the hotels of
this section but the private hospitality of the people of Stonington. It is believed, however, that the arrangements that
have been perfected will prove equal to the occasion, and that
all who attend will be able to find comfortable quarters either
in Stonington or its immediate vicinity. The literary programme for the occasion is quite elaborate, and cannot fail to
prove of great interest. No doubt one of its most attractive
features will be the address of welcome by Capt. Stiles T. Stanton.

[STONINGTON MIRROR, AUGUST 12, 1882.]

The attendance at the second annual reunion of the Palmer
family, now being held in this place, must be gratifying to the
officers of the Palmer Re-Union Association, as well as to the

members of the family generally. For several days, in fact during the entire week, indications of the great gathering have been manifest in the arrival of small parties of Palmers and the pitching of one monster tent and a large number of small ones on the lot northeast of the upper railroad station. On Wednesday evening the Palmer Band, of Whitefield, N. H. arrived here and took rooms at the Ocean House. About ten o'clock, at the request of a number of the attending Palmers, they assembled in front of the family headquarters and rendered several selections in a manner which at once stamped them as musicians of no mean order.

Early Thursday morning the committees were astir perfecting the arrangements for the meetings.

THE OPENING SERVICES.

At eleven o'clock, A. M., the opening ceremonies were held in the large tent, President Elisha H. Palmer calling the meeting to order. A selection was acceptably rendered by the Palmer Band, after which Prayer was offered by Rev. Caleb A. Lamb, of Ypsilanti, Michigan, the chaplain of the re-union association, Rev. E. B. Palmer, of Bridgeton, N. J., being unable to attend. Mr. Lamb is a descendant of Walter Palmer, and although ninety-three years of age is apparently in good health. His great interest in the affairs of the association is attested by his presence at the re-union, which rendered necessary a trip of several hundred miles. ·Mr. Stiles T. Stanton, of this place, was then introduced by the president and in a graceful address welcomed the Palmers, on behalf of the Wardens and Burgesses, to the hospitality of the borough. His remarks were at times of a humorous character, but bid the Palmer host a hearty welcome. President E. H. Palmer responded briefly.

The band then played a piece. It having been stated upon the street that the players were not all of Palmer descent, the leader, Mr. Frank H. Palmer, was called upon to testify to that fact. Gen. George W. Palmer, of New York, delivered an able address, abounding in good points, and Mrs. Isabella Grant Meredith, also of that city read a graceful poem written by

her for the occasion. The regular programme having been finished, business relating to Friday's exercises was transacted.

AFTERNOON EXERCISES.

The attendance at the afternoon session was much greater
than in the morning, the large tent being filled and surrounded
by many people unable to procure seats within it. The exercises were opened by the Hon. T. W. Palmer, of Detroit, Mich.,
who made an exceedingly happy address. Music by the Palmer band with a cornet solo by Mr. F. H. Palmer of Whitefield,
N. H., followed and was very heartily applauded. Miss Sara ·
A. Palmer of this village then read a poem written for the occasion. It was one of the pleasantest features of the occasion,
the subject, " The New Crusade " being treated with much
freshness of thought and marked by the grace of expression
which characterizes all her poems. Miss Palmer was very warmly received, after which C B. Palmer of Sing Sing, N. Y., spoke
at some length on " The Modern Palm Bearers. " The Rev.
A. G. Palmer contributed a beautiful love story in delightful
verse and there was more music by the band. The President
then presented the names of the members of the committee on
finance and the programme for the following day was announced.
One or two gentlemen spoke briefly relative to further arrangements for the celebration and the exercises closed with the
Palmer Hymn written by Miss Sara A. Palmer and sung by all
the Palmers to the tune of "America."   ·

A MAGNIFICENT PYROTECHNIC DISPLAY.

In the evening, commencing at eight o'clock, a beautiful display of fireworks took place on the re-union grounds under the
direction of parties from Middletown. The number of specta-
tors is thought to have been equal to that of last year, and the
exhibition, although not quite so elaborate, reflected great credit upon the persons having it in charge. A number of set pieces
were given, the largest and most beautiful being one gotten up
for the occasion showing the words " Palmer Reunion, 1882. "
About nine o'clock a slight shower dampened the spirits and

jackets of the assembled multitude, but happily the display was nearly finished before the rain began to fall.

The evening trains from the east and west came crowded and the extra trains at the conclusion of the exercises were literally packed with the returning excursionists.

From opening to close the first day of the reunion was of a most pleasant character and a grand success.

FRIDAY AND SATURDAY

the reunion exercises were continued, but at the hour of going to press we are unable to make a report of the meetings. Fri day's programme included a trip to the burial place of Walter Palmer at Wequetequock, a clambake, and a meeting in the big tent at which the following gentlemen spoke: J. U. Palmer, Brooklyn, N. Y.; A. L. Palmer, Auburn, N. Y.; L. T. Palmer, Chicago; Courtlandt Palmer, New York; Ephraim Williams, Stonington; Dr. G. D. Stanton, Stonington; Prof. Joseph H. Palmer, Yonkers, N. Y.; N. B. Palmer, Pittsburg, Pa.; Wm. Pitt Palmer, C. B. Palmer, Sing Sing, N. Y.; Robert Stanton, Frank Palmer, Norwich; Prof. A. B. Palmer, M. D., L.L. D., Michigan University; Rev. Hiram Stone, B. Frank Chapman, Oneida, N. Y.

THE LOAN EXHIBITION

at Palmer Headquarters contained many articles of interest, including Walter's portmanteau and photographs of Col. Jonathan Palmer's family.

[BROOKLYN DAILY TIMES, AUGUST 11, 1882.]

The second gathering of the clans of the Palmer family began yesterday at Stonington, Conn. The success of the Re-Union of last year so far exceeded the expectations of those who set on foot the enterprise in fear and trembling, that they were encouraged to go forward this year with the expectancy of even greater success. Last year about 1,500 Palmers nearly all of whom could trace their descent to the original Walter Palmer, who settled in Wequetequock, now Stonington, in 1650, assembled to revisit the home of their ancestor, and a thoroughly enjoyable family party was the result.

A PERMANENT FOOTING.

Since that re-union the participants have united upon a permanent footing and have formed the Palmer Re-Union Association, the object of which "shall be the perpetuation of the re-union of the Palmers and their paternal and maternal kindred through the Palmer lineage; to collect and preserve information respecting the history of the family, and to promote social and literary intercourse among its members." The constitution of the Association provides for re-union at least once in five years. This year however, it was deemed wise to appoint the second re-union, as so large a number of persons were unable to be present last year, and at least two-thirds of those present agreed to come again.

*   *   *   *   *   *   *

The present meeting is held as the last was, upon the anniversary of the historical day in Stonington, that upon which its naval battle was fought. The Re-Union grounds are in the north part of the borough, near the railroad depot. Here all the public meetings are to be held in a large tent, and smaller tents upon the grounds are put up to accommodate the overflow from the hotels and boarding houses. It is expected that not less than three thousand persons will be in attendance in the three days that the exercises will continue. Every possible provision has been made by the Local Committee of Arrangements for the comfort and care of all those who attend. In addition to the hotels, of which there are several in Stonington and Watch Hill, as well as in New London and Westerly (accessible in a few minutes by rail), there are many private houses thrown open for guests.

EXERCISES OF THE OCCASION.

The varied programme for each day has been provided. The first address was assigned to General George W. Palmer, of New York City. Various branches of the family and different localities are to be spoken of by their representatives, and poems

and music will diversify the public exercises. Business connected with the Association and its maintenance will be attended to.

One feature of the gathering is to be a collection of relics and
curiosities held by members of the family, and a curious and
unique exhibition is promised by Mrs. Isabella Grant Meredith
and Miss Emma W. Palmer who have supervised this feature.
This Loan Exhibition is also designed to show the works of
Palmers by pen, pencil and chisel, and art work of all sorts.
One evening will be devoted to a concert by a band composed
altogether of Palmers, and an exhibition of fireworks will be
given upon another.

A PALMER VOLUME.

Since the re-union of last year a neat volume of 300 odd pages
has been compiled by the indefatigable Secretary, Noyes F.
Palmer, giving an account of the origin of the enterprise, the addresses and features of the first gathering, and sketches of the
most notable men there. It is embellished with artotype illustrations of many of those who attended the exercises and contributed to their success. It is the first of a series of Palmer
books, the second to contain the genealogical lists of the various branches of the family, including already over 7,000 names.
The first volume has met with much success in the family,
which is as large as a small city in itself. The present Re-Union
is expected to intensify the interest in the family and all of its
belongings.

PLANS FOR THE FUTURE.

Not a few Palmers have been going to Stonington in the fort-
night past in order to be on hand for the Re-Union, and Stonington bids fair to be the Palmer Summer Seaside Resort.
Already a plan has been broached to buy a large hotel and con-
vert it into a Palmer House. * * * * There
is a likelihood, however, that the gatherings of Palmers will become fixed facts in Stonington history. It is expected that the
season which commenced yesterday and which will continue to-
day and to-morrow will be a thoroughly successful affair.

[NEW LONDON DAY, AUGUST 11, 1882.]

A bright hot summer sun rose into a deep azure sky, unobscured by a single speck of cloud, over the old borough of Stonington on Thursday morning, as the descendants of the pioneer Palmers from far and near began gathering on the tented meadow for their second annual re-union. The large central pavilion with a seating capacity of about 1200 was conveniently arranged with chairs and benches in amphitheatre form, fronting on a raised dais for the officers of the organization and speakers. To the left was the kitchen and dining pavilion and all around, smaller tents to the number of twenty-five dotted the ground and gave the whole a decidedly sylvan and picturesque character.   In the first of these smaller tents a register is kept where all who would might leave their autographs. Next was a tent in which Noyes F. Palmer issued certificates of membership to those of the family who desired them at the cost of $1.   Then came the striped tent of the president, E. H. Palmer, of Montville, with the colors of the clan and the motto " Palman Qui Meruit Ferat, " in which he received and welcomed the arriving guests. * * * * Another tent contained Palmer fancy work, bric-a-brac and souvenirs, the work all done in the family and each article marked with its price which ranged all the way from ten cents to $100.

Before the time announced for the commencement of the exercises, 10:30 A. M., all the trains, regular and special were depositing their freight of Palmers at the depots, but it was not until 11:15 that the committee of arrangements could arrange and accommodate the crowds that thronged to the main pavilion.   The order of exercises opened with prayer by Rev. C. A. Lamb of Ypsillanti, Mich., age 93, after which the president introduced Capt. Stiles T. Stanton of Stonington who in behalf of the warden and burgesses extended a cordial welcome and the hospitalities of the burough to the great and prolific family whose heroic ancestor was so intimately identified with the locality, whose ancient homestead can still be pointed out and whose bones still rest under the green turf he loved so well, and near the sounding sea whose heaving billows sing an eternal requiem. The address was received with unbounded applause and Capt. Stanton received a perfect ovation as he stepped down from the rostrum.

President E. H. Palmer replied, acknowledging the courtesy with his usual happy bonhomie. The Palmer band of White-field, N. H., composed exclusively of scions of the race, gave some fine original selections, after which Gen. Geo. W. Palmer of New York, for the literary committee delivered a greeting to Palmers, relatives and friends which was in reality a cursory history of the origin, genealogy and peculiar characteristics of the family from the middle ages to the present day, elaborated by quotation and comment from ancient and modern history and drawing deep draughts of inspiration from Walter Scott's heroic novel, Ivanhoe, where the Lady Rowena accosts the Palmer with : " The defender of the absent has a right to favorable reception from all who honor truth, honor and manhood " and where the Palmer himself asserts, in speaking of his brother warriors " Second to none, sir. " The poem of Welcome was read by Isabella Grant Meredith and elicited prolonged applause.

Part of the opening stanza only is given below :

> Friends ! Kindred ! it hath been accorded me
> The grateful part, to greet and welcome ye,
> To this old city by the sounding sea.
> An honorable task—in days of yore,
> When came some way-worn Palmer to the Hall.
> The Chatelaine brought forth the choicest store ;
> Her pages flitted at his beck and call ;
> In gentle cares her bower-maidens strove,
> And pretty zeal displayed in deeds of love.
> While with her own fair hands, the noble dame
> Dispensed the manchet, as her rank became,
> And served her venerable guest in Christ His name.

After Mrs. Meredith's poem the president asked for an expression from the assemblage as to whether they would visit the home and grave of Walter Palmer in Wequetequock at a cost of twenty-five cents for the round trip. It was unanimously voted that they would. The president then said that this meeting was called mainly to ratify the constitution and by-laws informally adopted at the centennial celebration in Stonington last year and subsequently confirmed at a Palmer meeting in New York last winter. At the last named meeting it was voted to continue the present officers until now and to hold an election for their successors at this re-union. The Palmers also voted to accord the right of suffrage to men, women and children. All can vote who are accredited Palmers and who pay $1 to Noyes F. Palmer, who is Recording Secretary, on the grounds. The president then appointed Senator Thos. W. Palmer, of Detroit ; Loomis T. Palmer, of Chicago ; Courtlandt Palmer, of New York City ; and Geo. W. Palmer, of New York, a finance committee.

This closed the forenoon exercises, and the concourse adjourned to the hotels or to the dining pavilion where for lack of clams they were disappointed in the chowder, but the way cold ham and tongue disappeared from the groaning tables was absolutely startling, and it took considerable time to appease those appetites stimulated by the bracing salt sea air that swept refreshingly across the moor. At 2:30 P. M. the large tent was again filled, many having arrived in the interim. Hon. T. W. Palmer, of Detroit, Mich., opened with an address in behalf of the Palmers of Michigan, in which he carried them back to the fountain head, bringing down the house frequently by his sallies of humor as he caught on to some funny Palmer trait. F. H. Palmer's cornet solo was finely rendered and received with an expressive encore. Miss Sara A. Palmer of Stonington read very effectively an excellent original poem on the New Crusade, and C. B. Palmer of Sing Sing, made an address on the Modern Palm-bearers, which was replete with interesting reminiscences and delivered in a masterly style of oratory. Rev. A. G. Palmer of Stonington read The Courtship of Betty Noyes and Ichabod Palmer, a historical epic written expressly for the occasion. Then the band gave the memorial hymn, a musical selection by the leader, and very creditable to his genius as a composer and arranger of music. Brief responses to family names were next in order. Some were brief and some were not, but all of them were more of a puzzle to the reporter, as they meandered through the lines and angles of families, than the differential calculus. Richard A. Wheeler, of Stonington, mixed some Irish blood, from Cork, into the clan through the Celtic tribe of Fanning

and proved himself one-fifth a Palmer. Rev. Mr. Stone, of Bantam, traced his family to Simeon Palmer, of Taunton, and claimed a quarter degree of blood relationship. Mr. Chapman, of
Oneida, but not of the community, knew more about the Palmers than any Palmer on the ground and told what he knew in
a graphic and humorous but very intricate style, and after he
got through with 115 Palmers—father and son, sisters, cousins
and aunts—the reporter put his fingers in his ears and stopped
his reckoning. The president and Mr. Chapman then announced
the following speakers for the exercises to-day, which they char-
acterized as the grand love feast of the Palmers : J. U. Palmer,
Brooklyn, N. Y. ; A. L Palmer, Auburn, N. Y. ; L. J. Palmer,
Chicago ; Courtlandt Palmer, New York ; Eph. Williams, Stonington ; Dr. G. D. Stanton, Stonington ; Jos. H. Palmer, Yonkers, N. Y. ; N. B. Palmer, Pittsburg, Pa. ; Wm. Pitt Palmer,
of Stockbridge, Mass. ; Wm. C. Palmer, Sing Sing, N. Y. ; Robert Stanton, Frank Palmer, Norwich ; Prof. A. B. Palmer, M. D.,
L.L. D. Michigan University ; Rev. Hiram Stone, Loomis T.
Palmer, Chicago, and B. Frank Chapman of Oneida. The Pal -
mer Hymn, written for this re-union by Miss Sara A. Palmer
of Stonington, was then sung by the whole audience, standing,
to the accompaniment of the band, and was a brilliant finale to
the exercises of the afternoon. This concluded the business
portion of the day's doings, and at the request of an enterprising photo man, the crowd left the tent and posed outside for a
quarter of an hour to have their pictures taken. It was interesting to see the girls saying prunes and prisms with their silent
lips, as they struggled for good positions to give the machine a
point blank shot at them. The president told all unlodged
Palmers where they could procure beds or hammocks in Westerly and New London or under the A tents on the grounds.
He also said that the concert to-morrow evening by the Palmer band and vocal singers would be held in the large tent. Admission 50 cents. The pyrotechnic display in the evening, commencing at 8 o'clock, was attended by large numbers from the
adjacent cities and villages, and was eminently successful, not-

withstanding a moderately heavy shower threatened to throw a damper over the exhibition.

On Friday morning the Palmers began gathering on their camping ground at an early hour. The air was cool and pleas. ant and a brisk westerly wind shook out the national and Palmer ensigns that floated bravely from the central pavilion. At 10:30 A. M. the officers arrived and shortly after the large tent was filled to the extent of its seating capacity which is at least 1000. The exercises opened with prayer, after which several speakers arose to respond to family names, tracing their origin, and descent from the Palmers. Ephraim Williams, of Stonington, said that the descendants of the Palmers in the female line were superior in physical endowments to those who inherited the name through the male line. He said it was one of the instances where the gray mare proved to be the best horse. B. F. Chapman, of Oneida, is a Palmer enthusiast. He went back to the days when a Tudor or a Stuart abrogating despotic rights over their subjects, compelled by their tyranny the best blood of Britain to leave the land where there fathers lived and died, and seek in the untried and virgin soil the freedom which they were denied in the land of their nativity. The speaker eulogised the hardy pioneer race, and claimed for them the development of the country which they adopted, and her progress through the centuries from an almost unknown and unsurveyed region to the highest pinnacle of power and civilization. In no other country has science, art, literature made such rapid strides, and in no other is the heaven born boon of civil and religious liberty enjoyed by its people to the fullest and most liberal extent. Several speakers whose names were announced on the programme were compelled by business exigencies to leave without fulfiling their engagements.

This closed the morning exercises, and the assemblage adjourned from the pavilion, some to their hotels, others to the restaurant tent and still others to the number of seventy- five took advantage of the special excursion train to Wequetequock, where two hours were consumed in visiting the ancient homestead and venerated tomb of the noblest Palmer of them all—the great and glorious Walter—whose name has made a brilliant page in the history of his adopted country. The old grist mill came in for its full share of admiration, and the party returned deeply impressed with the retrospective memories which the historic old spot awakened. The afternoon exercises did not commence until after 3 o'clock.

The President introduced Dr. Eugene Palmer, of Texas, an old gentleman of 80, who gave interesting reminiscences of the family in the far southwest. He was followed by his grandson, Albert G. Leoning, Esq., of N. Y. City who delivered a brief but eloquent laudatory address. Dr. Eugene Palmer was the furthest traveler to this re-union, except the Misses Nash—two beautiful girls whose maternal Palmer lineage is warmed by the hot blood of Castile and the dark liquid eyes and rich olive complexion, favors more the Andalusian than the Saxon extraction. The Misses Nash are orphans, natives of Mexico, and this is their first visit to their mother's land. Lawyer Palmer of Oneida, read from a deep mourning card a greeting sent by Mary Palmer Pitkin, who was the soul of the last re-union, to the officers and guests at this re-union and regretted that the recent death of her mother compelled her absence. Miss Sara Palmer read in a very effective manner a poem by her father, Rev. A. G. Palmer. Gen. George W. Palmer proposed a vote of thanks to the ladies whose efforts in collecting and exhibiting relics and souvenirs of the family were largely instrumental in making these re-unions the magnificent success they have been. The names of Mrs. Isabella Grant Meredith of New York, and Miss Emma W. Palmer of Stonington, were deserving of especial honor. The resolution was adopted with enthusiasm. Gen. Geo. W. Palmer offered a resolution of thanks to the president for the ability he displayed as a presiding officer and the herculean efforts he made to perfect this great family organization. The resolution was unanimously adopted. President E. H. Palmer gracefully returned thanks for the courtesy, and pledged his faith to continue with all the ability he was possessed of to work for the organization which had so honored him. Rev. A. G. Palmer then presented the first prize, a beautiful gold-headed ebony cane, to Rev. Elliott Palmer, of North Coventry, as the oldest clergyman, bearing the name of Palmer, in attendance at the re-union. This presentation address was the feature of the day. The venerable gentleman said that the gift reminded him, by its strength and stiffness, of the character of the recipient, who in the face of new creeds, new schisms and the assaults of infidelity, moved through life in the even tenor of his way, hewing to the line, according to the doctrine of Christ his Savior, and yielding nothing to force nor flattery, from the disciples of Ingersoll, and others less open in their expressions, but for that reason more dangerous by their insidious heresies.

He concluded by invoking the blessing of Christ on his friend and fellow minister, and as the two white-haired old men clasped hands in greeting their feelings overpowered them, and it was easy to discern that the vast audience was in sympathy with their emotions. Rev. Elliott Palmer replied in a very few words which were not half as expressive as his moistened cheeks and trembling hands.   *   *   *   The concert in the evening began at 8 P. M. The programme was good, excellently rendered and received the applause it deserved from a very fair audience. To-day's programme will consist mainly of election of officers, reports of the old, and appointment and organization of new committees.

PROCEEDINGS.

PRAYER,

BY REV. CALEB A. LAMB, OF YPSILANTI, MICHIGAN.

" Lord thou hast been our dwelling place in all generations. Before the mountains were brought forth, or ever thou hadst formed the earth and the world, even from everlasting to everlasting thou art God," as the Psalmist says. Lord we render the thanksgiving for thy creating power and thy preserving mercy and for thy kind providence which has watched over us and permitted so many of us to meet and mingle our kindred greetings. We invoke thy divine blessing to rest upon us, and especially upon the association, its officers, and its managers: that kindred ties may be strengthened, so that we may feel that it is good that we have come together: Lord grant that we may all so live here upon earth as at last to be brought to participate in that glorious Re-Union, where high hills and deep water, and broad lands should separate us no more, forever:

In the name of Christ. Amen.

ADDRESS OF WELCOME,

BY GEN. GEO. W. PALMER, OF NEW YORK.

[Note Illustration and Biography on pages 107 and 104—Vol. I.]

Palmers, Relatives, Friends: I am bidden by the Literary Committee, and others in authority, to extend to you a most cordial and hearty *welcome.*

I greet you all! Welcome, thrice welcome to this Re-union, ye Palmers of the East, ye Palmers of the West, ye Palmers of the North and ye Palmers from the regions where the Palm

trees grow. *Welcome* friends and relatives—one and all of you
descendants of Pilgrims, who brought order out of chaos on
this continent, and assisted in spreading light where before there
was darkness. Welcome every one to this historic field in the
heart of classic New England, where the giant Walter Palmer
and the sturdy William Palmer lent their strong arms and willing hearts toward practically illustrating that self reliant manhood, which here in this very section of our noble land sowed
the seeds that brought forth, a century later the tree of Liberty, under whose benignant and manifold branches we are this
day enjoying peace, good will and happiness.

Who is there among you that doubts the great share every
one of the Palmers of old contributed toward establishing upon
this soil that beacon light of freedom—resplendent in all its
glories—which in this century of ours has become the day star
of hope—the rock upon which mankind all over the world rests
its unwavering faith for the welfare of the generations that are
to come after us? No battle-stained castles, no armored halls,
no frowning towers mark the valleys where these ancestors of
ours first planted the seeds of civilization. The sturdy Pilgrims
of those days had already cast behind them the helmet and the
lance of the middle ages. They had come to conquer new fields,
but with weapons far more effective than those which for centuries have reddened the hills and dales, the rivers and lakes of
the old world with the blood of man. They had come to build
up, and not to destroy. They had come to infuse blood and
not to shed it. Industry was their weapon. Civilization was
their aim.

The humble cabins were their castles, the free fields, domed
by the glorious sky above, were their palatial halls. Thence
rung forth in tones that were heard all over the colonies, those
songs of toil and labor well performed, that one hundred and
fifty years later brought out the first Battle Cry of Freedom, "
and with it that matchless Declaration of Independence.

" The rights of man " were firmly planted in the soil by our
forefathers by the aid of the ploughshare and the spindle , but

where danger threatened, they knew how to, and did wield the sword to victory, returning quietly to their homes, and resuming the habitiments of labor, the ploughshare and the pruning-hook, when war was over.

And yet—but not in this land, of toil, there must have been in the dim past, Palmers who devoted their entire lives to the profession of arms; but only—and let us be thankful for it—in behalf of a cause dear to us all, the Christian religion. Not that can be traced directly, the line of genealogy to the ideal Palmer now in my mind. According to Sir Walter Scott, however, we read in his charming book "Ivanhoe" of a Palmer who had participated in the crusades of the middle ages, when religion was yet spread with the aid of the sword. We find in Ivanhoe, the Pilgrim Palmer upon his return from the Holy Land, imbued with all the sentiments of chivalry, truth and manhood, which should at least make us anxious to claim this heroic character as representative of one of our veritable ancestors. When in a conversation in regard to the courage displayed by various nationalities during the battles about the Holy Sepulchre, a Knight of the Temple claimed that the English warriors were second to others which the Knight mentioned, the Pilgrim Palmer arose and exclaimed :

" Second to *none*, sir! I say that the English chivalry were second to NONE who ever drew sword in defence of the Holy Land. I say besides, for I saw it, that King Richard himself, and five of his knights held a tournament after the taking of St. John D'Acre as challengers against all comers. I say that on that day each knight ran three courses, and cast to the ground three antagonists. The first in honor as in arms, in renown as in place, was the brave Richard, King of England. "

When subsequently the Pilgrim Palmer spoke in behalf of the absent Knight of Ivanhoe, and pledged his honor that upon his return from Palestine, he also would be ready to answer the challenge of the Knight Templar, the Lady Rowena, seated upon a throne and anxious to hear about Ivanhoe, the companion of her childhood, addressed Palmer saying : " The defender of

the absent has a right to favorable reception from 'all who
value truth and honor manhood. '" The eminent author points
other traits of character, honorable to the name of Palmer, but
this may be sufficient to show that even by one of the greatest
minds of English Literature, the word Palmer was considered
synonym with all that is great and noble in human nature.

Let us leave, however, the domain of story, fiction and tradition, and contemplate with the powers at our command, the living fact of this grand Re-Union, composed of many minds and
yet all bent on perpetuating the ancestral name, that ever re-
liable connecting link, between the past and the present, and—
judging by the well-known productive forces of the Palmers—
also of the future. We see before us the grave and the gay—
the young and the old—the farmer and the merchant—the soldier and the statesman—the artisan and the representatives of
the learned professions, all united in celebrating what? a simple
idea.

And yet the American people are frequently taunted by foreign critics with being solely devoted to the mighty dollar.
Do we gain anything in the shape or way of lucre by this Re-
Union? No. It is an idea, a simple but great and glorious IDEA
that brings us hither from the Prairies of the West, from the
granite hills of the East, from the chilly mountains of the
North and the majestic rivers of the South. It makes us greater men and women to commingle on this beautiful field for and
on behalf of this idea, in order to show the world at large that
the blood which courses through the veins of a Palmer gives
sustenance to a heart full of feeling and sentiment. to a head
full of understanding as to the importance of this most interesting Re-union of a great and growing family.

There are two ways of looking at these family Re-Unions or
gatherings, namely : in their moral, and also political aspects.
When I say *political*, I do not mean it in the narrow partizan
view, but the broad, vast political system which is synonym
with order and government We meet here with a full understanding that the family is the foundation stone of the State.

It is after the pattern of the family that the government of our country is constructed. In fact, the family being the narrowest limit in which people are united, is the real source of all power. It has a head, represented by the parent, whose duty, defined to him or her by the laws of nature, compels him or her to maintain order among the different members. Without such order, without such discipline there would come division, unhappiness and misery. " Honor thy father and thy mother that thy days may be lengthened," has been written and unwritten law ever since the thunders of Sinai first proclaimed to mankind the ten great commandments which were ever after to be the fundamental principles upon which all just laws must be based. The patriarchs of old in this respect have been no more scrupulous in its observance than are the savages of our day. Christians and Pagans, Jews and Gentiles have ever laid this solemn obligation to their hearts. " Honor thy father and thy mother." Aye. the Romans of old, were so imbued with the meaning and spirit of this command, that the thought of a child ever assaulting or murdering a parent never entered their heads. To them such an atrocity was *impossible*, and hence the renowned Roman laws contain no provision for the punishment of such a crime and totally ignore the word "parricide," leaving it to modern vocabulary to coin the designation of this crime, and to modern law to provide the punishment.

Acknowledging then, that mankind, ever since the beginning of history, has endowed the parents of the family with authority for the purpose of maintaining within its circle harmony and unity of action, we find that this system stands the test—nay, it is the necessity of the highest civilization. Here in our Republic, as I have already said, it lies at the foundation of our governmental system and contains the original source of power. Next to the family comes the municipality, which is an aggregate of families ; next to the municipality comes the province or as we term it, the State, its government stretching its authority over the various municipalities. The States again form a family which is governed by the Federal Power, called the Union. (We call our government the *Family Re-Union*). Now, again look at the beautiful structure composed of the just mentioned integral parts. While the government of the Union is restricted in its powers and in its authority, there is a corresponding strength of authority as we descend stage by stage from the Federal to the State, to the Municipal and finally to the Family power. The larger the extent of territory over which these various powers expand themselves, the fewer are the restrictions which they impose within their respective jurisdictions, until we finally come back to the family where the parental power is making itself felt in the minutest details of life, of habits, of manners, of food, of raiment, of religion and of education. These Re-Unions teach us to respect and honor the family—nay, make us more proud of it, and thus render it stronger for good in the body politic.

Nor will any one deny that such an organization as this is wise and proper. If one should, I ask him why he commingles in this Re-Union with the fathers, mothers, brothers, sisters, uncles, aunts, cousins, nephews, nieces and all those connected with him through the multiplicity of grades of consanguinity, gathered here to place a crown of garlands upon the family system and family name?

Within this Re-Union we have no questions of State to consider; no treaties to conclude or ratify, unless indeed it be the treaty of Love which the bold Palmer youth desires to conclude with the blushing Palmer maiden. But mind you! let us whisper it so low that it may not awaken the echoes in yonder nooks, under the shade trees, or in the quiet of the cozy parlor,—parental authority reaches far, but may not arbitrarily attempt to *command* in those sacred precincts. Mutual confidence between parent and child should always exist respecting the delicate relations of lovers and the all-important and serious contemplation of wedlock. The one should kindly and freely give and the other take the advice and the wisdom which experience brings; but arbitrary commands seldom, if ever, have any other than mischievous effects upon those whose affections are plighted.

Ah! would that all mankind in general, and the Palmers in particular, might lay to heart the lessons that ought to be in-

culcated by a Re-Union of hands and a Re-Union of hearts
such as seems to exist here, and feel the ennobling effects and
influences such gatherings have upon the young and the old
alike.

Why should not the Palmers stand at the head of that growing class of eminent souls who continually point with pride
toward any event of great contemporaneous human interest?
If we cannot be the pioneers in movements like these, we can
at least be the most active promoters of a cause such as we here
represent at Stonington. And why should we not? Casting
aside all care, all troubles, we have come here to sit at the feet of
those mature in years, and listen to the tales and songs of ancestral fame, as we heard them while still in our cradles, just as
they were told and sung when still being fed by our mothers.
This to us is a season of peaceful reflection: a wandering back—
if I may so express it—to the days of our childhood, when
peace and innocence held sway over our tender years.

It is meet and proper that we should have, now and then,
days like these ; not only for the purpose of enjoyment but for
the purpose of contemplating ourselves—our real selves. In
this busy life of ours, composed of so few and short years, we
pay too little attention to the betterment of ourselves and our
kind. We permit—too frequently, alas!—events to drive us
on, and perform our work in a hap-hazard way. Here, at
least, in this Re-Union we have an opportunity for study, for
reflection, for thought. We can compare notes as to the different modes of life indulged in by the various Palmers, as to the
different principles which guide their lives, as to the views entertained by them in regard to questions dear to us as citizens
and as men. As then we become acquainted with these various
phases of thought, of action, of habits, entertained by them, all
of us by contemplating the same, thereby become better Palmers, for we then learn to practice that great and noble cardinal
virtue, *Tolerance*. The time has passed, my friends, in this age
of thought for one set of men or women imposing their ideas,
their principles, *their* formulas upon another set of men or

women.   We will listen, study, reflect and choose for ourselves
what seems good and valuable to be our charts and guides of
life.   No man is so well informed but that he can always learn
something from what others may tell him, and if he does not
associate or cares not to associate with all those with whom he
comes in contact in daily life, a Re-Union like this teaches him
at least, that for the time being he must—in the common phrase
of the day—" put up " with those around him.   In other words,
this Re-Union teaches all of us, as I said before, tolerance, good
will to men and to women also.

Probably, while dwelling on this subject of our duty toward
our fellow men, while showing that we should never belittle the
attainments, the talents, the character of others, unless we have
ample proof of unworthiness, I ought also to speak of the respect
we owe to and for the matters and things of the past.   Henry
Thomas Buckle, in his unparalled work " History of English Civilization, " teaches us, in this regard, a valuable lesson.   Unlike
other historians who measure everything of the past by the
standard of the time in which they are writing, Buckle has set
himself to show the good that was done to humanity even in
those dark ages which are generally thought profitless to man.
He draws instructive lessons even from the monks and friars of
the time who kept themselves in seclusion from the world they
did not care to commingle with.   So, also, let us regard with
respect the men and things of the past, and endeavor to find
the good that was done by them or with them.

You here, for instance, will see during this Re-Union many
things your ancestors possessed, queer in their shape, odd in
their make up, stranger withal to your modern ideas.   But
there is a history to all of these relics, a history that may or
may not come to your ears, but a history nevertheless.   Your
paternal or maternal ancestors may have been happy in their
possession at a time when your very existence was not even a
subject of thought to them, while these relics were.   Human
nature is so constituted that we love to retain such relics, if
simply for the contemplation of the various associations sur-

rounding them, at a time that is now gone, a time that can never more return.

In this good work of collecting relics of the past, none have been so industrious, so untiring, so discriminating as the ladies of our organization. God bless them for it ! They always lead in works where the heart and sentiment preside, and often where the sterling intellect is brought into requisition.

My friends, I have already taken up more of your time than I ought, but let me say to you on behalf of the officers of this organization, that it affords us infinite pleasure to see so many Palmers present at this our second Re-Union, and apparently in such excellent health. We trust that the time you will spend in and around Stonington will not only prove pleasing, but also instructive ; and that it will be an incentive to you to urge other Palmers, who have not yet joined our ranks, to send in their names and enroll themselves under the family banner bearing that time-honored motto, " *Palma Virtuti.* "

And now, while yet standing upon the threshold of the precincts of this Re-Union, I again bid you welcome ! You have traveled the causeway—the gates are wide open. Let us enter and enjoy the poetry, the eloquence, the song, and all the varied entertainments which are in store for us. And may the events of this Palmer Re-Union be so pleasing—so fraught with all that is charming and delightful in the relations of social life—that their memory will ever be cherished in our hearts of hearts as among the sweetest and most beautiful experiences of our lives. Together let us labor, together let us rejoice, and in the language of Dickens, put into the mouth of "Tiny Tim, " may " God bless us every one. "

POEM OF WELCOME.

BY ISABELLA GRANT MEREDITH.

[Note Illustration, etc., on page 177, Vol. I.]

To the Palmers—Greeting:

I.

Friends, . . . kindred! . . . it hath been accorded me
The grateful part to greet and welcome ye
To this old city by the sounding sea.
   An honorable task. . . . In days of yore
      When came some wayworn Palmer to the Hall,
   The Chatelaine brought forth her choicest store,
      Her pages flitted at his beck and call;
   In gentle cares her bower-maidens strove,
   And pretty zeal displayed in deeds of love.
While with her own fair hands the noble dame
Dispensed the manchet, as her rank became,
And served her venerable guest in Christ His Name.

II.

Though wild those days when, for a zealot's scheme,
Mere tender Babes shared the Crusaders' dream,
Athwart that gloom, thank God! shone one faint gleam;
   One little taper burned with steadfast ray
      Till it dispersed the wavering shades of night;
   When Love illumined Faith, lo! dawned the day,
      And Force was fettered, Error shorn of might.
   No more brave Palmers strove by doughty deed
   From hands impure, that served an idle creed,
The Holy Land and Sacred Tomb to wrest.
Their worthier care, the temple in each breast,
By outward life the inward grace to manifest.

III.

Adown the ages shone that beacon clear
On Covenanters' ranks, Cromwell austere,
On faithless King, and loyal cavalier.
   On sturdy Puritans who home forsook,
      Heaven's counsel guiding their prayer-guarded deeds,

High-hearted, strong, with ne'er a backward look
  To England's storied woods and sweet, green meads.
From pleasant granges 'midst the flower-prankt glades,
Forth fared the Pilgrims, matrons, sires and maids,
Yet not as erst, with Paynim foes to fight,
Nor panoplied like the Crusading knight;
They went self-exiled in the cause of Human Right.

IV.

What welcome met the wandering Palmer here?
No eager servitors brought dainty gear,
Stayed him with flagons, cates and royal cheer.
  Yet sure this virgin solitude did thrill
    Before the Master of its savage moods;
  And the lark lilt with wilder, sweeter trill
    O'er rippling waters and o'er whispering woods,
That here a nobler race brought milder ways.
Methinks e'en Nature felt some soft amaze
When here the Pilgrim's gentle daughter, Grace,
Bent o'er the Wequetequoc a moment's space
To meet the wistful smile that flitted o'er her face.

V.

Once more the peaceful Pilgrims seek the strand
Two centuries have made *our* mother land:
Once more we meet and grasp each other's hand.
  And still ye strive, knights errant and Crusaders,
    With arms far nobler than the lance and brand,
  'Gainst foes more fell than Saracen invaders,
    Against insidious Circe, bright and bland;
Sin, that now lurks obscure in loathly nest,
  Now stalks abroad and flaunts its shameless crest.
Ye track the hydra, Vice, with hearts of ruth,
For Age dishonored, and for blighted Youth,
Your bright, resistless weapons, Beauty, Virtue, Truth.

VI.

For some of ye are poets, some are preachers,
Some artists, statesmen, editors and teachers;
All—like Ben Adhem—love your fellow-creatures.

And, howsoe'er ye tend the quenchless Light,
 Instruct a nation. strive in its defence,
Limn English meads ([1]), sing of " Love's Second sight ([2]),
 Chisel the dimpling dream of innocence ([3]),
Transfix in marble, Beauty's matchless face.
And touch our souls with the pathetic grace
Of Resignation's sweet, submissive calm,
Your faithful works uplift, your hands bring balm ;
Unto such noble labor God awards the Palm ([4]).

VII.

But better welcomes than my poor verse meet you
In the kind eyes that cordially entreat you
From yonder chair, whence genial smiles now greet you.
 When these bright days are ended and we sever,
  Be mine, yet once again, the grateful part,
 In the serene and beautiful Forever,
  As now, to bid you welcome from my heart.
There melody shall help the halting phrase,
And Pentecostal tongues teach truer praise.
And, oh ! my friends, let it be pardoned me
The lack of grace in words that welcome ye
To Walter's home and grave, beside the sounding sea.

NOTES TO THE POEM OF WELCOME.

1.

Limn English Meads.—Reference is here made to Mr. Robert Minor, the artist, whose studies of English scenery are well known.

2.

"Love's Second Sight"—A poem by Wm. Pitt Palmer.

3.

Dimpled Dream of Innocence.—"The Sleeping Peri," one of the PALMER MARBLES, as is also the bust of "Resignation," alluded to in a succeeding line. Both are works of art from the hand of the sculptor, Mr. Erastus Dow Palmer.

4.

Unto such noble labor God awards the Palm.—"Palma non sine Labore" is the motto which has been handed down for six generations in the branch of the family of which Mr. E. D. Palmer, the sculptor, is a member. The crest surmounting this legend is the scallop, or cockle-shell, worn by those Palmers who had visited the shrine of St. James the Less, at Compostella ; this shell being the cognizance of the great apostle.

ADDRESS OF SENATOR THOMAS W. PALMER,

OF DETROIT, MICH.

The Palmers of Michigan send their greeting to their kinsmen. Common report had long pointed to Stonington as the
parent hive; but until the gathering of the clan last year the
fact was involved in and only supported by the vagueness of
tradition.

They are grateful to the promoters and organizers of this
family Re-Union for the opportunity to formulate into history
the shreds, scraps and memories which, until now, had their
uncertain abiding place in anecdote and rumor.

In early life our hopes and aspirations are our motive power.
As we see the purpling of the dawn brighten into day, buoy-
ancy, strength and certainty of the future is a subtle quality
of the blood. If we study the past, we do so for its uses and
not for a solace; but as the shadows begin to lengthen in the
west all philosophic souls, healthfully weary of the struggle for
and possibly the possession of what men strive for, turn to the
past for consolation and repose. We delight to treasure up a
remembrance of traits in the characters of those to whom we
owe our being, and collate incidents in their lives which may
throw light upon the impulses which controlled them; nay,
more, he desires to know of those who in like manner were
dear to them, and to learn how they in turn wrought, suffered
and enjoyed.

In primitive times this was the beginning of history, and as
the family relation was the foundation of the State, so was the
knitting together of families by common memories the beginning of patriotism.

But aside from the sentimental aspect of the question, I
think the Re-Union has a scientific value. I must confess that I
had a great curiosity to come down and meet my kindred to
compare notes and to see how we had differentiated, as the sci-
entists say, in the last two hundred years; to note the effect of
the introduction of different strains of blood upon our mental
and physical structure.

The Palmers of Michigan represent two branches of the Walter Palmer tree. One of these branches, which I will designate as the Stonington and Voluntown branch, is briefly reported in Vol. I of the Palmer Record, in the notices of Hon. C. H. Palmer and Rev. William Ledyard Palmer. They are both gentlemen of character and position, and one of them I am happy to call my personal friend. Their line of descent from Walter Palmer is established.

The other branch, which I will call the Windham County branch, is the most numerous in Michigan. It had for its progenitor Dr. Joseph Palmer, who went up into Ashford, Conn., and made a home one hundred and fifty years ago. It is to this branch that I belong, and it gives me pleasure to come back and pick up the missing links, if any there be, which will render indisputable our claim to a descent from the staunch old pioneer whom we are all proud to claim as our common ancestor.

Our staying away so long may recall to some of you the story told of an old man and his son down here in Connecticut. The old man treated his boy with very little consideration ; in other words, he was rough in addressing him, and sometimes a little profane. His legs were paralyzed, and he generally sat in one position before the old-fashioned open fire-place. One evening, as night drew on, he raked out the coals, and, turning his head, said with an oath, " Ben, bring in a back-log." Ben went out with his feathers badly ruffled. After meditating a little while, he concluded to let the old man wait for his back-log, and starting off he went down to some seaport and shipped before the mast. Ten years wore round with varying fortune to Ben, till finally, one day in port, his heart yearned for a sight of the old faces, and he concluded to make the old home a visit. As he drew near the old farm, misgivings took possession of him. He wondered whether the old man, helpless and paralytic as he was, still lived, and then he questioned, as a feeling of tenderness came over him, whether he had not been too hasty, and again he felt guilty that he had stayed away so long. While stirred by these emotions, he drew near and entered the old yard. The light beamed from the same windows, and looking through he saw the old man in the same attitude in which he had left him. He had the hoe in his hand with which he was wont to rake out the coals preparatory to making the evening fire. Ben saw by the pose of his head that he was the same as of yore, that the same spirit animated him—stern, hard and unrelenting. Ben thought he would try what the French would call a *coup d'etat*, that he would conquer him by one stroke. He looked around, and seeing a back-log of the right size he shouldered it, walked in, and putting it down end first, said, " Dad, here's your back-log!"

Ben expected a revulsion of feeling, a throwing of arms around his neck such, as he had seen in the print of the prodigal son in the old family Bible. The old man looked up for a moment, but he never flinched, and then said, " Well, Ben, you have been a confounded long time about it, but put her on."

Now, whether old Dr. Joseph Palmer left Stonington in a huff one hundred and fifty years ago tradition does not say, but he has come back to-day in the person of his descendants—has brought in the back-log, and proposes to again take his place with his kindred around the old hearth-stone.

Dr. Joseph lived and died in Ashford, leaving five sons. From two of these sons, Benjamin and John, sprung all of the Windham County Palmers living in Michigan.

Benjamin Palmer married Martha Barbour, of Simsbury, Conn., by whom he had eight children, five of whom are buried in Michigan.

John Palmer, his brother, had five children, two of whom are buried in Michigan.

Thomas Barbour, of Simsbury, father of Benjamin Palmer's wife, had taken goods to barter for furs to Detroit as early as 1760. He bought his stock in Albany, and freighted it in batteaux up the Mohawk, thence by stream, lake and portage across to Lake Ontario, up Lake Ontario and by Indian trail around Niagara Falls, thence up Lake Erie to Detroit, at that time a British garrisoned fort. After exchanging his stock for furs, he returned by the same route. By two ventures of this kind he made a snug sum, which enabled him to live in comparative affluence. He undoubtedly would have continued his ventures in this direction if it had not been for the Indian troubles fomented by Pontiac, who was perfecting his great conspiracy to drive the. English from the valley of the lakes.

It was the recital of his adventures around the Winter fire in old Ashford that stirred the imaginations of Thomas and Friend, sons of Benjamin, and in 1809 Thomas went to Detroit and thence to Malden, in Canada, now Amherstberg, eighteen miles below the present city, at the mouth of the Detroit river, and there started a store. At the breaking out of the War of 1812, Thomas was thrown into jail as an American citizen, and after five weeks imprisonment was liberated, put across the river, whence he walked to Detroit and joined the legionary corps just in time to be included in the surrender of the town by General Hull.

He and his brother Friend returned in 1816, and for many years were engaged in large enterprises. They had stores for general merchandise at Canandaguia, Ashtabula. and at Palmer, Mich., now St. Clair, with a large establishment for headquarters at Detroit. They took contracts from the governor and judges, then the executive administration and judicial power in the Territory, for the building of government roads and the construction of the Capitol for the Territorial Legislature. They also built and freighted several vessels on the lakes.

In 1825. George, a younger brother, came out and settled on a farm at Palmer, St. Clair County. Catharine Palmer, who had gone out with her brothers, married Mr. Felix Hinchman. Titus followed his brothers, and engaged in the mercantile business.

In 1826, John Palmer, a cousin of Thomas and Friend, and son of John above named, came out and engaged with the brothers under the firm name of F. F. & J. Palmer. For some years they did a successful business, when John withdrew from the firm and started business alone. His brother Mason came out in 1828, and engaged in business alone.

The above is a complete list of all the Windham County Palmers of the last generation who settled and remained in Michigan. They were all persons of high character and good repute. The first of them went to Michigan when there were only 10,000 white people in the Territory. All save, one, lived to be eighty years old. They all, save one, Mr. George Palmer, died within a period of twelve years, and when the last one died, in 1880, the State had a population of 1,700,000. Few families had more to do than they with the material development of the State, and none, I believe, exercised a better influence by their moral, energetic and unostentatious lives. With one exception all the families live where they lived fifty years ago. All save one left children, most of whom live in the State. They were men of strong convictions and positive character, but kindly, genial and hospitable. They were all men of temperate, pure lives.

The sons of Benjamin were men of large stature and great endurance. The sons of John were delicate men and slight stature.

They were men of independent thought, as is evinced by their denominational connections. Friend was a Baptist ; Thomas never joined a church, although an attendant of one ; George was a Congregationalist ; Mrs. Hinchman was a Presbyterian ; Titus belonged to no church ; John was a member of the Presbyterian Church, and Mason of the Episcopal.

None of them nor their descendants were ever accused of a misdemeanor. They were not litigious, seldom appearing in court as plaintiff or defendant. Some of their descendants are rich, and all in comfortable circumstances, through wealth acquired or through their individual efforts; but none of them, to my knowledge, regard wealth as the be all and the end all of life. Both branches are people of good repute.

They seem never to have had a taste for public life. One only from each branch has held a State office respectively, Regent of the University and State Senator, and I imagine that those instances were the result of accident rather than of design.

And now, my kindred, the Palmers of Michigan have made their report. After a wandering of an hundred and fifty years, in which they have seen the great chief Pontiac, and spoken to the great chief and statesman Tecumseh, they have come back to the old homestead to look in the eyes of their kindred, to exchange congratulations, and to invoke the spirit of old Walter Palmer, that he may determine whether we have brought back his escutcheon untarnished.

"THE NEW CRUSADE,"

BY SARA A. PALMER.

[Note—Illustration, etc. on Page 177, Vol. I.]

One year ago to-day,
Our Pilgrim feet astray,
    Sought this green land ;
Our hearts were free from care,
Pleasure reigned everywhere,
The skies smiled bright and fair
    Upon our band.

We sang brave Walter's praise,
Cheered his grand old-time ways,
    With hearty zeal.
Proud we his children felt,
Gazing where erst he dwelt ;
As at his grave we knelt,
    Our hearts were leal,

And full of reverence strong, .
To him who well and long,
    This new land ranged.
And steady since that day,
Our love has burned alway
A never flickering ray,
    By nothing changed.

To-day more firm we stand,
More strongly hand grasps hand
    In kinship rare ;
We've learned to know the worth

Of honest Palmer birth;
Second to none on earth
    The name we bear.

Stronger our purpose grows,
As swiftly on time flows,
    To use life well.
Worthy our grand old name,
We mean shall be our fame ;
Not vain shall be our claim,
    All to excel !

Now planning let us drop,
And for a moment stop ;
Leave vows and pledges here,
And backward turn a year.
A merry sight we'll see,
Gay faces full of glee.—
This in the morning hours ;—
But by-and-bye—ye powers !
A shadow dark and deep,
Doth o'er our spirits creep.
And in our inmost hearts,
A sad foreboding starts ;
Remembering how in pain
We wanderers asked in vain
For sofas, lounges, beds,
Or shelter for our heads ;
How often meekly said,
" A Palmer wants a bed, "
Only to hear again
That wearisome refrain,
" The Palmers lodge, oh where,
We neither know nor care. "

   *   *   *   *   *   *

Astronomy that night
Was studied with new light,
For many a student wise
Beneath the starry skies,
Fancied he'd " plan-et " better
And make the Palmers debtor
If e'er they " com-et " again.
Were all these plannings vain ?
To-night the truth will show,

Our fate we soon shall know!
Now, too, we feel a gnawing,
A sudden awful clawing,
To think of that clam-bake
Which we had hoped to take,
And which, alas, we lost,
Though some found to their cost.

Oh bitter was the lay,
Of those who on that day,
Strolled up and down the street,
Seeking for " bread to eat. "
The Palmers in old times,
Wandered in distant climes
With scrip and staff in hand,
Seeking their holy land.
Did they our sorrows know,
Hungry and homeless go?
Did they as vainly try,
As we the land to spy?
Did they find only rocks,
Huge boulders, massive blocks,
Most glorious to see,
But surely they'd not be
Fit pillow for a head,
With weariness half dead;
Tired out, with Palmer lore,
And Palmer poetry; that's more
To bear than Palmer ways,
Their wit, their many days.
Their families so great,
(Twelve was the common rate),
And that wise man so tall,
Ancestor of us all.
The many men of note,
We almost learned by rote,
The night we heard them told;
And almost felt it bold
To claim our little place,
Among that giant race,
Described with graphic power,
In that dim-lighted hour,
By our historian small,
Who over-tops us all,

At least, in names and dates,
In old homes and estates,
With now and then a blunder,
Which fills us with " grave " wonder
And sorrow, that his pages,
Designed for coming ages,
Should misplace or mistake
A name or place or date.

*   *   *   *   *   *

If *height* the passport be,
How does our G. H. P.
Make good his presence here?
Why that is very clear,
Because with genius true,
He knew so well, to do
The thing that should be done,
That victories might be won
Knew, too, the time to take
A proud success to make.
Or tall or short, 'tis sure,
His Palmer blood is pure ;
We honor him to-day,
The man who led the way
In this, our new " Crusade, "
So worthy of our grade.
Proudly to every eye,
Lifting the " Palm " on high,
So long shall live his fame,
As lasts the Palmer name.

*   *   *   *   *   *

No more must we rehearse,
But turn to our first verse,
And throw one longing look
At that close-sealed book—
Our future. One glance cast
O'er now-to-be and past ;
Our deeds, our hopes and fears,
The joys we've had, the tears,
The plans we've made, and may,
And then the " Good-bye " say.

*   *   *   *   *   *

'Twas thus we planned last year,
And now we're gathered here
    The page to show,
To tell if dreams, or deeds,
If golden fruits, or weeds,
If failures, or won meeds,
    We Palmers know.

If, as the days went by,
We've used, or let them fly,
    No laurels won;
If we have e'er proved true,
To all we've vowed to do,
Stood strong, e'en when a few,
    To have right done.

No record *this* will show,
But every heart will know,
    In depths profound.
We trust our Palmer blood,
To stand for God and good,
E'en though wrong, like a flood,
    Surges around.

And so with gladsome hearts,
Albeit the tear-drop starts,
    Our kin we greet.
We give all, " welcome " smiles,
And use our sweetest wiles,
To make it worth their whiles,
    With us to meet.

And tribute we would pay,
E'en on this festal day,
    To those gone higher.
So many from our ranks,
Stand on the other banks,
Singing and giving thanks
    With heavenly choir.

Children that we have known,
Up into angels grown,
    So far above ;
Mothers and fathers dear,
Seeming to heaven so near,

'Twas but a step from here
To God's own love.

Thus grief must cloud this day,
God help us all to say,
    "It was Thy will."
Help us to give Thee praise,
For all their lengthened days,
For all their loving ways,
    For memory still.

And grant that by-and-bye,
We all may find on high,
    The rest we crave.
Then with all fightings done,
Then with all victories won,
Then with new life begun,
    Our Palms we'll wave.

MODERN PALM-BEARERS.

C. B. PALMER, OF SING SING, N. Y.

[Note—Illustration, etc., on page 107, Vol. I.]

Mr. President, members of the Palmer Re-Union Association—Ladies and Gentlemen :

I speak to-day of knightly conflict on other fields than Acre or Ascalon. I recount not the valor of a Godfrey or a Cœur de Leon, but the deeds of a later day and the conquests of a newer crusade. I shall not speak of the panoply of arms, or of a sheen of spears in the cause of sentiment, and an empty sepulchre, but rather tell you of achievements in behalf of the living principles of the teachings of the man of Nazareth. You, who bear derivative title in name and lineage from the palm-bearers of the thirteenth century, have gathered here on this second Palmer Day to do honor to the names and memories of an ancestry who had a part in this conflict, a conflict more glorious in its results than any on the Plains of Palestine.

One born of a parentage on the one hand paternal from that

non-conformist element that convulsed England in her political and religious policy for a century, and planted vast empire on this continent, founded upon the principles for which they contended, and, on the other hand, maternal from the sturdy Dutch who conquered the ocean with the dikes of Holland; protected the early Puritans by their liberal policy; and sent to that same England the man who calmed her troubled state when, in the words of Lord Macauley, the cry went up from Land's End to John O'Groat's house, "Welcome the Prince of Orange!" I say such an one may be pardoned on this occasion, in addressing this company of modern palm-bearers on the crusade for civil and religious liberty.

With the last years of the thirteenth century expired the dying spark of the crusades, leaving the world in social and moral darkness for two hundred years. When dawn appeared, it struggled through the doors of that little monastry at Erfut, and with that dawn came the new crusade for light and liberty to the human soul in the doctrine of a justification by faith alone.

It gave rise to the terrible wars of the sixteenth and seventeenth centuries—conflicts for principles—and from the smoke of battle and the incense of blood was diffused knowledge to the struggling masses of humanity.

Shall I speak of the leaders in the vanguard of this crusade? of Luther and Melancthon, of Zwingle and Calvin, of Cramner and Latimer, and of young Patrick Hamilton, or later of Pym Hampton and Cromwell, soldiers of the sword as well as the spirit?

I say these were conflicts of ideas, contests for principles. Man contested with man on the thirty-nine articles, or the five points of Calvinism, either but offspring of human thought. Both followers of the lowly Nazarine, brother battled with brother if he follow a clergy investments from the Aaronic priesthood or the simpler forms of the Genevean Church; men died for the doctrine of predestination, and shed blood for the form of a surplice.

Reviewing the events of these times from our standpoint in

Republican America, it seems absurd. Yet these questions deluged England in blood and woe, and drove from her throne an hereditary prince of the house of Stuart. But beneath these surface questions was the vital issue, Should the civil government regulate the individual responsibility of man to his God?

The pulpit of the Puritan became the forum of the common people, advancing step by step in that onward progress of the human race up to higher and nobler plains of Christian civilization.

In that portion of old England known as the north shire of Nottingham, in the Hundred of Bassett Lawes, was the little town of Scrooby. Here, under the shadow of the manor house of the Archbishop of York (that manor house where the great Cardinal Woolsey dwelt when, "if he had served his God with half the zeal he served his king, he would not, in his age, have been forsaken to his enemies"), was a congregation of Puritan separatists. Scrooby may be known as the mother of American Puritans. A leading man in this congregation was one William Brewster. He had been a secretary and devoted follower of that Davidson who had clipped off the head of the one fair woman who seems destined ever to be alike the contention of historian and theme of poet—Mary of Scotland.

The meetings at Scrooby and the preaching of Brewster soon attracted the attention and invited the interference of the authorities. From trial and tribulation there was no escape save exile. With longing eyes and heavy hearts they bid adieu to those fair Nottingham hills, and crossing the channel sought refuge in Amsterdam. This Scrooby company was twenty years after the Pilgrims of the Mayflower.

From Nottinghamshire, possibly, probably, of the Scrooby congregation came William Palmer, and Walter Palmer, and Abraham Palmer, and Matthew Palmer, palm-bearers in the crusade, bearing their palms across the broad Atlantic and planting them deep down among the foundation stones of a new commonwealth.

Argonauts on an unknown sea, standing upon an inhospitable coast, before them an unexplored, mysterious wilderness inviting physical contést, behind them, across the water, all they held dear in this life, but with it a fiercer spiritual combat:

I summon brave Ulysses
From the mists of Ancient Troy,
And knightly names of other days,
From the Cid to DeMaloy;
In heroic deed and action,
'Gainst savage craft and power,
The pilgrim of New England
Is the hero of my hour.

He came like John the Baptist,
In the wilderness he wrought,
Preaching in this world Judea,
What the holy teacher taught;
We revel in his visions,
And our hearts with rapture ring,
When he strikes the harp of glory,
Like the Israelitish King.

But there were other palm-bearers left at Whitehall bearing soiled palms. Roger, Earl of Castlemaine, lives solely in history as the husband of Barbara Palmer, the celebrated Duchess of Cleveland.

But our ancestry, casting behind them all favor of King and Crown, boldly planted their palms in the virgin soil of a new world. Palmer descendants—scions from the old palm stocks—have carried these palms and principles across the continent in all the walks of life—martial, educational, on sea and land, in art, science and literature. Of the Palmer patriotism let the roster roll of three wars tell, from Bunker to Malvern Hill.

A Stonington ship-master,

" Far voyaging, he struck the strand,
Now blazoned on charts as Palmer land."

We have searchers in the South seas and in the starry heavens. Inventors of machines for the destruction of mankind, and an honorable array of names devoted to their cure. Wealth may be the creature of chance—frequently the result of com-

binations ; and politics are not always a criterion of either ability or respectability ; but we do claim the man who introduced
stage-coaches in Great Britain, and the one who first brought
to this country Pekin ducks. The combative qualities of our
soldiery, and the doctrines and devotion of our clergy, the
character of our ancestry may clearly indicate. But what, you
may ask, is the Palmer peculiarity ? for what the family famous ?
And I challenge any other family in this broad land to produce
a dozen not unknown poets, male and female (not the least our
fair cousins of to-day), a score or more prose writers, and at
least one purely American sculptor. Shades of William and
Walter ! whence these poetical Palmers ? whence this art and
literature ? " My Faith Looks Up to Thee," or " Hymns of
Holy Hours," might echo back in the old colony without effect,
and " I'm a Pilgrim and a Stranger," sound natural, but that
" Smack in School " would cause tumult and commotion. And
then our sculptor, Palmer, must hide his Sleeping Peri and his
White Captive behind the colossal figures of his Landing of the
Pilgrims. Have these old Puritans deceived us ? Was there
hidden behind that sombre demeanor heart fancies of life's
amenities, suppressed because forbidden, which has developed
in their descendants to-day ?—You, who true to your pilgrim
name, have gathered here from the St. Lawrence to the gulf,
from the hills of New England to the canon of the Sierra
Nevada, from the populous city and the open plain—gathered
on this old ancestral ground, gathered around this family altar
that our fathers set up and dedicated to civil and religious liberty two hundred years ago.

Puritanism meant freedom of thought ; liberty of conscience ;
but the Puritans of Massachusetts Bay Colony limited it to the
measure of truth they had attained. It was heresy to go beyond. This seems bigotry. It was bigotry. Let us be truthful ; let us be fair. Being intolerant, they were no less sincere.
They had borne so much, suffered so much ; yet great suffering
had not taught them charity. If they drove forth from the colony
that man whose only crime was having advanced a step beyond
their standard, and who founded your adjoining great little State

—Roger Williams and also, perchance, Walter Palmer from Rehoboth—let us be truthful, let us be kind; let us not forget
their human frailties. For this Puritan belief was solemn; it
was profound. Men who stood face to face with God: men,
who by faith entered into his councils, joined with him in his
work. The slightest incident, to ordinary mortals trivial, was
to them unmistakable indications of Divine approbation or dis-
pleasure. Was it unnatural, then, that the first code of laws
for their guidance was taken entirely from the Old Testament?
On it was subsequently engrafted precepts from the Roman or
civil law, at least admitting that society in the seventeenth
century required something more modern. Was this a mistake
of Moses?

Their jurisprudence was severe; they were severe men; and
it may be a question to-day if we do not sacrifice quality for
quantity on our statute books. For instance, enactments pun-
ishing the crime of blasphemy was first the whipping-post.
This audience may consider the deplorable condition of a noted
orator of to-day had he lived in Massachusetts Bay Colony in
sixteen hundred.

If the Puritan conflict developed the zeal of fanatics, it also
developed the hearts of heroes. In the words of Whittier:

> " For there he stands in memory to this day,
> Erect, self-poised, a rugged face half seen,
> Against the back-ground of unnatural dark;
> A witness to the ages as they pass,
> That simple duty hath no place for fear."

Such, Palmers, was the character of the ancestry it is your
privilege to commemorate to-day. And I raise my voice in
humble tribute to their many virtues.

In religion the Puritan recognized the personal responsibility
of man to his Maker; in temporal affairs, that the governor
derived his just powers from the governed. They built with
circumscribed views of these principles, yet they builded greater
than they knew; for it was the outcome of society, founded
upon these principles, that brought on the conflict between the

colonies and King. It permeated the original thirteen States; it hastened that struggle of popular freedom against the divine right of a king to rule over men, called the revolution, which involved the destiny of a continent; yea! of half the world. Samuel Adams, the son of a Massachusetts Puritan, drove the entering wedge that separated the colonies from the mother country, and culminated in that second Magna Charta of human rights—the Declaration of Independence.

These results could not have emanated alone from the sturdy Dutchman of New Amsterdam, for by nature he was a conservative; nor from the disciples of William Penn, for they were non-combatants; nor the followers of Lord Baltimore on the shores of the Chesapeake, for they were churchmen; nor the cavaliers in the trains of Raleigh and Oglethorpe, for they were King's men. The moral lever, the educator of pre-revolutionary days, was New England Puritanism, and by and through it the Calvinist and Baptist of New England, the Reformed Churchman of New York, the Quaker of Pennsylvania, the Papist of Maryland, and the Episcopalian of Virginia, Georgia and the Carolinas, all combined, without guide or precedent, in the formation of a government of separated State and Church —the first in the history of the world from the days of Constantine.

A searcher around that monument that stands behind the White House on the flats of the Potomac, may read on a stone this inscription, " To George Washington : Hero, Soldier, Statesman. Founder of well-named Modern Liberty. The Native Country of Solon, Themistocles and Pericles—the Mother of Ancient Liberty—Dedicates this old stone from the Parthenon."

It is a hand grasp across the gulf of ages. From the Demos of Attica to the States of America. From the Pagan liberty of the Ancient to the Puritan liberty of the Modern Republic.

Yet this Puritan liberty was impure. With greed for gold came clank of chains. They legislated liberty for the white man, but slavery for the black man. A perfect government was not formed. There was other and fiercer conflicts in the crusade.

It was a beautiful Sabbath morning in early April, 1861, that I, a youth, stood in State street in the city of Albany. On my right, mingled with the sound of church going bells, I heard the roll of a drum. In front of the exchange I saw a mass meeting of excited citizens. I asked a bystander, What means this demonstration? and he replied, The rebels have fired on Fort Sumpter! It was one of the opening scenes in that drama history bears record as " The Civil War in America." The causes that may have led to it, time and the occasion forbid I should discuss. It has been charged to New England and Puritanism ; and indirectly they might plead guilty to the indictment with pride, for one result stands pre-eminent ; one fact established that civil liberty in this commonwealth shall be a misnomer no longer. The emancipation of three million human bondmen consummated the grand ideal, that under the broad egis of the Republic all men are born free and equal.

It was the same conflict fought at Naseby and at Marston Moor, at Concord and at Lexington, at Antietam and at Gettysburgh ; it was the same zealous longing of humanity for liberty that possessed the soul of good old John Knox when, wandering an exile in foreign lands, he cried, "Give me Scotland or I die." It was wafted through Cromwell's army on the notes of the seventeenth psalm. It burst from the lips of Virginia's great orator when he cried, " Give me liberty or give me death." It rustled among the leaves on the table where the Declaration was signed, when John Hancock said, " Let England read that without spectacles," and thus reverberating down the ages, it echoed in that round house at Harper's Ferry with Ossawatomic Brown and his Spartan band, when above the rattle of musketry might be heard :

" God never leaveth utterly
    This world that he hath rounded,
All human stress is by the sea
    Of his dear pity bounded ;
Upon no Israel, to its ill,

The grip of Pharoah closes,
Beyond the liberating skill
Of some anointed Moses."

As if, with prophetic vision, they saw through the smoke wafted across the sacred soil of Virginia the form of that man before whose name the great names of history pale, and whose character coming generations will behold colossal—Abraham Lincoln—and at his side that stalwart palm-bearer and modest soldier, U. S. Grant.

Yes, there were palm-bearers in this conflict. All may not have worn the blue; some wore the grey, and learned through bitter defeat the lessons all must learn—" The mills of God grind slow but sure." Some of these palm-bearers sleep to-day under velvet sod, fanned by gentle breezes, on Southern hillsides. and some sit here with us.

I am one of those who believe that " God ruleth among the armies of heaven and the inhabitants of earth," and that in his special providence for six thousand years of the world's history, this vast continent was hid from civilization ; that through the progress of principles and the evolution of events, as I have endeavored briefly to narrate, it might be, in these latter days, an asylum for civil and religious liberty.

Is there danger awaiting us as a nation ? Are we not slowly drifting away from the landmarks set by the Pilgrims of Plymouth and the fathers of the Republic? Is there not an indifference to the precepts they preached, and the principles they practiced? Is that a cloud just above the horizon, not larger than a hand yet a cloud? May we read on it aristocracy or anarchy? Aristocracy means State Church. Anarchy means no Church. The accumulation of great wealth in the few ; the interference of powerful ecclesiastical bodies and of corporations in affairs of State ; appropriations of large subsidies of public moneys for sectarian and other purposes ; and a rapidly-increasing population, without patriotic pride, and wanting sympathy with our governmental system, assaults on that moral nursery of the Republic, our common schools. A want of purity and morality in public affairs and among public men —nay, open and boasted infidelity, and disregarded that "righteousness exalteth a nation"—all indicate in the near future a conflict between aristocracy and too much religion, and anarchy and no religion.

Let the Palmers plant their palms on the middle ground.

God grant that in this land we may never have persecution for conscience sake ; that on our ears may never sound the jingling of the stirrups of the troopers of a Claverhouse. God grant we may not witness what France once saw, when a maddened crowd carried through the streets of Paris draped in the insignia of freedom an abandoned woman as the Goddess of Reason, and wrote on the tombstones in their cemeteries, "There is no hereafter."

Palmers! Palm-bearers! you who bear the motto, "*Palma Virtuti*," when this conflict shall come, if come it may, forget not the faith of your fathers. Let our palm-leaf be to us a signal, like the white plume of Henry of Navarre.

And in that congregation that John of Patmos saw, a great multitude, that no man could number, of all nations and kindred and people and tongues stood before the throne and before the Lamb, clothed in white robes and palms in their hands. And as that congregation shall pass up, up, higher, higher, higher, through the light of the throne of the ever-living God, foremost in their ranks, we pray, may march with their palms, the Palmers.

ICHABOD PALMER AND BETTY NOYES.

A POEM BY REV. A. G. PALMER, D. D.

[Note Illustration, etc., on page 90, Vol. I.]

I have a little tale, of olden time,
   Which I would like, in some way to rehearse;
Truthful, dramatic, thrilling and sublime,
   And worthy of the poet's highest verse;
The story is of fair young Betty Noyes,
And Ichabod Palmer, her first maiden choice.

Ichabod Palmer, son of Ichabod,
   Through Gershom, fourth, from Walter Palmer down,
Six feet and six, full in his boots he stood,
   The tallest, strongest man in all the town;
A fine physique, high-browed and open face,
A model man in build and strength and grace.

Five leagues, due north, from Walter's home domain
   Lived Ichabod, on bold Pauchunganuc
Hill, whence sweeping o'er the underlying plain,
   The eye took in the silvery Pawcatuc,
Discharging its bright waters, as to-day,
Into the Little Narragansett Bay.

Around The Bridge, where navigation ended,
   A nascent village early sprang to birth,
By store, and mill, and smithery attended,
   Adjuncts of village life in all the earth;
Now, Westerly—a city soon to be—
Four miles, by steam, from Watch Hill and the sea.

Here lived a fair young girl, our heroine,
   Referred to in our opening verse above,
Of chastened beauty and of modest mien,
   Whom but to see was to admire and love;
And many an offer for her heart and hand,
Came from the first young gallants in the land.

Still, Betty Noyes could not be wooed; but why,
   Though spinsters gossipped much, yet none could tell
For she, with quiet humor in her eye,
   Kept her sweet secret to herself, and well;

She only archly said: "I know my heart,
And have no mind at all with it to part."

" I am not in the market," she would say,
    " Not ready to be auctioned off just yet,
I want a little longer my own way,
    For all know therein I am strongly set ;
I could not my sweet liberty forego
For any unengaged young blood I know."

And so, girl like, she held the beaux at bay,
    Now smiled on them, now jilted them at will,
Now soberly, now in sheer sport and play,
    She tortured them with hope and fear, until
They'd turn away with wounded pride and pain,
Only, with her first smile, to come again.

A maiden's smile—who has not known its power,
    Who has not felt its half bewildering spell,
Who has not, in some fragrance-laden hour,
    Beneath its flash and brightness swooned and fell?
But who shall fail to know its thrill and bliss,
The ecstacy of life and love will miss.

But at a social gathering, one young man,
    Some miles outside the village, seemed to be
That evening present by design and plan,
    As if some one awaited him to see ;
And when he strode in, kingly-like and bold,
And towered above the rest like Saul of old,

And there was gathered round a radiant cluster
    Of flashing eyes and cherry lips to greet him,
'Twas noticed *Betty Noyes* was in a fluster,
    And did not press in with the rest to meet him ;
But timidly, stood just apart awhile,
Awaiting his affianced glance and smile.

But when he did not turn, her blushes fled,
    And pallor followed the retreating flow
On cheeks, where but just now the crimson red
    Of life was burning with a fevered glow ;
And then came over her a *stifling chill*,
She gasped and fainted—*Betty Noyes was ill.*

But why, none knew save two who knelt beside her,
    One, with maternal instincts quick and true,

Saw what it meant, and with no heart to chide her,
    Knew that there was but just one thing to do—
Restore her consciousness and vital sense,
Then leave her to herself and reticence.

So on her mother's couch the young man laid her,
    Kissed her white hand, the mother bade adieu,
And since 'twas plain he could no longer aid her,
    He bowed in courtly form and then withdrew :
Mounted his charger, and with morning's ray
Was at his Highland home, ten miles away.

But Betty's secret, though, at length revealed,
    Was locked securely in her mother's heart—
For mother-like she must her daughter shield,
    And in the threatening conflict take her part ;
Softening the father's hot, indignant wrath
Against the young man who had crossed his path.

For she herself had bitter memories still,
    Of sore heart troubles in her girlhood's days,
Constrained to yield her preference and will,
    A sacrifice to cold, prudential ways ;
She could but shelter, with indulgent care,
Her darling writhing in her sufferings there.

The father's wrath was not to be appeased,
    He stormed and chafed like a wild beast at bay,
He was not barely angry and displeased,
    But wild and furious, in his own blind way ;
His pride of family was deeply stirred
Against his child, who had, at most, but erred.

For, like most fathers in that early time,
    He ruled his household less by love than fear,
And every little fault became a crime
    To be reproved by penalties severe ;
His autocratic will alone was duty,
Alike for slave, and wife, and childhood's beauty.

The family, once kindly in its schooling,
    Had lost its tone of grace and gentleness,
For a severe and magisterial ruling,
    Holding the household under sheer duress ;
Not even childhood's prattle could assuage
The sternness of this Puritanic age.

At once the line of duty was decided,
  The love-sick daughter must be sent away,
The Island of Conanicut provided
  A safe retreat, in Narragansett Bay;
And thither she must go, allowed, in pity,
Sometimes to see her friends in Newport City.

For Betty Noyes was high-born, well connected
  On both sides, of a gentle pedigree,
Reverend James Noyes her grandsire, learned, respected,
  Of Yale's first corporate fraternity;
The Newport Sandfords and Governor Brenton,
The mother's side, the father proudly leant on.

Of course *his* daughter could not wed a farmer
  From the backwoods of Pauchunganuc Hill,
A plebian and democratic Palmer,
  With nothing but his beauty, strength and will;
That was a thing not even to be thought on,
And by no measure suffered to be brought on.

For though of princely qualities possessed,
  Of manly vigor, bearing proud and high,
He walked an open democrat confessed,
  Dark scorn and hatred flashing from his eye,
Against all aristocracy of race,
But toward the lowly, gentleness and grace.

The mother wisely urged entire submission,—
  On Betty's part there must be no resistance,
The trusting child saw in this sharp decision,
  A mother's strategy for her assistance;
So with an effort to be bright and gay,
She kissed her parents, and so went away.

But on her mother's lips she pressed a kiss
  Of fevered, loving trust, as if to say,
" I understand it, mother, you will not miss
  To help your Betty through this stormy way ;"
To this appeal the mother's tearful eye
And long caress were nature's own reply.

Ichabod Palmer, from Pauchunganuc
  Hill, rode south one day just as eve drew on,
By chance as he the little hamlet struck,
  Under the deepening gloam, upon the lawn

He met the mother who, with faithful heed,
Told the whole truth and gave him her God speed.

Eastward he faced for Narragansett Bay,
    And put his charger to his highest speed,
The loyal beast swept foaming o'er the way,
    As if he knew his master's urgent need ;
And ere the dawn twelve leagues were measured o'er,
And beast and rider halted at the shore.

The ferryman in early waiting stood,
    As if on guard against some rude invasion
Of his official trust, and in no mood
    To take our hero o'er ; and when persuasion
Failing, he was, as fit, severely chidden,
He said that he had been straightly forbidden

To take a traveler like him across ; •
    And he had been described so in advance
That when he saw him he was at no loss,
    But knew him by his build, and height, and glance ;—
He had been advertised a vagrant rover,
And he could not be bribed to take him over.

The young man looked out, o'er the white-capped tide,
    Measured the distance to the other shore,
Then boldly sprang his faithful horse astride,
    And plunged in reckless mid the breakers' roar ;
And while the ferryman, pallid with fright,
Gazed after him in the dim morning light,

He saw him standing on the farther bank,
    His horse caressing with a loving care,
Rubbing him down on neck and side and flank,
    As if he would with him the honor share,
Of that triumphant ride across the ferry,
Better and safer than by boat or wherry.

Just how the lovers met we cannot say,
    For here tradition fails ; we know but this,
That some *how* and some *where* they met that day,
    For when to meet did ever lovers miss ;
When drawn by hearts in dualistic action,
That subtle influence that we call attraction.

Ah ! who can think with what supreme surprise
    He looked on her and she on him at first,

How they embraced, and with what hungry eyes
   They gazed and gazed with a delicious thirst ;
She with a flush and tremor of confusion,
Lest it should prove a dream or bright illusion ;

He, with a manly strength and honest pride,
   In having foiled the father's poor design
To rob him of his long-affianced bride,
   Triumphant smiled on her with grace benign :
Talked low and deep, as only a strong man
When sanctified by woman's chaste love can.

Then mounted once more on the faithful steed,
   The dear girl pillioned trustfully behind him—
Her arm encircling him, delicious need,
   For she had long in her chaste heart enshrined him—
He dashed again into the swelling flood,
Confiding in his horse, himself and God.

The tide was at its height and full ebb flow,
   And seemed in wonderment to hold its breath
To see this slight young girl so bravely go
   Into the black, engulfing waves of death :
And watched, aghast, the terrible issue
That must o'ertake her half the passage through.

Even the winds were breathless with affright,
   And not a breeze the glassy surface stirred,
The "sea fowl," awe struck, ceased their sportive flight,
   And not a note of wild delight was heard ;
All nature seemed to watch, in consternation,
The ending of such blinded desperation.

The horse himself, as if conscious that beauty
   In double trust was given to his care,
Put every sinew to its highest duty,
   As if of all the facts fully aware
Knew what his mission was, and had a sense
Of its importance from intelligence.

So with unflagging courage on he pressed,
   With steady stroke and spirit in his eye,
And when his master his proud neck caressed,
   He whinnied back a strong and brave reply.
As if to say, " I know what I can do,
And I shall bear you both in triumph through."

On, on he struggled through the placid tide,
  Eyeing with eagerness the nearing sand,
With ears erect and nostrils open wide,
  With every sinew like an iron band ;
At length the shore was reached, and solid ground
Became a cause for gratitude profound.

Ashore, he shook his sides and heavy mane,
  Then waiting quietly his master's will,
Nibbled the scanty grass along the plain
  Skirting the shore, with heartiness, until
Remounted both, they took their homeward way,
And bade adieu to Narragansett Bay.

A farmer's house soon reached, dank garments changed,
  Her golden braids relaid with simple grace,
Her toilet made and tastefully arranged,
  She beamed on him from her bright girlish face,
Like Venus, goddess, rising from the sea,
His rescued love, and soon his bride to be.

And so it fell out—when do not things fall
  Out right and timely for true trusting hearts?—
A country clergyman was within call,
  And soon arranged were all the marriage parts ;
The bans declared, the "knot of true love tied,"
And *Betty Noyes* was *Betty Palmer*, bride.

The homeward course lay o'er the " Old Post Road,"
  Beskirting pleasantly the Atlantic shore,
The leagues with rapid pace the horse bestrode,
  As if he proudly felt the trust he bore ;
Bravely, till five miles east of Pawcatuc,
They faced northwest for bold Pauchunganuc.

The foliaged woods—it was the last of June—
  Were in their deepest green, and wild flowers gay
Decked copse and hedge. The air was full of tune
  And melody from birds, as if the day
Had been created and arranged for this
Sweet complement of long awaited bliss.

To me there is no sight of deeper beauty
  Than youthful matrimonial affiance,
Two young hearts pledged in words of faith and duty,
  Man's robust love and woman's strong reliance ;

With mutual confidence and admiration,
Waiting in hope the blissful consummation.

For nature will be nature, right or wrong,
   Will chastely rule, or misrule,—wildly free ;
Its instincts, though instincts, deep-seated, strong,
   Ungratified, will turn to anarchy ;
Marriage is *holiness ;* bridegroom and bride
In wedded love are nature sanctified.

Ten miles or more, a winding, narrow way,
   Secluded from too captious ears and eyes,
Brought them, toward the falling of the day
   As shades were gathering on the western skies,
Near to their journey's end—three miles aloof,
The shelter of the Palmer Manor roof.

These last three miles in conversation low,
   Which could not be reported if we knew,
Were passed with footsteps intermittent slow,
   As if the moments all too quickly flew ;
They lingered till the night shades round them fell,
By what enchantment, who does not know well ?

And here we leave them. Only this we say,
   That through long years they lived in peace and health,
And by industry worked their upward way
   To comfort and to satisfying wealth ;—
In the old cemetery, side by side,
Ichabod Palmer slumbers with his bride.

THE PALMER HYMN.

1653.   AUGUST 10.   1882.

BY SARA A. PALMER, STONINGTON, CONN.

O Lord to Thee we raise
A hymn of grateful praise
  For boundless love.
To us throughout the year
Daily hast Thou been near,
Bow down this day and hear,
  From Heaven above.

In Thy great presence now
Our hearts we humbly bow
  Asking Thine aid;
Asking Thy help, to stand
As a true Palmer band,
Showing through all our land
  Hearts undismayed.

Help each to hold his life
Free from all stain and strife,
  All sin and shame;
Help us to "Palmers" be
Striving the world to free
From wrong and tyranny,
  Sorrow and blame.

May the new coming year
Bright, and more bright appear
  In noble deeds;
May we prove faithful to
All that we've vowed to do,
Seeking the right and true
  Where'er it leads.

Once more Thy praise we sing,
Making the heavens ring
  With the full strain.
Glory we give to Thee,
Who e'er our guide shall be,
Through all eternity
  We'll praise again.

ADDRESS OF B. FRANK CHAPMAN,

ONEIDA, N. Y.

[Note—Illustration, etc. on Page 153, Vol. I.]

Mr. President, Relations and Friends:

The question is often asked how the Chapmans got into this Palmer Re-Union? It is easy answered: 1. Walter Palmer; 2. his son Gersham; 3. his son Ichabod; 4. his son Ichabod; 5. his son Elias S.; 6. his son Sanford; 7. his daughter Katurah Palmer, my mother, who married Col. Stephen Chapman; 8. your humble servant, B. Franklin Chapman.

On my father's side, John Chapman, the settler, was born near London, England, a weaver by trade ; while on a visit to London, he was pressed on board a man-of-war. The ship, some time afterward, visited Boston, and John availed himself of an opportunity to regain the liberty of which he had been deprived ; he fled to Wakefield, R. I., where he worked at his trade ; after a while he went to Stonington, Conn., where he was captured by the charming smiles and the beautiful Sarah Brown, whom he married in February, 1709; so coming down with our genealogy, we have—1. John Chapman ; 2. his son Andrew ; 3. his son Joseph ; 4. his son Stephen ; 5. his son B. Franklin Chapman, etc.

Chapman is a Saxon name, and is derived from trades or occupations ; and the name itself indicates labor, not ease ; strength, not weakness.

Walter Palmer and John Chapman were both Englishmen, and both settled in Stonington, Conn., but at different periods of time, and many of their descendants were educated in the same school-house ; and a large number of the families emigrated about the same time, just prior to the war of 1812, to the towns of Lenox and Manlius, in central New York, where many of their families yet reside.

If I shall mention the name of "Columbus," do not think that I am to navigate all the unknown paths of the sea; if I mention " our forefathers," do not think that I am to go through all their trials and sufferings, or fight all the battles of the Revolution.

The discovery of America, however, was one of the greatest events that had occurred since the downfall of the Roman Empire; and a greater number of coincidences are said to have occurred about the time the old world was introduced to the new world. Among them was the discovery of the art of printing, the use of gunpowder, the mariner's compass, the improvement in navigation, the revival of philosophy and literature, and the introduction of the Protestant religion.

Columbus was a volunteer, and begged the privilege from kings and queens of crossing the ocean to find a new continent.

Not so with our forefathers; they were driven from England by the religious tyranny under the reign of the Tudors and the Stuarts. They came to this country not to gain wealth nor honor, but with a full knowledge of the perils of the sea, with its unknown paths to travel, and the toils and sufferings they would encounter in landing among cruel savages of the forest; they braved it all for the privilege of worshipping God according to their own conscience.

The moment they landed they formed themselves into a civil body politic for the purpose of framing just laws, ordinances and constitutions; it was a voluntary confederation of independent men instituting a government for the good of the governed.

The axe came in contact with the forest; log cabins were raised, the families increased and multiplied, and every little hamlet was a republic by itself. Schools in log school-houses; teachers were self-educated, they had no colleges or seminaries of learning; they had fewer books, but knew better what was in them than we do to-day.

We remember, and recount with pride, the mighty battles of the Revolution, from the first gun at Lexington to the last shot at Yorktown, wherein the principle of self-government was firmly established, and that brains and not blood was to rule our country.

During a life of activity and toil it has been my privilege to see quite a considerable portion of our own country, and whether riding on a canal boat, in a stage coach, on a steamboat, or in a swift-moving train on a railroad, the mighty sweep of vision, taking in the hills, the long range of mountains, the valleys, the lakes, the rivers, the broad fields of grain, the meadows, the magnificent rich prairies with their flocks and herds, the illimitable fields of corn, the forest, dwellings, villages and cities, upon the right hand and the left, presents a panorama to the eye more beautiful than language can describe or tongue can tell; and add to this the great inventions springing up like magic from a thousand brains in our own country, like the steam-engine and steamboat by Fulton, which made its first trip a few miles up the Hudson; and the distingushed men on board made and published a certificate that it was propelled up stream and against the current at the rate of four miles an hour.

Compare it with the magnificent steamers of to-day on our lakes and rivers, and our ocean steamers ploughing their thousand paths across the Atlantic and Pacific oceans; the cotton-gin by Whitney, followed by the power-loom, by which a new product, cotton, was brought into the market, and to-day it is supplying the world with clothing; the telegraph and cable by Morse, which, to-day, if put in one continuous line would spin its way seven times around this globe; it is distributing news and business matters to every part of the inhabitable world with the exact rapidity of lightning; the power press by Hoe, which will print twenty thousand newspapers an hour; the sewing-machine by Howe, the poor cobbler, who invented the stitch and was unable for many months to raise sufficient funds to get a patent; the reaper and mower by McCormick, by which farming is made easy; the telephone and electric lights by Edison, the telephone relieving every branch of business of much of its arduous labor, and the electric light throwing the light of the sun into a shade, and converting darkness into light; the railroad by Stephenson, an Englishman; this is the great civilizer of the world, it passes over the plains and tunnels the mountains, it fills up the valleys, it leaps over the rivers, it slays down the forests, and plants civilization wherever it goes; wherever it stops almost every industry in life instantly springs up and is planted there.

Fortunate, indeed, was it that our forefathers were men of thought and brains; they were honest men and had convictions of their own, and to-day we are reaping the benefit of their bold act in fleeing from tyranny in the old world and planting freedom in the new world.

To-day the words of Loch, Pluto, Milton, Shakespeare, Emerson, Bryant, Longfellow, and a host of others, belong to the world. Chinese walls and national boundaries are of no account when a thought seeks passage.

English Gatling guns and her ponderous steel cannons, lately introduced before Alexandria, by which a cannon ball could be thrown with such force as to pass through a solid plate of wrought iron fifteen inches in thickness at the distance of three miles, and yet go on miles beyond in its path of death and destruction, will virtually put an end to wars as a means of settling national difficulties. International laws are fast spreading over continents; their tendency will be to bring all nations nearer together as one government, one people, and to use one universal language.

And what a glorious thought is it for us to-day, at this Palmer Re-Union, to know that the Palmer blood is on the farm and in the work-shops; it is in every trade and industry, in all the learned professions, in poets, orators and authors, in a president, governors, cabinets, legislators, and upon the bench, throughout our country; we have our relatives and kinsmen here to-day from South America, Mexico, and almost every State in the Union.

Oh! glorious the thought, that the Palmer blood and patriotism was in the Revolution from Bunker Hill to Yorktown, by which the principle of free government was firmly established! Glorious the thought that it was in the War of 1812, and upon

this very battle-ground where we stand to-day, by which the
freedom of the seas and the rights of the American sailor was
forever secured! Glorious the thought that it was in the last
great struggle for human rights, where prejudice had to yield
to humanity; where freedom won and slavery fell!

GRACE PALMER.

A POEM BY REV. A. G. PALMER, D. D.

OF STONINGTON, CONN.

[Note—Illustration, etc., on page 90, Vol. I.]

I.

Grace Palmer, Walter Palmer's child,
On whom, at birth, the angels smiled,
As snow, new fallen, undefiled,

Grew up, in sheltered innocence,
All artless and with no pretence
To premature intelligence ;

So reticent and so demure,
That one who knew her not, would sure
Have thought her birth-endowment poor.

A lone, sad child, without a mother,
Without a sister; had she a brother,
Friend of her own sex, or the other;

Playmates, with their rout and rattle,
Shout and laughter, noise and battle,
Answering to her low-voiced prattle?

Did her father have a caring
For her early childhood's faring,
Sheltering her with love unsparing?

Was he gentle, was he tender,
Of his child, so frail and slender,
Did he strength and courage lend her ;

Did he kiss away her tearing
When, all tremulous and fearing,
At a bound the darkness clearing,

Rushing to his arms affrighted,
By some ghostly phantom sighted,
Face as marble, pallid, whited?

Did he to his bosom press her,
Warmly, tenderly caress her,
And with words of brightness bless her?

We will think so, for 'twere not good
Even to dream in saddened mood
Of a young child's fatherhood.

And if, to any, it should seem,
Of gushing sunshine, just a gleam,
Would brighten up our shaded dream;

Our answer is, that what we see
In dreamland, for our minstrelsy,
With what is written must agree;

These visions that so fleetly glide,
Our waking thoughts and dreams inside,
All truthfully we must transcribe.

Should we the vision kindly lent,
Allow to be asunder rent
Or marred, no other would be sent.

The spirits that control the will,
And wisely our ideals fill,
Are of their own rights jealous still;

If we are true to them and leal,
They will to us new truths reveal,
And all our imperfections heal.

II.

Grace Palmer, then, as we have seen her,
Amid surroundings that ensheen her,
With but her father's arm to screen her,

So timid, bashful and retiring,
So gentle, winsome and inspiring,
As if our warmest love desiring

And craving, haunts us in all places,
And with her sweet and childish graces,
All else from heart and mind displaces.

She seems resolved that we shall know her
Just as she was; and so to show her—
Nor shade above, nor shade below her—

Her chaste simplicity discerning,
Our hearts go out to her in yearning,
Warm admiration, glowing, burning.

III.

We see her in her English home,
Amid the evening's deepening gloam,
As wont the heather wide to roam;

In rustic gown, of antique style,
With hat and shoes to match, the while
Prim, Puritanic, modest, guile.

Less as the wild flowers round her feet,
And like them breathing fragrance sweet,
In girlhood's loveliness complete;

Returning to her humble door,
While evening's shadows gather o'er
Thatched roof and porch and polished floor;

The ivy and the eglantine
And sacred holly intertwine
This English cottage to enshrine.

Within, the evening meal is spread,
Then Walter Palmer bows his head
And thanks God for his daily bread;

While little Grace, with pious ken,
And folded hands waits the amen,
Then smiles up in his face again;

And fills with light the lowly place,
The father's rugged form and face,
Made beautiful by his child Grace—

The image of her mother, high
Of birth, and hair of golden dye,
And eyes blue as the far-off sky.

IV.

That night Grace Palmer had a dream,
And from a distant land a gleam
Of sunlight flashing o'er a stream

So wide and dark, the farther shore
Seemed hid in mist forevermore,
So far away none might explore ;

But as she dreamed, this shadowy land
Came nearer, till with open hand
She gathered up the golden sand.

And then the wilderness withdrew,
And smiling landscapes rose to view,
And meadows bright with sparkling dew ;

A frith or cove from out the sea,
Opened as if designed to be
A pathway to the ocean free ;

And there, upon the eastern side,
A cottage rude, but well supplied
With food for man and beast beside,

Stood with its English vine-clad thatch,
And open door with outside latch,
And front and rear a garden patch.

Her father, too, with cheerful mood,
She saw in strength of full manhood
Clearing away the forest wood.

And the broad acres stretched away,
Northward and eastward from the bay
On which this dreamland homestead lay.

V.

And then another vision fell
Upon our little demoiselle,
Of which we have not time to tell ;

Save this, that it was very bright,
And golden to her raptured sight,
And filled her with a strange delight ;

Latent the while and unsuspected,
And now but timidly detected,
Because imperfectly reflected ;

An embryonic interjection,
A shadowy outline introspection
Of bliss, perspective in perfection.

A new world opens to the view
Of this young girl, as she peers through
The mists, love's paradise into.

Another sense is o'er her stealing—
An unknown sense to her revealing,
The fount of maiden love unsealing ;

As yet an indistinct conception,
Inconstant, easy of deflection,
Almost too frail to claim protection.

A tremulous, ecstatic flame,
A thrilling, subtle, chaste regime,
A passion strong, but without shame ;

A pungent yet delicious pain,
So grateful, waking she would fain
Have brought the vision back again.

Of course it was a young girl's dream
From out the future—just a gleam
Across the dark Atlantic's stream ;

But it was like a golden ray,
Kindling with rainbow hues the spray
And dash of billows far away ;

And with its sweet prophetic light,
Rifting the sorrow-clouded night
Of this young child with visions bright.

Blessed be childhood, chaste and pure,
For its young dreams are pledges sure
Of opening life in miniature.

VI.

Soon Walter Palmer bade farewell
To English soil, and came to dwell
In New England as we know well ;

At Charlestown first, Rehoboth then,   ·
Lastly at Wequtequock, when,
Grace Palmer found her dreamland glen :

And more than all, the man who sought her,
In vision far across the water,
And all the wealth of his love brought her.

VII.

The passing years, a full decade
Twice told, have rapid changes made,
And brought with them a higher shade

Of face and character, not less
Of form and maiden comeliness,
And lips, that challenge a caress,

Like threads of cherry red, between
Which rows of well-set teeth are seen,
Like pearls of highly-polished sheen ;

And eyes blue as the far-off sky,
Whence it is said the angels fly
When o'er the earth they hover nigh ;

And with a crown of golden hair,
Befitting well a face so fair,
And such as any queen might wear ;

With open countenance, serene,
High-browed and goddess-like in mien,
In girlhood, ene she walked, a queen.

Her skin is like the driven snow,
Save where the vital current's flow
Kindles a warm and crimson glow ;

As when the blood with sudden rushing,
Driven by some strong impulse gushing
Baptises all the face with blushing.

Nature's own chrism, kindly sent,
An index of the heart's intent,
And purity's chaste compliment.

VIII.

We wonder not that Thomas Miner
Thought her than any girl diviner,
And asked in his heart to enshrine her ;

And made her his affianced bride,
And married her in manly pride,
And walked through life by her dear side.

IX.

Beneath a huge moss-covered stone,
Sleeps Thomas Miner's dust alone,
The grave of Lady Grace unknown.

No matter, for beyond the sky,
Like angels robed in white on high,
They walk in love, no more to die.

Poetic license kept in view,
A picture, beautiful as true,
In outline I have drawn for you

Of Lady Grace, the fairy child,
On whom at birth the angels smiled,
As snow new fallen, undefiled.

ADDRESS OF COURTLANDT PALMER,

NEW YORK CITY.

Mr Chairman, my sister and brother Palmers: I have, on rising, to express my thanks for the honor of being called upon to reply to the toast, " The Palmers of the City of New York."

In looking over the Directory of that mighty hive of human beings I find that our name there is legion, covering several columns of that bulky and finely-printed volume. In a word, the Palmers of New York alone are numerous enough to constitute of themselves quite an extensive village. That these are all inter-related I strongly doubt, but that they are largely so connected I am quite sure from an experience that befel me some years ago. I was subpœnaed to serve on the jury of the U. S. District Court of our city. Next to me in the jury-box sat a gentleman whose name was announced by the clerk as Walter Palmer. I turned to him and said : '' Why, this is quite a coincidence, I had an ancestor whose patronymic was the same as yours, and who was said to have been a giant in his day. Tradition relates that he was nine feet high, and lived to be one hundred and fifty years old. He came over with Christopher Columbus in Her Majesty's ship, the Mayflower, in the year 1629, and landed on the top of Plymouth Church." " Why," replied my fellow-juryman, " that is the very progenitor from whom I boast *my* descent." " Well," rejoined I, " then we must be at least one hundred and sixteenth cousins." " We must," said he. " Shake," said I. And we grasped each other in the mutual recognition of our family relationship. But seriously, I found on further inquiry that this Mr. Walter Palmer was a thrifty merchant, doing business under the Bible House, and a man, as far as I could learn, of character and culture.

Perhaps, as another type of the Palmers of New York, it may not seem out of place on an occasion like this to pay my tribute to my own father. Born in Stonington, his life was passed in New York, and I doubt not that many of the potent grave and reverend seniors of this borough, now within sound of my voice, have played kite, tag and peg-top with him in the happy days of childhood. At ten or twelve years of age he shipped⌡by sloop for Manhattan Island, railroads being then unknown. He disembarked with the traditional shilling in his pocket, but fortunately found employment with his brother Amos, then engaged in the hardware trade on the corner of Pearl street and Maiden lane. Half clerk, half porter, he toiled from early morn till noon, from noon till dewy eve, learning his business in every detail. At length—he often told this inci dent—desiring to embark on his own account, he requested—on the basis simply of his good American self-assurance—a credit from three auctioneers, which, probably to his, and perhaps even to their own surprise, was granted him. But he was thus enabled to purchase his goods at great bargains, and by turning them quickly met his notes before they were due. Such was the beginning of a career which finally resulted in his admission as partner to a firm doing the largest hardware trade between New York and New Orleans.

It is needless to cite further individual cases. The shortest biographical sketch of each worthy Palmer in our great city would exhaust my powers of speech and your patience. Suffice it to say that in all the departments of human achievement and effort, in the army and navy, in law, medicine and theology, in sculpture, architecture, painting, poetry and literature, in mechanics and the practical arts we, as a family, have set the stamp of our intelligence, perseverance, honesty and skill.

Such are the Palmers of the *present*. And why loom they up so well? Is it not because behind them stands the race of the strong and sturdy Walter Palmer and his descendants? Along with myriads of other worthy citizens of this Republic have not our forefathers delved in the mines ; have they not tickled the soil with the plow and .made it laugh with the harvest ; have they not agonized for us, battling against rude nature's firm decrees, and taming her hard forces into our service? Have they not suffered that we might enjoy the fruits of their conquests? Are we not products of the epoch they have made—products in character as well as inheritors of mere material gain?

Such is a glance at the Palmer empire of the past. May I now try to forecast the coming empire of the future, in order that hereafter as heretofore our extensive family may thus, perchance, be enabled more grandly to walk worthy of the vocation whereunto they may be called?

Change is the primal condition of existence. Without it progress cannot be. In visiting the room where the Palmer relics are exhibited I chanced to see an ancient wooden loom, standing about as high from the floor as an ordinary table, from off which old tape was slowly and wearily woven. Comparing this poor contrivance with the present power-loom, which in our time produces fabrics by the flowing yard, we can readily see the wonderful mechanical advance our age evinces, as we do also in the brilliance of the electric lamp as compared with the tallow dip of Walter Palmer's time, or in the rush of the railroad train contrasted with the tedious travel of the stage coach era. Ay! even the very mountain tops, impregnable as they appear in all their granite strength, crumble before the mild attacks of the Summer rains, or rend themselves to fragments when shattered by the bolts of Winter and the resistless shafts of the frost.

And can it be supposed that changes such as these can come to our external and material life without some corresponding variation in the province of ideas? Gen. George W. Palmer, in his most able address, stated, in truth, that this Re-Union only represented an *idea*, the sentiment, to wit, of family unity and brotherhood, wherein, gathered together in a spirit of mutual tolerance for each other's opinions, we might take counsel together to our general benefit.

It is in this spirit that I would speak of the empire of the future. "*Palmam qui meruit ferat*," "Let him bear the palm who deserves to bear it." As Goethe says: "He only conquers liberty and life who daily conquers them anew," and also as Tennyson affirms:

" I hold it truth with him who sings
    To one clear note in divers tones,
    That men may rise on stepping-stones
    Of their dead selves to higher things."

And while quoting in this strain, I might most appropriately add right here these words from the talented pen of our own sister poetess, Miss Sara A. Palmer:

" Help us to 'Palmers' be,
        Striving the world to free
        From wrong and tyranny,
        Sorrow and blame."

All this, my friends, is simply introductory to the statement that as far as I can look abroad and read the signs of the times I see the human race passing through, perhaps, the most remarkable transition the history of man has yet revealed. In order to outline this empire of the future, so that the Palmers, if they will, may adapt themselves thereto, allow me to consider it in several of its aspects.

We can all of us recall the anathemas of yore which the pulpit hurled against the stage. Between the actor and the clergyman there seemed a great gulf fixed. But now the gown assumes a different attitude towards the buskin. In very many of our New York churches no longer is the entrance to the theatre called the gate of hell. In a similar manner, the pulpit formerly leveled its invectives against the novel, against portions of the press, against art, and many innocent amusements, while now it has practically come to recognize all of these not only as inevitable, but, under proper guidance, as useful forces. In a word, its function has come to be not to extirpate them but to *moralize* them, and thereby lift them up to loftier human purposes. Instead any longer of seeking to slay these cognate institutions, it now seems content to harness itself by their side, so that in place of wasting strength in vain contentions amongst themselves all of them together may draw onwards the glorious car of civilization.

Such is one vast change in what may be called the domain of sentiment and art.

But turn we to another field. Throughout the world there seems to be arising the thrilling cry, the sterner demand for a larger industrial justice. In distant Russia Nihilism lifts its voice in the name of land and liberty—the *land*, without which people cannot live, and *liberty*, without which life is not worth the living. I read the manifestos of these much-censured revolutionists and find that all the rights they ask is less than we of this republic enjoy as commonly as the air we breathe.

If we turn one glance to the German fatherland we also there behold the spirit of unrest. I see by recent statements in the newspapers that Socialistic thoughts have so pervaded every rank that even the army no longer can be counted on, and that the man of iron, Bismarck, seeks to satisfy the masses by stealing the very thunder of the malcontents, himself, with admirable statesmanship, becoming the leading one to advocate and for_ ward many of their measures.

In France, as I càn read the way that nation tends, I see that they would there create not only a democracy in politics, but that they aim to found a socialized republic.

The throes of troubled Ireland chant their pregnant lesson. It is a nation rising in revolt against a thraldom that has grown into a tyranny. It is the stand that a wronged race has taken wherein they give their edict to the world that it is contrary to every law of human justice that the soil of a whole country should be held in toll by the tens among its populace, while the thousands, through the landlords' power, are bound thereby in practical servitude. And all throughout the British Isles, I'm told, the Irish refrain is being echoed from hill-top unto hill-top.

But here, three thousand miles away from these old-world disturbances, here in free America, 'tis said, where we have ample space and almost limitless land for every settler, here such dangers cannot show themselves. But even here, I think, I see the writing on the wall. We find most palpably among

ourselves the tendency of wealth to gather in the clutches of
the few, while relatively the many go lacking. Even such a
conservative authority as Mr. David A. Wells affirms that the
rich are continually growing richer and the poor poorer. And
the murmurs of discontent are beginning to make themselves
only too plainly manifest as the masses, in their increasing sense
of something wrong, perceive that the present processes of
trade all tend to concentrate wealth—the wealth *their* labor
makes—in the pockets of the plutocrats. And is not this brood-
ing feeling exhibiting itself in politics? Does it need much
power of prophecy to state that the olden parties—the democratic and republican parties—are really dying out for want of
vital issues on which to subsist? And in place of them, like
threatening heads arising on the vast ocean of politics, do we
not perceive such organizations as the Anti-Monopoly League
proclaiming deadly war on bloated corporate aggrandizement;
do we not see the old Greenback party—not dead, but only
sleeping—still loudly maintaining that we must have a money
of the people for the people instead of a money of the banker
for the banker and by the banker? The Socialistic Labor party,
too, they tell me, with its slogan, that all profits are robbery, is
a rapidly-growing clan. And more than all of these, and far
more threatening as regards this coming strife between labor
and capital, is the vast extension of trades-unionism throughout
the length and breadth of our land, wherein the laborers throw
their gauntlet down in defence of labor's rights.

But this is enough, for this occasion, to indicate the empire
of the future in the line of industry that seems to be casting
upon us its coming shadow, and unto which, as in the previous
case that I have stated, I would have the Palmers adapt themselves as their good hearts and active brains may dictate.

And now, for a moment, let us bend our thoughts to the last
department of the empire of man in the future that I shall now
allude to, I mean the department of Religion. I know how
delicate is the ground I stand on, but without it my subject
were incomplete and my purpose unaccomplished. Be it

enough for me to say, that I shall advance no dogmas of my own nor assail a single cherished doctrine held by any here, and if I state, as my opinion, that faith itself must undergo a change, I also, in the self-same breath, affirm that this will only be because worship must enlarge to grander, nobler issues. It will be like Saul, the son of Kish, who, being sent to seek his father's asses, found himself possessor of a kingdom.

A great man has said : "Without religion civilization dies;" but yet everywhere around us the signs of altering creeds obtrude themselves at every turn. If America has produced any one divine more prominent than another, we must confess that Henry Ward Beecher is that one, and yet this is the clergyman who, in the August number of the "North American Review," openly pronounces that the time-honored faith of Christendom must step onwards to the music of the century or else itself must be left behind.

And here another name straightway suggests itself, the name of one now gathered with the mighty dead of our own America, I mean Ralph Waldo Emerson, the sage of Concord, of whom, like Spinoza, it might almost be said : "He was a God-intoxicated man;" and yet even Emerson, descended as he was from a long line of clergymen ancestry, himself educated for the pulpit. was forced to leave his inherited limitations and find his church in nature, his inspiration in humanity.

I sat some four years ago beneath the venerable and consecrated roof of Westminster Abbey. Around me I could almost fancy were flitting the shades of the heroic personalities whose tombs from adown the ages have been built against its walls. Around me in the pews a crowded throng were gathered. They had come to listen to that brave and wise and gentle man, Dean Stanley. It was Trinity Sunday, and of the trinity the reverend preacher spoke. But oh, in what a different, in what a clearer, holier light than that we were accustomed to! God, the Father, in his hands became the underlying though unknowable force which flows with never dying energy, and which manifests itself to us in all phenomena; the Son, the Christ,

enlarged to all Humanity, as in its daily death, its daily martyr-
dom, its daily resurrection, it lives and suffers for the sake of
man, while the Holy Spirit became transformed to the saving
grace of the individual conscience.

My friends, it is folly for us to play the ostrich ruse and bury
our heads in the sandy desert of conservatism and imagine that
no change is going on around us. Thousands of lives like Stanley's are being lived. In Germany, but a few decades since,
great Goethe passed away. His Faust is being read, or else, in
the form of opera, is being sung in every land; and, mind you
this, that Faust was *saved* not *lost* as for the most part is supposed. And Faust, that wondrous play, the divine comedy of
this new era, is the revelation of the new salvation, wherein
"for all our failings a pure humanity atones." In France Au-
guste Comte has written—Comte, whom Gambetta pronounces
the greatest thinker of the nineteenth century, and whose
teaching is the creed of science, and whose religion is the religion of humanity. In England, Darwin, vilified only twenty
years ago as the prince of evil writers, has been lately buried
with princely honors in the same cathedral pile to which I have
alluded. Herbert Spencer is still toiling, honoring now this
country with his presence, while Harriet Martineau and George
Eliot, the two leading women thinkers of this time who spoke
our mother tongue, have only, as it were, just gone away before us, leaving their works to follow them.

And so I might continue by the hour citing these heroic
souls, these hearts devoted to humanity, and these deeply-
thinking brains; but enough has been said, I think, at least to
suggest that as in the realm of mechanical invention, as in the
field of art and industry, so in the wider domain of religion
itself "our knowledge grows from more to more;" therefore
here also I would admonish my kinsmen to so live and so enlarge their lives that our Palmer orators in Re-Unions of the
future may say of us, as we affirm now of our past ancestry:
"Well done, good and faithful servants!"

One more reflection and I have finished. New York City is

called the Empire City of the Empire State—New York State is called the Empire State of the great Republican Empire of the United States. I would, my friends, live to see the Palmers acknowledged as the Empire Family of this our Empire Country. Xenophon it is who in his history of the anabasis, tells the tale of how the Greeks, ten thousand in their numbers, made a brave *retreat* from Asia back to Hellas. Our own genealogist informs us that in all their ramifications the Palmers, also, doubtless aggregate to some ten thousand. My friends and relatives, I trust we may never hear of a Palmer retreat, even though it a courageous one, but instead thereof always of a Palmer *advance*.

ADDRESS

BY EPHRAIM WILLIAMS (EX-WARDEN), OF STONINGTON, CT.

[Note Illustration, etc., on page 106, Vol. I.]

Mr. President and Kinsfolk:

The name for which I have been requested to speak has had, until perhaps in the present generation and branch of the family which I have the privilege to represent, so little connection by blood and marriage with the vast concourse who have emanated from your worthy ancestor, Walter Palmer, that I had many misgivings, and felt that it would be almost intrusive for me to attempt by participating in your family Re-Union, in the manner suggested by the kind invitation of your venerable and revered Vice-President, the Rev. A. G. Palmer, to assume any claim as a Williams to be taken into your fellowship and association. And so I delayed and deferred, after receiving that invitation, to signify my acceptance of the appointment (for which I hope the Rev. Dr. will accord me full pardon) until, finally, with some reluctance and doubt as to the propriety of my putting in an appearance, only the other day endeavored to see if my ingenuity could devise some form of words whereby

I could associate Palmer and Williams, and comply with the Dr.'s polite invitation. And I am fearful that in the time allotted, or without great weariness to your patience, even if I possessed the literary abilities and mental force of the most intellectual now present who represent those names, or who have passed away, and have adorned various professions and gained the reputation of the historian, the scholar, the orator, the poet, that it would hardly be proper for me to attempt more than simply ask you, in the enjoyment of these festivities, not to forget, but to preserve and cherish the remembrance of those whose lives were famous and whose good example it should be the legitimate purpose of these Re-Unions to perpetuate; for I think whatever can be most appropriately said on such occasions, must emanate from and revolve around the idea that we are met to commemorate the virtues of the ancestors. And with this intention, it may be justifiable for me to briefly show by what right I respond to the names of Palmer and Williams, and how in my branch the Palmer blood came down.

As for the Williamses whose remains now mingle with the dust of their native town, I have intimated that so far as my genealogical knowledge extends their infusion with the Palmer blood would not warrant my going into the details or history of the Williams family or portray the part they performed in building up the wealth, intelligence and prosperity of the community where they lived. My ancestor, Robert Williams, was not among the first settlers here. He and his sons, Samuel, Isaac and Stephen, resided at Roxbury, Mass., where they arrived from England in 1637. He lived to the good old age of one hundred years, having been born in 1593, and died in September, 1693. His wife, Elizabeth Stretton, died July 28, 1674, aged eighty years, and saw the commencement of the fulfillment of her dream that from her should spring a long line of gospel ministers; and, without doubt, through her sons, Samuel and Isaac, for many generations there were more in New England eminent in that profession of her lineage than of any other, and the record of her offspring for a long period had an honorable and conspicuous position in the history of the colonies; there was scarcely a battle fought either with the Indians or a foreign enemy in which one or more of the name does not appear. On Groton Heights among the martyrs for their country's independence, whose self-sacrifice and patriotism the State and nation ceremoniously and grandly commemorated on the centennial anniversary of their massacre at Fort Griswold, in the sublime language written upon the monument there, John, Henry, Thomas, Daniel, "were a people that jeoparded their lives unto the death in the high places of field." The wife of the brave Col. William Ledyard, who commanded the garrison and was brutally murdered after laying down his sword, was the grand-daughter of Ebenezer Williams, who came to this town about 1685. She died in 1789, a few hours after her son Charles, who was a babe but ten days old when his father was killed, and at her request this boy whose infancy and childhood were impressed upon her heart by the blood of the heroic father, was buried in her arms.

Ebenezer Williams, who was the son of Samuel, and his two cousins, John and Eleazer, the sons of Isaac, came from Roxbury here together and took up land adjoining; and they and their descendants, although not as numerous as the Palmers, have acted a respectable part in the early history of this town in developing its resources and in forming its social, civil and religious society. It would not be interesting for me to particularize or hold any up to view, " for they have rested from their labors and their works do follow them;" but it is due to their memories to say that the early settlers of this town had not the opportunities for study and education and the public display of acquired powers that others of their family enjoyed who remained at or near the historic Plymouth Rock and Boston harbor, which then, more than now, was supposed to be the "hub of the universe;" yet, as pioneers in the wilderness here, causing it, if not "to blossom as the rose," to yield a decent subsistence, in originating industries and improvements in various business occupations, and in their views of self-government in town meeting assembled, upon which the fabric of our great republic, to be secure, must always depend; and in their organization of those local methods which we now follow in the management of our civil affairs, they exhibited eminent qualities and those inherited natural abilities which were more necessary here then to make the land give forth its increase, and by toil of the hands and sweat of the brow to open the way of prosperity and happiness for themselves and others, than were the exclusive wisdom of colleges and the circumscribed duties and accomplishments of the learned professions. And in my opinion it would be to the general advantage now if we had more of their old-fashioned, straight-forward integrity and hard-headed business method in public matters, and less new-fangled notions, vain babblings on law, hair-splitting technicalities, and wordy, pettifogging oppositions of science of government, falsely so-called.

It would at least save some worriment and just criticism if we could throw off a few delusive theories, a little false style and pride in daily living, and snobbish imitation of foreign manners, which the Pilgrims never intended should cross the Atlantic, and are a severe reproach to the professions of their descendants that they are a free and independent people; for what can be more slavish than servile worship of imported fashions, and aping the habits and usages that surround monarchial governments and a titled nobility; and it would infuse more of original, genuine manhood into our body politic if, instead of soaring quite so high after "Æsthetics and High Art," we would cultivate more the rugged simplicities of our ancestors, Palmer, Williams, Denison, Wheeler, Chesebro, Stanton, Noyes, Gallup, Miner, and all those worthies whose characters and customs it is to be hoped your Re-Unions will recall, and make us profoundly realize that if we live in more cultured days, with greater opportunities of ease and affluence, that the wisdom, the economies, the patriotism and sturdy uprightness of the forefathers laid the foundation of it all. And you who are to-day glorifying the name of Palmer, do not forget that you had foremothers as well as forefathers, and that in very many cases "the grey mare was the better horse," that in mental capacity, in that perception or intuition which is more valuable than experience, because it prevents mistakes and comprehends in advance the wise course to take, in that painstaking prudence in domestic duties and economy in saving what was earned, which are essential to success, that the woman was often the better help-mate ; and if the assertion be true that the sons usually inherit the traits and characteristics of the mother, and the daughters those of the father, then the name of Palmer is for you only an empty boast ; you are not Palmers at all, for the blood of old Walter Palmer went down through his daughters to a variety of names, perchance a Williams, a Denison, or some other name ; and while I would not have you feel any less cheerful because you have inherited the Palmer *name*, yet I deem it my duty to account for my being here by telling you that I claim the Palmer *birthright* through the fairest and perhaps the wisest of the immediate family of our honored progenitor, who was Grace by name, and was all that name implies as the consoler and counsellor of her father in the loneliness of his widowhood, as the dutiful daughter in attending diligently to the ways of his household, and afterwards as the devoted wife of Capt. Thomas Miner, by whom, if my friend the Palmer genealogist tells true, she had sons and daughters whose descendants have been known in this State and everywhere where ex-Gov. Miner and Gen. Grant are known.

And so may we all, by whatever line we claim descent and right to participate in this gathering, do all honor to the women who have borne the Palmer blood. The deeds of its men may seem grander and more conspicuous as you trace back your family history to that modest home at Wequetequock Cove, but who can measure the quiet, subtle essence of the mother's influence through all these years in shaping the lives of the men whose achievements in different walks of life have made honorable the name you call your own. And permit me to add, Mr. President, that you have contributed a creditable part towards making that name respected and esteemed. It is woman's in-

fluence much more than any other forms, and as civilization
progresses will the more and more form the character of the
people, and on through manhood the lesson learned at the
mother's knee, like the voice from an angel, shall arrest the err-
ing sons of men in their wayward career and call them back, if
not to innocence, to their duty and their God. And though
that mother may have lived so long ago that your lips have almost ceased to pronounce the name, and in the sunshine of
your domestic happiness, with little ones climbing your knee
and young tongues calling you father, the momory of your own
childhood appears like a distant dream, yet you may be sure
that somewhere down in your heart, though the wound made
by her grave may seem entirely healed, that there is a chord
which is always whispering low to the old-time lullaby of her
gentle voice, and ever saying, "A mother's influence, a mother's
love never dies, for it was made only a little lower than the
angels."

ADDRESS

BY REV. HIRAM STONE, OF BANTAM FALLS, CT.

My Kindred:

When introduced to a promiscuous audience, as on the present occasion, it is common for the speaker to address them as
" Ladies and Gentlemen." But in this instance I salute you as
my kindred, for such you are. Though looking upon hundreds
of faces which I have never seen before, and speaking to people
gathered from different parts of our wide-spread country, I recognize you as members of a numerous family heretofore to me unknown. We are descendants of a common ancestry ; our remote
forefathers left England some two hundred and fifty years ago,
and braving the terrors of savage war tribes and the unbroken,
desolate wilderness, settled upon this Western Atlantic shore.
Could those sturdy ancestors of ours but revisit this spot to

day, doubtless they would be as much surprised as me to behold such a numerous posterity sprung from that little family which cast their destiny upon this then inhospitable land.

But in this how has a "little one become a thousand." From William and Walter Palmer, who settled in southern Massachusetts and Connecticut, have sprung a posterity literally representing every section of our country from the great lakes on the north to the Gulf of Mexico on the south, and from the Atlantic to the Pacific shores. The Palmer family thus widely disseminated, represents every honorable trade, pursuit, calling and profession. The ministry, the bar, the medical faculty, the army, the navy, the State and National Legislature, the press, the maratime and commercial interests are all honorably represented by Palmer name and blood.

It is gratifying to meet so many of you on this occasion, to make so many new acquaintances, and to establish new relations for the future with those who hitherto were entire strangers. In looking around upon this assembly I feel much like a person lying down to sleep in a solitary place with hardly a recognized face about him, and without a knowledge of a relative near. On awakening, what a strange metamorphose has risen to greet the eye! Hundreds of family kindred appear before me of whom I knew nothing before; I find myself in the midst of friends of whom I never dreamed. I seem to have entered upon a life almost new; a vision surrounds me which it is rapturous to contemplate. To awake to such a *reality* is better than awakening from a pleasant dream. Permit me, therefore, to tender my sincere congratulations to you all as my newly-found friends and kindred.

For several years past I have been seeking out the four family lines of my ancestry in order to trace them back to our fatherland. The Palmer line I had traced back to Taunton, Mass., about one hundred and fifty years, and there I lost all further trace. But on receiving the circular of Noyes F. Palmer, Esq., to whose indomitable perseverance and unflagging interest the whole Palmer family owe an unspeakable debt of gratitude, I was put upon the direct line of research, and on my maternal side trace my pedigree to England.

And now I close this brief address, hoping that much good and many happy experiences may grow out of our family gathering.

ADDRESS

BY FRANK PALMER, ESQ., OF NORWICH, CT.

It was to a *Thomas* Palmer that in the village church of Snodland, County of Kent, Eng., a tablet was erected bearing these words:

> " Palmers all owre Faders were ;
> I, a Palmer, liuyd here,
> And trauyld stil, till, worne wyth Age,
> I endid this Worlde's Pylgramage
> On the blyst Assension Day
> In the chereful Month of May,
> One Thowsand wyth fowre Hundryd
> Seauen ;
> And took my Jorney hense to
> Heuen."

And for a *Thomas* Palmer I have been invited to speak. Both the invitation and response, amid this present company, would bear out the spirit of the opening sentence of that old epitaph —for our fathers were " Palmers all," and therefore we are here ; they were Palmers, though many be the number of our various originals, and scant the blood relationship between them.

The Thomas Palmer of whom I would speak was among the company which founded Rowley, Mass., in April, 1639. The leader of the company was the Rev. Ezekiel Rogers, a man of note in England, who by his own exertions had gathered together the little church at Brough, Rowley, Yorkshire, and had ministered to them there for many years, till at length he led them away into the wilderness of America to found the *new* Rowley in the *new* England.

The history of our Thomas, preceding this establishment in the new home, is as yet a blank page to be filled only by ingenious conjecture and brilliant imaginings.   One theory is that he was one of those friends of the Rev. Mr. Rogers who accompanied him to this country in 1638—a theory that has many things in its favor, and which has yet to be put to the final test. Another theory is that he is the Thomas Palmer who, in his twentieth year, sailed for Barbadoes on the ship *Expedition*, the vessel leaving London the 20th of November, 1635.   This theory, too, is supported by certain strong facts of circumstantial evidence.   So much for the *time* of his coming; as to his English *home*, Bradford and Rowley have both been claimed, though the former has now been discarded, while there are facts that point away from Yorkshire to the County of Essex.

On the 10th of September, 1643, the first town survey of Rowley was made, and the seventh house-lot on Bradford street, the principal street, was set to Thomas Palmer—he having taken to himself his good wife Ann in the August preceding. His previous occupation had been that of a weaver, at which occupation it is presumed he labored while here; yet, like all the early comers, his heart was set on the acquirement of land. A strange story does his purchase of a salt-marsh, one of his earliest acquisitions, tell of the slavery of his mind to the old-time English thoughts and traditions.   We of to-day, in this land of boundless fertile fields, would fain inquire what he could see to desire in a salt-marsh while this whole fair land lay yearning for possessors?   Nevertheless, with scrupulous care, the deed of this precious purchase has been preserved to this day.

The fruit of Thomas Palmer's marriage was three sons, Samuel, born in 1644; Timothy, born in 1647; and Thomas, born in 1650.

In August, 1669, after living in the main a quiet life, in which he took a more or less active interest in the affairs of the new town, Thomas Palmer died.   His widow outlived him by nearly a score of years, she being buried the 22d of February, 1686.   This is not the time nor the place to descant on his vir-

tues or his graces; suffice it to say, therefore, they were such
as were peculiar to the days in which he lived, and the spirit of
the old Puritan—a spirit typical of one reared in the famous
John Evelyn's district—may be read in this single fact, that he
was the progenitor, in one line at least, of a race of deacons,
devout and earnest men.

Two of the children of Thomas and Ann remained in Rowley—namely, Samuel and Thomas. The former married in 1671,
two years after his father's death, Mary Pearson, of Rowley, the
daughter of the founder of the first fulling mill in America, and
through his son Thomas he became the ancestor of the Norwich branch of the Rowley Palmers.

Thomas 2d married Hannah, the daughter of Capt. John
Johnson, of Rowley—he went to the wars, and came home to
marry the captain's daughter—and he has numerous descendants living in Maine, eastern Massachusetts and New Hampshire. The second son, Timothy, in company with his brother-
in-law, John Huggins, the celebrated Springfield lawyer of later
years, and Capt. Anthony Austin, as well as with others, removed to Suffield, Conn., becoming one of the proprietors of
that town in 1674. Timothy's descendants are mainly to be
found in that vicinity—in Springfield, Westfield, Agawam, Amherst, etc.—a sturdy and honored race ; while we are all indebt-
ed, so our corresponding secretary gracefully acknowledges in
his words of dedication, to the inspiration and effective support
of one of these descendants, Mr. Lorin Palmer, of the Brooklyn
" Union-Argus," for the existence of " Volume I of the Palmer
Records "—one of the many exemplifications of the fact that
the Palmers, though of various clans, unlike the Greeks in the
old adage, are ever ready to assist one another.

The branch which I represent runs back to the first Palmers
of Norwich, Conn., Thomas 3d, the grandson of the original
Thomas, who came to Norwich in 1723, and bought lands there
that have ever since remained in the family—a period of about
one hundred and sixty years—though his descendants have migrated in many directions. These lands lay in that part of

Norwich which was ceded to the town of Preston in 1786. Their present owner and occupant is Mr. Charles Palmer, and his grandchildren are the sixth generation in direct line born thereon. The same peculiar love for the "old homestead" is found in other lines of this family, and the branch which went to Maine in 1765 retains still its original purchase, as do also, I believe, other branches which settled in other States. Though many of the descendants of Thomas, of Norwich, have found homes elsewhere, notably in Vermont, where three separate families settled in the last century, yet taking the male and female lines together they are still numerous in this vicinity. This last branch, together with the branches that settled in Massachusetts and in Maine, make up the greater part of the race of Thomas Palmer, of Rowley, so far as that race is known, and doubtless many of them are present here to-day.

Such is a brief outline of the generations of the Puritan of 1639; though not so numerous as the descendants of Walter, they still show quite a company.

And now, friends, whether sprung from Walter, or from Thomas, or from the numerous other Palmers who came as pilgrims to this shrine of liberty, let us rejoice in this Re-Union because of the emphasis such a gathering places on the memories and aspirations that our name suggests; let us rejoice together in the friendships that we here have found, and though while we bear a common name, we may not bear a common ancestry; yet, as our fathers became of kin by their devotion to a glorious cause, let us, too, prove ourselves heirs of a like fellowship by our united service to our country and our age!

ADDRESS

BY ALBERT G. LEONING, ESQ., OF NEW YORK CITY.

Mr. President, Ladies and Gentlemen of the Palmer Re-Union:

I feel deeply the honor my venerable grandfather, Dr. Eugene Palmer, of Texas, has thus thrust upon me by saying that

Texas, as a young State, would prefer being represented by the rising than by the setting sun, and I also feel how inadequate I am to the occasion. I am proud of the privilege of coming before you, for it gives me the chance to proclaim myself a member of the Palmer family, and to eulogize the Palmer name.

Although I was not present at the last Re-Union, I have been informed that the genealogical tree of the family was displayed before, and its history given from the first exotic that took root in this soil down to the generation of the hour; its trunk was described, also its branches, with the fruit and flowers that they bore, together with the Palmer scions that were grafted on other stocks, and it would seem that the subject of Palmer was then and there entirely exhausted, yet I know of no other theme so appropriate to this occasion.

But why is Stonington the chosen place of meeting for all time? Is it because the ashes of our old patriarchs repose within its borders, or is it not rather that Stonington is the *seed-bed* of the Palmers which raises plants to be set out in other climates and on other soils? Wherever this plant has taken root in a congenial soil, it has flourished like the "cedar of Lebanon;" and in the universal adaptation of the cedar to climate and soil, and in its longevity, how much that species of tree resembles the Palmer family—for the cedar has a wider climatic range than any woody plant on the continent of America, or for aught I know on the surface of this planet. It is found growing in the torrid and in frigid zones. It maintains its vitality in the coldest climate on the most barren soil, it grows also on the rich lands midst the orange bloom and fragrance of a golden Southern shore. It rears its green foliage above the white surface of the snow-clad hills of New England, and is a gladsome sight to the weary traveler on the arid prairies of the West. It is the only tree that the tropical sun-heat, or the long-continued tropical drouths cannot kill.

It is found on the high bluffs of the Missouri and Canadian rivers where, above the reach of prairie fires, it attains its perfect development, where the trunk of trees measure four feet in diameter, and from their exceeding slow growth such trees must be of immense age. They may have stood for centuries, thus resembling the longevity of the Palmer family.

Has not the Palmer family some towering cedars that have lived and grown on a higher plane, above the prairie fires of religious schismatics or political detractions? Why, at the sacred desk to-day, teaching peace and good will to all men, the Palmer name can boast of a pulpit orator who stands almost without a peer.*

The Palmer lineage has another towering cedar, a military chieftain,† who has won laurels of victory, has smoothed the angry brow of "grim-visaged war" and made it wear the smiles of peace. I need not call the name, for the man I speak of cannot, in this world, be singly counterpoised.

Has not the Palmer name furnished successful agriculturists? You may find in every township in this State and other States, where the rugged bramble heath has been changed to the tasteful landscape with its groves, its lawn and embowered home, all planned by a Palmer taste, wrought by a Palmer hand.

And when you come to that semi-amphibious class of New Englanders, the daring and intrepid seamen, the name of Palmer stands pre-eminent; for this village has furnished one,‡ whose sea record is not only an honor to the name, but an honor to the generation he lived in, for he pushed his prow beyond the circuit of waters that had hitherto been navigated, discovered a new land, and called it Palmer land.

> " Honor and fame, from no condition rise;
> *Act well your part, there* all the honor lies."

And did he not act well his part when, as a star actor in the drama of life, he was applauded in every scene till the last act and the dark curtain fell.

---

* Rev. Dr. B. M. Palmer, of New Orleans.
† Gen. U. S. Grant.
‡ The late Capt. "Nat." Palmer, of Stonington.

The early boyhood of distinguished men has ever been a subject of interest. I am told that his free spirit, like that of Patrick Henry, would never be chained to the dull bench of the school-room : that he played the truant, and when found was always afloat on his sail-boat. Was he an idle truant? By no means ; with the blue waters beneath, and the blue sky of heaven above him, he was all this time studying the profession of his choice. Adapting his canvas to the veering winds, his "jib" was his grammar lesson, his "mainsail" his class-book ; and how did it come to pass that, without a store of academic acquirements, without the regular training of mathematics in the schools, how did he become one of the greatest navigators of the nineteenth century? What was the grand secret of his success? Why, it was a self-educated Palmer brain!

And take the Palmers where you will, in peace or in war, with the ploughshare or the sword, on the land or on the ocean, afloat or ashore, the Palmer name or the Palmer lineage has borne the Palm!

For the fruits of the Palmer scions that have been grafted on other stocks, in whatever market they may have been displayed, their surpassing excellence and high quotations are justly claimed by this *Palmer Re-Union.*

ADDRESS

BY ALANSON L. PALMER, ESQ., OF AUBURN, N. Y.

Mr. President and Kindred :

There is a proverb often applied to human affairs which says, "the unexpected always happens." Certainly that is true in my case to-day. When the committee came and asked me to deliver an address about the Palmers in central New York, I said "No, I could not do that, because the Palmers whom I know do not make speeches. I do not remember such an event in the life of any one of them I ever knew. They make pretty sharp remarks about people and affairs and then go about their work, but no speeches." "Well," the committee said, "if you were at a family dinner you could answer questions and talk, could you not? That is all we want from you." "Yes," I said, "I can do that." But behold! instead of sitting at a dinner and conversing I find myself on this platform, and this great audience of Palmers looking with some expectation evidently for an address.

The impression made upon me at this Re-Union, and the one you make upon me now as I look into your faces, is indeed peculiar. I came here an entire stranger. I have not seen a face in Stonington into which I have ever looked until this visit. Not one of you have I ever spoken with or seen before in my life. One hundred and fifty years or more have passed since there has been any intercourse that I am aware of between our branches of the family and those I see represented here. And yet I know you are my kindred. The evidence is beyond question. Personal appearance, tones of voice, manner of speech, quality of temper and spirit—a thousand things you say and do and think are Palmer traits—so like our own peculiarities at home that there can be no mistake. You are all Palmers and my kindred.

The resemblances I see here to nearly all of our immediate family and relations are most striking My father's features are before me—his profile, complexion and partial baldness. The forms and tones of voice of my uncles have startled me as I have looked and listened. I have seen to-day, as it were, the very face of an older sister long since departed—the eyes, lips and form of teeth were exactly hers. The stout forms of my brothers and cousins are all about me, while the large, full form and happy face of our good Aunt Sally have approached me more than once, suggesting an accustomed hearty embrace, and yet a century and a half has passed since these same branches of the family have stood in each other's presence. So I can but say what a strange and unique experience is this to me.

I had been here but a few hours when I learned something of the difficulties our president has had to encounter in endeav-

oring to make this Re-Union a success. Some blamed the
Palmers in Stonington, because it was said among them that
there was too much pretense and self-laudation about it, and
therefore they declined to give their aid.   When I heard that,
I said they are true Palmers; for that is a trait which belongs
to all of them in our region.   A sham they hate, with a good,
honest hatred, and they speak of it with freedom.   Sometimes
they make mistakes, and call things insincere which are not;
but the matter gets a "piece of their mind," you see, just the
same.   And perhaps all the Palmers in Stonington have not
been able to see all the good there is in this Re-Union; but
they have faithfully expressed their opinions, I find, like true
Palmers, and I therefore welcome them as my kindred.

Now, in carrying out his plans, our president has felt himself
somewhat hindered and embarrassed by these things; and, I
have been told, he was very patient for a long time, but at
length the proper limit was reached.   Things became close and
hot.   Then there was some forked lightning and thunder, followed by the peaceful success which has attended all these
arrangements for our comfort and profit.   Now this quality of
mind and temper is exactly like the Palmers I know.   They
are over-kind, over-generous, many times bearing too much;
but when matters have gone about so far, look out for thunder
storms and clearing weather.

I have said Palmers are generous—many times over-generous.
In fact, it is a proverb among us that a Palmer always gives
away his best things.   And this comes not from recklessness,
but from conscientiousness; for if they have one trait more
marked than others, it is that of having a tender conscience.   I
think I can say this truthfully and without egotism.   I learn
from the historical addresses made here, and what I otherwise
hear of our ancestors, from Walter Palmer down, that they
have been, as a rule, a people with strong religious faith.   God
and the unseen world are real to them; so real that the conscience becomes educated in sensitiveness and controls the life.
Now, when this is the case, you have a character that will do
its duty in the family, in society and in the State; and this is

true of the Palmers in our locality. They do not become very rich ; they are never very poor ; their families are well provided for and well educated. They are industrious and frugal, and thrifty as far as is compatible with generosity. You will find them in churches, and always interested in schools. They rarely hold office or are politicians, but are uniformly at the caucus and at the polls. Central New York was represented by many Palmers among the 75,000 men who responded to the first call of President Lincoln for soldiers. They do these things because they are right and conscience requires them done. And I feel very grateful to good old Walter Palmer and all our ancestors who have followed him, that they have given us some measure of this inheritance of conscientious Christian principle.

ADDRESS

BY PROF. A. B. PALMER, M. D., LL. D., OF ANN ARBOR, MICH.

Mr. President, Ladies and Gentlemen :

I scarcely need to say it gives me pleasure to be here at the home of my ancestors, and to meet with those whom I can regard as kindred. We have all a common heritage in a Puritan ancestry and in New England institutions, and I have the satisfaction of claiming, with most of you, a descent from the Pilgrim, Walter Palmer. There must have been in that old hero much sturdy vigor—I say hero, for peace, and civilization, and religion have their heroes as well as war. When we look upon these rocks and this meagre soil, and remember the forests which were to be subdued, and the ferocious beasts and the more ferocious savages to be resisted ; when we consider that a livelihood was to be extracted from this soil and these surrounding waters ; when we reflect that churches, and schools, and towns, and States, and a great Nation were to be established, we may well call those heroes who commenced the task. There must have been, I repeat, much sturdy vigor in that old hero to have commenced a new and untried life in this wilderness, and to have been the father of a race so numerous, to say nothing of their activities, their deeds, and the results of those deeds.

At first view it might have seemed unwise for our ancestor, with the whole continent before him, to have commenced the new life among these rocks; but there is "a Providence that shapes our ends, rough hew them as we may," and results have shown that the struggles of Walter Palmer and his more immediate descendants with this rugged, reluctant nature, developed qualities which would not have had an existence in a milder climate and upon a richer soil.

We are here to-day from various and many distant parts of this great country—a country which has survived many perils, whose present and prospective prosperity and greatness exceeds those of any other nation; a country whose greatest peril now is its unprecedented prosperity—we have come here to remind ourselves of the virtues, the struggles and the successes of our progenitors, to receive inspiration from their history, and to excite each other to stronger efforts for improvement; to receive a stimulus to exert ourselves for the preservation and continuance of our family, and to make our name respected and honored.

Whatever may be our philosophical notions, we must admit that "the survival of the fittest" is, at least, a general law, however many exceptions there may be; and we, as a family, must submit to the conditions of this law. We shall survive if we are fit for survival.

Now, it seems to me, that the principal object of these Re-Unions is to take counsel together as to the proper methods of preserving and strengthening all that is good and commendable among us, and of repressing all that is evil and reprehensible—of making ourselves the fittest to survive, and thus promoting our survival, and with our survival the promotion of our honor and our efficiency for good.

I appeal to you, Mr. President, and to you the originators

and sustainers of this Re-Union Association, whether this is not its chief object and the justification of its existence?

With this understanding of your object, it would have given me pleasure to have endeavored to contribute my mite to the accomplishment of that object, and to have stated in a somewhat orderly manner some of the means of self-preservation, and of physical, mental and moral improvement. Had I been trained as a minister of religion I should have been inclined to set forth the claims of spiritual influences in renovating the heart and purifying the characters of those I might have addressed. Had I been a general educator of youth, I might have dwelt upon the influence of common school, academic and higher education in elevating the mind and increasing the power of the family. Had I been a statesman, I should have been inclined to dwell upon the importance of proper political institutions, and just and beneficent laws; or had I been a financier or manufacturer, I might have made suggestions respecting economy in living, care and uprightness in business, and industry and skill in useful pursuits. All these, it seems to me, are proper themes for discourse on these occasions.

But being a physician—having devoted my life chiefly to the study of the human organism, of the physical laws which govern its existence, and the influence of physical agencies upon the body and through it upon the mind—upon the intellectual and the moral characters—I was inclined to make some remarks upon the influence of these physical agencies upon the vigor, the continuance, the power, and the honor of the Palmer family. This, I thought, was a theme worthy of the occasion, however unworthily it might have been presented; but having been prevented by illness in my family from arriving here until this late hour, when so few remain, when you have all been satisfied if not surfeited with the good things you have received, and are now anxious to return to your homes, I must content myself with expressing my gratification at meeting even this number, and of saying that should all the Palmer family obey with strictness the physical laws established by the Ruler of the universe, avoiding all injurious articles and influences avoidable, should they lead temperate, and, in every way, proper physical lives, not neglecting mental and moral energies and spiritual influences, their existence would be perpetuated, their power and influence would be progressively augmented, and their name and honor preserved until the latest generation.

Many families commenced in this country with more wealth, higher position, and, to all appearance, with better prospects than the family of Walter Palmer, who are now almost unknown, or have become entirely extinct. Few families are as numerous or have been as successful as his. There have doubtless been natural, intelligible causes for this.

Among the influences which have determined these results must be placed physical agencies ; and among these physical agencies strong drinks are not the least. Family after family has been extinguished by intemperance, and its entailed vices and defects. The evils of this great error are not confined to those who are drunkards, but those who indulge to a less extent are more or less .injured ; and the evil effects are often manifested more in the progeny of the drinking men than in themselves. These sins of the fathers are visited upon their children to the third and fourth and later generations.

So far as my observation and information extends, the Palmers have generally been a temperate race. I have known very few drunkards among them, or even habitual free drinkers ; and if this general absence of intemperance is the fact, as I believe it is, it will go far to account for the numbers and character of the family. The inferences are too evident to require to be urged. Other influences might be mentioned, but the time and the occasion do not justify a further continuance of these unprepared and hasty remarks ; and thanking you for your attentions and kindly greetings since I have 'been with you, I will leaveyou to the closing exercises of this Re-Union.

ADDRESS

TO THE PALMERS OF WESTCHESTER CO., N. Y., BY PROFESSOR
JOSEPH H. PALMER, OF YONKERS, N. Y.

Mr. President, Ladies and Gentlemen of the Palmer Re-Union :

Westchester County is a small part of the great territory of
the Palmer family. It was so closely allied to the State of
Connecticut that for many years it was impossible to determine
a boundary line of separation ; but now Westchester County
contents herself, lying between the Hudson River and Long
Island Sound, and having for its southern boundary the great
city of New York.

In population Westchester ranks as the ninth county in the
State of New York. It contains the city of Yonkers and numerous villages, among them White Plains, Peekskill, Tarrytown
and New Rochelle. From its proximity to New England and
New York, and its beauty of situation, it is not surprising that
the Palmers were among its first settlers.

The first settlement was made at the present village of Westchester in 1642, by John Throckmorton with thirty-five English
families from New England, with the consent of the Dutch who
had acquired title from the Indians. These, and others immediately following them, were refugees from New England persecution, and among them was William Palmer, who died in
Westchester about 1670.

The Palmers were not only among the early settlers, but they
were among the most active participants in the affairs both of
Church and of State. As early as 1673 Joseph Palmer and
Edward Waters were appointed the first magistrates of Westchester. In 1688 Joseph Palmer was appointed a trustee for
Westchester; and in 1692 John, Joseph and Samuel Palmer
were appointed as commissioners for the repurchase of the land
from the Indians. John Palmer was a vestryman of St. Peter's
Church, Westchester ; other Palmers were Baptists, Methodists,
Independents and Quakers. Some shared the independent
spirit of Ann Hutchinson, and deeply lamented her untimely

and cruel death, which occurred near the creek which bears her name.

As the population increased and the settlements extended, we find the Palmers in the adjoining towns—Pelham, New Rochelle and Mamaroneck, and in other parts of the county, and finally in other counties and other States.

City Island, originally called New City Island, in the town of Pelham, takes its name from an organized effort to make it a great trading port—a great commercial city. The waters are deep, and the tides from both extremities of the sound meet there.

Benjamin Palmer owned the island, consisting of 230 acres, and with his consent and co-operation it was granted to a company or corporation consisting of thirty persons, and laid out and mapped into city lots. The plans of the company were interrupted by the Revolutionary War. Benjamin Palmer, in the beginning of the war, at once took an active part in favor of independence. He was driven from the island, where he had retained an interest, and was a great sufferer during the entire war, losing almost everything for his attachment to the American cause.

In 1789 he set forth his grievances in a petition to Gen. Washington for redress, Aaron Burr being his advisor. The petition, among other things, stated "That himself and his family were taken prisoners by the British who used us very ill, and then ordered us off my plantation, which I then had on said island, to New York, where I have continued with my family ever since."

In order to give the original lines of the Palmers of Westchester, we must go still farther back, and begin with:

William Palmer, accompanied by his son William, a lad of nine years, came from Nottinghamshire, England, in the ship *Fortune*, in 1621—the second ship after the *Mayflower*—landed at Plymouth, Mass., and settled at Duxbury, Mass., and thence to Scituate. It is supposed he died in 1637. His will was probated March 5, 1638. His wife, Frances, followed her husband to America in the vessel *Anne*, in 1623.* His son William it

* See Palmer Records, Vol. I, p. 114.

is supposed migrated into Westchester Country, and died there in 1670. Children, William, Joseph, Benjamin, *Samuel*, Obadiah and Thomas. *Samuel* settled in Mamaroneck, and became the propritor of Mangopson Neck. Children, *Obadiah*, Nehemiah, Sylvanus and Solomon. Obadiah died in 1747. Children, William, Samuel, Benjamin, David, Obadiah, Caleb and Mary Anne. Nehemiah died in 1760, leaving a son and a daughter. The son died, leaving Harrison, Drake, Aaron, Nathan, Benjamin, Nehemiah and Elihue. Sylvanus died in 1741. Children, Robert, Sylvanus, John, Marmaduke, Edward, Anne, Susannah, Charity and Mary.

John, son of Sylvanus, grandson of Samuel and great grandson of William, of Westchester, married Rebecca. Children, Joseph, Philip, Marcus, Lewis, Benjamin. The brothers Joseph and Benjamin became proprietors of City Island.

John Palmer, of Rockland County, N. Y., was probably a son of Joseph and nephew of Benjamin, of City Island. He lived in Rockland County as early as 1750, and called his little settlement New City, from New City Island where his father had lived. The Palmer homestead is about one mile north of New City, which has long been the county-seat of Rockland County. I have been unable to trace with certainty the relation between Benjamin Palmer, of City Island, and John Palmer, of New City, but there are old deeds and other papers in possession of John Palmer's descendants which establish a connection between him and the City Island property; and the dates indicate that he was the son of Joseph. He married Martha Brown. Children, John, Joseph and Jonathan. Joseph never married. The descendants of John and Jonathan, with dates, are more fully given in " Family Sketches," by Rev. David Cole, D. D., Yonkers, N. Y. In these remarks I can only trace the Westchester branch from Rockland County back to Westchester.

Jonathan Palmer, born at New City, date unknown; married Elizabeth Wood, daughter of Sheriff Ebenezer Wood, born at Tappan, July 4, 1762, and died at Camillus, Onondaga County, N. Y., December 10, 1832. Children, Elizabeth, Jonathan

Mary, John, Sarah, Benjamin, Jacob, Hannah, Ebenezer, Joseph and Daniel.

Benjamin Palmer, born at New City, April 1, 1793; married, December 8, 1814, Clarinda Frink, daughter of Isaac Frink and Phebe Pendleton; born at Cherry Valley, Otsego County, N. Y., July 28, 1795. The husband died July 20, 1857, and his wife, December 12, 1872. There were seven children, all born at Camillus, Onondaga County, N. Y., Phebe, Hannah Etta, Jane, Joseph H., George W., Warren W., and A. Judson.

Joseph Howard Palmer (myself), born at Camillus, Onondaga County, N. Y., September 16, 1824; married first, December 25, 1851, Hannah Maria Van Cott, daughter of John G. Van Cott and Sarah Wyckoff; born at Bushwick, L. I., April 18, 1830, died at Yonkers, N. Y., March 17, 1859. Married second, July 19, 1866, Frances A. Bingham, daughter of Horace B. Bingham and Emeline Jones; born at Coventay, Conn., March 31, 1835. Children of the first marriage :

Sarah Clarinda Palmer has the professorship of mathematics since September, 1876, in Wells' College, Aurora, Cayuga Lake, N. Y.

John Garrison Palmer is a partner in the *Pure Gold Manufacturing Company*, Fairport, Monroe County, N. Y.

Anna Maria Palmer has charge of a kindergarten in Allegheny, Pa.

Phebe Etta Palmer is a teacher in the Park Heights Seminary, Ocean Grove, N. J.

Children of the second marriage, Horace Bingham Palmer, Frank Howard Palmer, and Maria Whitney Palmer.

But few of this numerous race remained in Westchester. The enterprises of New York City and the surrounding country became inviting; and as westward the star of empire takes her course, thitherward from every eastern county and State went many of the Palmers to act their part among the first in peaceable possession, among the first in places of honor and trust, among the first in war, in peace, and in the hearts of their countrymen. In the wide stretch across the continent their dwellings ere found in almost every county, from Plymouth Rock to the Golden Gate. From every point of the compass on land and sea the Palmers rejoice over this Palmer Re-Union—this reuniting of heart and home. The home in all ages has been the center of love and affection. Its surroundings and associations engage our earliest attention, and the words father and mother are the last of all things forgotten. The pictures of our old homes awaken commingled emotions of joy and sorrow, reminding us of the sunshine and shadows of the past.

The remembrances of kindred and friends are precious endearments. Art has been taxed to its uttermost to present in photography, in painting and in sculpture the forms so dear to us. These remembrances are sacred—our penates, our household gods. And when these, like all earthly things, shall perish from the earth, the memory they faintly embodied. the story of virtue or valor and of useful lives, will be told to children's children. Yes, when all who now live, and their children's children, have been carried to their last resting-place, their successors throughout all time will read the story of Plymouth Rock and Stonington, Bunker Hill and Saratoga, Valley Forge and Yorktown.

If memory is so enduring, and the story of one's life so indestructible, then let our lives be lives of virtue and honor; let us be exemplary parents and citizens, known and blessed by doing good amoung our fellow-men.

BRIEF RESPONSE,

BY N. B. PALMER, ESQ., OF PITTSBURG, PA.

Having had the pleasure of attending the last Re-Union of the Palmers at Stonington, Conn., and after spending a season of unequalled comfort, I was led to believe that a word to this effect would be of interest, and act as an incentive to induce others to attend future calls of the Association.

On these memorable occasions of Re-Union, it is not possible that all interested would be able to assemble and smoke the family calumet ; there will always be some, from various causes, less fortunate ; they must be content with reading of the joyous time their more favored brethren experienced, and in contemplation thereof find their pleasure and source of knowledge of these transcendent affairs pertaining to and concerning them peculiarly as dwellers upon this mundane sphere.

At the Mecca of the Palmers, quaint old borough of Stonington (which, by the way, is worth a day's journey to see), you would find here the stranger could not dwell as such—all are acquainted, each vieing with one another to make all happy. Here might one, had they the stature of a Colossus, plant one foot in the State of New York or Rhode Island whilst the other remained in the State of Connecticut ; and historic, too, as having been the scene of conflict, of which relics may yet be seen in her streets, but of most interest, that beautiful cove, " Wequetequock " by name, where our great ancestor was wont to rest in his canoe, and as it gently made its way to the sea he might view the broad acres, of which he was monarch of all he surveyed. Words cannot picture the delightful scenes, moving, as it were, in a panoramic dream : and as encomiastic friends pour into your ears well earned praises of those of your ancestors gone before, it will prove quite elevating. If you desire, willing friends will accompany you to the very place where once dwelt our grandfathers; here you will find the old mill that ground their meal for ten generations still faithful to the last, and grinding away at the post of duty (although almost gone from infirmities of age) whilst all else has passed away, and with them should have been forgotten had it not been for these Re-Unions. So with that little sacred spot where dwelleth the dead ! How suggestive of the unwritten things of earth ! Can we realize that here relative lie—born, served their calling, made their election sure, and have passed out as an extinguished star, leaving little else behind them save a good name ?

Had I the silver tongue of the orator I should spend the happiest moments of my life in proclaiming the praises of the

Palmers who have, upon this American soil, implanted that which from effects it would be impossible to lose sight of the cause. The corner-stone of American civilization, imbedded in the strong bonds of virtue and morality, was laid by the Pilgrims; then why should we not reunite to recall the past? Where is there one so base as to decline to show forth to the welkin the praises of those who walked in full faith, and gave expression and impression of and to them that should follow? Their mantle has fallen upon our shoulders; shall we acquit ourselves nobly? If so, now our opportunity occurs. Shall we emulate their example, and so teach our children? You may say, How emulate? One way, I answer, by gaining, with proper motives, an extended knowledge from each and every one; by imparting and receiving ideas and items, one with another, of the good deeds and virtues of those gone before; then you can sit in delightful reverie and contemplate that which is beyond the stars; slowly rolling back the ponderous curtain of the past, then shall be revealed to your anxious eyes the silver lining of that light beyond the clouds which shall enable you to more fully realize the object and appreciate the worth of these family Re-Unions. How commendable the desire to perpetuate the memory of those we love, to keep green in the garden of our remembrance the family tree to which we may repair and partake, in our leisure moments, of a refreshing change, after buffeting with the waves and storms on the ocean of life.

Brethren and friends, one and all, be ye a Palmer, then your duty is evident; complete your library by securing all the books and papers relating to these Re-Unions, so that you may be able to entertain your friends, read your title clear, and have on stated occasions a family Re-Union of the little Palmers that may gather around your hearthstone there to be made acquainted with their history, so that they can pass it along down the line from generation to generation until time shall be no more.

Hoping to experience, as the cycles of time allotted shall

roll around, more of these Re-Union occasions, and perhaps see
relatives for the first time in life ; may you, kind reader, if such,
be numbered among them.

CONCERT.

The concert given on the second evening, August 11th, was
an interesting and enjoyable entertainment.   The Palmer Band,
of Whitfield, N. H., consisted of leader and cornettist, Frank
H. Palmer, G. F. Palmer, Chas. W. Palmer, John W. Palmer,
Fred. A. Palmer, and some others—twelve pieces in all ; vocal-
ists, Mrs. R. G. Coit ; soprano, Mrs. H. F. Palmer ; alto, Mr. H.
E. Stevans ; tenor, Dr. F. W. Holbrook ; and pianist, Miss Ada
L. Crandall, who took part in the quartette.   Miss Amy Palmer
and sister, Mrs. Jessie Clayton, both of New York City, also
added their cultivated voices to the evening's melodies.   The
Stonington " Mirror " speaks of the concert thus :

"The ' Palmer Band ' from New Hampshire was one of the
notable features of the late Re-Union.   The concert given by
them in the pavillion tent, evening of August 11th, was well
attended and received.   At the close an impromptu dance was
indulged in, and after a general hustling of seats to make room,
the tripping of the light fantastic toe on the mother earth was
really novel and hugely enjoyed.   The barrister from Oneida,
with a lady from New York City, first led off, and soon a general dance was inaugurated.   None enjoyed it more than the
lookers on, and they ached for an opportunity to participate."

ARTICLES IN THE LOAN COLLECTION OF THE PALMER RE-UNION.

Mrs. Isabella G. Meredith, *Chairman.*   Miss Emma W. Palmer, *Secretary.*

Punch bowl of 1750, loaned by Mrs. Jos. Chesebro.
Glass bowl of 1750,   "   "
China cup and saucer, 100 years old,   "   "
Two table-spoons,   "   "   Mrs. F. Larkin,

Cockle-shell tea-spoon, very rare, Miss Fannie Chesebro.

Shell harpa, Miss Fannie Chesebro.

Majolica-leaf plate, rainbow glaze, old and rare, Miss Fannie Chesebro.

Two pictures, silhouettes, in gold leaf on black, very rare, Miss Fannie Chesebro.

China cup and cream pitcher, 100 years old, Miss Fannie Chesebro.

Linen towel, 100 years old, Miss Fannie Chesebro.

" 75 " " "

Old-fashioned toilet cover, " "

Book, 100 years old, " "

Indian amulet, with Masonic emblems engraved on it, supposed to be ancient Masonry, Miss Fannie Chesebro.

Arrow and spear heads, dug up at Wequetequock, Miss Fannie Chesebro.

China plate, 1739, Mrs. F. Larkin.

Black lace veil, worked by Mrs. Jos. Chesebro 50 years ago, Mrs. F. Larkin.

Panel tidy, modern, Mrs. Jos. Chesebro.

Tape loom, 100 years old, Mrs. Jos. Chesebro.

Old paper and song of 1728, Sara A. Palmer.

" House-wife," 100 years old, "

Three pieces of crewel work of 1730, worked by Prudence Hallam on linen spun by herself, Miss H. R. Hallam.

China tea cup, 80 years old. Miss H. R. Hallam.

Masonic pocketbook, Mrs. Dr. Wm. Hyde.

Miniature, very quaint, " "

Red morocco bag of 1812, " "

Lace scarf, imported from France in 1812, Mrs. Dr. Wm. Hyde.

Towel made in 1768 from flax grown on Lem'l Palmer's farm, H. Stanton.

Skeleton leaves, painted by the Japanese, E. W. Palmer.

Bead work, over 70 years old, E. W. Palmer.

Malines lace, worn at Washington's inauguration ball, E. W. Palmer.

Portrait of B. Frank Palmer, E. W. Palmer.

B. F. Palmer's journal, written in Dartmouth prison in 1812, E. W. Palmer.

Bible, 1797, Amos Palmer, E. W. Palmer.

Old school-book, 130 years old, Rev. A. G. Palmer.

Four large books, printed in 1618, "   "

Modern table-spread, made by Mrs.   "

Photos of Jonathan Palmer, first postmaster of Stonington, Dr. Geo. D. Stanton.

Letter from Timothy Pickering, Postmaster General, to Jonathan Palmer, in 1793, establishing post-office at Stonington, Dr. Geo. D. Stanton.

Letter from Jonathan Palmer to Timothy Pickering, Dr. Geo. D. Stanton.

Survey of lands, 1675, Dr. Geo. D. Stanton.

Two samplers of 1782, Mrs.   "

Concordance, printed in Amen Corner, London, 1726, Mrs. John Brown.

Spanish coin, 1734, Mrs. John Brown.

Old pocketbook, 1732, Rich. A. Wheeler.

Piece of wedding-dress, silk, 1735, Rich. A. Wheeler.

Diary of Thomas Miner, 1654,   "

Bond of Capt. Kidd, 1699,   "

Wig worn by Israel Hewit, 1740,   "

Autographs of the first settlers of Stonington, Rich. A. Wheeler.

Diary of Manassah Miner, 1797, Rich. A. Wheeler.

Plan of Indian Pequot fort at Groton, fac simile of fight (by Lieut. Underhill), 1637, Rich. A. Wheeler.

Will of Geo. Denison, 1693, Rich. A. Wheeler.

Book printed in 1510 at Venice, afterwards owned by Jos. Palmer, very rare, Dr. David Hart.

Manuscript black-letter, written on vellum, 870 years old, very old and curious, Dr. David Hart.

Drawings of the ships of war of 1812, drawn by C. T. Hart, Dr. David Hart.

Pitcher with picture of the attack on Stonington, 1814, E. P. Hubbard.

Penny token of the first stage coach, W. P. Hopkins.

Portrait of I. H. Palmer (æt. 10 yrs.), Ira H. Palmer.

Writ served in 1729, Mrs. F. A. Denison.

Two portraits of Elijah and Mercy Palmer, Mrs. D. C. Hyde.

Whale teeth carved with a jack-knife, Mrs. E. Chesebro.

Two rugs, modern work, made by Mrs. Mitchell.

Watch of 1770 which, after a rest of 50 years, keeps perfect time, Miss Nellie Cornell.

Reed musical pipe, over 100 years old, Miss Nellie Cornell.

Afghan and umbrella, lace work, modern, made by Mrs. J. G. Palmer.

Specimens of minerals, F. F. Palmer.

Old sampler, crewel work, W. H. Palmer.

Old mourning piece, embroidered on satin, Mrs. Emeline P. Stanton.

Cane, over 200 years old, J. H. Wilcox.

Razors of five generations of Palmers, H. C. Palmer.

Indian spear-head, Harvey C. Palmer, Greenville.

Warming-pan of Roger Williams, Mrs. Eunice Noyes.

Landscape belonging to Lady Ann Borodel, 1640, Mrs. Eunice Noyes.

Lace collar, worked by hand, very old, Mrs. Gen. Geo. W. Palmer.

Crewel-work, material spun and dyed by the lady who worked it over 70 years ago, Mrs. Gen. Geo. W. Palmer.

Indian samp stone, Mrs. Chase.

Miniature of Hon. E. H. Palmer at 17 years, Mrs. Mitchell.

Plates and platter, painted by Mrs. Appelman.

Wistaria, painted by Miss E. W. Palmer.

Pewter platter, over 100 years old, H. A. Murphy, Mystic.

Pewter plate marked B. P. (Bridget Palmer), H. A. Murphy, Mystic.

Jabez Brewster's chopping knife, 110 years old, H. A. Murphy, Mystic.

Jabez Brewster's wedding stockings, H. A. Murphy, Mystic.

Handkerchief with prints of the attack of the " Leopard " on the "Chesapeake " in 1807, H. A. Murphy, Mystic.

Walter Palmer's chopping knife, W. P. stamped on it, over 200 years old, Emilie Pendleton, Norwich.

Commission of Thomas Palmer, T. W. Palmer.

Tea cannister, 120 years old, very curious, Mrs. Lois Appelman.

Wooden sugar-bowl, 120 years old, very curious, Mrs. Lois Appelman.

Lem'l Palmer's hymn-book, Mrs. Lois Appelman.

Deeds (1681) with autographs of Anna (Lord) Stanton, Dr. Geo. D. Stanton.

Yellow quilted skirt of the last century, Miss Julia W. Palmer.

Confederate scrip, collected by Mrs. Appelman.

Chinese embroidery, Sara A. Palmer.

Lace caps, worked by Mrs. Geo. Sherman over 5c years ago, E. W. Palmer.

Pewter plates, kept in the Stanton family over 150 years, Dr. Geo. D. Stanton.

Silk handkerchief of 1770, Dr. Geo. D. Stanton.

Cups and saucers of Mrs. Eunice P. Stanton, 100 years old, Mrs. Appelman.

Plate, belonging to Marvin Palmer, 1739, Mrs. Sam'l M. Stanton.

China bowl, supposed to have belonged to the Rev. James and Dorothy (Stanton) Noyes, 1674, Mrs. Sam'l M. Stanton.

Linen coverlet, woven by Palmers over 100 years ago, Mrs. Appelman.

Photo of Warren Palmer, born in 1776, emigrated to Ohio in 1800, Dr. Corydon Palmer.

Set of dental instruments, designed and made by Dr. Corydon Palmer.

History of Job. 1727, Mrs. Appelman.

Book, "No Cross, No Crown," written by Wm. Penn, 1747, Mrs. Appelman.

Portrait of Parson Fayweather, painted on copper, Mrs. T. Mallaby.

Portrait of Rev. A. G. Palmer at 21.

Silver spoon, 1749, Mrs. S. M. Stanton.

Certificate of membership in the Baltimore Union Lodge of A. F. & A. M., 1788, Dr. Geo. D. Stanton.

[Stonington " Mirror," August 19, 1882.]

THE RE-UNION IN RETROSPECT.

The second annual Re-Union of the Palmer family has transpired, and its record is already on the historic page. In many respects it was unlike the first Re-Union. Many circumstances had a tendency to detract from the attendance, but on the whole it was a success—much criticism to the contrary notwithstanding, The opposition element in our midst, so manifest prior to the first Re-Union, long since became of little account, and was virtually extinct, except in a few individual cases. Even time is not long enough to educate such. But to that portion of this community that by its willingness to accommodate the late Re-Unionists, the management desire to express unqualified thanks, and state that their hospitality was appreciated by the recipients.

Not until 1886 will the people of Stonington be called upon to again lift the latch of their doors to a Palmer Re-Unionist. By that time it is to be hoped a general and hearty welcome will be extended to the Palmers that will then be here. During the intervening Summers, without a doubt, the social element of the family will assemble here or elsewhere for the purpose of a good time, and to keep alive the coals of enthusiasm left burning at the late Re-Union. The acquaintances made at the first Re-Union and renewed at the last have bacome too strong and pleasant to expire by limitation, consequently demand an annual "coming together" of those that affiliate, and by nature and taste enjoy social intercourse and all things collateral thereto.

NECROLOGY.

DEATHS DURING THE INTERVAL OF THE RE-UNIONS.

AGE.

Abbie Palmer, Mrs., East Avon, N. Y., December 31, 1881 77
Alva Palmer, Byron, Wis., May 27, 1882 72
Arthur C. Palmer (child), Montville, Ct., May 11, 1882 . . . .
Braman, Milton Palmer, Auburndale, N. Y., April 10, 1882 83
Bert L. Palmer (child), Brooklyn, N. Y., January 24, 1882 4
Brewster, Mrs. Olive, Corning, N. Y., September 10, 1882 . . . .
Cullen Palmer, Madison, Ohio, August 28, 1881. . . . .
Chapman, Mrs. Lydia, July 27, 1882 . . . .
Case, Ann E., Norwich, Ct. . . . .
David Palmer (Dr.), Pittsburgh, Pa., July 8, 1882 32
E. W. Palmer, Mrs., Portsmouth, March 11, 1882 . . . .
Edward Palmer, Rev., Barnwell, S. C., September 30, 1882 94
Fanny Palmer, Mrs., Syracuse, N. Y., December 12, 1882 72
Geo. W. Palmer, Union Park, Ct., November, 1881 . . . .
Gideon Palmer, Capt., Newport, R. I., March, 1881 . . . .
Geo. W. Palmer, Boston, Mass . . . .
Hoadley, Mrs. Ella P., Branford, Ct., September 4, 1881 32
Huldah Palmer, Mrs. (widow of Stephen W.), Norvell, Mich., Jan. 30, 1882 . . . 82
Harriet N. Palmer, Norwich, Ct., October 31, 1881 . . . .
Hutchins, Mrs. Sophia P., Fayetteville, N. Y., May 20, 1882. 86
Hannah E. P. Stanton, Lebanon, Ct., February 14, 1882 65
Helen M. Palmer, Lanesborough, April 23, 1882 24
Harriet Palmer, Mrs., Dover, April 7, 1882 . . . .
James Woolsey Palmer, Jersey City, N. J., December 5, 1881 71
Jacob P. Palmer, Mrs., Boston, Mass., January 29, 1882 . . . .
Kingsley, R. A. H., Hartford, Vt., May 17, 1882 . . . .
Kathie Palmer (child), Glasgow, Mo., May 5, 1882 . . . .
Lura Palmer, Mrs., Canastota, N. Y., March 13, 1882 77
Minnie B. Palmer, Stonington, Ct., March 9, 1882 9
Paul S. Palmer, Mrs., Stockbridge, Mass., March 13, 1882 77
Roswell C. Palmer, Rev., Stonington, Ct., July, 1881 . . . .
Ray Palmer (child), Minneapolis, Minn., March 9, 1882 . . . .
Safford, Mrs. Huldah P., Syracuse, N. Y., August 17, 1882 . . . . 95 yrs. and 5 mos.
Tallman Palmer, Hartford, Ct., March 30, 1882 79
Woodward, Emeline, July 6, 1882 . . . .
Williams, Geo. P. (Rev. and Prof.), Ann Arbor, Mich. . . . .
Wm. Brown Palmer, Covington, N. Y. January 30, 1882 . . . .
Walter Palmer, Winfield, N. Y., January 30, 1882 . . . .
Wm. Walter Palmer, Jamaica, N. Y., February 5, 1882 . . . . 1½
Wm. H. Palmer, Boston Highlands, Mass., April 17, 1882 70
Walter Palmer, Mrs., Woodstock, Vt. 90
Wm. Palmer (Judge), Gardiner, Me., June 4, 1881 . . . .

[NOTE.—More appropriate notices of the deceased will be given in "Vol. III, Palmer Records, Historical and Biographical."

CONTENTS.

www.ingramcontent.com/pod-product-compliance
Lightning Source LLC
Chambersburg PA
CBHW032305280326
41932CB00009B/709